An International Civil War

An International Civil War

Greece, 1943–1949

André Gerolymatos

Yale UNIVERSITY PRESS

New Haven & London

Published with assistance from the Louis Stern Memorial Fund.

Portions of this book appeared in an earlier work titled *Red Acropolis, Black Terror* (New York: Basic Books, 2004).

Yale University Press books may be purchased in quantity for educational, business, or promotional use. For information, please e-mail sales.press@yale. edu (U.S. office) or sales@yaleup.co.uk (U.K. office).

Set in Adobe Garamond type by IDS Infotech Ltd., Chandigarh, India.
Printed and bound by CPI Group (UK) Ltd, Croydon, CR0 4YY

ISBN 978-0-300-18060-2 (paperback : alk. paper)

Library of Congress Control Number: 2016935986

10 9 8 7 6 5 4 3 2 1

To my sister Areti,
With love,
whose courage and stamina in adversity is an example to all of us

The sufferings which civil strife entailed . . .

were many and terrible,

such as have occurred and always will occur,

as the nature of mankind remains the same.

THUCYDIDES, *History of the Peloponnesian War*, 3.82.1

Contents

Map 1. The Balkans, 1878. Map by Costa Dedegikas.

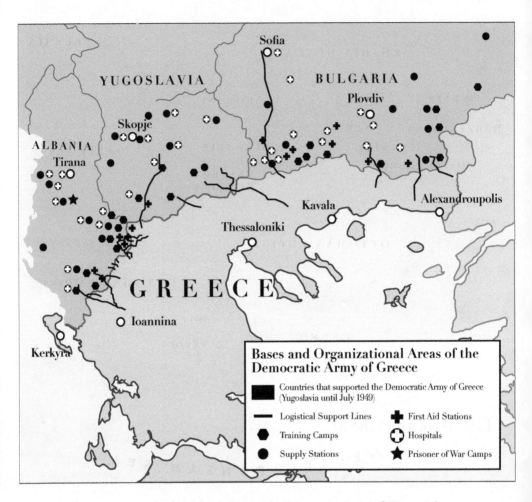

Map 2. Bases and Organizational Areas of the Democratic Army of Greece, July 1949.
Map by Costa Dedegikas.

Preface and Acknowledgments

The Greek civil war was actually three civil wars: three phases of a conflict that raged across Greece and some of the islands, and engaged countries from around the region and beyond. In all three phases, communists and communist-backed insurgents sought to seize control, first of the resistance against the German occupying force (October 1943–February 1944), then from the restored Greek government of national unity after liberation (December 1944), and finally, in what historians commonly demarcate the "civil war," from 1946 to 1949. But the Greek civil war was also an international war, as competing interests maneuvered for position in the postwar world.

Between 1945 and 1947, Greece was caught in the vacuum of a world in transition. The period just after World War II was a time of change and global realignment. Old empires were in eclipse, and new ones, such as the Soviet Union and the United States, were poised to instigate and dominate world events. The British Empire, which once ruled the waves and controlled one-fifth of the world's surface, was rapidly declining, forced to relinquish large tracts of its colonial possessions in Asia and Africa and under pressure to relinquish the Middle East. The British, however, were not prepared to surrender every "jewel in the crown," particularly in the Middle East. In 1945, the Abadan oil refinery in Iran produced more oil than all the Arab states together—80 percent of British petroleum supplies relied on the Middle East—and was critical to Britain's economic recovery. Furthermore, a significant part of

Britain's trade, including petroleum, was carried on ships that depended on the Suez Canal.

Greece was an essential part of London's new Middle East strategy, and failure in Greece would have repercussions in Britain's postwar grand strategy in the region. In 1945, as had been the case since the nineteenth century, Greece was still within the British sphere of influence. London's interest in Greece was part of Britain's postwar policy that aimed at replacing colonial rule in the Middle East by co-opting the newly independent Arab and Muslim states in a reconstituted British sphere of influence based on mutual interests and security. The new Labour foreign secretary, Ernest Bevin, underlined in a policy paper to the cabinet on 11 August 1945 that "we must maintain our position in Greece as part of our Middle East policy, and that unless it is asserted and settled it may have a bad effect in the whole of our Middle East position."[1]

The British were prepared to accept assistance from the Americans to secure the Middle East, but not to relinquish military or economic primacy. In another memo to the cabinet on 17 September 1945, Bevin insisted that Britain "should not make any concessions that would assist American commercial penetration into a region which for generations has been an established British market."[2] Events, however, undermined British plans to maintain their suzerainty over the Middle East with only a subsidiary role for the United States. The Iran crisis and the Turkish Straits crisis in the spring and summer of 1946, respectively, followed by the outbreak of the Greek civil war in the same year, made it clear to the British that they lacked the resources to defend the Middle East and Greece; it also convinced President Harry Truman that the United States had to intervene in order to stop Soviet aggression. It is within this context that Greece became an American concern—not so much because of the country's Balkan location, but because of its geographic proximity to the Middle East through the eastern Mediterranean.

The Truman administration decided to intervene in Greece with financial and military assistance in the form of supplies and advisers partly in response to London's dramatic announcement that the United Kingdom could no longer provide military and economic sustenance to Greece and Turkey, and that Britain's failure to do so would undermine the security of the Middle East. Washington was convinced that Moscow intended to gain control of the Aegean and undermine Turkey and Iran, thus expanding Soviet influence over the emerging postcolonial Arab and Muslim states. In 1946, the communist uprising in Greece was merely a small insurgency. Hostilities quickly

FIG. 1. President Harry S. Truman reviewing the troops on "Army Day" in Washington, D.C., 7 April 1947. On 12 March he had implemented the Truman Doctrine. Abbie Rowe, photographer. U.S. National Archives and Records Administration.

spiraled to a full-scale civil war that engulfed northern Greece, parts of the Peloponnese, and some of the Aegean islands. What was, in effect, a Greek domestic crisis quickly escalated into a contest pitting the United States, and, to a lesser degree Britain, against the Soviet Union and its satellites, particularly Yugoslavia, Bulgaria, Albania, and indirectly Romania, Czechoslovakia, and Hungary—at least to the perception of American policy makers. The participation of all these states transformed the Greek fratricide from a regional concern into an international civil war, at least by proxy, and helped inaugurate the Cold War.

The suggestion for a new history of the Greek civil war originally came from John Donatich, then at Basic Books, who left the company before a previous edition of this book was published. John became director of Yale

University Press, and he encouraged me to undertake an updated version of the original publication, *Red Acropolis, Black Terror: The Greek Civil War and the Origins of the Soviet-American Rivalry, 1943–1949* (New York: Basic Books, 2004). Although my intent was to provide some updates on the original chapters, a great deal of new material both primary and secondary has surfaced, which required significant rewriting and the addition of five new chapters. At Yale University Press, I had the good fortune to work with Christopher Rogers, whose patience and understanding brought about the completion of this work. I would also like to thank Erica Hanson for her help in preparing the manuscript. I am very thankful for the work of manuscript editor Noreen O'Connor-Abel.

Recent studies on the Greek civil war are effectively micro-histories of the conflict that depend on extensive interviews with victims and participants and, in most cases, the descendants of the victims. The intention of these studies is to offer an alternative to the grand narrative histories. Most new publications on the Greek civil war are available only in Greek, which is beyond the reach of many individuals in the English-speaking world. These works continue to reflect the polarization in Greek society and highlight the ongoing left-right schism that has dominated the study of the conflict. The monograph of Nikos Marantzidis, *Demokratikos Stratos Elladas (DSE), 1936–1949,* has offered insight into the logistics and most notably the armaments of the Democratic Army of Greece, providing Greek-speakers the research available in Charles R. Shrader's English work, *The Withered Vine: Logistics and the Communist Insurgency in Greece, 1945–1949.*[3] Georgios Margaritis' two-volume history, *Istoria tou Ellinikou emphiliou polemou 1946–1949,* remains the most extensive account of the Greek civil war, but is entirely from the perspective of the left.[4] A spate of new books has been published in Greece, but since they are available only in the Greek language it would not be very useful for the English reader to list them here.

The standard works in English are, most notably, Edgar O'Balance's *The Greek Civil War: 1944–1949* and C. M. Woodhouse's *The Struggle for Greece, 1941–1949,* which remain important sources for the general political and military history of the conflict. The major drawback of both accounts is that the authors had to rely exclusively on secondhand accounts and primarily British sources.[5] Over the past twenty years, however, there has been a range of articles and books in English on the subject of the Greek civil war which follow, more or less, two trends. Stanley G. Payne's *Civil War in Europe, 1905–1949* and Philip B. Minehan's *Civil War and World War in Europe: Spain,*

Yugoslavia, and Greece, 1936–1949 are examples of an attempt to place the Greek civil war within the broader context of European history.[6] The second trend includes John Sakkas' *Britain and the Greek Civil War, 1944–1949: British Imperialism, Public Opinion and the Coming of the Cold War,* as well as Loring M. Danforth and Riki Van Boeschoten's *Children of the Greek Civil War: Refugees and the Politics of Memory,* which, like the micro-histories, focus on specific aspects of the conflict.[7]

This volume is a narrative political history that includes the major military events of the conflict and is intended to bring the full scope of the war to English-speaking readers. I have included a few interviews for the sake of atmosphere and to offer readers impressions of the civil war from the perspective of the participants and observers. I will always be grateful to the individuals on both sides of the Atlantic who generously shared their experiences of the war and who were acknowledged in the original edition.

Writing is a solitary experience and the final result would have been impossible without the assistance of many individuals who contributed their time, comments, and advice. I am grateful to my doctoral graduate student and research assistant James Horncastle for his exceptional work and help during the course of the research and writing of the final manuscript. James' dissertation, "The Pawn that Would Be King: Macedonian-Slavs in the Democratic Army of Greece, 1946–49," will add a new chapter to the study of the Greek civil war and wade into the uncharted waters of the role of Slavophone Macedonians in the Greek fratricide. I am grateful to him and my other students for helping me see the Greek civil war and other historical conflicts through their young eyes.

My colleague Eirini Kotsovili provided inspiration, assistance, and essential research to help me place the civil war within the current Greek cultural context, and offered advice on how to interpret Greek literary and autobiographical texts that have come to the forefront in recent years as part of the debate on the war. Colleen Pescott has been invaluable not only for typing and proofing last-minute changes to the manuscript, but also for her continuing assistance to this and other projects. I am also grateful to the staff of the Stavros Niarchos Foundation Centre for Hellenic Studies for their organizational support and for keeping the center functioning on the days that I worked on this book. And I thank the Simon Fraser University Publications Fund for support. Special thanks go to the late Michael Ward, a veteran of Britain's Special Operations Executive in Greece, for his generous comments on the original monograph that enabled me to add new and relevant information to this book. I am equally in debt to James Warren, who worked to implement the Marshall Plan in Greece. It is gratifying to have validation from individuals who held key positions in Athens during the course of the Greek civil war. As always, my agent, Bill Hanna, has been a source of advice and inspiration.

I am forever grateful to my wife, Beverley, for her patience, putting up with long periods of silence as I worked on the manuscript, and most of all for her invaluable editing. She is the best part of my life. Tigger, my faithful canine, is the ideal writing companion and quietly waited as I finished each chapter. In completing the book I thought of my parents, who lived through the occupation, the December Uprising, and the Greek civil war. For them, rather than a story of political and military history, the war was a matter of life and death.

Chronology

1821	Greek War of Independence against the Ottoman Empire.
1830	Great Britain, France, and Russia recognize Greece as a sovereign state.
1833	Otto of Bavaria is crowned Othon I of Greece.
1844	The new constitution establishes Greece as a constitutional monarchy.
1897	Greek-Ottoman War. Greece is defeated in just three weeks of fighting.
1910	In the wake of a coup by military officers, Eleutherios Venizelos wins a landslide victory in the elections and institutes major reforms.
1912	First Balkan War. Greece, Serbia, Montenegro, and Bulgaria defeat the Ottoman Empire.
1913	Second Balkan War. Greece, Serbia, and Montenegro defeat Bulgaria.
1914	Outbreak of World War I.
1916	Venizelos forms a revolutionary government in northern Greece. The beginning of the Great Schism.

1917	Great Britain and France force King Constantine to abdicate in favor of his son Alexander.
1922	Greek-Turkish War. The Greek army is defeated in Asia Minor; Constantine is forced to abdicate for a second time.
1923	Treaty of Lausanne (24 July) establishes the borders of Greece and Turkey. Both countries also agree to a population exchange in which more than 1.5 million Greek Orthodox are forced to relocate to Greece.
1924	Greece becomes a republic.
1924–1926	A succession of military coups undermines the new republic.
1935	The Venizelist faction in the armed forces attempts a coup and fails. The officer corps is purged of antimonarchists.
1935	The monarchy is restored after a fraudulent plebiscite; George II returns to Greece.
1936	(4 August) Ioannis Metaxas, with the support of King George, establishes a dictatorship.
1940	Italy attacks Greece. The Greek army scores a number of impressive victories and pushes the Italians back to Albania.
1941	(6 April) The German army, with support from Bulgaria, invades Greece.
1941	King George leaves Greece, and a Greek government-in-exile is set up in London and Cairo.
1941–1944	Greece is occupied by the Axis (Germany, Bulgaria, and Italy). A resistance evolves but is divided between left- and right-wing organizations.
1942–1943	The Special Operations Executive (SOE) establishes the British Military Mission in Greece to coordinate the Greek guerrilla forces.
1942	The British SOE, along with the Greek Popular Liberation Army (ELAS) and the National Democratic Greek League (EDES), destroys the Gorgopotamos viaduct.
1943	(April) Ioannis Rallis, with permission from the Germans, creates the Security Battalions.

1943	(August) A delegation representing the Greek resistance travels to Cairo, but all efforts at a political compromise with the Greek government-in-exile and the British fail.
1943	(8 September) Italy surrenders.
1943	(12 October) The first phase of the Greek civil war begins.
1944	(29 February) The Plaka Agreement ends the first phase of civil war.
1944	(March) The Political Committee of National Liberation (PEEA) established.
1944	(17–20 May) The Lebanon Conference and the creation of a government of national unity.
1944	(July) The British Military Mission is joined by the U.S. Office of Strategic Services (OSS) and is renamed the Allied Military Mission.
1944	(28 July) A Soviet Military Mission arrives in ELAS territory.
1944	(August) National Liberation Front (EAM) agrees to join the government of national unity.
1944	(26 September) The Caserta Agreement is concluded.
1944	(9 October) The Churchill-Stalin Percentage Agreement divides the Balkans into spheres of influence.
1944	(17 October) The Greek government returns to liberated Athens.
1944	(3 December) Demonstrators are fired upon by police in Constitution Square.
1944	(4 December–February 1945) The December Uprising.
1945	(4–11 February) The Yalta Conference.
1945	(12 February) The Varkiza Agreement ends the December Uprising.
1945–1946	Period of White Terror as ultra-right-wing gangs persecute former members of ELAS as well as those in EAM and the Communist Party of Greece (KKE).
1946	(30–31 March) Communists attack Litochoro, launching the third round of civil war.

1946   (31 March) First postwar Greek general election.

1946   (July) Markos Vaphiadis organizes communist forces into
            military units.

1946   (Summer) Fighting escalates in the countryside.

1946   (1 September) Plebiscite restores monarchy.

1946   (28 October) KKE proclaims establishment of the Democratic
            Army of Greece (DAG).

1947   (12 March) Proclamation of the Truman Doctrine.

1948   (May) Murder of CBS correspondent George Polk.

1948   (15 November) Markos Vaphiadis is removed and Nikos Zach-
            ariadis completes the organization of the Democratic Army of
            Greece into a conventional force.

1949   (10 July) Tito closes Yugoslavia's border to Greek communist
            refugees.

1949   (5–16 August) Offensive of the Greek National Army in
            Grammos and Vitsi.

1949   (24–31 August) Final offensive in Grammos.

1949   (26 August) Albanian communist government disarms and
            detains Greek insurgents.

1949   (16 October) Radio Free Greece (the KKE radio) announces
            the end of the insurgency.

1952   Greece becomes a member of NATO.

1967–1974   A junta of colonels establishes a military dictatorship.

1974   Turkish invasion of Cyprus.

1981   Greece joins the European Community.

1981   (October) The Panhellenic Socialist Movement (PASOK),
            led by Andreas Papandreou, brings to power the first Greek
            socialist government since the end of the civil war.

1991   The breakup of Yugoslavia and the reemergence of the
            Macedonian issue.

1992   Mass rally in Thessaloniki on the Macedonian name issue.

2001   Greece adopts the euro.

2004   Athens hosts the Summer Olympics.

2007–2008   Global financial crisis sends shockwaves through the
            Eurozone.

2009   Greek sovereign-debt crisis begins.

2015   Syriza emerges as the largest party in the Greek Parliament.

Dramatis Personae

ALEXATOS, GERASIMOS, aka Odysseus: SOE agent

ALTENBURG, GÜNTHER: the Reich Plenipotentiary in Athens, 1941–1943

ANASTASIADIS, STERGIOS: member of the KKE central committee

ARMATOLI: Christian Ottoman militia

ATKINSON, JOHN: MI9 officer

BAKIRDZIS, COLONEL EURIPIDES: Prometheus I

BALTAZZIS, GEORGIOS: foreign minister of Greece, 1921–1922

BARTZIOTAS, VASSILIS: minister of agriculture, KKE provincial government

BELOYANNIS, NIKOS: senior member of the KKE

BILIRAKIS, KOSTAS: EAM member

BYRON, LORD: British poet and hero of the Greek War of Independence

CADOGAN, ALEXANDER: British permanent under secretary of the Foreign Office, 1938–1946

COAT, RANDALL: British information officer in Thessaloniki

CONSTANTINE I: king of the Hellenes, 1913–1917 and 1920–1922

CURZON, LORD: British Foreign Secretary, 1919–1924

DAFNIS, GEORGE: Greek historian of the 1930s

DAMASKINOS: Archbishop of Athens, 1941–1949

DEMERTZIS, KONSTANTINOS: Greek prime minister, 1935

DIMIKIS, ILIAS, aka Gotsis: important commander of SNOF

DIMITROV, GEORGI: leader of the Comintern and head of Bulgarian Communist Party

DJILAS, MILOVAN: leading member of the CPY, 1938–1954

DODIS, DIONE: young Athenian resident and translator

DONOVAN, WILLIAM: head of U.S. OSS

DREW, GERALD: American delegate to UNSCOB

ECONOMOU, KAITI: Greek actress and collaborator

EHRGOTT, CAPTAIN WINSTON: member of AMM

ERBACH, PRINZ ZU: German ambassador to Greece

FLORAKIS, CHARILAOS: secretary general of the KKE, 1972–1989

FORD, LIEUTENANT BOB: member of the AMM

GEORGE II: king of the Hellenes, 1922–1924 and 1935–1947

GEORGIOU, VASOS: editor of *Rizospastis* during the occupation

GONATAS, GENERAL STYLIANOS: Venizelist leader

GORKIC, MILAN: head of CPY until 1937

GOUNAIRIS, DIMITRIOS: Greek prime minister, 1915, 1921–1922

GRIGORIADIS, COLONEL NEOKOSMOS: Greek officer in charge of the execution of the Six

GRIGORIADIS, PHOIBOS: ELAS officer

GRIVAS, GEORGIOS: led X organization

HADJIMICHAELIS: member of the ELAS central committee

HADZIS, THANASIS: part of KKE leadership

HADZIVASILIOU, CHRYSA: member of the KKE central committee

HAMMOND, NICHOLAS: SOE liaison officer

HATZIANESTIS, GENERAL GEORGIOS: commander-in-chief of the Greek army in 1922

HAWKESWORTH, GENERAL JOHN: commander of fighting British forces, 1944 Greece

HOXHA, ENVER: head of the Albanian Communist Party

IOANNIDIS, YIANNIS: member of the KKE politburo

JEBB, GLADWYNE: British undersecretary, Ministry of Economic Warfare, 1940–1942

KANELLOPOULOS, PANAGIOTIS: prominent Greek politician

KARAGKITSIS-SIMO: member of the KKE central committee

KARDELJ, EDVARD: leading member of the CPY, 1937–1979

KARLIS, CHARILAOS: victim of KKE atrocity

KATSIGIANNAKIS, COLONEL: deputy commander of the gendarmerie

KENNAN, GEORGE: American diplomat

KIRIAKOPOULOS, VASILIOS: Greek minister of justice, 1945

KITSIOS, GENERAL CHRISTOS: commander of Greek forces in Crete, 1941

KONDYLIS, GENERAL GEORGE: Greek prime minister, 1935

KORYZIS, ALEXANDROS: Greek prime minister, 1941

KOTSIS, SPIROS: member of the Tsigantes mission

KOUKOULOU, ROULA: second wife of Nikos Zachariadis

KOURONIOTIS, MIKES: KKE assassin

KOUTSOYIANNOPOULOS, CHARALAMBOS: Prometheus II

KYROU, ANDONIS: KKE assassin

LEEPER, REX: British ambassador to Greece, 1943–1946

LEVIDIS, ALEXANDER: head of an escape and espionage cell in Greece

LIKERI, BERO: Italian sergeant at Paros

LIPPMANN, WALTER: American journalist

LIST, FIELD MARSHAL WILHELM: commander of the German Twelfth Army in Greece, 1941

MACASKIE, FRANK: *Telegraph* correspondent in Athens

MACMILLAN, HAROLD: British resident minister of state in the Middle East

MAKARONIS, VASES: KKE executioner

MAKKA-PHOTIADI, DESPINA: victim of KKE atrocity

MAKRIYIANNIS, YIANNIS: hero of the Greek War of Independence

MALTEZOS, KITSOS: young poet, murdered by the KKE in 1944

MAMAS, HELEN: stringer for the Associated Press

MANDAKAS, EMMANUEL: member of the ELAS central committee

MANIADAKIS, CONSTANTINE: minister of security during Metaxas dictatorship

MARINOS, THEMIS: member of the Harling mission

MARKEZINIS, SPIROS: Greek politician and historian

MARSHALL, GEORGE: U.S. secretary of state, 1947–1949

MATTHEWS, KENNETH: British journalist

MAXIMOS, DIMITRIOS: Greek prime minister, 1947

METAXAS, IOANNIS: Greek dictator, 1936–1941

MONTGOMERY, GENERAL BERNARD: commander of the British Eighth Army

MOUSKOUNDIS, MAJOR NICHOLAS: head of Greek General Security Service, northern Greece

MYERS, EDMUND: general head of the BMM, 1942–1943

NIKOLOUDIS, THEOLOGOS: minister of propaganda during the Metaxas dictatorship

ORESTES: pseudonym of a sadistic KKE executioner, Andreas Moundrichas

OTHON I: second son of king of Bavaria and first king of Greece

PALAIRET, SIR MICHAEL: British ambassador, 1939–1942

PALAMAS, COSTAS: major Greek literary figure

PANGALOS, GENERAL THEODORE: Greek dictator, 1925

PAPADAKI, ELENI: well-known actress, murdered by the KKE

PAPADIMITRIOU, ELLI: SOE link with KKE

PAPADOPOULOS, GEORGE: leader of the 1967 colonels' coup

PAPAGOS, GENERAL ALEXANDER: the commander-in-chief of the Greek army, 1936–1941, 1949

PAPANASTASIOU, ALEXANDROS: Greek prime minister 1924 and 1932

PAPANDREOU, ANDREAS: first socialist prime minister of Greece, 1981–1989 and 1993–1996

PAPANDREOU, GEORGE: Greek prime minister in 1944

PAPANDREOU, MIRANDA: stepdaughter of George Papandreou

PAPARRIGOPOULOS, CONSTANTINE: nineteenth-century Greek politician and historian

PAPAS, ELLI: wife of Beloyannis and KKE cadre

PARTSALIDIS, MITSOS: head of the KKE provincial government

PATRIKIOS, ANDREAS: ELAS judge

PAXINOU, KATINA: actress and KKE supporter

PEARSON, DREW: *Washington Post* columnist

PEPONIS, COLONEL: secretary of the court-martial of the Six

PETROTSOPOULOS, KOSTAS: collaborator and Gestapo agent

PLASTIRAS, GENERAL NIKOLAOS: nominal head of EDES and military and political leader

PLOUMPIDIS, NIKOS: head of the outlawed KKE in Athens

POLK, GEORGE: CBS Middle East correspondent murdered in Greece

POPOV, COLONEL GRIGORI: head of Soviet Mission to Greece

PORPHYROGENNIS, MILTIADIS: member of the KKE central committee

PROTOPAPADAKIS, PETROS: Greek minister of the economy, 1920–1922

PSARROS, DIMITRIOS: Greek officer and resistance leader

PSARROS, DIMITRIS: member of the Tsigantes mission

PYROMAGLOU, KOMNINOS: general secretary of EDES

RADOSAVLJEVIC, DOBRIVOJE: CPY envoy to Yugoslav Macedonia

RALLIS, IOANNIS: puppet prime minister of Greece during the occupation

RANKOVIC, ALEXANDER: head of OZNA

RENDIS, CONSTANTINE: Greek minister of public order and foreign minister

RIGOPOULOS, RIGAS: leader of a clandestine group

ROUSOS, PETROS: part of the KKE leadership

SAKELLARIOU, ALEXANDROS: Greek admiral and politician

SARAPHIS, STEPHANOS: military head of ELAS

SCOBIE, LT.-GEN. RONALD: commander of British forces in Greece, 1944

SEFERIADIS, ALEKOS: member of EAM

SIANTOS, GEORGE: acting general secretary of the KKE

SIMITIS, KOSTAS: prime minister of Greece, 1996–2004

SMITH, HOWARD K.: CBS correspondent

SPILIOTOPOULOS, GENERAL PANAYIOTIS: head of the Gendarmerie

STAKTOPOULOS, GRIGORIS: condemned falsely for the murder of George Polk

STRATOS, NIKOLAOS: Greek minister of the interior, 1920–1922, prime minister, 1922

SVOLOS, ALEXANDER: EAM minister in George Papandreou government

TALBOT, COMMANDER GERALD: British naval and intelligence officer

THEOTOKIS, NIKOLAOS: Greek minister of war, 1920–1922

TSALDARIS, PANAGIOTIS: Greek prime minister, 1932 and 1933

TSIGANTES, COLONEL IOANNIS: led SOE mission to Greece

TSIRIMOKOS, ILIAS: head of the Greek Socialist Party and EAM member

TSOLAKOGLOU, GENERAL GEORGIOS: prime minister of first collaborationist government

TSOUDEROS, EMMANOUIL: prime minister of Greece, 1941–1944

VANSITTART, SIR ROBERT: British permanent under-secretary for foreign affairs, 1930–1938

VAPHIADIS, MARKOS: head of the Democratic Army

VELOUKHIOTIS, ARIS, aka Thanasis Klaras: Andartes head of ELAS

VENIZELOS, ELEFTHERIOS: eminent Greek politician

VENIZELOS, SOPHOCLES: son of Eleftherios Venizelos, Greek politician

VLAHOV, DIMITAR: chairman of the Presidium of the Peoples Republic of Macedonia, 1946–1947

VOULGARIS, ADMIRAL PETROS: commander-in-chief of the Greek navy

VUKMANOVIĆ-TEMPO, SVETOZAR: senior Yugoslav partisan commander

WARD, MICHAEL: SOE officer in Athens

WARNER, EDWARD: head of the Southern Department in the British Foreign Office

WATERLOW, SIR SYDNEY: British ambassador to Greece, 1933–1939

WAVELL, GENERAL SIR ARCHIBALD: commander-in-chief, Middle East Theater of Operations

WILSON, GENERAL MAITLAND: commander-in-chief, Middle East Theater of Operations

WINES, MAJOR GERALD K.: head of OSS part of AMM

WOODHOUSE, COLONEL C. M.: head of the BMM, 1943–1944

YIOTOPOULOS, DIMITRIS: leader of the Archive Marxists

ZACHARIADIS, NIKOS: general secretary of the KKE

ZACHARIADIS, SIFIS: son of Nikos Zachariadis

ZANNAS, ALEXANDER: head of resistance group

ZAOUSIS, ALEXANDER: Athenian writer

ZERVAS, NAPOLEON: leader of EDES

ZEVGOS, YIANNIS: member of the KKE politburo

ZEVGOU, KAITI: wife of Yiannis Zevgos and senior KKE cadre

ZHDANOV, ANDREI: head of the Cominform

Abbreviations and Terms

AAA	Struggle—Restoration—Independence
ACP	Albanian Communist Party
AJ	Arhiv Jugoslavije
AKE	Agrarian Party of Greece
AMFOGE	Allied Mission for Observing the Greek Elections
AMM	Allied Military Mission
Archive Marxists	KKE splinter group
Arvanitis	Greek Orthodox Albanians
ASKI	Archeia Synchronis Koinonikis Istorias
AYE	Istoriko Archio tou Yrourgio Exoterikon
BCP	Bulgarian Communist Party
BEF	British Expeditionary Force
BMM	British Military Mission
C	head of British Secret Intelligence Service
CAB	Cabinet Papers
CC	central committee of a communist party
Chrysi Avgi	Golden Dawn, an extreme right-wing party

Cominform	Information Bureau of communist parties
Comintern	Third Communist International
Committee of Six Colonels	minor resistance group in Athens
COS	Chiefs of Staff
CPSU	Communist Party of the Soviet Union
CPY	Communist Party of Yugoslavia
DAG	Democratic Army of Greece
DGFP	Documents on German Foreign Policy
DSE	Democratikos Stratos Elladas (Democratic Army of Greece)
EAM	National Liberation Front
EDES	National Democratic Greek League
EKKA	National and Social Liberation
ELAS	Greek Popular Liberation Army
ELD	Union of Popular Democracy
EON	Greek Youth Organization
EP	National Civil Guard
FO	Foreign Office (British)
FORCE 133	SOE in Greece
FRUS	Foreign Relations of the United States
FYROM	Former Yugoslav Republic of Macedonia
GAK	Genika archia tou kratous
Gendarmerie	national provincial police
GHQ	general headquarters
GNA	Greek National Army
HMG	His Majesty's government
HS	Records of Special Operations Executive
IAEA	Historical Archive of the National Resistance (Greek)
IDEA	Sacred Association of Nationalist Officers
JUSMAPG	Joint U.S. Military Advisory and Planning Group—Greece

KKE	Communist Party of Greece
KUTV	Communist University for Workers of the East
MI5	British security and counterintelligence service
MI6	military designation of British Secret Intelligence Service
MI9 (N Section)	British service assisting the escape of prisoners of war
MID	Military Intelligence Directorate (British)
Midas 614 SOE	Greek espionage and sabotage group
Military Hierarchy	monarchist faction of Greek generals in 1943
MIR	Military Intelligence Research
NARA	National Archives and Records Administration (U.S.)
NOF	National Liberation Front
November 17	Greek Marxist-Leninist Terrorist Group
OKNE	Communist Youth of Greece
OPLA	Organization for the Protection of the People's Struggle
OSS	Office of Strategic Services
OZNA	Yugoslav Secret Police
PASOK	Panhellenic Socialist Movement
PEAN	Panhellenic Union of Fighting Youth
PEEA	Political Committee of National Liberation
PESE	Philiki Etairia Stratou Eleftheroseos
PRO	Public Records Office (UK)
Prometheus I and II	SOE espionage network in Athens
RG	record group
Rimi Brigade	Greek royalist unit
RN	Royal Navy
Sacred Company	Greek elite company
SAS	Special Air Service
Section D	forerunner of SOE

Security Battalions	German-controlled collaborationist security units
SIS	British Secret Intelligence Service (also known as MI6)
SKE	Socialist Party of Greece
SNOF	Slavic National Liberation Front
SOE	Special Operations Executive (British)
UNRRA	United Nations Relief and Rehabilitation Agency
USAGG	United States Army Group Greece
WO	War Office
X	ultra-right-wing organization
Yiafka	communist clandestine cells
YVE	Defenders of Northern Greece

Prologue

The city of Athens was shrouded in a gray pall as 29 November 1922 dawned, a fitting backdrop for a day that would soon be weighed down by drama and history. Despite the cold rain that drizzled from early morning on, approximately 150 men clustered in a field adjacent to the Goudi military barracks just a few kilometers north of Athens, filled with restless anticipation. They had come to witness the execution of six men who had individually and collectively directed the Greek state for two years. Now prime minister Dimitris Gounaris, foreign minister Georgios Baltazzis, minister of the interior Nikolaos Stratos, minister of war Nikolaos Theotokis, minister of the economy Petros Protopapadakis, and Georgios Hatzianestis, the commander-in-chief of the Greek army, were the most despised men in Greece, tried by military court-martial and condemned to death for high treason.[1] Under their stewardship, the Greek army had been defeated in Turkey, terminating any hope of reclaiming the ancient Greek territories in Asia Minor that had for centuries been under the control of the Ottoman Empire. Thousands of years of Greek habitation in what was once ancient Ionia had come to a tragic and abrupt end.

Three officers had been charged in the court-martial: Hatzianestis, Xenophon Stratigos, and Admiral Michael Goudas were all condemned to military degradation, but the latter two were spared the death penalty; only Hatzianestis faced the firing squad with the politicians, who had also been found guilty.

The execution of "the Six," as they came to be known, was, however, an aberration in Greek politics. Although coups and countercoups were part of the political landscape of Greece, they tended to be relatively bloodless affairs. Before 1922, being on the wrong side of a political conspiracy usually meant the loss of office and influence and the inability to compensate followers with the rewards of government largess. Even the more extreme measures were usually confined to internal exile or a limited period of imprisonment. And the shift in fortune would usually be temporary, rectified by the next election or coup. While strong emotion and violence often accompanied major shifts of political power, the prospect of death as punishment for political failure represented a finality that few were prepared to countenance.

Indeed, most Athenians, including some of the officers who took part in the events that were intended as a national exorcism, assumed or hoped that an external power would intervene to stay the executions—a sentiment that stood in direct contrast to the demonstrations and headlines screaming for blood and retribution during the course of the trial. Even so, few Athenians believed that the executions would take place. Foreign intervention had been an integral part of Greek political life since 1821, and many assumed that the Great Powers, especially the British, would stop the executions. (The expectation of foreign intervention was a recurring theme in the history of Greece. In effect, the modern Greek state was created when the British Navy, along with Russian and French squadrons, destroyed the Ottoman fleet at the Battle of Navarino on 20 October 1827.)

But the condemned men had sinned against the Great Idea, a short phrase that encompassed all the hopes and aspirations of generations of dreamers, ambitious politicians, and kings. A vision of a greater Greece that hearkened back to the glories of classical Greece and the grandeur of Byzantium, the Great Idea had also served as the common bond and a source of identity for Greeks both within and outside Greece. Although the appetite for territorial expansion may have perished on the battlefields of Turkey in 1922, the aftershock of that costly delusion generated a continuum of upheavals that lasted well after 1949. The notion that Greece could someday incorporate all Greeks living within the bounds of the Ottoman Empire as well as the territories that were historically part of the Byzantine Empire was born from the idealism of nineteenth-century Greek nationalism. Its failure generated a frenzy of blame.

In 1922, assigning blame had become the order of the day. Someone had to pay for the Asia Minor catastrophe and atone for the sin of defeat, and the military took on the task of choosing the sacrificial victims. In the second week of September, following their defeat by the Turks, the remnants of the Greek army had retreated to the islands of Lesbos and Chios, where they rebelled against the royalist Greek government. A group of angry officers then took control of the state, supported by ordinary soldiers who, bone weary and hungry, had little other choice. The government in Athens appeared helpless and overwhelmed by the magnitude of the defeat and the daunting problem of Greek refugees fleeing Turkey.

In late September, a few army units had reached Athens and, with almost no resistance, took over the country and proclaimed a provisional government.[2] The Greek military seized Athens quickly, well aware that control of the capital meant control of the state. By establishing a government in Athens, the army was able to secure international recognition for their coup.

The principal leaders of the 1922 coup and members of the subsequent Revolutionary Committee that controlled the country included Colonel Stylianos Gonatas, Colonel Nikolaos Plastiras, and Captain Nikolaos Phokas. For the sake of appearances and under pressure from the British and French, the colonels set up a puppet government led by S. Krokidas. A short while later Krokidas' government was replaced by one headed by Colonel Gonatas, dropping any pretense of civilian rule. Almost immediately upon gaining control of Athens, the army had arrested six politicians, a prince, a general, and an admiral.[3] Ultimately, only the general and five of the politicians were chosen to pay with their lives for crimes against the state. On 26 September, the military issued an ultimatum to the government demanding, among other things, the removal of King Constantine, who agreed to step down and left Greece on 30 September (he died in Palermo a year later). George, the eldest son of the monarch, replaced Constantine, but in 1924 he also went into exile when Greece became a republic.

The real crimes for which the minsters and military commanders were tried, underlines Michael Llewellyn Smith, the author of the most comprehensive and compelling account of the Greek disaster in Asia Minor, were "inefficiency, failure, panic, corruption," and "their political views." An additional charge of mental imbalance was laid against Hatzianestis, who, according to several accounts, was under the delusion that his legs were made out of sugar and were so brittle that if he stood up they might break.[4]

On 29 November, at 11:30 A.M. these once powerful men confronted the end of their lives. For most of them, the journey to the firing squad had begun at the Greek Parliament, where the court-martial was held, within the

highly charged political atmosphere of Athens, and led to the city's Averoff
prison, where they had spent the night waiting anxiously for a decision on life
or death by a military court that was interested less in justice than in the
politics of retribution.

Colonel Katsigiannakis, the deputy commander of the gendarmerie, had
the onerous task of informing the Six that the decision of the court-martial was
death, but the officer could not bring himself to face the condemned. He tried
to pass on the responsibility to a subordinate, and when that failed, he even
pleaded with a prison inmate, but he, too, declined. Finally, Colonel Katsigiannakis worked up sufficient courage to inform the Six that at 11:00 A.M. they
were to be transferred. The authorities in Averoff prison were simply unable to
put into words the fact that these men were going to die.[5]

The possibility of foreign intervention in the matter gained plausibility as a
result of the activities of Commander Gerald Talbot, who had been dispatched
to Athens by Lord Curzon, the British foreign minister, specifically to try to
prevent the executions. Talbot had close ties to Eleftherios Venizelos, the most
prominent member of the Greek government and an opponent of King Constantine. Lord Curzon believed that Talbot could use Venizelos' relationship
with the colonels (who looked on him as their spiritual leader) to persuade them
to commute the death sentences. Talbot arrived in Athens on 28 November, too
late to stay the executions but just in time to save Prince Andrew (Constantine's
son), who had also been held responsible for the Asia Minor defeat.

Andrew had commanded the Greek Second Army Corps in the Asia
Minor campaign, and during the Battle of Sakarya in 1921 he had refused to
execute a direct order to attack the Turkish positions. A military court would
find him guilty of insubordination on 2 December, and the British believed,
as did most of the Greek royalists, that if he were convicted he too would face
a firing squad. Since Andrew had ties to the British royal family, Lord Curzon
had instructed Talbot to negotiate with the leaders of the coup. After a series
of secret meetings, a compromise was reached. Instead of the firing squad,
Andrew was condemned to perpetual banishment. The prince, along with his
family, departed Athens on board HMS *Calypso*.[6]

Andrew's narrow escape and Talbot's intervention added further credence
to the widely held notion that the Great Powers, and the British in particular,
were the ultimate arbiters over Greek affairs. According to the politician and
historian Spyros Markezinis, Talbot was in reality an agent of British intelligence, which is depicted in many Greek accounts as the primary mechanism
for foreign interference in Greece.[7] When the Americans replaced the British

after World War II, however, the CIA supplanted Britain's Secret Intelligence Service as the perceived éminence grise of Greek politics. Despite the conspiracy theories, and the ingrained conviction among the Greeks that foreign intervention was inevitable, in reality no one could have prevented the execution of the Six.

At a little past 10:30 on the morning of the 29th, the families of the prisoners were permitted a last farewell. This was only granted at the insistence of the British ambassador, Sir Francis Lindley—a testament to the bitterness and lack of sympathy for the accused among the military revolutionaries. The condemned men were given last rites. A monk was brought into the prison and reluctantly performed the ceremony, protesting that he could not minister to men responsible for the deaths of priests and the destruction of churches.

Twenty-five minutes later, the prisoners and their guards were herded into two trucks, accompanied by about a dozen officers and gendarmes in automobiles. The procession, led by an ambulance that would later serve as a hearse, then headed to the place of execution. The small convoy sped along Alexandras Avenue, one of the main boulevards in Athens, toward the military barracks of Goudi at the foot of Mount Hymettus. The street was lined with soldiers, who stood in the rain hoping to get a glimpse of the men who had cheated them of victory, but the trucks were covered. Even if most Athenians nursed a secret desire for the Six to be spared, the army needed and demanded a human sacrifice.

At 11:05, the trucks disgorged their reluctant passengers. The clusters of soldiers and nervous spectators milling about in the chilly November morning formed three sides of a rectangle. An army captain collected the prisoners and with his sword pointed each one to his last patch of earth. The first four moved quickly to the designated firing zones, but the last one, Dimitris Gounaris, still suffering from typhoid fever, had to be assisted by Protopapadakis. Behind each man, a shallow grave had been prepared to accommodate his body before burial in a proper cemetery.

Six firing squads (one for each prisoner) presented arms, but the officer in charge, Colonel Neokosmos Grigoriadis, noticed that one squad had six men, one more than the others. He ordered one of the soldiers to retire, but the man demanded to keep his place. The spectators whispered that the soldier had to be from Asia Minor and wanted to take a personal revenge. Colonel Grigoriadis proceeded to read the charges and specifications; however, soon his voice failed, as did his courage. After a few vain attempts at preserving his dignity, he collapsed to the dank ground, and Colonel Peponis, the secretary of the court-martial, finished reading out the document. The officer in charge of the firing squads offered each of the condemned men the traditional option of saying a few last words, followed by the ritual presentation of the blindfold, but the Six refused both. Once again the command was given to the firing squads to present arms.

The privilege of completing the execution was awarded to a veteran of the lost war in Turkey, an amputee. The man, struggling with his crutches, slowly approached the line of soldiers, took his place, and in a clear voice gave the commands to "aim" and "fire." Thirty-one rifles concentrated on the Six, and in a split second, the air seemed to explode. Five of the six collapsed almost immediately; the sixth, Hatzianestis, hesitated and, clutching his throat, spun downward onto the wet earth, gasping for life.[8] Before the officer in charge could administer the coup de grâce, the soldier from Asia Minor, who had held his fire, took matters into his own hands. He dropped to one knee, took aim, and shot the field marshal in the head. A light rain fell on the spectators, who stiffly abandoned the field, some only partly conscious that this particular execution had now solidified the political schism that had dogged Greek society since the beginning of the nineteenth century.

Many of the key individuals who later contributed to the events that led to the civil wars of the 1940s had a role, directly or indirectly, in the trial and execution of the Six. Key among them was Colonel Nikolaos Plastiras, "the Man on the Black Horse," as his friends and followers liked to call him. Plastiras was typical of the professional Greek officer of that time: of humble origins, he had found success and social mobility through a military career. As one of the primary leaders of the Revolutionary Committee, Plastiras held the greatest responsibility for the execution of the Six. Later he argued that he had condoned it to prevent a larger massacre of royalist officers, politicians, civil servants, and even ordinary civilians. Plastiras was a determined antimonarchist and had led two abortive coups in the 1930s to prevent the restoration of the monarchy. Ironically, they paved the way for the return of George II in 1935 and the establishment of the Metaxas regime a year later. In 1945, Plastiras became prime minister, and under his stewardship Greece descended into the final stage of the civil war that broke out in 1946.

Another character in the drama of 1922 was General Theodore Pangalos, an erratic and rabid antimonarchist member of the Revolutionary Committee. Pangalos organized a coup in 1925 and ruled Greece as a petty dictator for six months. The Pangalos interregnum was brief and ridiculous, less of a fascist dictatorship and more an opéra bouffe. The more outrageous examples of his legislation included the devaluation of the currency by having all the paper notes cut in half, the imposition of a dress code for women that decreed that skirts could not rise above the ankle, and the hanging of two civil servants for corruption. With the exception of the last, which for a brief moment shook up the civil service, the rest of his legislation was consigned to comic obscurity. Inflation continued to soar despite Pangalos' intervention, and the result of his foray into fashion was that for at least six months, Greek policemen could legitimately stare at women's legs.

During the occupation from 1941 to 1944, however, Pangalos and his associates played a much darker role. Many of his supporters joined the infamous Nazi-controlled Security Battalions who fought the left-wing resistance. In 1944, under British command, the officers of these Quisling units participated in the December Uprising and afterward contributed to the White Terror that forced many on the left to take up arms and organize guerrilla bands. In 1946, these units formed the nucleus of the Communist Democratic Army, which began its own terrorist retaliations.

In 1922, George Papandreou was a rising star in the Venizelist camp, closely linked with the leaders of the military coup that toppled King Constantine, though he was not a participant. In the fall of 1944, he was brought out of occupied Greece by the British Special Operations Executive (SOE) to head a government-in-exile that included communist and socialist representatives. Less than two months after liberation, the government of national unity collapsed, but Papandreou remained prime minister, and under his tenure the British and Greek government forces fought the left-wing resistance during the December Uprising.

Some of the lesser figures from the events of 1922, such as Colonel Stefanos Sarafis (a junior member of the revolutionary committee), played a greater role in the resistance after 1941. During the occupation, Sarafis was appointed commander-in-chief of the National Popular Liberation Army (ELAS), the left-wing resistance force controlled by the KKE (Communist Party of Greece), which came close to enabling the Greek communists to take over Greece after liberation. Sarafis was not a communist; he remained a committed Venizelist with social democratic views. Yet like many officers of his generation he opted to join ELAS in order to fight the Axis as well as to prevent the return of a British-imposed monarchy.

There were many others present on that cold November morning who in one fashion or another had a hand in turning the pages of history, initiating a cycle of division, revenge, and retribution. Yet individually none of these men possessed the charisma to attract a mass following and impose his will on events. Many were middle-rank officers who later achieved higher office because circumstances created opportunities for advancement, not because of contributions to a particular movement or party. Allegiance to the monarchy or the Venizelist-republican cause was motivated by loyalty to a specific faction to secure promotion more than to a political ideology. Collectively the officer corps lacked a common ideology and vision for the Greek state; that was left to the KKE.

Certainly on that fateful November day, it was unlikely that anyone from the KKE would have been welcome at any official event, let alone permitted to witness the execution. In 1922, before the Asia Minor disaster, the Greek communists could boast about 1,500 members. As a party, the KKE remained on the periphery of the political scene and had been further marginalized by opposing Greek irredentist policies. For the most part, KKE members were in the throes of an ideological bloodletting, consumed by the ebb and flow of events in the Soviet Union and the Communist International.

The communists were concentrated in the poorer districts of Athens and Piraeus and had failed to make an impact on mainstream voters. Their focus was on the small working class in Athens, Piraeus, Thessaloniki, and some of the larger towns. Most KKE activity was confined to penetrating labor organizations, distributing leaflets and the party newspaper, *Rizospastis* (the Radical), or huddling in small coffee shops to debate endlessly the finer points of Marxism. Greece was a country of small farmers, shopkeepers, a limited number of professionals, and artisans, with a modest industrial base employing small numbers of workers. Greek society was not fertile ground for a class struggle that could have swelled the membership of the KKE.

All that changed in 1922. The tidal wave of refugees from Asia Minor provided the KKE with its only consistent supporters. A large number of the members of the central committee and politburo, including Nikos Zachariadis, the secretary general of the KKE from 1931 to 1956, and Markos Vaphiadis, the commander of the Greek communist forces in 1946, came from the working-class neighborhoods of Constantinople, Smyrna, and other large cities of the Ottoman Empire. Later, Greeks from Asia Minor filled the higher ranks of the left-wing resistance and the Democratic Army, but in the 1920s and 1940s the refugees provided the KKE with votes; they elected the first communist deputies to the Greek Parliament in the interwar period. During the civil war of 1946–49, the refugee-dominated regions of western and central Macedonia and Thrace became the principal bases of operations for the Democratic Army.

The harsh life of the refugees in the sprawling shantytowns of Athens and Piraeus became a breeding ground of discontent and political dissent, as well as a source of the malaise that permeated Greek society in the 1920s and 1930s. In 1922 hundreds of thousands had left the shores of Turkey on anything that floated and were dumped on the quays of Greek harbors, while others made the long trek from eastern Thrace. They arrived half starved, stripped of possessions and dignity, and were consigned to makeshift camps stalked by disease and famine. Thousands were packed into overcrowded churches, and still more overflowed into the streets, finding shelter in doorways and alleys.

The helplessness of the refugees was compounded by the Great Depression. Thousands perished, and for the survivors hope was an extravagance few could manage. The Greek authorities had been overwhelmed in 1922 when the refugees first arrived; in 1929 they simply gave up. The limited and modest welfare services of the Greek state could not deal with the more than 1.5 million unexpected new residents in addition to the swelling ranks of the poor and unemployed caused by the collapse of the Greek economy.

Throughout this period, the political establishment remained impotent and, instead of confronting these upheavals, turned inward. Since the foundation of the Greek state in the nineteenth century, irredentist policies had offered a convenient distraction for politicians and the general public from the complex social and economic issues that confronted the new country. The end of the Great Idea exposed the stark realities of a divided society and a fragile financial infrastructure. The military coup of 1922, coming in the wake of defeat in Asia Minor and after such a dramatic sociological upheaval, not only imposed political change but also undermined the notion of legitimate authority.

The causes of the three Greek civil wars from 1943 to 1949 are manifold and complex. The process of political fragmentation that marked the years 1922–44 was triggered on the morning of 29 November 1922. Both this and the postwar period were dominated by the constitutional issue, which forced the Greek people to align with or against the crown. Moderates were squeezed out and compelled to join either the left, which placed them on the side of the KKE, or the right, which forced them to accept the monarchy and by extension an authoritarian political system. The radicalization of Greek society created a harsh and unforgiving environment in the postwar period that made compromise next to impossible. To some extent, the story of the Greek civil war revolves around these political realities and the personalities who attempted to impose their will on events, unleashing a cycle of violence that pitted Greeks against Greeks, killed thousands, and condemned the country to poverty for generations.

CHAPTER I

Origins

Who controls the past, controls the future:
who controls the present controls the past.

—George Orwell

There is no doubt that the Greek civil war arose out of the inequalities and injustices that originated with the inception of a modern Greece following the war of independence in 1830. And yet the emergence of the Greek state was as much a result of the ability of the Great Powers (Britain, Russia, and France) to force the Ottoman sultan to concede the establishment of modern Greece. The Great Powers in 1878 granted the Greeks additional territories, which expanded Greece to include Thessaly. In 1912–1913, during the Balkan Wars, the Greeks acquired more territory in the north, Macedonia and western Thrace, and, thanks to the British, the island of Crete. Foreign intervention was even enshrined in the Greek constitution by assigning Britain, Russia, and France a protecting role, a privilege they exploited in 1917 to remove King Constantine when the monarch refused to drag Greece into World War I on the side of the Entente. In 1922, then, on that gray November day when the six men held responsible for the devastating losses in Asia Minor were lined up in front of the firing squads, it seemed natural that the Great Powers would step in and spare the Greeks from political murder. For most, the verdict of capital punishment in and of itself had been sufficient to soothe the national conscience, but actually going through with the executions was another matter entirely.

The army, or more specifically the officer corps, desperately needed to distance itself from the defeat in Asia Minor. As was the case with the military of the other Balkan states, the army officers saw themselves as the embodiment of the nation and the protectors of the state. Any stigma of defeat or humiliation had to be deflected and consigned to either unscrupulous politicians or to the Great Powers. Consequently, the Greek military chose scapegoats to explain their part in the 1922 defeat in order to preserve the role of the army as the guardian of Greece.

The army's contempt for accountability, however, only perpetuated a cycle of military interventions that frequently destabilized Greek society and guaranteed the army a disproportionate influence in the state. The condemnation of the Six was simply another step in a self-serving process that enabled the military and the political opponents of the Six to avoid direct responsibility for the defeat. Although the disaster in Asia Minor was the immediate responsibility of the government in power, almost the entire Greek political and military establishment had played a part. Tragically, the execution served to enshrine the political schism that had plagued Greek society almost from its inception, and later a mutated form of this division would loom over the bloodletting of the civil wars in the 1940s.

The political, social, and economic divisions that fractured the Greek nation in 1922 were fundamentally the outcome of geography and history that had become part of the cultural baggage of the new Greek state in 1830. It was difficult to shed four hundred years of Ottoman rule that had exulted absolute power and demanded subservience. In effect, the Ottomans stifled political evolution and sustained an intellectual paralysis over most of the Greek communities in the empire. This condition was further compounded by the disparate state of Greek society, which, in turn, fostered regional social, economic, and cultural particularism. Effectively, the Ottoman sultans ruled over a collection of Greek communities clustered in the southern Balkan peninsula, predominant in the Aegean islands, along the south coast of the Black Sea, and dotting the coast of Asia Minor in Turkey.

Life under an alien regime was often harsh, and the fate of individuals and groups depended on capricious sultans and, more often than not, on rapacious pashas. For the most part, the Ottomans were content to allow the Greeks a measure of self-rule, but local Christian notables remained hostage to the whims of the Ottoman administration. Consequently, four centuries of Greek political experience and the exercise of limited civic responsibility developed out of the peculiarities of the Ottoman system, which was predisposed to religion as the main catalyst for social and political organization. Under these circumstances, the idea of civil society did not take hold in mainland Greece.

Even after Greek independence, the political differences that divided the country, combined with the use of rewarding the party faithful, meant that the government in power lacked legitimacy in the eyes of its opponents. This was not the case, however, with the Greek communities in Asia Minor who, in the absence of population upheavals and poverty that beset the mainland, were able to develop the organizations and institutions of civil society that mirrored those of the West.[1]

For the Christian subjects of the empire, the Church was the primary mechanism to any degree of civic autonomy and access to the sultan's court. By the eighteenth century, a powerful financial Christian (and predominantly Greek) aristocracy, based in the Phanar district of Constantinople, assumed a predominant role in the affairs of the Orthodox Church. Effectively, these men achieved through the Church a significant but limited role in the affairs of the empire.

The Phanariots,[2] the collective name for this group of Ottoman Orthodox Christians, possessed linguistic and financial expertise as well as the mercantile networks deficient in the Muslim communities of the Ottoman Empire. Over time, the Phanariots secured almost exclusive control over Ottoman banking and trade, as well as establishing a significant role in the diplomatic affairs of the empire. The sultans were grateful for these services and the Phanariots achieved considerable wealth and influence. Some became patrons of the arts, endowing schools and building churches, but most of them focused on amassing greater fortunes. Wealth not only bought high office, but also could stave off arrest and sometimes execution. Traditionally, Phanariots administered the semi-independent principalities of Wallachia and Moldavia in Romania, which they exploited to recoup the extensive bribes it cost to secure the position in the first place. Significantly, the Phanariot rise to power, comments Christine Philliou,

> flew in the face of religious dogma and political ideology underpin-
> ning Ottoman governance, which forbade Christians a formal share
> in Ottoman sovereignty. Their political success transcended (and
> often effaced) their mercantile origins and connected them with
> Ottoman governance in several ways: as translators, purveyors, tax
> farmer-governors, and diplomats, and through their association with
> the Ecumenical Patriarchate in Istanbul, itself deeply connected to
> Ottoman administration.[3]

In the provinces and islands of mainland Greece, an equally small group of Primates (Christian landlords, tax farmers, and ship owners) formed a powerful oligarchy that set them apart from the landless peasants and poor farmers. Both the Phanariots and Primates were an extension of the Ottoman regime and not inclined to oppose a system that ensured their wealth and status. For most of these privileged few, the prospect of a Greek state, as defined by nineteenth-century nationalism, was an alien and dangerous concept that they outright rejected. Although as a group they opposed revolution and liberalism, some, such as the Ypsilanti family, worked and died in the cause of Greek liberation. In fact, Alexandros Ypsilanti's abortive revolt of 22 February–6 March 1821 demonstrated the appeal Greek independence had for some Phanariots and its futility in the absence of the intervention of a foreign power.

The Ecumenical Patriarch of the Orthodox Church, also a member of the Phanariots, was even less inclined to encourage a movement toward a Hellenic state or any action that threatened the special relationship between the Church and the sultan. In the words of Yennadios, the first Ecumenical Patriarch in the Ottoman era, in a pastoral letter, "only by obedience and submission to the church and its protector (the sultan)" will the Orthodox faithful live in security. Anything that went contrary to the Ottoman regime placed the Greek Orthodox community at risk. In this respect, the Ecumenical Patriarch had condemned the French Revolution, whose ideas threatened to foment rebellion and earn the wrath of the Ottoman authorities. Without a powerful external ally and a substantial military force, there was little that the ideas of the French Revolution could do for the Greeks except bring about Ottoman retribution and at the same time destroy the Greek Orthodox establishment.

In 1821, the Ecumenical Patriarch excommunicated any Greeks who rebelled against the sultan, and a few months earlier also had issued an anathema on Ypsilanti. In practical terms, the patriarch had little choice, as the rebellion was concentrated in mainland Greece, while the center of Greek Orthodoxy was based in Constantinople in the heart of the Ottoman Empire. The revolutionaries could espouse the glories of an independent Greece, but the fact remained that three-quarters of the Greek world was trapped within the Ottoman Empire and could not participate in the rebellion or join the prospective new state.

In addition to these practical considerations and potential liabilities, the Church was fundamentally opposed to the precepts of the French Revolution. During the first two hundred years of Ottoman rule, the influence of the West and the ideas emerging out of the Renaissance were perceived as threats to the Orthodox Church as an institution as well as to its dominion over

Ottoman Orthodox Christians. Until the czars of Russia presented an Orthodox alternative, the Ottoman Empire was the only bulwark against Western
intervention and Catholic penetration of the Orthodox world. According
to L. S. Stavrianos, a historian of the Balkans, the Orthodox Church was
repelled by the "exaltation of reason in place of dogma, the turn to Greek
antiquity. . . . In short, Balkan Orthodoxy opposed the West not only because
it was heretical but also because it was becoming modern."[4] To the Church,
modernity threatened to unravel the monopoly of Orthodox theocracy over
the Balkan Christian communities.

Four centuries of Ottoman rule had reinforced subservience to central
authority, a concept strengthened by the legacy of the Byzantine period, while
the anti-intellectual and anti-science attitude of Muslim clerics had also permeated the mindset of the Orthodox hierarchy in the Ottoman Empire.[5] As
a consequence, the Orthodox Church did not encourage mass learning or
develop teaching orders such as the Jesuits and Franciscans. It is doubtful that
a dynamic clergy educating the mass of *rayia* (sheep, as the Christians were
defined) would have been permitted by the Ottoman authorities or the Muslim establishment. The Patriarchate in Constantinople, consequently, was
primarily concerned with survival and maintaining the privileges of the clergy
and control over the secular affairs of the Greek and other Balkan societies
under its jurisdiction.

Under the Ottoman Empire, the intellectual development of Greek society stagnated. Literacy and education in general practically vanished in Greece
during the Ottoman period. Most communities were unable to support
schools financially and the Church was unable to fill the vacuum. The Patri-
archal School in Constantinople, established in the sixteenth century, was
one exception, but it primarily catered to the Phanariot elite and the families
of the higher clergy in the Ottoman capital. At the end of the sixteenth century, the Church began to fund new schools in Greece, but these were isolated
examples and did not represent an effort at mass education.

Meanwhile, by the eighteenth century, the courts of the Phanariot princes
of Wallachia and Moldavia, as well as their palatial homes in Constantinople,
became centers of learning and the arts. In practice, this only benefited a small
group of individuals, but the Phanariots also offered employment and protection for the handful of Greek professionals and artists who would otherwise
have had to seek work outside the Greek world. Later, some of these professionals, along with a few Phanariots as well as the wealthy Greek merchants of
the diaspora, represented part of the odd collection of revolutionaries who

championed the creation of a Greek state. After the outbreak of hostilities in 1821, the Peloponnesian Primates, the ship owners of the Aegean islands, and the bandits of mainland Greece and the Peloponnese also joined them.

Unlike the Phanariots and primates, the diaspora merchants did not constitute a collective entity and were exposed to the intellectual trends of their adoptive countries. Those in France and Britain were influenced by the liberalism of Western Europe, whereas the Greek merchant communities in Russia were predisposed to the authoritative administration of the czars. Each diaspora group attempted to superimpose its political and constitutional ideas on the Greek independence movement, but in terms of influence was limited to providing money and guns for the 1821 uprising. A few idealists traveled to Greece and participated in the war, but most remained in their adopted countries and used their influence to secure eventual recognition of the fledgling country. In this respect, the role of the European Diaspora Greeks in the nineteenth and early twentieth centuries was that of sources of finance and informal ambassadors between Greece and the Great Powers.[6]

In contrast, the Primates of the Peloponnese and the mainland had deep roots in Greece but remained distinct from the ordinary peasants and shepherds that made up most of the population. Individually, and as a group, they enjoyed considerable autonomy under the Ottomans and represented the wealthiest landowners in Greece. In addition, they augmented their wealth by engaging in tax farming and controlling the commerce of the region.[7] "The Peloponnesian Primates," writes John Petropoulos, "were very much a social class—self-perpetuating, cohesive and alike in their style of life."[8] Unlike the cosmopolitan Phanariots, the Primates were provincial and to a degree reactionary. Although most of them eventually opted to join the movement for Greek independence, they did so reluctantly and only after it became apparent that the Ottomans had lost control of mainland Greece and the Peloponnese. These men understood, however, that the new Greek state was to replace Ottoman absolutism with an indigenous and equally authoritarian regime.

Although the Phanariots and the diaspora elites provided the intellectual momentum and financial resources for the Greek war of independence, they could not agree on the form of government or boundaries of the new state. Their views were influenced by their immediate environment and particular social and economic disposition. The Phanariots and the Greek diaspora merchants were physically and culturally removed from the primarily agricultural and pastoral communities of mainland Greece. The Phanariots, because of their position in the Ottoman Empire and their wealth, constituted a de facto aristocracy with direct participation in the center of an established empire. Cosmopolitan and sophisticated, they had little in common with the landless Greek peasants and shepherds. Most of them preferred a future in which the Ottoman regime would gradually give way to a secular and multicultural empire dominated by an economic elite. Some even believed that after the Muslim element was displaced, it would be only a matter of time before a Christian ruler assumed the sultanate and the Ottoman Empire would follow in the footsteps of Rome and transform into another Greek Byzantium.

The competition between the authoritarianism of Byzantium and the liberalism of classical Greece remained and later mirrored the political and cultural struggles in the modern Greek state in the twentieth century. The nostalgia for Byzantium and autocracy later served as an ideological base for dictators, monarchists, and any political faction in modern Greece that opposed liberal democracy. The Metaxas regime of 1936–1941 not only defined itself as antiparliamentarian and anticommunist but also proclaimed it ushered the dawn of a "Third Christian Civilization," implying a hazy succession from classical Greece to Rome and Constantinople. The conservative right-wing governments that followed World War II, and certainly those after the civil war, preferred the Byzantine to the classical Greek heritage. The junta in 1967 identified with the perceived absolutism of Byzantium and went so far as to ban many of the works of classical antiquity.

For over half a millennium, Greek cities, towns, and villages lived under a flexible despotism that permitted a degree of local administration but at the discretion of the Ottoman sultan and his pashas. The only exception was the bandit groups in the mountains who were a law unto themselves. Although during the war of independence the bandits represented the foot soldiers of the uprising, only a small number of their leaders played any role in the new Greek state. The most prominent or notorious were pensioned off and most of the others simply resumed their former occupation. This was possible because after 1830 the authority of the Greek government was confined to the cities and towns. Large areas of the countryside and the mountains were beyond the reach of the state. Later in the twentieth century these isolated communities would become hostage to guerrilla armies and serve as both the staging areas and battlegrounds of insurgencies opposed to foreign occupation and the political order in Athens. The bandits, however, remained a distinct element and one that could be harnessed to serve the interests of the political factions.

The Greek state that emerged after 1830 was dominated by the factionalism left over from the Ottoman period, the lawlessness of the bandits, and the divisions between the indigenous population and influx of refugees that had arrived in the aftermath of liberation. The inhabitants of mainland Greece and the Peloponnese had been startled and disconcerted by the unexpected influx of refugees, along with Greeks of the diaspora (mostly idealists who had fought in the war of independence) and some Phanariots, who settled in Greece between 1821 and 1830. The indigenous population concentrated around small and essentially isolated communities was suspicious of any newcomers, viewing them as a foreign element.

Another factor in the establishment of the Greek state was that the Great Powers dictated the boundaries and the constitution of the country. The Greeks had to accept a very small state and a foreign monarchy as the price for independence. Both concessions contributed to a national restlessness that fueled irredentist ambitions and created a polarized political environment.

A monarchy was thrust upon the Greek nation by the Great Powers to ensure that the new country adhered to the old regime system in Europe that followed the collapse of Napoleon and the French Revolution. The concept of monarchical rule, however, did not fall on sterile ground, and some of the Greek revolutionary leaders were content to accept an authoritative regime as long as they could form part of the new ruling elite. Others found the institution abhorrent, and once the dust of creating the new state settled, they proceeded to chip away at the powers of the crown, setting in motion a dynamic that engendered almost an ongoing political schism. For almost one hundred and fifty years, the obsession with the constitution suffocated Greek society, sucking up all creative political energy at the expense of any other issue.

In this environment, domestic and national interests gravitated between the king, a small coterie of hangers-on, and clusters of small political blocs. It is indicative of the period (1830–1864) that the Greek political factions that vied for the right to govern the Greek state not only lacked a party structure but even their names linked them directly to the Great Powers. During the rule of King Othon, the first king of Greece, the political factions were labeled the French, English, and Russian parties, respectively. To some degree, the leaders of these factions identified with or were strong proponents of British, French, or Russian influence in Greece with respect to the fulfillment of the Great Idea.[9]

Remarkably, a foreign policy based on the mantra of the Great Idea dominated the discourse and policies of the competing factions. On a pragmatic level, the country's paucity of financial and natural assets left little room for domestic development and modernization and nothing at all for foreign adventures. The Great Idea, in contrast, was flexible, nonpartisan, and sufficiently intangible. As a concept, it fired the imagination of all Greeks regardless of political affiliation and provided a link with the unredeemed communities that had been left in the Ottoman Empire. The only question that remained was how the Great Idea could be implemented, and the sole realistic answer was that the unification of the Greek world could come about only with the help of one of the Great Powers.

The so-called Russian faction was convinced that if the Russian Empire did nothing else it would assist Greek irredentism by simply waging war against the Ottomans. The French faction assumed that France would facilitate the establishment of a greater Greece, but both groups were adamant in their opposition to Britain. This left the British party at a disadvantage since the British were not only occupying the Ionian Islands, but also insisting on maintaining the integrity of the Ottoman Empire. The English faction nonetheless argued that Greece could not expand without British support, pointing out that the Royal Navy dominated the eastern Mediterranean and could intervene at will for or against Greece.

Fundamentally, this argument underscored the crux of the Greek foreign policy dilemma—maritime vulnerability. No matter how the factions positioned their irredentist ambitions, they could not escape the realities of Britain's intervention for or against the future expansion of Greece. Indeed, the creation of the modern Greek state owed a great deal to the involvement and support of the British Empire. Consequently, a rather special relationship developed between the two countries, represented on the one hand by the romanticism of Lord Byron's death at Missolonghi while fighting for Hellenic liberty, and, on the other, by the Royal Navy, which on more than one occasion imposed a British outcome on Greek and, for that matter, Ottoman ambitions. As long as the focus of the Greek state was the Great Idea, foreign policy and the relationship to the Great Powers played a disproportionate role in the political life of the country.

Regardless of the lofty ambitions for a greater Greece, independence from the Ottoman Empire did little to change the fact that the country was poor in resources and economically unviable. Furthermore, the rugged and mountainous terrain of Greece as well as poor communications concentrated the exercise of political power in Athens. With few exceptions, most of the political leaders lived in the capital or had the resources to maintain a home there and a separate residence in the countryside—success in government depended upon wealth and establishing a political base in Athens. Consequently, the

Greek political establishment, even in the twentieth century, was small, self-contained, and fed from a complex system of clientage that revolved around an even smaller group of powerful individuals. Although the new Greek state had adopted European political institutions, the use of patronage, structural corruption, and servile (yet fickle) obedience to authority remained a legacy of the Ottoman Empire.

The century of internal struggles produced a strange assortment of characters who emerged from obscurity and came to the forefront of the tragic events of the 1940s. In this context, Nikos Zachariadis, as the head of the Communist Party (KKE), bears a measure of responsibility for the onset of the civil war. He was not the only one: a parade of politicians, military officers, and resistance leaders from the left and right made their own contributions that collectively pushed the country into the cataclysm of civil war.

Zachariadis was born in Adrianople (present-day Edirne) on 27 April 1903 and died on 1 August 1973, in Surgut, Siberia.[10] He hanged himself after having written to the leaders of both the KKE and the Communist Party of the Soviet Union (KPCC/CPSU) that he would do so as an ultimate act of political protest in response to his illegal detention in the Soviet Union. Nonetheless, the authorities concealed the true cause of his death and announced that he had suffered a heart attack. The Soviets wanted to suppress any reaction to his suicide from his supporters and swiftly proceeded with the funeral in Tyumen. Maria Novakova, Zachariadis' first wife with whom he had two children, Cyrus and Olga, was the one chosen to write to his family in Greece about the bad news. The letter was sent on 7 August 1973 and made references to the last wishes of the deceased; namely to have a handful of Greek soil, which he kept all those years among his belongings, thrown into his grave and for a bouquet of flowers to be placed on his mother's grave every year on the first day of August, on his behalf. His last wishes are indicative of the level of nostalgia that must have both tormented Zachariadis and sustained him while in exile.[11]

In the days prior to his suicide, Zachariadis wrote to various members of the Communist Party of Greece and its general secretary, Charilaos Florakis, and to the CPSU, led by Leonid Brezhnev. In these letters, Zachariadis expressed his intention of taking his own life as a final act of protest if his rights as a political refugee were not finally reinstated, so that he would be able to leave the Soviet Union.[12] He had been desperately seeking to end his exile and to be able to travel to Greece, even amidst the dictatorship, to undergo a trial, if necessary, in order to clear his name.[13] In Greece, only a few individuals knew that Zachariadis had taken his own life. Among them was his second wife, Roula Koukoulou, who was part of the KKE leadership and did not believe that Zachariadis would have committed suicide. After receiving a letter from Zachariadis soon after his death, she made their only son Sifis swear not to share with anyone that he had killed himself. Sifis Zachariadis kept his promises, something his father had taught him for seventeen years.[14] The truth was published in a local Russian newspaper with information provided by KGB Colonel Petruskin and reprinted in 1990 in the Moscow newspaper *Komsomolskaya Pravda*. The Greek press soon picked up the news and in the process revived public interest in Zachariadis. It also set in motion his family's efforts for the repatriation of his remains, which arrived in Greece on 21 December 1991, with the burial taking place in the presence of KKE members and Zachariadis supporters.[15] Ten years later, the KKE rehabilitated Zachariadis. Unfortunately, forty years after his death, one still cannot access the records kept about him in Greece and Russia.[16]

Zachariadis' tragic end was the culmination of his life under Soviet surveillance. Sifis Zachariadis recounted that his father lived in a small room, six to seven meters long, and spent hours writing letters and notes to ensure that his case, his plight, and his existence were not forgotten. For an office he used a table, on top of which he usually kept several of the books he had acquired over the years. Until the very end of his life, he tried to keep informed of international developments and read voraciously newspapers he had access to, usually a week or two after their publication date. Furthermore, after his oldest son Cyrus was able to secure a transistor radio for him, Zachariadis would listen to the news broadcast as often as possible.[17]

As a young man Zachariadis was restless and sought adventure. He wanted to join the Greek army during World War I, only to be forbidden by his parents. By 1923, he had twice visited the Soviet Union, attracted by its proclaimed lofty ideals and the scale of the social experiment being implemented. He entered the newly established Communist University for Workers of the East (KUTV) and became a member of the Soviet Communist Youth. Zachariadis remained in Russia until 1925, having lived most of his life in the Ottoman Empire and the Soviet Union. Even when he moved to Greece he only spent just over a decade as a free man, nine years in Greek or German incarceration, and four years conducting the communist insurgency from the northern mountains of Greece. Although by the end of his life, confined to dreary exile, he longed for Greece, but was it for a chance of political rehabilitation or to return to a country and people he hardly knew? It may be that Zachariadis was less a Greek and more a Soviet man—a creature fashioned by

Stalinist ideals that remained with him until that fateful day when he realized that he could not escape the Soviet system.

Meanwhile, in 1923, the KKE was facing a serious challenge from a break-away communist organization. The Archive Marxists included members of the KKE who had ideological objections to how the Greek Communist Party administered and utilized Marxism. The Archive Marxists focused on theory and quickly contested the KKE's appeal to the working class. Members of the organization began translating notable theoretical texts, while at the same time criticizing the KKE for not educating the working class in Marxist theory,[18] which they sought to remedy with their journal, the *Archive of Marxism*.[19] Dimitris Yiotopoulos assumed the leadership of the organization and joined the Trotskyite movement, becoming the mortal enemy of the KKE.[20] The main objective of the Archive Marxists was to create dedicated and disciplined supporters who, guided by Marxist theoretical texts, would be able to assume control of Greece just as the Bolsheviks did in Russia.[21]

When Zachariadis returned to Greece in the mid-1920s, he was able to galvanize the KKE and counter the inroads achieved by the Archive Marxists for the hearts and minds of the Greek workers. Shortly after Zachariadis arrived in Athens he was elected to the KKE's central committee and the Communist Youth of Greece (OKNE)'s representative from the Soviet Communist Party. He remained in Greece for four years and then returned to the USSR in 1928–1929 to continue his studies on communist ideology. It is not clear why he left Greece, but while in Russia he became a member of the Communist Party of the Soviet Union. He came back to Athens in 1931 a more fervent communist, with an unshakable faith in Stalin's interpretation of Marxism, and quickly rose to the leadership of the party. His credentials were impeccable and with his Russian pedigree, the support of the Comintern, and more important that of Stalin, he was elected Secretary General of the KKE in 1934. As head of the KKE, Zachariadis instilled discipline in the party and quickly imposed his authority over the Greek communists. Furthermore, under his leadership the organization and membership flourished. As a reward for his success in bringing the KKE under the sway of Stalinist discipline, he was admitted to the Comintern.[22] Unfortunately for Zachariadis, following the 1936 establishment of the Metaxas quasi dictatorship, he was arrested and imprisoned on the island of Corfu.[23]

The Metaxas regime was remarkably enlightened with respect to the segregation of political and criminal offenders, allowing the former some latitude in keeping contact with the outside world and even permitting them to wear ordinary clothes. Under these conditions, Zachariadis maintained a prolific correspondence and produced several substantial texts. He wrote treatises on the poet Kostis Palamas (1869–1943), a study on Greece's prevailing economic and political difficulties, a provisional blueprint for the KKE's future course of action, and, finally, interpretations of the history of the KKE.[24] When the Italians invaded Greece, Zachariadis published several open letters to the Greek people urging them to unite and fight against the fascists, even if they had to do so under the Metaxas regime.[25] At this point, however, Zachariadis' tragedy of missteps began.

In the excitement of the moment when Greeks of all stripes banded with the Metaxas government to fight the common enemy, Zachariadis over-reached himself. In the first open letter to the Greeks, he urged them to fight the Italians. It was the right move and one that placed the KKE alongside the sentiments of mainstream society. Unfortunately, the KKE's call to arms against fascism was contrary to Stalin's rapprochement with Hitler and, by extension, with Italy, Germany's Axis partner. Zachariadis, not for the first time, had to choose between loyalty to Greece and devotion to Stalin. In a second letter, 10 November 1940, he condemned the Greek struggle as an imperialist war and called for the intervention of the Soviet Union. The Greek communist leader had his appointment with history, but chose to subsume the interests of his country to those of the Soviet Union. In so doing, he cheated himself and the KKE of the miracle of the Greek victory against the Italian Empire and the first victory against the Axis in World War II.[26]

The feat of arms that gave the Greek army incredible victories against the Italians provoked Hitler into action, and in April the German army overran Greece. Although the occupation authorities released many Greek communists because of the Russian-German Pact of 1939, Zachariadis was not so fortunate. The Nazi authorities transferred him to the notorious Dachau concentration camp in southern Germany, where he would be confined for the remainder of the war.[27] Once again, Zachariadis missed a historic opportunity; while he was languishing in Dachau, events in Greece passed him by, cheating him of securing a reputation in the resistance.

In Zachariadis' absence, the KKE founded EAM (Ethniko Apeleutherotiko Metopo—National Liberation Front), and a few months later (January 1942) established its military wing, ELAS (Elinnikos Laikos Apeleutherotikos Stratos—Greek Popular Liberation Army). The former would evolve into a mass-based anti-Axis organization in Greece, expanding well beyond its original communist origins to include an estimated two million members.[28] The latter, under the military command of Aris Velouhiotis, nom de guerre of Thanasis Klaras, undertook military operations against the occupying forces, but from October 1943 until February 1944 waged an armed struggle against the nonleft resistance groups.[29]

The communist-led EAM-ELAS achieved considerable success not only in fighting the Germans and Italians, but also in bringing about a social evolution, particularly in the mountain villages that served as places of supply and sources of recruits—all these accomplishments, however, occurred without Zachariadis. Joseph Broz, or Tito, Zachariadis' Balkan counterpart, emerged as a major international personality within and outside the Communist International, while the Greek communist leader was consigned to insignificance as an inmate in a German concentration camp. Perhaps this bitter reversal of fortune and lost opportunity to make his mark in wartime drove Zachariadis to seek a new battlefront in 1946. Indeed, after four years in Dachau, he was a man in a hurry. He was liberated by the U.S. army and returned to Greece in the spring of 1945.[30]

Despite the failure of the KKE to seize power at the time of liberation and the defeat of ELAS in the December Uprising, Zachariadis' return to Greece was a significant morale booster for the KKE membership. The party had expanded and many of the new members were attracted to the KKE less by ideological affinity than by the exigencies of the occupation. The reliability of the wartime recruits was questionable, while the finger-pointing within the KKE leadership over who was responsible for the defeat of EAM-ELAS in December further exacerbated the fissures that had developed in the party since 1944. Zachariadis was not tainted by defeat, and as Moscow's man he was in a position to purge and guide the KKE back in an orthodox Marxist direction. In 1945, Zachariadis had little faith in guerrilla warfare as it had been waged in the Greek mountains during the occupation, but he believed in the Marxist notion of a workers' uprising in the cities.

Initially, however, Zachariadis proceeded with caution, trying to gauge the situation not only in Greece generally, but also the postwar dynamics of the KKE and the Greek left. To the surprise of many hardliners, he approved of the Varkiza Accord that had ended the December Uprising and had underscored the defeat of the left.[31] Zachariadis then took the first steps in regaining control of the party by denouncing the well-known ELAS chief, Aris Velouhiotis, who had publicly rejected the peace accord.[32] The exact reason for Zachariadis' actions is unclear. Perhaps this was a signal to the government that the KKE were abiding by the treaty, or he needed to buy time to reorganize the party and reaffirm his authority as well as eclipse any potential challenger to his leadership.[33] Increasingly, however, he began to sound ambiguous about the possibility of returning to an armed struggle.[34]

The defining moment for Zachariadis and the future of the KKE, and the left in general, came at the end of March 1946. The government called for a national election under international supervision, which posed a dilemma for Zachariadis. If the KKE participated in the election it faced two possibilities: first, despite the presence of international observers its members, particularly those outside the main urban areas, would face intimidation and not vote; second, even if all went well, the communist vote would not be enough to give the KKE strong representation in the new Parliament. Either outcome could have marginalized the KKE, and coming so close to achieving power, only to suddenly lose it, was not acceptable to Zachariadis. According to some KKE estimates, if they had fielded candidates and encouraged their supporters to vote they could have secured about a third of all the Parliament seats.[35] Despite strong indications from Stalin to adopt a gradual approach and to participate in the political process, Zachariadis ignored his Soviet patron and opted for military confrontation.[36]

Unknown to Zachariadis and the KKE leadership, the Soviet Union had abandoned the Greek communists. At the Yalta Conference in February 1945, Stalin had reassured Churchill that he would stand by their agreement, made in Moscow in 1944, not to interfere with British policy in Greece. Unfortunately, neither Zachariadis, nor anyone else in the KKE, had any idea of the arrangements made between Stalin and Churchill. Accordingly, in February 1946, the Central Committee announced that the supporters of the left should not register in the electoral lists and should abstain from the March elections.[37] The Greeks went to the polls on March 31 and elected a government that did not represent a sizable segment of the population both in the cities and in the countryside. By all accounts, however, the election was, albeit with some incidents, as fair as it could have been under the circumstances. In June, Zachariadis had also denounced the Plebiscite Bill, which was to decide the fate of the monarchy, as fraudulent and ordered that the KKE and the left were not to take part when the referendum was held on 1 September.

As a result, in September 1946, a legitimate referendum restored the monarchy and George II returned to his palace. Within six months, the political status quo ante was reestablished. Zachariadis had miscalculated and in so doing marginalized the KKE and the left and in the process created the conditions for civil war. It is impossible to speculate on the future of Greece if the communists and the left had taken part in the election and the plebiscite; perhaps the country would have eventually evolved into a liberal democracy. At the very least Zachariadis' legacy would not have been civil war and complete defeat.

By abstaining from the election and launching an insurgency, the KKE abandoned its role as a legitimate opposition and almost overnight was transformed into an outlaw organization. The communist bloc eventually provided arms and supplies to the KKE, but denied them official recognition, thus guaranteeing that both the Provisional Communist Government in the Mountains—in reality based in Yugoslavia—and the Democratic Army of Greece (DAG) remained an insurgency for the duration of hostilities rather than an acknowledged belligerent. The absence of recognition from any government robbed the KKE of legitimacy, and permitted the government in Athens to label the DAG forces as bandits.

The DAG, despite these liabilities and an erratic supply situation, achieved remarkable tactical victories, confounding the Greek army as well as its British advisors. The KKE guerrilla war was the first post–World War II insurgency that challenged the limits of a conventional military. In March 1947, the Truman Doctrine brought the United States into the affairs of Greece and elevated the civil war from a domestic fratricide into an international concern in which the combatants became the proxies of the United States and its allies against those of the Soviet Bloc. The Americans poured massive supplies of war material and economic aid into Greece, but in the end the war was not so much won by the Greek army and its backers as lost by the communists. In 1949, Zachariadis staked everything by committing his forces to conventional battles and faced defeat by a reorganized and well-disciplined Greek army.

The remnants of the DAG escaped to Albania and some even into Yugoslavia (despite the Stalin-Tito split and Zachariadis' decision to remain loyal to the Soviet leader), which put them beyond the reach of their pursuers. Zachariadis also escaped and initially found refuge in Romania, where KKE and DAG survivors were accommodated temporarily, before settling in the USSR. During the period of de-Stalinization and the Khrushchev "thaw," he was deposed as the KKE's General Secretary.[38] "You must have heard my news," he wrote to Alexis Parnis, an already politically excommunicated comrade: "I was expelled from the Party after thirty-six years! That way we are both in the same denominator. Let it be. The wheel will turn, and the poor man will rejoice."[39] But he did not. Zachariadis was sent into a protracted forced exile until his eventual suicide in the summer of 1973.

The Greek communist leader, like many of his counterparts in the Balkans, Europe, Russia, and China, viewed the world through the prism of ideology set by Stalin. It was a harsh creed that permitted no compromise, and even the hint of disloyalty invited immediate retribution. Mistakes, failure, or being caught in the wrong place on the shifting communist spectrum meant catastrophic defeat resulting in confinement—at least for most communist leaders—and possibly execution. The death of Stalin and the rise of Khrushchev spelled the end of many of the Soviet dictator's followers. Men such as Zachariadis understood this dynamic and as long as death was not the result, they could anticipate that circumstances would change. They had mimicked Stalin's style of leadership and imposed the Soviet interpretation of communism and history in their respective parties.

Zachariadis did not have the luxury of condemning his opponents in Greece to death or to a gulag, but he did have the power to excommunicate those he deemed schismatic from his and Stalin's version of the communist faith. By the 1930s, Zachariadis had fashioned the KKE into a Stalinist communist party purged of any cadres who had views contrary to his and those of the Moscow leadership. The decade was also ripe with opportunities for the Greek communists to find a foothold in the Greek body politic. The Great Depression, the impact of the Asia Minor refugees, and the failure of the traditional political establishment to deal with the ongoing economic crisis, along with a succession of coups and countercoups, created opportunities for the KKE to move from the fringe to mainstream politics.

CHAPTER 2

Authoritarianism, War, and Occupation

He who establishes a dictatorship and does not kill Brutus, or he who
founds a republic and does not kill the sons of Brutus, will only reign a
short time.

—Machiavelli, *Discourses on Livy*

The dynamics of Greek politics in the 1920s and 1930s were shaped by the
tumultuous events that had buffeted Greek society in the late nineteenth and
early twentieth centuries. The course of Greek irredentism, launched successfully by Eleftherios Venizelos in the Balkan wars of 1912–13, culminating with
the Asia Minor disaster during the summer of 1922, came to an abrupt end.
In the decades to come, notions of a greater "Greece" surfaced occasionally
but were confined to the incorporation of Cyprus.[1] The rest of the decade was
marked by military coups, the abolition of the monarchy, the establishment
of a short-lived republic from 1924 to 1935, followed by monarchy, then by
Metaxas' authoritarian regime.[2]

The collapse of Greek financial institutions and the mass unemployment
resulting from the Great Depression, as well as problems created by the influx
of over a million refugees from Asia Minor, greatly undermined the credibility of the republic and hastened its demise. On 3 November 1935, after another attempted military coup, a fraudulent plebiscite led to the restoration
of the monarchy. The return of King George II was less the result of increased
popularity for the crown than a symptom of national malaise, brought about
by the 1929 stock market crash and the subsequent international financial
collapse, the never-ending political intrigues on the part of the major parties,
but most of all the intervention of the military.

FIG. 2. Eleftherios Venizelos, Greece's most prominent politician, whose followers
overthrew the monarchy. Library of Congress.

Individual members of the armed forces have played significant roles in
Greek politics from the inception of the modern Greek state. Nevertheless,
until 1922, the army had refrained from assuming power directly, and had only
occasionally attempted to influence the political leadership.[3] A major factor
that impeded such ambitions was the factionalism and system of clientage that
permeated the officer corps. Indeed, the officer corps simply mirrored the
divisions within Greek society, each faction looking to a different political
leader or the monarchy for professional favors.[4] In 1915, Greek officers were,

for the first time, compelled to choose sides over participation in World War I, the choices being either neutrality, as advocated by King Constantine, or alignment with the Entente, espoused by Venizelos.[5] In so doing, the officer corps lost its cohesion as a corporate body. The ensuing fracture created in the army (and throughout the country) became permanent with the military coup of 1922 and the blood feud after the execution of the Six.[6]

The revolution of 1922 not only forced the abolition of the monarchy, but also heralded a new era of direct intervention by the army in the making and unmaking of governments. Each coup, whether successful or not, was followed by a purge of the armed forces. In 1922, the royalists were drummed out of the military, but in the succeeding coups of 1933 and 1935, the ax fell mostly on republican officers so that by 1940, almost all antimonarchists had been forced into retirement.[7] As a result, control of the armed forces reverted to royalist officers, who, in conjunction with some members of the Populist Party, began to clamor for the restitution of the monarchy. In 1932, the Populists (the traditional party of the royalists) had disavowed their allegiance to the crown, but as George Dafnis observed, their rejection was superficial and three years later (in 1935) they reasserted their support for George II.[8] As indicated above, after the Populist victory at the polls and immediately following the March 1935 coup attempt, tremendous pressure was placed on Panagiotis Tsaldaris, the Populist premier, to bring about an immediate restoration of the monarchy.

Tsaldaris had promised a referendum on the issue of the monarchy, but following the landslide victory in the 1935 general election, many in his party, and primarily senior army officers, demanded that he abolish the republic and invite George II to return to Greece.[9] Tsaldaris refused, and his government was promptly overthrown by the military. He was replaced by General George Kondylis, one of the conspirators and a former republican who, upon assuming office, declared the end of the republic and set a referendum on the return of the monarchy for 3 November 1935. The results of the plebiscite were outlandish even to the most credulous supporters of the monarchy; out of 1,492,992 votes cast, only 34,454 opposed the return of George II.[10] The restoration of the monarchy, according to John S. Koliopoulos, "brought in a new and decisive factor, the King, who held the undisputed loyalty of the military."[11] Other factors, however, emerged that not only secured the position of the monarchy, but also brought Greece closer to the totalitarian regimes of Germany and Italy.

The reinstatement of George II did not heal the fissures of Greek society, and the elections of 1936 showed this clearly by producing a parliament divided almost evenly between the Liberals and Populists, along with fifteen communist deputies. Since the bitter divisions between the Venizelists and monarchists made it impossible for the major parties to cooperate and form a coalition government, the other practical option was for one of the major parties to work with the communists. In 1936, the Greek Communist Party was on the fringe of the political scene and although they did not enjoy widespread support, with the fifteen seats they had won they were in a position to hold the balance of power in parliament.[12] Both major parties initiated talks with the communists, and the Liberals actually managed to reach an agreement with them, but these efforts at political compromise were unsuccessful. When news of a possible Liberal-KKE coalition leaked out, Alexander Papagos, the minister of army affairs, with the support of the chiefs of the air force, navy, and gendarmerie, informed the king that the armed forces would not countenance a government that included communists.[13]

In the period preceding and following the election, Greece was undergoing labor unrest accompanied by strikes and violence, which occasionally led to serious casualties.[14] On 8 May 1936, a strike in Thessaloniki by 6,000 tobacco workers broke down in violence, which prompted railway and tram workers to strike in sympathy. The government was then forced to deploy army units to support the gendarmerie and issued a decree mobilizing the railway men and tram workers. These measures were ineffective, and the number of strikers reached 25,000. On 9 May the gendarmerie clashed with demonstrators around Government House, and in the ensuing battles twelve died and two hundred protestors were wounded.

In the absence of a majority government or coalition, a caretaker government, headed by Konstantinos Demertzis, administered the country. Unfortunately, Demertzis died in April and Ioannis Metaxas, the deputy premier and the leader of a small right-wing party, succeeded him as head of the government. The death of Demertzis had been preceded by the demise of a number of other prominent political figures including Kondylis, Venizelos, Tsaldaris, and Alexandros Papanastasiou, which at this critical juncture deprived the country of some of its most influential and experienced leaders. The coincidence between the deaths of these individuals and the labor unrest sweeping over Greece provided an opportunity for Metaxas, with the support of the king, to gain control of the state. The Workers' Federation had declared a twenty-four-hour general strike for 5 August, and on 4 August, Metaxas persuaded the king to suspend certain articles of the constitution and declare martial law in order to avert a communist revolution.[15] After 4 August 1936, King George II gave Metaxas the authority to rule by decree, thus establishing, in effect, a royalist dictatorship that lasted until the king reinstated the constitution in February 1942.

Unlike the totalitarian regimes of Germany and Italy, the Metaxas regime was not based on a political party nor did it seek to secure a mass following. Although supported by the military, it was not given power by the army and did not develop a Fascist or Nazi ideology, beyond some vague references to the establishment of a "Third Greek Civilization."[16] It had some of the trappings of a dictatorship, and Metaxas has often been labeled a dictator, but his power rested on the sufferance of the king. Metaxas is better defined as a strongman and the head of an authoritative regime, one whose conservative credentials were akin to those of the governments that had preceded it.[17]

According to Metaxas, the regime established on 4 August 1936 was "an anti-Communist Greek state" that was totalitarian with an agricultural and labor basis and therefore antiplutocratic. It did not depend on a political party, but rather constituted the whole of Greek people, excluding the communists and reactionary old political parties and factions.[18]

The dictatorship, in essence, was a royalist dictatorship that functioned through Metaxas, and a small but devoted group of lieutenants propped up by the armed forces. The military depended on the monarchy for their rank and to keep their Venizelist counterparts out of the armed forces. In addition, an efficient security service quickly weeded out any opposition to the regime. Unlike Hitler and Mussolini, Metaxas did not make a conscious attempt to distance himself from the military in order to avoid the appearance of relying on the army for support, because the officer corps remained loyal to the king, and his authority was maintained entirely at the king's discretion.[19]

The leaders of the major parties failed to mount an effective opposition or attempt to undermine the dictatorship and, for the most part, they did not pose a serious threat to the regime. Their activities were confined to written protests or efforts to convince the king that they could provide an alternative to Metaxas.[20] There were exceptions, most notably Panagiotis Kanellopoulos, but the noncommunist resistance effort came from Venizelist officers purged after the 1930s coup attempts. With the exception of a single abortive rebellion in 1938, the efforts of these ex-officers were restricted to plotting future coups and printing illegal pamphlets.[21]

For Metaxas, the communists constituted the most serious danger, and immediately upon assuming power, he outlawed the KKE.[22] Constantine Maniadakis, the minister of security, established a wide network of informants; through communist renegades and police agents he was able to infiltrate and ultimately dominate the local communist organizations. A month after the declaration of martial law, the authorities apprehended the general secretary of the KKE, Nikos Zachariadis. By April 1938, all members of the Politburo had been arrested with the exception of George Siantos.[23] Hundreds were arrested, imprisoned, or sent to internal exile on remote islands, while thousands more were coerced into signing declarations of repentance in order to avoid incarceration.[24] Just before the Italian invasion in October 1940, a proud minister of propaganda, Theologos Nikoloudis, claimed that 57,000 had signed declarations. Remarkably, these figures exceeded the total membership of the Communist Party, which did not surpass 14,000, and must be attributed to the excessive zeal of the police, who often seized individuals assumed to have communist sympathies.[25] Eventually many of those unjustly arrested or condemned to prison drifted to the KKE.

The tactics used by Maniadakis quickly undermined the communists, with most of their leadership in prison, while the few who managed to escape were forced to live a clandestine existence that later proved invaluable during the occupation.[26] In addition to the use of informants and infiltration of police agents into communist organizations, Maniadakis created a fake KKE central committee as a counterweight to the existing central committee, which, along with the numerous declarations of repentance, came close to destroying the Greek Communist Party. Throughout this period, the police, the gendarmerie, and the security service were the principal forces used not only to combat the communists but also to be the main prop of the Metaxas regime. Unlike the police forces, the army remained exclusively loyal to the king despite Metaxas' efforts to secure the loyalty of the officer corps.[27]

Aside from the persistence and audacity of its loyal cadres, the continued survival of the communist party is partially attributable to Zachariadis' policy of decentralizing some of the KKE underground into independent self-contained cells.[28] Although many of these units were penetrated by the Metaxas security services, enough survived to provide a core for the party's reorganization after 1941.[29] Another important, albeit inadvertent, contribution was made by the Metaxas regime's policy of keeping arrested communists together in special political prisons and islands of exile. The imprisoned communists transformed their incarceration into useful activity by conducting classes on Marxism and training the less experienced cadres in clandestine work.[30] To some extent, these factors explain how the KKE, although seemingly at the point of extinction during the Metaxas period, was capable by autumn of 1941 to begin organizing a wide and effective underground.[31]

Despite the vigilant efforts of the dictatorship's security services, some opposition remained and communist cells and groups of Venizelist officers continued to work underground. Their survival and reemergence during the occupation would play a pivotal role in the resistance. Each year, however, the Metaxas regime tightened its grip on the country and made it progressively more difficult for anyone to organize effective opposition. The general population continued to remain indifferent to Metaxas even though the strongman instituted a number of reforms which, if they did not inspire popularity for the government, assured it benign toleration. In the face of public apathy toward Metaxas and the king, some individuals in the underground became willing recruits for the British intelligence services. It is impossible to discern their motives except that the increased presence of the British intelligence services after 1939 raised the specter of possible British intervention—a situation that had historical precedence in Anglo-Greek relations.

For most of the 1920s and 1930s, Great Britain, the foreign protagonist in Greek affairs, had little interest in the small Balkan country. The Greek debacle in Turkey was a major setback to British ambitions in the Near East and after 1923, the British had to reconsider their policy toward Greece, Turkey, and the Balkans. On 14 October 1922, the chiefs of staff of the military services in a memorandum to the Foreign Office recommended closer ties between Britain and Turkey, rather than with Greece. The chiefs of staff also warned that an aggressive attitude toward Turkey could endanger the allegiance of Britain's Muslim subjects, who regarded Turkey as the champion of their faith. The chiefs of staff also suggested that friendly relations with Turkey would allow Britain to maintain control over the Bosphorus and Dardanelles Straits with minimal forces.[32]

Within this new geopolitical context, Greece ceased to be a factor in British policy and strategy in the eastern Mediterranean. The British government regarded the internal political situation in Greece with indifference and for the most part lost all interest in the country. According to Sir Robert Vansittart, "Those who helped Greece into a mess (the Greek invasion of Asia Minor) did nothing to help her out."[33] After the Chanak crisis in 1922, Britain had little enthusiasm for foreign adventures, and the prime ministers who followed Lloyd George were more concerned with domestic and imperial matters. "When they looked to Europe at all," comments C. M. Woodhouse, "Greece fell within their blind spot. The Near East was insensibly superseded by the Middle East, which meant the Arab states and the problem of carrying out the Balfour Declaration on Palestine."[34]

During the next sixteen years (1923–39), British-Greek relations remained dormant except for the occasional disturbance by the Greek population of Cyprus. Despite the flare-up of Greek nationalism in Cyprus and demonstrations of anti-British feeling, politicians in Athens were content to maintain the status quo in Cyprus and avoided doing anything that might have antagonized the British.[35] The Greeks felt that it was imperative to maintain good relations with Great Britain, not only because of her military influence in the Mediterranean, but also because London was one of the main sources of foreign loans.

The service of these debts, which amounted, in some years, to one-third of Greece's budget, became due in the years when the Depression was at its height. At the same time, Britain's slower recovery from the Depression tended to work against client states, such as Greece, who were forced to seek other trading opportunities. Germany clearly provided such an opportunity due to its more rapid recovery in the mid-thirties. Between 1932 and 1935, Greek exports to Germany rose from 14.5 percent to 29 percent. Concurrently, Greek imports from Germany doubled to 18.7 percent from 9.7 percent. After 1935, German imports superseded goods from Great Britain and reflected the growing influence of Germany in Greece. During the same period, Greek exports to Britain fell from 23.4 percent to 12.8 percent, while imports rose slightly, from 13.6 percent to 15.5 percent. Trade with the United States fared better. Although imports fell from 15.3 percent to 6.2 percent, Greek exports to America went from 14.4 percent to 17.1 percent.[36]

The growing trade dependency of Greece on Germany increased during this period by the system of payment the Germans implemented in the 1930s. Exports to Germany from Greece were not paid for in currency but settled through a clearing account in Berlin and could only be liquidated by making purchases in Germany.[37] German influence upon the Greek economy peaked on 24 September 1937, when a trade agreement was signed between the two states that attempted to regulate their economic relations. Under the terms of the economic treaty, official representatives from both countries were to meet once a year in order to establish a fixed rate of imports and exports between the two, thus bringing Greek-German trade under joint control.[38]

In 1935, the Abyssinian crisis during which Italy invaded Ethiopia forced the British to reconsider the strategic relevance of Greece, and once again raised British interest in Greek affairs. For example, it was while British attention was focused on Ethiopia that General Kondylis, with the support of the chiefs of the armed services, staged his coup in order to restore the Greek king to his throne. Ultimately the British response to the events in Greece was the final blow to Greek parliamentary democracy. Koliopoulos writes, "The British Government was faced with a serious dilemma: they wished to stay out of the internal affairs of Greece; yet they needed the co-operation of the Greek Government in the present international crisis, and in a possible emergency in the Mediterranean." He adds: "Recognition of the new regime, however, was tantamount to recognizing a restoration of the monarchy by force. But from now on the Abyssinian crisis acted as a catalyst in the formulation of British policy towards Greece and Greek affairs. Hitherto, the British Government had followed events and issues in Greece as an interested spectator; thereafter, the British Government became a participant in Greek affairs."[39]

On 15 October 1935, the Foreign Office instructed the British ambassador in Athens to establish contact with the government of Kondylis and personally assure him of British support. Accordingly, the ambassador was told by the Foreign Office,

> We think that the present political situation, in which we might at any time require the goodwill and friendly co-operation of the Greek Government, renders it desirable that you should enter into personal relations with General Kondylis and other ministers, whether there be official recognition of the new regime or not. As for official recognition, the sooner it can be safely affected the better from the point of view of British interests. Delay merely on technical grounds is, in view of the international situation, to be deprecated.[40]

King George II, unlike his father Constantine, was pro-British in both sentiment and action. From 1924 until his restoration in 1935, he lived in London while enjoying the life of an English gentleman and made several useful contacts with influential British politicians and senior civil servants.[41] He was greatly admired and trusted by members of the Foreign Office, who, in turn, were sympathetic to the exiled monarch. Sir Robert Vansittart, the Permanent Undersecretary of the Foreign Office, for example, described George II as "a companionable man, who preferred his affections in Britain to rickety eminence in Greece."[42] Before George II left London he met with the Foreign Secretary, Sir Samuel Hoare, who informed him that while the British government could neither endorse nor discourage the restoration, Great Britain would not delay recognition and would wish to see the new regime established as securely as possible.[43]

The Foreign Office, in effect, wanted to secure Greek support in case of a military confrontation in the Mediterranean, and a pro-British monarch was added insurance.[44] After the end of the Abyssinian crisis, British policy focused on restoring good relations with Italy while placating Greece, Yugoslavia, and Turkey with assurances of military support. On 18 June 1936, the British Foreign Secretary, Anthony Eden, declared in the House of Commons that Great Britain would continue its assurances to the small Mediterranean states, as outlined under Article 16 of the League of Nations, after it lifted sanctions against Italy.[45] The Foreign Office also considered going a step further and turning the declaration of British support into a military pact with Greece and Turkey.

The issue of military assistance for Greece, however, troubled the British chiefs of staff, and a lengthy analysis concluded that a military understanding with Greece would burden Britain with the liabilities of a weak ally and offer little in return. The report suggested that Greece was difficult to defend and went on to underline that Britain risked becoming involved in local Balkan disputes, whereas an alliance with Turkey would offer valuable military advantages in a war against either Italy or the Soviet Union. The chiefs of staff recommended that the best method of securing the Mediterranean was the restoration of Britain's former friendly relations with Italy.[46]

The report of the Joint Planning Sub-Committee influenced British policy toward Greece until the outbreak of World War II: it minimized the value of an Anglo-Greek alliance and underlined its liabilities for British security interests.[47] The report stated:

> The Greeks are poor fighters and the military problem of protecting their country against Italy in war would be a very difficult one. Greece lies so close to Italian airdromes that a heavy scale of air attack could be directed by Italy against any military bases established in that country. We should also be committed to the maintenance of Greek sea communications, which would be a commitment, in some respects, greater than maintaining our own, as for us there are routes alternative to the Mediterranean.[48]

After the end of the Abyssinian crisis, several new factors influenced the course of Anglo-Greek relations. The British government once again was reluctant to establish an alliance with Greece or with any of the Balkan states. At the same time, Greek foreign policy reflected the dichotomy of power represented by the king and Metaxas. The Metaxas regime appeared to steer a neutral policy while attempting to court a British alliance to counter the encroachments of Italy. According to Koliopoulos, "The long tradition of

Anglo-Greek co-operation and friendship made the Greek Government take for granted British support in all circumstances and this prompted it to follow, despite the serious and repeated warnings of the Greek Chiefs of Staff, a policy which depended to a great extent on Britain."[49] This interpretation, however, reflects the wishes of King George II and not necessarily the policy of Metaxas.

The reaction of the British government to the royalist dictatorship was mixed, and for the most part the British reconciled themselves to the new order. The appraisal of Sir Sydney Waterlow, the British ambassador in Athens, of the Greek political situation in August 1936 played down the abolition of parliamentary democracy and stressed that the king was in control of the situation; the dictatorship, he argued to the Foreign Office, was advantageous to British interests.[50] Metaxas, for his part, went out of his way to assure the British that he would maintain the traditional Anglo-Greek friendship. He informed Waterlow in December 1936 that Greece "was irrevocably and unreservedly devoted to the British connection."[51] These professions of friendship reflect typical polite diplomatic exchanges and are not indicative of enthusiastic British support for the new order nor do they suggest that Metaxas wished to abandon Greek neutrality in exchange for an alliance with Great Britain.

In the same vein, Metaxas, in the aftermath of the Czechoslovakian crisis during which Germany annexed the Sudenland, attempted to placate the German ambassador in order to preserve Greek neutrality. During the course of a meeting with the German Foreign Minister, Prince zu Erbach, in early October 1938, Metaxas admitted that the king would oppose a pro-German policy and that any movement in that direction would lead to the downfall of his government. At the same time, Metaxas told Erbach that if Greece sided with Great Britain, the Venizelists would use this opportunity to take control of the state. In his dispatch to the German Foreign Ministry, Erbach pointed out that during the Sudeten crisis Greek public opinion was overwhelmingly in favor of Britain and France, but he stated that the Metaxas government was not affected by the attitude of the general population. He also added that the Greek government saw "its salvation rather in collaboration of the European Great Powers and from this standpoint welcomed with sincere joy and satisfaction the happy solution of the European crisis through the Munich Agreement."[52]

As he indicated to the German ambassador, Metaxas had to tread very carefully with respect to Greek foreign policy since he required the goodwill of the king, and the monarch insisted upon close ties with Britain. Metaxas had to maintain at least a veneer of pro-British sentiment. He feared that the British did not like the dictatorship and that they harbored strong misgivings about his past affiliations with Germany as well as his loyalty to King Constantine, who had attempted to keep Greece from joining the Entente during World War I. On 12 March 1939, Metaxas wrote in his diary that he suspected that the British would try to remove him, and as late as April 1940 he was still suspicious of British intrigues against him.[53]

Metaxas' suspicions were not without foundation. Waterlow, originally a supporter of the dictatorship, had by 1938 changed his views. His dispatches included warnings that the dictatorship might soon be violently overthrown and recommended that the British government withhold any assistance to the Metaxas regime since this aid might cause an anti-British reaction.[54] Waterlow also attempted to use his influence with the king to convince him to drop Metaxas, but he met with no success.[55] In 1938, Metaxas met with Waterlow and proposed an Anglo-Greek alliance, and when this was rejected Metaxas confided in his diary that the refusal left him free to pursue his own policy, essentially one of neutrality.[56] His distrust of British commitment to the Balkan states was reinforced when Britain accepted the Italian invasion of Albania in April 1939 without much protest.

For their part, the British issued a mild reprimand to the Italians; in contrast, the Greek government began preparations to meet a possible Italian invasion of Greece. Meanwhile, Mussolini had assured the British that Italy did not have any hostile intentions against Greece, and Lord Halifax persuaded the Italian dictator to repeat these assurances to the Greek government.[57] Greek officials, however, remained skeptical and looked to Britain for support but the British government was not prepared to give any guarantees to Greece except in close consultation with Italy. However, after Mussolini's statement on 10 April 1939 reaffirming Italy's intention to respect the territorial integrity of Greece, Britain and France issued their guarantees to Greece and Romania on 13 April 1939.[58] The assurances of Britain and France to Poland represented a watershed in British foreign policy regarding further German expansion. The guarantees to Greece and Romania, although implemented in such a manner as to avoid a break with Italy, fell within the new policy of containment invoked by Great Britain in the spring of 1939.[59]

After the outbreak of war following Germany's invasion of Poland in September 1939, the Foreign Office requested from the Committee of Imperial Defense (CID) a strategic analysis of Greece. The CID was to determine what possible support Britain could provide the Metaxas government should circumstance brings the Greeks into the conflict. According to the chiefs of staff:

> It will be to our advantage for Greece to remain neutral as long as possible, even if Italy declares war against us. As a belligerent she will undoubtedly prove to be a liability and will tend to absorb allied resources which could be used elsewhere. It has already, however, become apparent that the use of Suda Bay for our patrols engaged in interrupting German sea-borne trade would be an advantage. If Turkey comes in on our side this need would be obviated since contraband control could be more effectively exercised from the Bosporus. If Turkey, however, remains neutral or even becomes hostile the use of a Greek harbour may become necessary. In this event Greece might submit to "force majeure" while remaining neutral in the best interests of the allied cause.[60]

Metaxas, however, was determined to keep Greece out of the war at all costs. He confided in his diary that the interests of Greece, as far as the major powers were concerned, received a very low priority. The only option for his country was to become self-sufficient and maintain its neutrality.[61] At the same time, the British policy of keeping Greece neutral enabled Metaxas to avoid a possible showdown with the king should the latter press for Greece to enter the war on the side of Great Britain. Despite Metaxas' repeated displays of friendship toward Britain and his strictly formal relationship with Germany, the British always had doubts about the Greek dictator. They accepted the situation, however, because they could do little else under the circumstances and because they could count on the pro-British attitude of King George II.

On 28 October 1940, Mussolini issued an ultimatum to the Greek government, which, if accepted, would have reduced Greece to the status of an Italian satellite. The immediate and uncompromising refusal of Metaxas to accept the Italian demands led to war. The Greek dictator's strong stand against Italy alleviated any doubts that the Foreign Office had over Metaxas' potential Axis sympathies, at least as far as Italy was concerned. There was still the question of Germany, and the British were particularly sensitive to the possibility that Metaxas could turn there for mediation and support. Germany, however, did not take sides in the matter.

The surprising victories of the Greek army over the Italians in Greece and Albania reinforced the British policy of support for Metaxas, despite pressure from the Foreign Office to encourage the Greek government to release political prisoners and cooperate with the opponents of the regime.[62] Metaxas ordered the release of a large number of political prisoners incarcerated on remote islands and even recommissioned Venizelist officers, albeit lower-ranking ones, back in the army. Although the Foreign Office was satisfied with Metaxas' aggressive response to the Italian invasion, the SO2 (later part of the Special Operations Executive or SOE) was not convinced that the Greek dictator would be equally steadfast in the face of a German attack. According to SOE officers in Athens, the Metaxas regime was honeycombed with too many pro-German sympathizers. Even if the Greek dictator did stand up to a German invasion, SO2 doubted if, in the inevitable occupation of Greece, Metaxas could head a credible government-in-exile.[63]

In December 1940, a meeting was held between the British Foreign Office and representatives of the SOE to discuss the situation in Greece. The SOE representative indicated that the SOE already had an agent in Athens—"with the object of promoting a united front."[64] He was attempting to secure the return of the exiled politicians, encourage the Venizelists to support Metaxas, and make it known to the Greek government the undesirability of having two pro-German ministers in the government. The Foreign Office had serious doubts about the use of such activity, and the SOE had to ensure that its representative would not undertake any action in such matters without the express approval of the British embassy in Athens.[65]

In fact, the newly created SOE had very little contact with the intelligence services, ministries, or individuals close to the Metaxas government. Its raison d'être was to prepare for sabotage and resistance: in Winston Churchill's often quoted phrase, to "set Europe ablaze." Its role in Greece was to organize a network of agents to conduct such activity in anticipation of a possible Axis occupation. Despite the assurances given to the Foreign Office by their London counterparts, SOE officers in Athens began to make contact with Venizelists, communists, and other opponents of the Metaxas regime because, as will be illustrated below, the SOE believed that such groups were capable of the type of underground work required to pursue its objectives in an occupied country. As a result, after the occupation of Greece, the SOE's contact was mainly with Venizelists and communists who opposed the Greek monarchy, which effectively was the Greek government-in-exile. In contrast, the Foreign Office and the British government were committed to the Greek king, and the traditional British intelligence services, such as the Secret Intelligence Service (SIS), had contacts in Greece with monarchists and with individuals who had been a part of or were in sympathy with the Metaxas regime.

The continued success of the Greek armies against the Italians in Albania, after the initial victories of the Italian army, and the appearance of British forces, even of token strength, on the Greek mainland and Crete made a German invasion a distinct possibility. As early as 4 November 1940, Hitler had decided that some kind of intervention in the Balkans was necessary to rescue his only major ally from a humiliating defeat. On 12 November Hitler directed the commander-in-chief of the German army to make preparations for the occupation of the Greek mainland north of the Aegean should it become necessary to attack British air bases in Greece.[66]

Although he had not yet decided on the outright occupation of Greece, Hitler was contemplating the seizure of bases for the German air force in order to dominate the eastern Mediterranean. His main concern, according to Directive 20, was to frustrate British designs against the Romanian Ploesti oil fields, Germany's main source of petroleum, and for this reason he ordered the planning for the invasion and occupation of northern Greece alone. Nevertheless, if necessary, he was prepared to overrun the entire Greek mainland.[67]

After the Italian attack against Greece, the Greek government was less reticent about receiving British military aid, but still wanted such support kept secret, for the Metaxas regime did not wish to antagonize Germany.[68] In addition to formal contacts between Greek and British military representatives, Military Intelligence Research (MIR) and Section D, the forerunners of the SOE, had begun preparations for the organization of clandestine networks in anticipation of a German occupation of Greece. Agents of MIR and Section D managed to procure substantial quantities of small arms, ammunition, grenades, and incendiary bombs and hide them in the British consulate in Athens. In addition, sabotage kits were manufactured out of four-gallon gasoline cans; they included explosives, a saboteur's handbook translated into Greek, Greek currency equivalent to £100, two pistols with ammunition, and a few knuckle-dusters. During this period, the British secret services managed to train three to four hundred potential saboteurs.[69] MIR worked closely with the Greek General Staff, but Section D activities were kept secret from the Greek authorities, since these efforts involved the organization of underground cells staffed by Greek subjects hostile to the government as well as to the monarchy.[70] The SIS had a station in Athens and managed to develop a good working relationship with the Greek security police. The Greeks, for their part, supplied the British Secret Service with considerable information on German activities in the country. After the Italian attack, the MI6 station also anticipated a German occupation and made plans for evacuation and clandestine networks.[71]

According to postwar accounts, the eventual employment of communists and republicans by the SOE can be attributed to their willingness and ability to function underground. In contrast, those loyal to the Greek government and to the king were not interested in these activities because they were content with the political situation in Greece. Some even believed in an ultimate Axis victory or sympathized with the regimes of Germany and Italy. C. M. Woodhouse, who played a pivotal role as head of the SOE's mission in Greece and became one of the principal historians of that period, claims that "the right wing and the monarchists were slower than their opponents in deciding to resist the occupation, and were therefore of little use to the Allies until it was too late."[72]

Nicholas Hammond, a member of Section D and later of the SOE, states that the "rationale for using communists and republicans as agents prior to Greece's entry into the war" was that the Greek king and the government, headed by General Metaxas, who had been trained as an officer in Germany, would side with Germany, which had cleverly remained neutral and was disregarding the war of its ally Italy with Greece.[73] According to Richard Clogg, many senior Venizelist officers became willing agents of the SOE in the fall and winter of 1940–41 because the Metaxas regime had refused them permission to fight the Italians. Clogg writes that these men were "almost by definition pro-British. . . . With British contacts going back to 1916, this group of officers was eager to contribute to the war effort but had been condemned by Metaxas' vindictiveness to kicking their heels in Athens."[74]

On the other hand, the *Report on SOE Activities in Greece and the Islands of the Aegean Sea*, composed by Colonel Julian Dolbey on 27 June 1945,[75] clearly states the premise for SOE dealings with left-wing organizations: "subversive activities must be based on a political concept. Effective sabotage and or guerrillas [sic] can only thrive if a revolutionary atmosphere has been created previously through political organizations."[76] This report was written after the war and with the benefit of hindsight. Dolbey further states: "The fact that resistance movements and eventually guerrilla warfare had to be built on left-wing political elements was well known to all concerned, and accepted in the SOE directives of the Chief-of-Staff for 1943 and by the Prime Minister in his directives on our policy to Greece."[77]

Initially, British strategy toward resistance in occupied Europe was to form secret armies inspired by revolutionary zeal that would rise up when the British or an allied army invaded the European continent. Although the concept of secret armies was not implemented, it continued to influence SOE policy toward resistance throughout the war.[78] Given this context, it is not surprising that Section D in 1940, and later the SOE, turned to the more radical elements in Greece for their recruits. Equally relevant is that for many Greek nationals, being employed by the secret service of a foreign power while Greece was neutral could be construed as an act of treason. At least this would have been the case up until the German attack against Greece. The communists and many republicans did not consider the monarchy and the Metaxas regime as the lawful representatives of the Greek state, and welcomed support from the British secret services to organize an underground that eventually they could use to achieve their own political ends.

In 1941, Section D had established contacts with several individuals and groups and had organized two clandestine cells in Greece: one of conservative republicans under Alexander Zannas in the north, and another of more liberal republicans and left-wing individuals under Colonel E. Bakirdzis in Athens.[79] Section D, through Elli Papadimitriou, a bitter opponent of Metaxas who maintained close contacts with republican circles, established the Bakirdzis cell. Papadimitriou introduced Ian Pirie and Pawson to Bakirdzis and shortly after secured for the SOE the services of Odysseus, one of the most successful agents of the British intelligence service.[80] Papadimitriou became an important conduit between these groups and Section D, which was able to recruit additional key figures in the resistance such as Charalambos Koutsogiannopoulos, Dimitris Bardopoulos, and Ilias Degiannis as well as others.[81] In the early period, Papadimitriou was also the main contact between the SOE and Greek communists.[82] However, neither group had much of an opportunity to get organized before the German invasion forced the British to withdraw from Greece.[83]

On 29 January 1941, Metaxas died from an infection, leaving King George II with the option to restore the constitution, but the Greek monarch could not bring himself to dismantle the authoritarian state. Instead, he appointed Alexandros Koryzis, the governor of the National Bank of Greece, as Metaxas' replacement. Sir Michael Palairet, Waterlow's successor, urged the king to take provisional control of the government rather than appoint a nonentity figurehead, because he feared that the death of Metaxas would cause internal dissent. "Metaxas," Palairet commented, was "unfortunately irreplaceable."[84] The king, however, was reluctant to take such a step. Koryzis became president of the council—the de facto head of government—and control of the army was left to the commander-in-chief, General Alexander Papagos. The Greek general was an Anglophile and even before the death of Metaxas had made his pro-Allied views known to the British military attaché in Athens, who reported that Papagos "definitely considered himself and Greece as being our allies in all except word."[85]

The continued defeats of the Italians in Albania, North Africa, Ethiopia, and the eastern Mediterranean as well as the presence of British forces in Greece, however, convinced Hitler to intervene in Greece. On 22 March 1941, Hitler ordered Operation Marita, which included the occupation of the entire Greek mainland as well as all the islands.[86] The only changes to Hitler's plans came as a result of the coup in Yugoslavia on the evening of 26–27 March, which caused the resignation of the regent, Prince Paul, and the fear that Yugoslavia would withdraw from the Tripartite Pact with Germany. This situation required the transfer of additional forces to participate in attacking Yugoslavia as well as Greece. The Yugoslav coup expanded Hitler's strategic options with respect to Operation Marita by simplifying the logistical and transportation difficulties anticipated by the German high command for the invasion of Greece. The Yugoslavs had inherited from the Habsburg Empire the railroad system that connected Austria, Hungry, Rumania, and Greece, which made the campaign much easier than if they had to rely on Bulgaria's rail network. Thus, it offered the German army a direct approach to Macedonia.[87]

On 6 April 1941, the German army launched its offensive and quickly overwhelmed the Yugoslav forces, reaching the Greek frontier within days and not the weeks anticipated by General Papagos. Meanwhile, the deployment of the Greek army and the British Expeditionary Force (BEF) was, according to Martin Van Creveld, "suicidal."[88] Papagos had divided his limited forces by keeping four divisions along the Metaxas Line, which protected eastern Macedonia and Thrace, but allocated only three divisions to join the BEF and defend the Aliakhmon Line a hundred miles to the rear. The British had assumed (from their discussions with Papagos on 21 February 1941) that Papagos would abandon the Metaxas Line and use those forces to reinforce the Aliakhmon Line. When the first elements of the BEF arrived in Greece on 5 March, however, Papagos refused to withdraw any divisions to the Aliakhmon Line because he feared the political repercussions of abandoning Macedonia and Thrace to Bulgaria. Instead, he recommended that the British commit their forces piecemeal to reinforce the Macedonian frontier. This suggestion proved unacceptable to the British, and a compromise was reached that left the BEF defending the Aliakhmon Line with the support of three Greek divisions.[89] These dispositions effectively created three defensive positions (the Aliakhmon Line, the Metaxas Line, and the Albanian front), which depended for their security on the Yugoslavs holding their ground against superior German manpower and equipment. Papagos' plan was not what the British had agreed to when General Sir Archibald Wavell had discussed with the Greek general the role that the BEF would play in the defense of Greece, but was rather the result of misinterpreting Yugoslav intentions and political expediency.

This turn of events was particularly disheartening for the British, especially since the decision to send troops to Greece was made over the objections of the chiefs of staff and the Middle East commander-in-chief.[90] Initially, Churchill was also reluctant to commit military forces to support Greece but quickly changed his mind. Aid to Greece was motivated less by military considerations than by Churchill's enthusiasm to support a "gallant" ally, but also because it would receive favorable American reaction.[91] In addition, there was the faint hope that it might result in a significant setback for the Germans. There was also the fear that if Britain did not support Greece it would have grave repercussions for relations with Yugoslavia and Turkey.[92] The chiefs of staff finally agreed to send help to Greece, but they cautioned that if British forces were to have any effect they had to be dispatched as soon as possible. The strategy of holding the Aliakhmon Line with the Greek forces withdrawn from Thrace and Macedonia, they concluded, would have been the only chance of success.[93]

The military situation, however, deteriorated within weeks and was followed by the near-collapse of the Greek government. By 9 April, the Germans routed the Yugoslav army and captured the Metaxas Line. Once they achieved this objective, they were able to turn the left flank of the Aliakhmon Line and advance into central Greece, while a detached force outflanked the Greek position in Albania. The Greek forces in Albania held their ground despite an Italian attempt to mount an offensive to coincide with the German attack, but the Italian army ultimately failed to achieve a breakthrough. The British, in contrast, did not have the opportunity to offer serious resistance since each defensive position proved futile, thanks in part to German superiority in equipment and air power. Once their position on the Aliakhmon Line was outflanked, they fell back from one position to another until the Royal Navy rescued them.[94] The commander of the First Greek Army in Albania, General George Tsolakoglou, realizing that his forces were cut off, decided on his own initiative to surrender to the Germans rather than give the Italians a victory they did not deserve.[95]

Koryzis took his life on 18 April 1941, and the king appointed a new premier, Emmanouil Tsouderos. On 21 April, General Papagos recommended that the British begin evacuating their forces from Greece.[96] On 23 April, the remnants of the BEF, the king, and his government were evacuated to Crete. The island, however, proved a temporary respite and, once again, the Royal Navy had to rescue the British forces, the king, and his ministers and take them to Egypt.

From this point on, the Greek government was a government-in-exile under circumstances that would undermine its credibility with the general population of occupied Greece. Ultimately, in the hectic weeks before the collapse, George II lost another opportunity to establish a national government that might have enjoyed the confidence of his people through the dark years of occupation. Instead, with the exception of Tsouderos, the monarch surrounded himself by a camarilla of ex-Metaxas ministers and some Venizelists who hardly qualified as true representatives of the Greek people. Meanwhile, some members of the Greek political and military leadership that remained in occupied Greece collaborated with the Axis powers, as was the case with Tsolakoglou, but most of the traditional political elite remained on the sidelines following the lead of Papagos.[97]

The government-in-exile contained few outstanding personalities: Emmanouil Tsouderos, who had been governor of the National Bank of Greece until Metaxas removed him, and Sakellariou, who had managed to evacuate part of the Greek fleet to Alexandria.[98] Although the Foreign Office suggested that the Greek king and his government remain in Cairo, at least until the Battle of Crete was over, it reconsidered after the Egyptian government refused to allow the Greek government to stay in Egypt. Eventually, the Foreign Office decided that it was more convenient to have the Greek monarch in England, thus London became the base of the exiled government, as was the case with all the other exiled governments. London, however, offered one serious drawback: it isolated the king from almost any contact with other Greeks, who continued to make their way to the Middle East throughout the occupation and could have given him a realistic picture of the transformation of the political situation in the country.

The Greek government-in-exile attempted, at least superficially, to distance itself from the Metaxas regime, but it was reluctant to grapple with the problem of constitutional reform. The king and Tsouderos did not consider the constitutional issue critical or immediate; the primary preoccupation of the government was the war. According to Tsouderos, only after liberation should the king and the government introduce constitutional changes.[99] The policy of the Greek government was mainly concerned with the organization of the Greek forces in the Middle East, followed by putting forth to the British and, later, the Allies, the Greek claims to northern Epirus, the Dodecanese, and Cyprus. The premier also argued for an adjustment of the frontiers with Bulgaria as well as with Yugoslavia and massive Greek immigration to the Italian colonies of North Africa. In addition, if Turkey were to follow a hostile policy toward Britain, Greece should demand the accession of eastern Thrace and insist that Istanbul become a free city with Greece participating in its administration.[100]

Much as he tried, Tsouderos could not bypass the problem of the constitution, and to avoid the appearance of bowing to British pressure he encouraged George II to terminate officially the 4 August dictatorship. The king issued a decree ending the Metaxas regime in October—four months later, in February 1942, he signed a new constitutional act revoking Metaxas' legislation of 4 August 1936 and reestablishing the constitution of 1911.[101] It is not evident from the extant sources whether this move was the result of British pressure, an attempt to placate the resurgent republican sentiments of the Greek political parties, or simply a response to the fact that, as Tsouderos had pointed out on 25 January 1942, the death of Metaxas had ended the dictatorship. At least this was a delicate way of distancing the king from his actions on 4 August 1936.[102]

The lack of popular support for the Greek monarchy in Greece left the king in a position of weakness when dealing in matters of Greek foreign policy and territorial claims. The problem for the Greek government-in-exile was complicated further by the fact that all Greek political leaders, with a few exceptions, had turned their attention to the constitutional question of monarchy or republic, while Greek territorial interests took second place. On 30 March 1942, the leaders of the prewar political parties, with the exception of Kanellopoulos and Tsaldaris, signed an agreement stating that the constitutional problem would be addressed after the war by a referendum. With this agreement, the political leaders, with some exceptions, moved to the sidelines and obsessed over who should govern Greece in the post-occupation period and in what manner.[103] This not only affected questions of foreign policy, but also created a political vacuum in occupied Greece that enabled the communists to dominate the resistance movement.

Indeed, the first approach by the KKE to the Greek republican factions to form a common front with the aim of organizing resistance was met with rejection. Certainly working with the communists to fight the Axis occupation was not appealing, but the Greek political establishment was equally uninterested in organizing its own resistance movement. The leaders of these parties and political factions went as far as to suggest that it might even be preferable to exploit the antimonarchist line of the Tsolakoglou regime, which the puppet government was advocating through the Axis-controlled press.[104]

The leading figures of the Greek prewar political parties concentrated on the constitutional issue and did not consider the establishment of resistance organizations as either premature or as an unnecessary hardship for the Greek people, who had done more than enough for the Allies in the campaigns of 1940–41.[105] To a great extent, they, and those now living in exile, preferred to challenge the right of the king and his government to represent the Greek nation. Under these conditions, it was extremely difficult for the Greek government-in-exile to pursue a policy of reclaiming Greek territory. Even more difficult was the prospect of organizing a resistance movement, which, because of the political climate in Greece, would be beyond their control and in due course manipulated to oppose the return of the monarchy.

The first major problem for the Greek government-in-exile, however, was not opposition but the growing famine in Greece, a result of the allied blockade of occupied Greece, undertaken as a strategy to deprive the German army of food and supplies. The impact of this tactic had severe repercussions upon the populace, so the king and Tsouderos had to persuade the British to lift the blockade, if only temporarily.[106] The crisis placed the Greek government-in-exile on the horns of a dilemma. Tsouderos understood the utility of the strategy of blockade as a tactic of war and as a means of defeating the enemy.[107] The question, however, was one of degree; depriving the occupation forces of external food supplies was one thing, while imposing a full-scale famine was entirely another. Tsouderos bombarded the British government with appeals and memoranda desperately pleading for the lifting of the blockade, but the interests of the Greek government-in-exile had very little impact on the British.[108] The British government did authorize the shipment of grain from Turkey, but the amounts were negligible and the grain had almost no effect on the food crisis that expanded considerably by the time winter arrived.[109] According to Ilias Venezis, in the winter of 1941, the British ambassador had assured the Greek premier, Koryzis, that in the event of the occupation of Greece, the British would permit the importation of 30,000 tons of grain per month. After the collapse of Greece, however, the British failed to honor this agreement, if indeed it had been made in the first place.[110]

Concurrent with the problem of the blockade was the attempt by the Greek government-in-exile to implement a foreign policy based on a postwar political alliance with Britain that would be instrumental in addressing Greek territorial demands. On 29 September 1941, Tsouderos proposed to Alexander Cadogan, the Permanent Under Secretary of the Foreign Office, a Greek-British alliance and offered the British naval and air bases in Greece. Cadogan responded favorably to the Greek proposal but assumed that such an agreement would also involve Greek territorial claims.[111] For this reason Edward Warner, the head of the Southern Department, was reluctant to endorse an alliance that included any postwar territorial revisions in the Balkans and the eastern Aegean. He proposed instead a military alliance along the same lines as that concluded with the government of Norway and suggested that the question of British bases and Greek territorial claims could be discussed later, without making any formal commitments.

Others shared Warner's view in the Foreign Office, fearing that Tsouderos aimed to establish, with British support, a greater Greece that would dominate the eastern Mediterranean. P. Dixon, also of the Southern Department, not only agreed with Warner's concerns about the implications of a postwar alliance with the Greek government but also suggested that Turkey was far better suited than Greece to play a pivotal role in the Near East.[112] As far as the issue of bases was concerned, the Foreign Office was inclined toward a policy that would lead to a postwar Balkan alliance, which could also have included British and even American military bases. To this end, the Greek and Yugoslav governments were encouraged by the British to conclude an alliance on 15 January 1941, which aimed at forming a Balkan union.[113] On 25 November 1941, Eden met with Tsouderos and proposed an Anglo-Greek military alliance. He pointed out that any territorial and political agreements would be considered only after the end of the war. Tsouderos had little choice but to accept Eden's offer, and after receiving the king's agreement, a military alliance was concluded on 9 March 1942, which also gave the British operational control of the Greek forces for the duration of the war.[114]

Another matter of considerable interest to the British government was the disposition of the Greek merchant marine fleet. The use of the Greek ships was a vital concern for the British since more than 80 percent of the Greek merchant marine operated from London and was chartered to the Ministry of War Transport. Some of the Greek owners wished to transfer their operations to New York, and the Greek Minister of Marine planned to open an office in the United States. The Ministry of War Transport, however, was opposed to this move and was anxious to keep control of the Greek merchant fleet in London.[115] According to Procopis Papastratis, the Greek government-in-exile failed to exploit this situation because they needed the wholehearted support of the British government and could not risk alienating Churchill or the Foreign Office.[116] It is unlikely, however, that relocating the Greek merchant marine fleet to New York would have afforded the Greek government-in-exile any leverage over the British, especially after the United States became a belligerent in December 1941. Regardless, the Greek government-in-exile had to grapple with these and other critical issues throughout the war, but always within the context of an alliance with Britain.

The British government supported the exiled king and his government in the expectation that he would be welcome back in Greece after the end of hostilities; only then, the British assumed, could demands for constitutional change be addressed in an orderly manner and through free elections. British policy, according to Sir Llewellyn Woodward (the official historian of British foreign policy during World War II), "could not have been based on any other assumption, but such a policy of moderation and common sense assumed a higher level of political education and restraint than was the case in the predominantly peasant countries of Yugoslavia and Greece."[117] The British historian also overlooks the impact of the famine, Axis reprisals, and the emergence of resistance that ultimately altered the political dynamic in Greece. Equally significant was that the Quisling occupation governments had all been affiliated with Metaxas and the monarchy. Later, the presence of SOE missions that worked closely with the left-wing resistance also gave the impression that the British supported the opponents of the monarchy.

Prior to the war neither Yugoslavia nor Greece had popular or democratic governments, and during the occupation, the left-wing underground in both states gained control of the resistance, leaving the British little choice except to cooperate, as military necessity dictated, with the communist-led resistance organizations. Woodward attempts to explain the difference between British policy toward Greece and that toward Yugoslavia by suggesting that had the Greek resistance produced a leader such as Tito, the British government might have followed a similar path in both countries.[118] He modifies his comments by adding that had Belgrade been as accessible as Athens, British policy toward Yugoslavia might also have been quite different.

British policy in Greece between the beginning of the Axis occupation and liberation was characterized by two uncompromising principles. First, the Greek king and his government were the legitimate representatives of the

Hellenic state, and second, that Britain would neither sanction nor impose any political change during the war. Within these guidelines, British policy was adapted and stretched to accommodate the Greek resistance groups in order to encourage them to play a useful military part in the overall efforts of the Middle Eastern Theater of Operations that included the Mediterranean. In his first book, *Apple of Discord,* Woodhouse defines British policy toward Greece as taking shape in an ad hoc manner and excludes the notion that the British government maintained any fixed policy: "There was no such thing as HMG's policy towards Greece, in the sense of a fixed set of objectives laid down in advance. British foreign policy has never been something that is laid down in advance, to be achieved regardless of what may happen between its formulation and its execution; it is rather an emergent character which can gradually be detected amongst the welter of *ad hoc* discussion."[119]

As far as the British government's support of the Greek monarchy was concerned, Woodhouse explains this was a commitment to the person of King George II. On the motives for Britain's loyalty to the Greek king, Woodhouse writes that they "sprang hardly at all from the consideration that the restoration of the King would ensure the friendship of Greece towards England, because as a matter of plain fact almost any Greek government that was not communist would be friendly to England; they sprung almost entirely from gratitude and loyalty to the man who had stood with us when everything seemed lost."[120]

A better question surely is whether the British had any other alternative. The king and the Greek government-in-exile were the internationally accepted representatives of the Greek state. Consequently, British denial of the legality of the Greek government could have given some credibility to the puppet regime in Athens.

During the course of the occupation from 1941 to 1944, British policy alternatives in Greece fell between military expediency, using resistance groups to hamper and inflict damage to the Axis forces in Greece and thus indirectly to support the war effort in North Africa, and a political agenda that strove to keep postwar Greece within the British sphere of influence. To ensure the latter, the Foreign Office remained loyal to the king of Greece. In addition, Churchill felt a sense of gratitude to George II for his allegiance to Great Britain in 1941,[121] but he was less eager to maintain the Greek monarchy than to preserve an orderly transition from occupation to liberation. In a statement to Rex Leeper, the British ambassador to the Greek government, Churchill outlined his policy regarding the Greek monarchy: "The King is the servant of his people. He makes no claim to rule them. He submits himself freely to the judgment of the people as soon as normal conditions are restored. He places himself and his Royal House entirely at the disposition of the Greek nation. Once the German invader has been driven out, Greece can be a republic or a monarchy, entirely as the people wish."[122]

The underlying factor influencing British foreign policy was that the Greek monarchy represented legitimacy. From the beginning of the German occupation of Europe, Churchill had resolved that during the war Great Britain would resist any changes that altered the political establishments of the occupied states.[123] He was resolute in this policy and only gave way in the face of new realities, as was the case in Yugoslavia, France, and Poland; where possible, Churchill remained steadfast to the concept of legitimate authority. Within these parameters, however, the British government had to pursue a military strategy that in some theaters of operations required the cooperation of resistance groups with paramilitary organizations such as the SOE. In these circumstances, it was necessary to ignore temporarily the overall guidelines of British policy in order to satisfy military expediency. Accordingly, throughout the war, the perceived usefulness of resistance organizations to military strategy had to compete with the policy objectives set by the Foreign Office.

During the first phase of the war (1939–1942), when victory seemed distant, the Foreign Office did not press its concerns over the potential friction between short-term military objectives and long-term political considerations. The Foreign Office, comments Gladwyne Jebb, tended to view the SOE "as a joke and then as a menace," whereas the staff of the SOE considered the Foreign Office "as a collection of timorous officials unaware of the supreme necessity of 'getting on with the war.' "[124]

British policy toward maintaining the war in occupied Europe was to be carried out by guerrilla forces inspired by revolutionary fervor and not the secret armies of patriots originally envisaged by the British chiefs of staff. Although the British government did not adopt the secret-armies strategy, it was incorporated into the idea of guerrilla forces as armies of resistance organizations and was part of the mandate of the SOE. The very concept of revolutionary upheaval, however, was anathema to the Greek government-in-exile as well as to the political establishment in Greece. Ultimately, the Greek government-in-exile had to accept responsibility for the consequences of the occupation of Greece. For George II and Tsouderos, instigating an organized resistance movement held the prospect of considerable reprisals and the devastation of the country, but to what end? In 1941–1942, the British were not in a position to attempt an invasion of the Greek mainland; they were barely holding their ground in North Africa. Ultimately, the brutality of the occupation forces and the ensuing misery that descended upon the population proved the primary catalyst for resistance. Meanwhile, once the king and his government left Greece, they no longer had firsthand knowledge of its circumstances and lacked the ability to influence events in the occupied country.

In the first days of the occupation, the German army behaved with almost extreme courtesy toward the general public. German soldiers paid for anything they bought and were particularly well mannered in encounters with Greek officers. Hitler, on the recommendation of Field Marshal List and Reich Plenipotentiary Günther Altenburg, had ordered the immediate release of all Greek officers and those of other ranks who had been taken as prisoners of war.[125] In fact, during the German invasion of Greece, Hitler had instructed the Wehrmacht to treat all captured Greek officers with military courtesy and permit them to retain their personal swords.

The hastily formed government of Tsolakoglou, a creature of the Axis, attempted to be as accommodating as possible and believed that Hitler could be prevailed upon to keep the Italians out of Greece. One of Altenburg's first reports from Greece was to pass on a message of thanks from the Greek government, supported by telegrams from medical and professional associations, with the request that Hitler take Greece under his protection.[126] Symbolic gestures made by the Germans such as maintaining the Greek flag on public buildings and the honor guard at the tomb of the unknown soldier made a positive impression during the first weeks of the occupation.

As Fleischer has pointed out, however, it is extremely difficult to determine the attitude of the general public toward the Germans. According to the Nazi press, the Wehrmacht was greeted with flowers and overwhelming enthusiasm, while the Greek underground press contends that from the beginning the population displayed its disgust and outright hatred toward the Nazis.[127] Between these two extremes, Fleischer writes, it is almost impossible to gauge the sentiments of the average Greek. The onset of the German occupation found a population that was war-weary and numb, one that felt Greece had fulfilled its duty to the Allied cause.[128] Between the entry of the German troops in Athens and the end of the Battle of Crete, most people, with the exception of opportunists and some old supporters of King Constantine, maintained an attitude of passive resignation toward the Germans.[129] However, after the Battle of Crete and the entry of the Italians into Greece as part of the occupation forces, the public attitude quickly turned to loathing.

The early gestures of the Wehrmacht aimed at softening Greek attitudes toward the new order, however, were negated by acts of symbolic oppression which, coupled with the presence of the despised Italians, quickly convinced most people that the Germans were not likely to treat them with any measure of respect and honor.[130] From simple irritants such as the way the Germans indulged themselves in numerous baths and wasted water to wash their automobiles despite a chronic water shortage, to more disturbing incidents such as confiscating automobiles, villas, and any other valuable possessions, quickly changed people's opinions.[131] The Germans confiscated numerous houses and apartments in Athens as well as in other parts of Greece. Usually, they simply gave the unfortunate owners a receipt from the Wehrmacht. In some cases, they requisitioned part of a house and relegated the occupants to a few small rooms. The new German occupants also took possession of all the furniture, but occasionally they either paid a small sum or allowed the owners to take with them some of their belongings.[132] German arrogance and insensitivity was also reflected by the double standard in restaurants, which permitted German soldiers to have access to meat, beer, and other commodities denied the Greeks.

In addition to the imposition of a curfew, Greek households were forced to keep their shutters closed day and night despite the oppressive heat of the summer.[133] Furthermore, the Wehrmacht in Greece purchased everything with freshly printed occupation currency that almost at once became worthless. At the peak of the famine that gripped Athens in the winter of 1941–1942, German soldiers were permitted to send food to their families in Germany, while the occupation authorities requisitioned foodstuffs in quantities that exceeded their needs and sold the surplus at prohibitive prices.[134] The German authorities took over most transportation and all communication networks as well as imposing a strict press censorship. The former was particularly significant, since not only did it inconvenience the general public, but the confiscation of private transport also made it almost impossible to supply Athens with foodstuffs from the islands and the countryside.[135]

The Greeks showed where their sympathies lay through their attitude toward British prisoners of war. Whenever the Germans transported these prisoners in the streets of Athens, people cheered the British and gave them cigarettes and food; from a population that now faced extreme deprivation of all such items, these were not merely symbolic gestures. Attitudes on both sides hardened considerably during the Battle of Crete, and then at the end of May 1941 two young men scaled up the Acropolis and took down the German flag.[136]

This nonviolent and symbolic act caused the Germans to overreact. On 31 May 1941, the German authorities issued a proclamation that clearly exposed the oppressive and brutal nature of the occupation, although it attempted to shift responsibility for the new policies onto the Greek population. According to this decree, the harsh policies that the Germans adopted resulted from the recent attitudes and reactions of the Athenians toward the occupation forces; from that point on, a curfew was set for 10:00 P.M. The taking down of the German flag and similar acts of symbolic and sporadic resistance in the first months of the occupation were benign and mostly ineffective. The response of the occupation authorities, however, escalated in severity and acted as a catalyst for more organized and violent acts of defiance that within a year led to the creation of guerrilla bands in the Greek mountains.

By the end of the summer of 1941, the combination of the encroaching famine and the increasing brutality of the occupation forces resulting essentially from minor and insignificant acts of defiance provided additional incentives for the Greeks to commit acts of violence against the Germans and Italians. On 19 June 1942, Archbishop Damaskinos, the head of the Orthodox Church in Greece, met with Altenburg, the Reich Plenipotentiary, to protest the execution of hostages by the German authorities. The Greek cleric pointed out to Altenburg that it was unjust to kill innocent individuals in order to exact reprisals for acts of sabotage committed by unknown parties. The Greek people, Damaskinos added, expected better treatment from the Germans. They believed that Germany would protect Greece from the Italians and were prepared to accept a German occupation. After the executions and other acts of reprisals, the Greek people, including the Germanophiles, considered the German occupation forces as despised enemies.[137]

Throughout the occupation the archbishop and other senior as well as ordinary priests undertook to save as many members of the Greek Jewish community as possible. The Orthodox Church issued Jews baptismal certificates and worked with the chief of the Athens police, who gave them identity cards that indicated their religion was Greek Orthodox. Parish priests and bishops throughout the country not only gave Jews refuge but also hid their sacred texts and objects in churches. When the Germans announced that Greek men would be conscripted as laborers and sent to Germany, Archbishop Damaskinos informed Altenburg that he would have all the church bells ring to signal a mass uprising. The Greek archbishop was the only senior cleric in occupied Europe to prevent the Germans from using Greeks as slave labor and the only one to officially condemn the persecution of the Jews.[138]

Despite the burgeoning and progressively violent opposition to the Axis, the Greek government-in-exile was reluctant to instigate organized resistance and remained on the sidelines until it was forced to react to events. According to the British ambassador to the Greek government-in-exile, Palairet, Tsouderos and the king were more anxious to consolidate their power against the encroachments from the Venizelist and antimonarchist exiles than to help form a resistance.[139] In 1940, the former commander of the Greek forces in Crete, General Christos Kitsios, returned to Athens and advised Greek officers that it was the monarch's wish that they should avoid getting involved with politics and should make sure that the younger officers did likewise.[140] John Hondros interprets "involvement with politics" to mean that the king and his government were against the idea of resistance.[141] Edmund Myers, who led the first British sabotage mission in Greece, writes, "There were indications that the majority of influential Royalist officers had been ordered by the Greek government-in-exile to remain in Athens, to have nothing to do with the Republican resistance movements and to await the return of the Royalist Government."[142] Ultimately, the Greek government-in-exile was not so much opposed to attacking the enemy within Greece as to the concept of mass resistance, which meant that the Greek population would have had to sustain terrible reprisals, since in 1941–42 there was little hope of an allied landing in Greece.

During the first year of the occupation, the defeat of the Axis was a very remote possibility. Essentially, the Greek government-in-exile and their supporters in Greece had to accept, at the very least, a long occupation period and possibly a German victory. Both outcomes would have dire consequences for Greece. A mass resistance, in any case, was beyond the control of the Greek government-in-exile. It also had the potential to devastate the country. Britain lacked the resources to support the Greek army in 1941, let alone arm and supply a large resistance organization in Greece. Although the situation changed in late 1942, the king and his ministers had to assume that their priorities were to keep the country intact so that if and when the Allies won the war, they could return and reestablish the former political and social status quo.[143]

Ironically, the puppet governments of occupied Greece adopted a similar policy. From Tsolakoglou, the first Quisling prime minister, to Ioannis Rallis, the head of the last occupation government, the main objectives of these regimes were to prevent the disintegration of the country and maintain the prewar social and political fabric of Greece.[144] Tsolakoglou was convinced that the Germans were winning the war and Greece had to make the most out of a bad situation. The second puppet prime minister, Constantine Logothetopoulos, had expectations of a profitable career, while Rallis claimed that his motives were to keep Greece under control in the wake of the anticipated German withdrawal and hand over the country to the Greek government-in-exile, thus preventing chaos and a possible communist takeover. All the puppet regimes as well as the Greek government-in-exile assumed that the officer corps would be instrumental in accomplishing these ends.

The obvious leaders of a Greek government-sponsored resistance were the veterans of the Albanian campaign, but the officers who had led the victorious Greek armies against the Italians also bided their time and were slow to react to events as a body. The professional officers of the Greek armed forces who had served during the campaigns of 1940–1941 formed a distinct group and, to a degree, identified with the established social and political order.[145] Another group included the purged officers from the 1930s who had remained loyal to the cause of Venizelos and continued to oppose the monarchy.[146]

At the beginning of the occupation, there were approximately 4,391 professional and 8,700 reserve officers.[147] The initial reaction of most of these officers to the occupation, as far as it can be determined, was one of resignation. At first, some Greek officers participated individually in several small underground organizations formed in the autumn and winter of 1941–1942. Later many officers joined or helped to establish various resistance groups, while others escaped from Greece to fight with the forces of the Greek government-in-exile. One major difficulty for the officers was that the Greek government and the king, through envoys from the Middle East, continued to discourage the military from participating in resistance organizations. At the same time, a large percentage of the senior officers believed that opposition to the Axis was futile; they assumed that Germany, because of its superior weapons and forces, would win the war. At any rate, this was the perception until the defeat of the German Sixth Army at the Battle of Stalingrad in December 1942.[148] Another obstacle was that no one in Athens was authorized to speak on behalf of the Greek government-in-exile and to maintain contact with the officer corps.

The initial policy of the Greek government-in-exile was to encourage its followers, particularly those in the officer corps, to focus on espionage and sabotage as a means of continuing the struggle in occupied Greece. Another consideration, which had important consequences for the future, had to do with access to and control of information concerning the situation in Greece by the British and Greek authorities in the Middle East. In the first year of the occupation, information about Greece came essentially from Allied soldiers who had avoided capture and had made their way to the Middle East. Another source was Greek politicians, businessmen, professionals, and military officers who left Greece because they were wanted by the occupation authorities or decided to join the forces raised by the Greek government-in-exile. Finally, the clandestine groups organized by SIS and SOE provided an abundance of intelligence on the political conditions in Greece, especially on the resistance groups, but that information was heavily censored before it was passed on to the Greek authorities in the Middle East and in London.

The Tsolakoglou regime also attempted to control or at least keep the officer corps neutral by maintaining a ministry of defense, despite the fact that the occupation authorities did not permit the existence of armed forces. Greek generals, many of whom were heroes of the Albanian campaign and exercised considerable influence over the senior and, to a lesser extent, the younger officers, headed the ministry. For the most part, these officers either were royalists or had been followers of the Metaxas regime. Regardless of these efforts, hundreds of Greek officers made the perilous journey to the Middle East to join the armed forces of the Greek government-in-exile. The tendency of the ministry of defense of the Greek government-in-exile was to employ officers who had royalist and conservative credentials. In some cases, "reformed" Venizelist officers were readmitted into the Greek army, but despite their newfound allegiance to the monarchy, their presence caused considerable resentment amongst the royalist officers and eventually was a contributing factor to several mutinies in the Middle East.[149]

During the occupation, the officer corps continued to maintain its two broad divisions—royalists and Venizelists—which had the effect of marginalizing the institution in the covert and guerrilla war against the Axis in Greece. Furthermore, many of the younger and middle-rank officers either found their way to the Middle East or joined the resistance groups that started to develop in early 1942. Both trends disrupted the control that senior officers exercised over their junior colleagues and weakened the cohesiveness of the officer corps. Indeed, the monarchist-republican rivalry was reestablished in the Greek armed forces in the Middle East, but in Greece the old schism underwent a metamorphosis that galvanized the country into pro- and anti-left coalitions that quickly took on the labels of communist and nationalist, respectively. The occupation presented the Greeks with a new reality that made the prewar political schism almost irrelevant. Men and women had to choose between fighting the Axis, collaborating, or remaining passive. To fight they had to choose between the forces of the left and those of the antimonarchists.

CHAPTER 3

The Politics of Violence

FROM RESISTANCE TO CIVIL WAR

So now what will become of us, without barbarians.
Those men were one sort of resolution.

—Constantine P. Cavafy

For Greeks today, occupation, resistance, and civil war invoke a parade of
images—some magnificent, others outrageous—most cataloguing a painful
period in their recent history. The Athenians define the occupation as the
period of darkness. Most remember the first day, 27 April 1941—a glorious
Sunday. In the capital, the bone-white marble of the Parthenon, the center-
piece of ancient and modern Athens, basked under a cloudless blue sky. That
morning, the Germans in a solemn ceremony raised the red and black swastika above the Acropolis. At 11:00 A.M., the German commandant of Athens
ordered the Greek Evzone, a soldier from the unit that traditionally guards
the Unknown Soldier and takes part in all official ceremonies, to lower the
Greek flag as a special tribute to Hitler. The Evzone, dressed in the traditional
kilt of the revolutionary soldiers of 1821, refused the command, and, as the
Germans watched in astonishment, he threw himself over the wall, plummet-
ing to his death five hundred feet below on the foothills of the Acropolis
rather than lower the Greek flag.[1] Although there is no hard evidence that this
act took place, it is a tragic yet beautiful image that lives in the imagination
of Athenians.

Three days later, on a moonlit evening, two young men, Manolis Glezos
and Apostolos Santas, scaled the Acropolis and climbed over the barbed wire
enclosing the Parthenon. They were determined to bring down the swastika
and thus, for a brief moment, leave the Parthenon free from the stain of the

Third Reich's flag. At a few minutes past midnight, the young men reached their objective and with some difficulty managed to pull down the swastika. The Athenians were jubilant—word spread quickly, as enough people had noticed the absence of the swastika from the Acropolis and passed the news. The Germans' response was disproportionate to the deed and a hallmark of their administration of Greece. They imposed a 10:00 P.M. curfew to punish the Athenians and declared the Acropolis off-limits to all Greeks.[2]

During the first month of occupation, the issue of flags on the Acropolis almost became an obsession with the Axis forces. A few days after they arrived in Athens on the heels of the German army, the Italians raised an immense Italian flag on the Acropolis, dwarfing the swastika. By noon, the wind had shredded the Italian flag, which was promptly replaced by a much smaller one. A few days later, the Italian authorities raised yet another flag, this one merely three times as large as the swastika. The Germans responded by replacing their flag with one significantly larger than the Italian flag. Twenty-four hours later, the wind tore the swastika to pieces, the Germans then raised a newer, smaller version but one still larger than that of their Italian allies.

The comic relief of the battle of the flags soon gave way to a harsher reality. The Germans seized all Greek hospitals, which were still overcrowded with the wounded of the Albanian war. The Greek soldiers, many with amputated limbs, were forced to leave, regardless of their condition. Some lucky few had a means of transportation, but most had to go on foot. For several days, Athens was awash with thousands of wounded soldiers making their way home. Shortly after, a new creature appeared in the capital—the pro-Nazi and pro-Fascist Greek.

The collaborators emerged almost immediately. A motley collection of businessmen, husbands of German spouses, petty criminals, members of the extreme Greek Right and, sadly, some of the senior commanders of the Greek army. General George Tsolakoglou, a corps commander on the Albanian front, agreed to form a government under Axis tutelage and served as the first in a succession of puppets to dance to the tune of the occupation authorities. Other collaborators assumed more humble tasks, such as being translators for the unspeakable horrors of Gestapo and SS interrogations, while the lowest form of Axis lackeys served as double agents and informants. During the occupation, they strutted about like peacocks in their leather coats, impervious to the suffering around them and protected by their German-issued identification cards.

Civil war was the price that the Greeks had to pay for organized resistance against the Axis—but the war also reflected the divisions in Greek society.

While the causes reach back to the inception of the Greek state in 1831, it was the occupation and resistance that spawned the culture of violence that made civil war almost inevitable. The forces that spiraled the country into fratricide during and after the occupation, however, resulted from the convergence of several factors, each of which played havoc with Greek society. First, the demobilization of the Greek armed forces by the German occupiers provided a large pool of trained men for guerrilla war. Second, the British strategy of instigating mass resistance, sabotage, and subversion prompted the newly established SOE to sponsor clandestine republican and left-wing networks in Greek cities and towns as well as guerrilla bands in the mountains. In sharp contrast, the British Secret Intelligence Service and the Foreign Office continued to support the royalist cause in Greece, thereby backing the sworn enemies of the major resistance organizations that were the SOE's preferred allies. At first, the exigencies of war overshadowed the divergence in British policy toward Greece. Over the course of the occupation, however, this division contributed to the right-left polarization of the Greek resistance and, by extension, Greek society. Finally, the famine in 1941 brutalized the urban population and shattered any illusions that the Greeks may have had about their security and survival under Axis rule. The failure of the Axis to prevent, or even try to address in any significant way, the disastrous effects of the famine fueled resentment and swelled the ranks of the resistance organizations.

The vast majority of the Greek population during the late summer of 1941 was still recovering from the shock of defeat and the anxiety and fear of living under foreign occupation. Greek society was in a state of turmoil, and nearly the entire country was on the move. Anxious people yearned for the security of familial surroundings and sought comfort in old neighborhoods or found a way out of the cities. The fortunate ones could return to ancestral villages and islands to weather the storm, but a great many, especially parents, spouses, and children of soldiers, had to stay put, waiting with apprehension for the return of the men who had fought in the war. The postal network between Albania and Greece was practically nonexistent, and the few prewar telephone and telegraph lines had disintegrated in the course of the fighting. The tens of thousands of demobilized soldiers (the future resistance fighters) were slowly making the arduous trek home and had no ready means of communicating with their families. Long columns of bone-weary men—some wounded, all gaunt—snaked their way through the few mountain roads in southern Albania as they headed back toward the Greek frontier.

For almost a year, they had fought with grim determination, relentlessly hounding the Italian army out of Greece and forcing it back into Albania. In the winter of 1940–41, the fighting was bitter and was waged under the harsh mountain conditions of northern Greece and southern Albania. Greek soldiers suffered from frostbite and unattended wounds, were tormented by lice, worn down with fatigue, and handicapped by dwindling critical supplies. When they ran out of ammunition they mounted bayonet charges in blizzards and fought hand-to-hand, but all to no avail. In the spring, a German army of mechanized and armored divisions poured over the northwestern frontier to rescue Hitler's vanquished ally.

It was over in less than three weeks. The Greek soldiers in Albania were outflanked, the British Expeditionary Force had to retreat in the face of the German onslaught, and, for the second time in the war, had to be rescued by the Royal Navy. Mussolini, with the false bravado of a cheat, insisted on a final Italian offensive in Albania to take advantage of the German victory, only to face yet another failure. The Greek lines held because the Greek army refused to concede defeat to a vanquished foe. In the early summer of 1941, the heroes of the Albanian campaign were simply anxious to go home and protect their families from the uncertainty of occupation. The Germans, in a rare gesture of compassion, did not intern the Greek army; the soldiers were simply given indefinite leave and sent home. The dispersal of thousands of hungry men, however, further aggravated the critical shortage of food supplies and accelerated the progress of mass starvation.

The famine remains the darkest legacy of the occupation and was the incubator of hatred that inspired mass resistance against the Axis. Starvation pervaded every city and town in Greece, felling its victims at an alarming rate. Thousands succumbed to the debilitating effects of malnutrition or died from the onset of disease triggered by the famine. More than 100,000 died of starvation and associated diseases in Athens alone, and thousands more in other cities and towns. For many, survival hinged on the drudgery of waiting in long lines to collect a bowl of watery soup delivered daily by the Greek Red Cross. People sought every means possible to survive. They sold whatever they had of value to purchase a loaf of bread, a couple of eggs, or any form of vegetable. Cats and dogs became a rare delicacy and when these were not available, rodents had to suffice.

Every morning vans collected the famine's victims and headed to the outskirts of Athens, disgorging their grisly cargo into open pits that served as makeshift graves. Soon, a lack of fuel curtailed these grim convoys and the backlog of decaying bodies posed a new hazard for the beleaguered Athenians. For many survivors, images of emaciated children standing vigil over a dead parent and small piles of corpses stacked by street corners haunt their memories of the famine.

Mass starvation was inevitable: the Germans had descended like locusts upon Greece, consuming or conscripting everything of value and paying for it with useless occupation currency. The Nazis awarded Macedonia and Thrace to their Bulgarian allies, who promptly seized the wheat fields and denied any supplies to Greece, exacerbating the critical food shortage. The Axis also mined Greek waters and appropriated most of the fishing fleet, allowing only a handful of boats to supply the mainland. In addition, the confiscation of all locomotives and rolling stock, trucks, cars, motorcycles, bicycles, horses, donkeys, and mules by the Axis severed the connection between the countryside and the cities for the duration of the occupation.

Before the war, the small mountain towns and villages in the hinterland constituted distinct societies, self-contained and remote from the political and social changes that buffeted the rest of Greece. For centuries, the only common denominator between the villages and cities was language and religion, with trade serving as the primary mode of communication. The villagers and farmers supplied the urban centers with basic staples of olive oil, dairy products, beans, wheat, and so on, in exchange for essential products, such as tools, plows, knives, shoes, fabrics, and glass, as well as a few luxuries. Nonetheless, centralized authority was the primary feature of the Greek state and power radiated from the city of Athens and dominated the villages. However, the famine and the guerrilla forces in the mountains served to reverse their roles and Greek political authority shifted to the villages.

The famine also dissolved civil society in Greece and discredited the authority of the state. Whatever limited influence over events the first occupation government may have had, the famine had exposed the effectiveness of the first German-sponsored Quislings as a cruel joke, nothing more than a collection of ex-soldiers and politicians addicted to the exaggerated pomp of petty bureaucracy. The writ of the regime had only limited efficacy in larger towns and cities, and even there it simply adjudicated trivial matters of state or cases of petty crime. Issues of organized crime such as the black market, homicide, and other serious offenses came under the jurisdiction of the Axis-controlled law enforcement. Under these circumstances, the police and gendarmerie too often were identified with the instruments of the occupation and, regardless of their contribution to the resistance, both officers and men were eventually tainted with the stain of collaboration. This was often the mantra of the communists, who considered all law enforcement as traitors.

In the countryside, and particularly in the mountain regions, the presence of the Axis was limited to towns near strategic passes, bridges, and viaducts that serviced major communication networks. The remaining villages along the naked mountain ranges of the rugged Greek hinterland provided the ideal setting for the organization of guerrilla bands. The mountains of Greece historically nursed the forces of armed insurrection; indeed, the tradition of Hellenic and Christian warriors descending from snow-covered peaks to vanquish the Turks was part of the cultural identity of the modern Greek state.

The embryonic guerrilla bands that took to the mountains in the spring and summer of 1942 were aware of the power of history, even more so of mythology, and they attempted to link themselves with the glories of the past. The Greek partisans or "Andartes" adopted the dress and style of the bandit freedom fighters who had fought in the War of Independence. It was common for some of these men to fashion themselves with thick beards, hair in long ponytails, occasionally sporting the traditional woolen kilt and stockings. The appeal to history was less for the benefit of city folk and more as a means of forging a bond with the simple villagers and shepherds that could be exploited for provisions and recruits to sustain the guerrillas in the field.[3]

Nevertheless, during the first year of occupation, opposition to the Axis was spontaneous and disorganized. The early resistance consisted of minor acts of defiance such as writing graffiti on public buildings, puncturing the tires of Axis military vehicles, and cheering Allied soldiers led to captivity by the Germans. When some of these Allied troops managed to escape, they found refuge in the homes of people willing to risk at minimum imprisonment in a concentration camp. In time, hiding and assisting the escape of British troops served as the initiation for many into the hazardous world of clandestine work. Dozens of small networks sprouted overnight to facilitate the transportation of these men to Turkey and Egypt.

The resisters' lack of skill in intelligence tradecraft, however, resulted in arrests as well as the instant reprisals by the occupation authorities, and quickly deflated the enthusiasm of these early resistance groups. Those who survived did so because they found employment and rudimentary training with either the British intelligence services, left-wing or republican resistance groups, or, in some extreme cases, even the Axis authorities. Nonetheless, the covert groups in the cities, more so than the partisan bands in the mountains, attracted a strange assortment of individuals from the fringes of society.

Left-wing radicals liberated from the grip of the Metaxas security apparatus, disenchanted army officers, smugglers, communist renegades, police informants, displaced persons, prostitutes, thieves, and bandits gravitated to clandestine warfare like moths to light. Some were compelled by adventure, others by patriotism, but most joined because hiding from the authorities had become as much a way of life as a means of survival.

A somewhat similar situation prevailed among the ranks of the British intelligence services—for the duration of the war, espionage, sabotage, and subversion were the domain of the gifted amateur, romantic eccentric, reckless volunteer, and the downright scoundrel. After World War I, the traditional disdain for espionage, along with misgivings about its value, led to deep budget cuts, which had left the British intelligence community with few active agents, let alone networks, in Europe. The SOE had managed to organize a few clandestine groups in Athens and Thessaloniki and equipped one of them with a radio transmitter before the debacle in Greece, but it could not establish contact until much later in the fall of 1941.[4] The other British intelligence services fared even worse. The Secret Intelligence Service, as well as the Military Intelligence Directorate (MID), also organized clandestine groups and equipped them with radio sets, but within a week of the occupation the Germans arrested all the operators because these British services had divulged the names of the agents to the Greek government.[5] Information about Greece came from the trickle of British and Greek soldiers, as well as civilians, who succeeded in reaching the Middle East (although often any information gathered was not reliable and almost always dated) and from the handful of agents who managed to travel back and forth between Greece and Cairo.

The principal SOE operative and key link with the republican and left-wing groups in Athens and Thessaloniki was Gerasimos Alexatos, appropriately code-named Odysseus, because of his native cunning and appetite for danger.[6] Alexatos was an enigmatic character hovering on the edge of society, a lifelong resident of the murky eastern Mediterranean underworld, and had been recruited by Elli Papadimitriou. In 1940, he volunteered to work for the British and graduated from the SOE's makeshift training school that operated out of a semiruined Venetian castle on the island of Crete. For the fledgling SOE intelligence directorate in Cairo, Odysseus was a godsend. As an accomplished smuggler, he was familiar with the "back alleys" of the eastern Mediterranean—small islands with natural harbors and deserted coastlines endowed with secret coves—that provided surreptitious transit in and out of Greece.[7]

It is somewhat of a mystery why this middle-aged smuggler decided to risk his life for the Greek resistance. But he did manage to combine espionage with smuggling and, on occasion, was caught sneaking precious gems past the customs officials in the Middle East. Equally baffling is why this barely literate man sympathized with the left, which played no small part in convincing the SOE that only radical republican groups and the communists had the desire and aptitude to organize resistance. After the war, he vanished into obscurity. In 1955, Michael Ward, a former member of the Greek section of the SOE in Cairo, saw Odysseus walking ahead of him on a street in Piraeus. Ward fondly recounts, "walking up behind him I tapped him on the back, saying 'Odysseus my friend' when he jerked his head over his shoulder, took one suspicious look at me and beat a hasty retreat round the nearest corner. One thing was certain: he was up to his old tricks."[8]

In the first months of the occupation, when the SOE had no contacts or agents in Greece, Alexatos laid out the secret routes between Turkey and the Greek islands that later enabled the SOE, as well as other British intelligence agencies, to smuggle people and weapons in and out of Greece. By November 1941, Odysseus had managed to bring to Athens the radio codes for the transmitter of the Prometheus cell, the only underground group that had survived the Axis invasion and the primary liaison between the SOE and the Greek resistance. For the next two years, Odysseus served as courier, saboteur, guerrilla fighter, and, perhaps, the most important link between the SOE and the KKE. Certainly he was the SOE's main source in Greece and his reports influenced the opinion of the British intelligence organization in Cairo to support the left.[9] Odysseus contributed to the impression created at SOE Cairo that the left was more active and committed to resistance. But it was the sophisticated and radical Elli Papadimitriou whose voice lent considerable weight in favor of the leftist semiliterate smuggler.[10] In part, thanks to him, as early as February 1942 the SOE Greek desk had become convinced that "the Royalist cause in Greece was as good as lost, and that when the country was liberated we should find Republican sentiment too strong to be imposed upon. We did however differ somewhat in our estimate as to what type of Republicans we should find rampant when liberation came."[11]

According to one historian, the information from Greece convinced the SOE Greek experts in Cairo that "preparation for resistance or acts of resistance, were the work of the Left, of Venizelists or of Communists."[12] To some extent, the information collected and passed on was selective and occasionally colored by the bias of the individual SOE officer. It can also be argued that an equal number of reports from Greece warned of the danger posed by EAM and described the organization as one opposed to accepting the government-in-exile and the monarchy.

In contrast to the experience of the SOE with Greek agents who opposed the Greek monarchy and the government-in-exile, the few operatives of the Secret Intelligence Service (SIS) either sympathized with King George II or were not concerned about the constitutional issue. As was the case with the SOE, potential Greek agents made contact with the SIS on their own initiative or by chance encounters. Others, such as Greek loyalists, had access to representatives of the British Foreign Office, namely consuls and ambassadors, and these officials led them to the SIS.

In the late summer of 1941, the British were desperate; the war was not going well, the Germans had overrun Europe, the Americans were committed to neutrality, and the campaign in North Africa was heading for another defeat. Covert action was one of the few methods available to slow down the German Africa Corps by cutting off its supplies from Greece. Few British political or military officials in London and in the Middle East had much faith in clandestine operations, yet they could not afford to ignore any means of striking at the enemy. In this atmosphere of desperation and doubt, the SOE undertook in Greece, almost from scratch, the complex business of espionage, sabotage, and guerrilla warfare. By so doing, the organizers of the SOE contributed to the radicalization of Greek society because circumstances ultimately left the British little choice but to work with individuals and groups opposed to the established order. This was partly the result of the SOE's reliance on only a handful of agents for information concerning the Greek resistance and partly the tragic outcome of the first major covert mission in Greece. The first skewed SOE policy in favor of the left; the second, by fatally damaging the moderate elements in the Greek underground, practically ensured that left-wing organizations would dominate the resistance movement.

The precise details of this event still remain convoluted and partly shrouded in secrecy. In large part it is the tragic story of junior officer John Atkinson, one of the many soldiers captured after the British withdrawal from Greece in April.[13] He managed to escape the Germans, however, with the help of Alexander Zannas, the head of the Greek Red Cross and one of the leaders of the nascent resistance movement.[14] For months, Atkinson shared an apartment with a Greek family, who also had to provide a room for an Italian colonel. Despite serious obstacles, Atkinson left Athens and reached Alexandria, possibly in early October 1941. He volunteered his services to the

SOE, which turned him down, but he eventually went to work for section N of MI9, the British service responsible for assisting the escape of prisoners of war.[15] By early fall, Atkinson returned to Greece and was operating a secret cell on the island of Antiparos for the purpose of establishing escape routes to the Middle East for allied soldiers and civilians.[16]

In late October or early November 1941, the British agent met Zannas in Athens and through him acquired intimate knowledge of the clandestine networks that initially were set up to help escaped British soldiers but that by now had expanded to espionage and sabotage activities.[17] As a member of Athenian society, Zannas was able to use his influence and position to support these groups, as well as to recruit other prominent individuals to work against the occupation forces.[18] During their discussion, however, Zannas noticed that Atkinson was keeping notes of everything discussed, including the names of those involved with clandestine activities.[19] When Zannas objected, Atkinson promised that he would later destroy his papers.[20] Atkinson, with Zannas' help, set up an escape route that ran from Athens to Antiparos via the small island of Anavysos and then by submarine to Egypt.[21] Indeed, shortly after this meeting, twenty-two British and five Greeks were able to leave Greece using that route.

In addition to organizing escape routes, Atkinson ventured into espionage and sabotage work. His first breakthrough came when he acquired the services of an Italian sergeant, Bero Likeri, a member of the Italian garrison on the nearby island of Paros. Likeri was able to give Atkinson and his group advance warning of Italian or German search parties coming to Antiparos as well as to provide information on the Paros garrison.[22] With the assistance of Zannas, as well as that of local fishermen, who were all anxious to play some role in the struggle against the occupation forces, Atkinson was able to establish an intelligence network that provided information about Axis naval movements in and out of the Cyclades islands.[23]

Early success, according to one account, encouraged Atkinson to extend his activities to sabotage, and he undertook to destroy two German tankers anchored at the island of Milos.[24] In November 1941, with help from a local fishing-boat captain, Georgios Anyfandis, and two of his men, Atkinson sailed to Milos and planted explosive charges against the hulls of the tankers. In the early hours of the morning, the explosives went off, sinking both ships.[25] The sabotage of the German ships increased Atkinson's prestige with the islanders and encouraged more volunteers to help with information and escape work, but the increasing level of activity also attracted the attention of the Italian garrison at Paros.

In early January 1942, Likeri, Atkinson's Italian accomplice, warned him to leave the island as soon as possible, but for some reason the British officer delayed his departure.[26] On 6 January, the Italians surrounded the white-washed house that served as the base for the clandestine group and within minutes, the barking of automatic weapons shattered the tranquility of the island. As the Italians burst through the front door, Atkinson shot the first man, who managed to toss a grenade before collapsing on the floor. Fragments from the grenade struck Atkinson, ripping through both his legs. A few minutes later, the entire group was captured.[27] To make matters worse, the Italians found Atkinson's code book, a list of current and potential agents indicated by their initials, a seventeen-page report on possible contacts in Athens prepared by the Greek embassy in Cairo, cash totaling $10,000 and £500, Atkinson's notes from the meeting with Zannas, and a diary of his activities in Greece.[28]

Atkinson was in a terrible physical state and one of his legs had to be amputated. Although the Italians treated the British officer well, he suffered considerably when they moved him from Antiparos to Athens. The other members of his party were less fortunate. One man was beaten every day and another tortured by being subjected to long periods of starvation. Perhaps due to depression caused by the loss of his leg, or the loss of blood and the pain of recovery, Atkinson's morale was undermined and after only a short time he broke down and confessed. The Italians, according to some accounts, did not torture him. Atkinson just gave up and provided his captors with names, organizations, and a list of all his collaborators.[29] In addition, some of the other British soldiers arrested with Atkinson betrayed the individuals at Antiparos who had helped hide them.[30] Atkinson's disclosures dealt a crippling blow to the burgeoning Athenian resistance groups and to those who had been involved with his network in the Cyclades.[31]

The Italians arrested at least fifty individuals, including some of the most prominent Athenians involved with the underground, who had given Atkinson refuge in the course of his first escape.[32] Atkinson's confession spared no one, including himself. Initially, the Italians were not inclined to execute the British spy, but their German allies demanded the death penalty for Atkinson and for all the members of the Antiparos group. On 24 February 1942 at the crack of dawn, the hapless British officer joined the other four marked for execution in front of a firing squad. He had to be carried on a stretcher and then tied to a chair because his injuries made it impossible for him to stand up. Atkinson asked and received permission to say a few last words and, looking up from his chair, in broken Greek he pleaded, "Please forgive me so that God can also grant me forgiveness."[33]

The arrests and subsequent trials astonished the Athenians almost as much as the fact that those apprehended were involved with espionage.[34] This event represented the first major success of Italian counterintelligence and a significant setback for the Athenian underground, particularly for those groups made up of individuals loyal to the Greek government-in-exile or, at any rate, those opposed to revolutionary change. Some who styled themselves republican members of these organizations represented the more conservative wing of the Greek Liberal Party, but they would have accepted a constitutional arrangement that included the Greek king. In their absence, control of the Athenian underground passed to less well-known individuals and fanatical opponents of the monarchy as well as to the left.

In the critical period of 1941–1942, when the resistance was being organized, the absence of moderates such as Panayiotis Kanellopoulos, one of the few prewar politicians willing to participate in a resistance movement and also prepared to accept the Greek government-in-exile, left the initiative to the Greek communists and the more radical republicans.[35] Kanellopoulos' name was in the papers found with Atkinson, and the Greek politician was forced to flee to the Middle East. Although a royalist, Kanellopoulos had opposed the Metaxas regime and was in the process of creating a large resistance group that could have served as a counterweight to the left-wing organizations established by the KKE. After his departure, the group fell apart because there was no one with his stature to fill the void. He arrived in the Middle East as a refugee and not as the head of a major resistance organization. Under these circumstances, when he joined the Greek government-in-exile as vice-premier, he quickly became marginalized.

Thus far, with the exception of Kanellopoulos, the response of the traditional Greek political leaders to the occupation had been at best passive and in some cases outright defeatist. The leaders of the Liberal and Populist parties, as well as of the factions that existed within these organizations, viewed the prospect of resistance as premature and did not entirely trust the former republican officers to lead such an endeavor.[36] The smaller parties either believed in an ultimate Axis victory or preferred to follow the lead of the communists in the creation of the EAM.

The Greek government-in-exile, however, did make one attempt at coordinating the underground organizations and resistance groups, but it ended in failure. The effort collapsed partly from the carelessness of the officer in charge of the operation, but also from the policy of the SOE to establish and maintain exclusive control over the Greek resistance. The Greek government-in-exile established contact, mainly through SIS, with a group of Greek officers known as the Committee of Six Colonels, who were planning to organize resistance and sabotage activity in Greece. The Six Colonels, led by General Panayiotis Spiliotopoulos, the former head of the gendarmerie, had links with most of the senior Greek officers who had fought in the Albanian campaign as well as with Kanellopoulos, now serving as a minister in the government-in-exile.[37]

In the spring of 1942, the colonels, through the efforts of Tsellos, a close associate of Kanellopoulos, had obtained a radio transmitter and attempted communication with the Greek government-in-exile.[38] Kanellopoulos believed that the Six Colonels, with adequate support, could instigate sabotage and guerrilla warfare in Greece and proposed the creation of an action committee based in Athens to be led by these officers. At about this time (July 1942) the SOE was planning a sabotage mission to block the Isthmus of Corinth as well as destroy a bridge in Lamia. Although it was not common practice to notify the Greek government-in-exile of their plans regarding operations in Greece, the SOE on this occasion required the use of a senior Greek officer and approached Kanellopoulos.[39]

Kanellopoulos not only agreed to loan the SOE a Greek officer, Colonel Ioannis Tsigantes, but also saw this an opportunity to set up an organization and coordinate the resistance under the direct control of the Greek government-in-exile. The SOE in Cairo accepted Kanellopoulos' proposal and agreed that the Tsigantes mission, in addition to the sabotage operations, would also get in touch with the colonels in order to set them up as the coordinating committee for the resistance.[40] This was a major breakthrough for Kanellopoulos in his goal of developing the resistance, as he had serious reservations over the isolation of the Greek government-in-exile with respect to events in Greece. He confided in his diary that the British intelligence services controlled all access to the underground groups in Greece and were basing their estimates of the situation there exclusively on reports from biased Greek and British agents.[41] The Greek government, consequently, could not ascertain the political developments in the country independently or have any say over the resistance.[42] He believed that by cooperating with the SOE, he could achieve a relationship of trust between the Greek government and the British intelligence services and thereby could secure some influence with the Greek resistance organizations.[43]

Three months later Kanellopoulos' efforts had borne fruit, as an Anglo-Greek committee was set up to oversee and direct all intelligence and guerrilla warfare operations in Greece (with the exception of EAM-ELAS). For a short period, the committee was kept informed about most intelligence and resistance activity in Greece, including the establishment of a British military mission in the Greek mountains in the fall of 1942. But after the resignation of Kanellopoulos from the Greek government, the effectiveness of the committee diminished and it became simply a propaganda outlet for the SOE.

The SOE mission to Greece, however, proceeded. The team codenamed Midas 614, assembled by the Cairo SOE, included Colonel Tsigantes, who was placed in charge of the operation along with eleven other officers and enlisted men trained for sabotage and espionage. The mission was subdivided into several groups, each assigned a specific task. One team was to block the Isthmus of Corinth, another to destroy a bridge near Lamia, and a third to bring supplies to an alleged resistance group in the southern Peloponnesus called Philiki Etairia Stratou Eleftheroseos (PESE), which the SOE mistakenly believed had over 3,000 members. A fourth team was to organize the transport of Allied troops who had evaded capture, while the rest of the mission, among them Tsigantes, was to go to Athens and assist in the organization of a center to coordinate all resistance activity, provide information on the food crisis and on the Axis intelligence and counterintelligence services, and undertake sabotage and subversive operations.[44]

Although all the members of the team were Greek, they represented different intelligence agencies stationed in the Middle East that included the SOE, SIS, MI5, and the Hellenic Intelligence Service.[45] Midas 614 left Alexandria aboard the submarine *Proteus* and reached Mani on the southeastern Peloponnesus on 1 August 1942. There they hid in a cave for ten days while one member of the team, Panagiotis Rogakos, attempted to make contact with the PESE—only to discover that the resistance group did not exist. His efforts to find the phantom organization, as well as to secure a means of transportation to Athens, alerted the Italian authorities; the group managed to leave the region just ahead of the Italian security forces. On 12 August, Tsigantes divided his team into two sections and each made its way to Piraeus by separate boats. From the harbor, they reached Athens individually or in groups of two or three.[46] Tsigantes had decided to trust the owner of the boat and left behind one of the radio transmitters and most of the explosives. All the members of Midas found accommodation in the homes of family or friends, but they had to keep changing locations to avoid detection by the occupation authorities.

The situation began to unravel almost from their arrival in Athens. The boat on which Tsigantes had left a good portion of their supplies was seized by the Italians, and to make matters worse the second group, along with the only other radio, failed to make contact. Eight days later, however, another boat arrived with the rest of the Midas team. Tsigantes began to initiate contact with his old associates and slowly set up groups to gather intelligence on the Axis forces in Greece. Nevertheless, his main preoccupation was to organize a center to coordinate the resistance.

The other priorities for the Midas teams were to block the Corinth Canal and to destroy the bridge at Karyon near Lamia (central Thessaly), thus disrupting the only rail link between Athens and Thessaloniki. Tsigantes dispatched Spiros Kotsis to survey the bridge, but after close examination, the latter reported that the bridge was too narrow and too well defended and that its destruction would cause minimal delays since repairs could be effected quickly. He suggested that the Gorgopotamos viaduct presented a much better target—it was 215 meters in length and supported by six piers, four of stone and two of steel. Tsigantes agreed with Kotsis and recommended to SOE headquarters in Cairo the destruction of the viaduct, requesting supplies of appropriate explosives. In the meantime he organized, with the help of Dimitris Psarros, a team of former Greek officers to attack the garrison at the bridge while the explosives were being set.[47] This, unfortunately, was as far as Tsigantes got in organizing the sabotage of the bridge or an attempt to coordinate the resistance movement. The explosives did not arrive and Tsigantes was later betrayed by a woman and killed in a shootout with the Italian security service in Athens. The SOE soon dispatched a British team to Greece, the Harling mission, which undertook the destruction of the Gorgopotamos viaduct and took over the effort to direct the development of guerrilla warfare.[48]

From this point on, the plans for both the direction of the underground in Athens and the organization of resistance, as envisaged by the Greek government-in-exile and the SOE, diverged. Kanellopoulos had wanted to establish an organization in Athens that would coordinate all major sabotage activity in Greece and organize the deployment of guerrilla bands. The key objective of the Tsigantes mission, from Kanellopoulos' perspective, was to establish an organization made up of Greek officers loyal to the Greek government-in-exile and moderate in political outlook.

A significant act of sabotage such as the destruction of a major communications link would have given Kanellopoulos' proposed organization tremendous political and moral authority in occupied Greece as well as in Cairo. Instead, the credit for this accomplishment went to the two organizations, EDES and ELAS, whose policies were contrary not only to the Greek government-in-exile but also to the British Foreign Office. Indeed, the arrival of the Harling mission represents a critical turning point in the evolution of the resistance movement and the road to civil war. The SOE, by destroying the Gorgopotamos viaduct, demonstrated to the satisfaction of the British government and the military chiefs the possibilities of large-scale partisan operations in Greece. The SOE, however, accomplished the first major act of sabotage in occupied Europe with the support of the fledgling communist-led and republican guerrilla bands.

For the communists and radical republicans, the Gorgopotamos operation was a remarkable opportunity to demonstrate to the Greek people that the left-wing resistance was working in tandem with the British in order to liberate Greece. The communists, from the onset of the occupation, did not hesitate to embrace the idea of mass resistance and the implementation of guerrilla warfare. Beyond the desire to fight the occupation forces for its own sake, the new communist leadership sought the creation of a resistance movement as a means to control and ultimately dominate the social, economic, and political future of Greece. Unlike the extreme right wing and a large percentage of the traditional ruling elite, most communists believed in an Allied victory because the alternative—the success of the Axis—meant perpetual imprisonment or extermination.

Despite such sentiments, in the early months of the occupation the KKE was still in disarray.[49] The Metaxas regime had incarcerated 2,000 communists, including most of the KKE's senior leaders, in special prisons and confined others to internal exile on several remote islands.[50] In May 1941, 190 communists escaped from the small islands of Folegandros and Kimolos, along with three members of the original central committee of the KKE (Petros Rousos, Chrysa Hadzivasiliou, and Karagkitsis-Simo), and arrived in Athens on 20 May 1941.[51] Another ten reached Crete just before the German assault against the island, accompanied by two other members of the central committee: Stergios Anastasiadis and Miltiadis Porphyrogenis.[52] By the fall, 300 out of the 2,000 imprisoned communists had managed to escape, and could thus take part in the reorganization of the KKE.[53]

After the Axis forces occupied Greece and assumed control over all the prisons, some important KKE members claimed Bulgarian nationality and, with assistance from the Bulgarian embassy, managed to secure their release.[54] The Bulgarians believed that freeing communists, especially those of Slavo-Macedonian origin, would enable them to use these individuals as propagandists for the Bulgarization of eastern Macedonia and Thrace.[55] The communists, however, knew how precarious their newly found freedom was, and once released they quickly disappeared into the underground. When the Greek security services realized what was taking place, they protested to the occupation authorities that they were freeing dangerous communists, but by the time the Germans reversed their decision it was too late.

Once free, these central committee members were able to revive the KKE by the end of the summer. An important factor in the reorganization of the party was that the central committee and Politburo now included men and women who, by virtue of their incarceration, had remained uncontaminated by the machinations of Maniadakis, the head of the Metaxas security apparatus. Furthermore, they had no connection with the prewar police-infested central committees.[56]

According to Thanasis Hadzis, who took part in the reorganization of the communist party, the KKE leadership ignored the existence of armed bands that were forming in the mountains. Hadzis explains that although the central committee was aware that the resistance would have to take on a military character, ultimately becoming the decisive factor, the KKE lacked experience in guerrilla war; it still had to progress from general strikes and small struggles to armed resistance.[57] First and foremost, the KKE had to create a strong political base and achieve legitimacy as a national organization by co-opting as many political organizations as possible into the proposed national front. Attempts to enlist the cooperation of the republican and populist factions, however, met with failure.[58] Ultimately, the KKE had to rely on the smaller parties on the fringes of the Greek political world in order to create the semblance of a national coalition.

The communists, in conjunction with the marginal Greek Socialist and Agrarian parties, established the National Liberation Front (EAM) on 27 September 1941, and invited other interested groups to join the new organization and fight the enemy.[59] The traditional political parties declined to join EAM, for different reasons;[60] the populists refused because the KKE controlled EAM, the liberals declined for the same reason, but also argued that organized resistance was premature and would lead to reprisals. Instead, the liberals proposed the creation of a common front with the aim of preventing the return of the monarchy and the dictatorship after liberation.[61] Despite the boycott by the traditional parties, EAM developed rapidly and attracted an impressive following. Joining EAM did not require any particular sacrifice; one only had to accept the organization as the common resistance front. Under these terms, EAM acquired thousands and ultimately hundreds of thousands of adherents who, by the simple act of becoming members, could believe themselves to be fighting against the occupation authorities.

In February 1942, the KKE leadership sent agents into the mountains to instigate armed resistance and on 10 April, the central committee of EAM, together with the KKE, officially approved the formation of the guerrilla bands.[62] As a result, a month later (22 May 1942), Aris Veloukhiotis established the first unit of what became known as the National Popular Liberation Army (ELAS).[63] Although Veloukhiotis started with fifteen men and his actions were originally limited to central Greece, by 1943 ELAS had grown into a major guerrilla force. Every effort was made to associate the guerrilla force with the revolutionary bands and heroes that had fought the Ottomans during the Greek War of Independence. Even the acronym ELAS, when pronounced, sounds like *Hellas*, or Greece, which gave that organization a powerful propaganda tool. Throughout the occupation, EAM and ELAS confined their propaganda to simple patriotic slogans that aimed to equate their organizations with national pride and Greek history.

Almost concurrent with the creation of EAM (on 9 September 1941), a group of Venizelist officers inaugurated a republican resistance organization that they named EDES (National Democratic Greek League); they could not secure the participation of the established political parties either.[64] Indeed, their own Liberal Party refused any kind of cooperation or support.[65] The founding members and most recruits came from the ranks of the discharged officers of the 1930s. In contrast to EAM, EDES had specific political and social aims that included the provision that the organization would prevent, by any means, the return of the monarchy and also outlined a detailed program of economic and political reforms. Among these reforms were the purging of royalists from the civil service, the armed forces, and the professional organizations, as well as creating programs to alleviate hunger and establish social justice.

Komninos Pyromaglou, who became the general secretary of EDES, related that the Democratic League intended to fill the gap on the Greek political spectrum between the Greek communists and the traditional political parties. In the end, it failed to accomplish this aim because the organization did not gain the support of the prewar republican movement. On the contrary, the republican leadership attempted to destroy the organization, some because they assumed an Axis victory, others because they feared reprisals against the population. Because of this, EDES was unable to establish even modest political bases in the cities or, for that matter, in most parts of Greece, with the exception of Epirus.[66]

The nominal head of EDES was General Nikolaos Plastiras, a former republican officer who had helped to topple the government in 1922 and a

principal conspirator of the abortive 1935 coup. Plastiras, however, found political asylum in France, where he remained until the end of the occupation.
The actual driving force and initiative for the creation of EDES came from
Napoleon Zervas and a handful of republican officers. Zervas, unlike Plastiras, lacked credibility in republican circles and needed Plastiras' name to
legitimize EDES. Zervas had a reputation as a gambler and womanizer, while
his role in the numerous coups from 1916 until his expulsion from the Greek
army in 1935 labeled him a professional conspirator rather than a committed
republican.

It is still not clear why Plastiras allowed his name to become associated
with EDES and with the disreputable Zervas.[67] According to one theory,
Plastiras' reputation remained sterling as long as he abstained from active
politics; he was, after all, the defender of the republican cause. The moment
he became associated with EDES, which was immediately labeled a political
organization, Plastiras ceased to be a nonpartisan statesman and was viewed
by many as a political opponent. A large number of his supporters refused to
join and either actively worked against EDES or created their own resistance
groups.[68] These organizations with their alphabet-soup acronyms (EKKA,
AAA, YVE), however, were doomed from the start and only served to fragment the republican forces. Over the next two years, ELAS disbanded, ab-
sorbed, or destroyed all of these organizations, and the remnants found their
way to EDES and in some instances joined the Greek Security Battalions
raised by Ioannis Rallis, the last puppet prime minister in the spring of 1943.

After the establishment of EAM and EDES, and later of ELAS, the SOE,
through its radio contact with Prometheus II (Prometheus I had to abandon
Greece, a victim of Atkinson's betrayal), was kept up-to-date on various
resistance organizations and groups that were forming in 1942. On 3 March
1942, SOE Cairo instructed Prometheus II to provide protection for agents
who would shortly be arriving in Greece by parachute as well as to find safe
places for the weapons and explosives that would be parachuted separately. In
addition, Cairo ordered Prometheus II to begin the process of recruiting individuals and their families and start preparations for partisan warfare.[69]

In April, the SOE's agent, Odysseus, arrived in Athens from the Middle
East with considerable funds and equipment to assist the budding resistance
groups to undertake espionage, sabotage, subversion, and guerrilla warfare
operations. Alexander Levidis, a Greek officer and head of an escape network
for MI9 and the SOE, arranged a meeting for Odysseus with several senior
Greek officers who represented various republican groups in Athens, as well

as with a representative from EAM. The meeting achieved little except to expose the cleavages within the republican-Venizelist movement and their divergent views about organizing resistance.

Alekos Seferiadis, an associate of Prometheus II, appealed to those present to encourage republican officers to lead the guerrilla bands and do so within EAM.[70] Despite his appeal, the officers disagreed with Seferiadis and insisted that they would terminate all contact with the Cairo SOE if they had to co-operate with EAM.[71] Levidis attempted in vain to make them understand that because the KKE controlled EAM, it was in everyone's interest that republican officers should direct the future armed forces of the left-wing organization. He argued that by refusing, they would not hinder EAM from establishing guerrilla bands, but if republican officers led these units, it would minimize the influence of the Communist Party.[72] A few days later, Levidis set up another meeting for Odysseus, this time including Zervas, Komninos Pyromaglou, and Charalambos Koutsoyiannopoulos, the head of the Prometheus II network. They agreed to instigate guerrilla activity in the mountains and even outlined areas of responsibility for each organization. Zervas undertook to concentrate his actions in Epirus and western Greece, Psarros received jurisdiction over central Greece, and Stefanos Sarafis agreed to concentrate on Thessaly.[73]

Finally, they directed Odysseus to report these arrangements to the SOE and to request that the 2,000 gold sovereigns he had brought from Cairo be divided among those who had agreed to set up guerrilla bands. Ten days later Levidis met again with Odysseus, but the latter informed him that the SOE had instructed him to divide the funds between EAM and EDES—there was to be no support for any other organization.[74] Because of this decision, the attempt by Odysseus, Koutsoyiannopoulos, and Levidis to establish a large republican resistance organization in Athens as well as to field several guerrilla bands in the mountains collapsed. Shortly thereafter, MI9 ordered Levidis not to involve himself with guerrilla activities and instead to concentrate on the evacuation of British soldiers to the Middle East. Odysseus gravitated closer to the KKE, and Koutsoyiannopoulos had to rely on EDES.[75]

It was not coincidental that during this period Veloukhiotis received formal permission from the KKE to establish the first ELAS band in central Greece. Although the SOE had instructed Odysseus to turn over his supply of gold sovereigns to EDES and EAM, Zervas was unhappy with his share and felt cheated, since he assumed that the British now favored only EAM. Odysseus, fearing that Zervas might exact revenge, sought refuge with the

KKE—according to postwar accounts, his reports to Cairo began to down-play Zervas' role in the resistance and to advocate more support for EAM-ELAS.[76] He remained with the KKE for four months and supplied them with money as well as a wireless set, thus enabling them to establish direct contact with Cairo and acquire arms and supplies for ELAS.[77]

Subsequently, the SOE in Cairo decided that Zervas was no longer trust-worthy and ordered Prometheus to end all contact. Koutsoyiannopoulos, however, decided that after all the effort and preparations to organize EDES forces, it would have been counterproductive to cut off Zervas and leave the field to ELAS. Instead, he threatened to denounce Zervas as a traitor and swindler on the BBC Greek Service, unless he proceeded to organize guerrilla bands. Zervas reluctantly left Athens on 23 July 1942 for the mountains of northwestern Greece to take on his role as the leader of EDES.[78]

In the summer of 1942, both ELAS and EDES, although numerically small and with a few antiquated arms, initiated sporadic attacks against the Italians. The Cairo SOE was fully aware of the chaotic political situation in Greece and its effect on the resistance. Through Prometheus II, they were in contact with EDES and EAM-ELAS as well as with other groups that were forming in the winter of 1942, and thanks to the transmitter left behind by Odysseus they also had a direct link with the KKE.

Before the battles of El Alamein and Stalingrad, "Set Europe ablaze" was the catchword in Whitehall and the raison d'être of the SOE. Any organiza-tion, whatever its political outlook, was a welcome addition to Britain's arsenal of secret armies that would rise against the Axis in Europe at the appropriate moment. Until the Gorgopotamos operation, however, the partisan bands were paper tigers. The SOE had mounted several small acts of sabotage, but these were few and of limited strategic value that paled in comparison to the crippling losses inflicted against the British by the Germans in North Africa and by the Japanese in Asia.

The SOE was an organization in search of a mission and one that could dramatically illustrate the potential contribution of guerrilla operations to the war effort. All that changed in September 1942 when General Alexander, the commander-in-chief of the Middle Eastern Theater of Operations, asked if the SOE could disrupt the supply lines of the German army that ran from Central Europe through Greece to North Africa. The SOE could hardly re-fuse; on the contrary, this request presented an opportunity for the organi-zation to validate its credentials as a fighting service. On the basis of these factors, SOE Cairo decided to send a British team—the Harling mission—to undertake the first major sabotage action in Greece and to do it in conjunction with the republican guerrilla band of Zervas.

The objective of the Harling mission was to destroy one of the main bridges in southern Thessaly and disrupt the Thessaloniki–Athens rail line. The operation was to coincide with a major British offensive at El Alamein (in Egypt) and stop the supplies reaching the German Africa Corps through Piraeus. The SOE persuaded Colonel Edmund Myers, an officer with little experience in clandestine operations but the only available engineer in the Middle East Theater of Operations, to lead the mission and destroy the viaduct. Following the sabotage, a submarine would evacuate the team, with the exception of Christopher Woodhouse and Themis Marinos, who were to remain behind and serve as liaisons between SOE Cairo and EDES. What exactly Woodhouse was to accomplish in Greece, in addition to this liaison work, is not clear. According to his own account, he was planning to transfer to the Special Air Service (SAS), and instead when he went to Cairo to negotiate his release from the SOE, someone asked him whether he wished to be dropped by parachute into occupied Greece.[79] There were several delays and abortive attempts, but on 30 September 1942, three groups of four men each boarded their aircraft. Two of the groups parachuted over Greece, but the third airplane could not identify the prearranged signal from the ground and had to turn back.

After Woodhouse landed in Greece, it took him over five weeks to locate Zervas, and along the way, he heard about ELAS, which had given refuge to the third SOE team that arrived in Greece on 30 October. On 10 November, Woodhouse finally reached Zervas' headquarters and shortly afterward they set out to join Myers to accomplish the destruction of the Gorgopotamos viaduct.[80] On the return journey, they came across Veloukhiotis' ELAS band, which also agreed to join the operation even though, according to Woodhouse, EAM did not permit ELAS to engage in any full-scale confrontations with the enemy.[81]

Eight days later, and after almost two months of delays, the Harling team, with the assistance of EDES and ELAS, destroyed the bridge on the evening of 25 November 1942. Unfortunately, the last phase of the Battle of El Alamein had begun a month earlier on the evening of 23–24 October. By 7 November, the Africa Corps was in full retreat, and on 9 November, the Allies successfully invaded French North Africa. In just over ten days, the Eighth Army pushed the Germans almost six hundred miles west, and on 23 November, General Bernard Montgomery, the victor of El Alamein, halted the advance of the

Eighth Army in order to regroup his forces. The Gorgopotamos operation, consequently, had little impact on the war in North Africa. Weeks before the Harling team destroyed the viaduct, Erwin Rommel's supplies had been arriving in Africa from Italy via Sicily, not Greece, since the Africa Corps had retreated so far west.[82]

The destruction of Gorgopotamos viaduct, however, provided excellent propaganda material for the Allies, who used the success of this operation to demonstrate that the resistance was fighting the Axis in occupied Europe. It also elevated the status of the SOE in Cairo and with it the future possibilities of guerrilla warfare in Greece.[83] To this end, SOE Cairo decided not to evacuate the Harling mission and with the stroke of a pen transformed it into the British Military Mission (BMM) in the Greek mountains. Over the next eight months, the BMM expanded rapidly; SOE teams mushroomed throughout the mountain regions of Greece, enabling the SOE to lay claim to the much promised guerrilla war envisioned by its planners.

Woodhouse writes that his new orders from SOE Cairo were to establish himself in Athens as a permanent liaison with the BMM and the resistance groups, which the SOE assumed would come under the control of the Six Colonels. To Woodhouse "this belonged to a world of fantasy," but he agreed to undertake an exploratory visit to Athens, although he was convinced that to remain in the city permanently would have been suicidal.[84] At the very least, it would have challenged the most adept expert in disguises to camouflage the redheaded, six-foot, five-inch-tall Woodhouse to pass as a Greek in Athens. For any SOE agent, let alone one with distinctly Anglo-Saxon features, Athens was a city rife with double agents, collaborators, and traitors who either had infiltrated or had knowledge of the major underground groups and individuals associated with them.

Despite the obstacles, Woodhouse stayed in Athens for several days and afterward reported that the Six Colonels were preparing to transform the guerrillas into an army after the collapse of Italy. He dismissed their usefulness as far as the resistance was concerned, but stated that they would prove valuable after the occupation. In the same report, Woodhouse recorded that the guerrilla forces would be more "easily directed from the field. . . . The EAM remote control is sure but slow. Luckily Ares (Veloukhiotis), their outstanding commander, pays only lip service to their system and acts as he decides."[85] In addition to making a strong case for the future prospects of guerrilla warfare, Woodhouse implied that it was much easier to control the partisan bands from the mountains than by any central authority in Athens.

Myers, the head of the British Military Mission in the Greek mountains, in his first series of reports on the Greek guerrillas, played up the importance of ELAS and indicated that although EAM was communist-controlled, most of its members were not aware of this. As he put it, "The Thessaly guerrillas [ELAS bands] are the largest and best organized of all. Athens attaches importance to them owing to their position astride the main North-South road." He went on to describe EAM "as a genuine body organized to free Greece. It has many royalist members including a general. After the war? [*sic*] they desire a plebiscite to decide the government and to be controlled by the Allies, followed by a General Election. The EAM would then dissolve."[86]

Woodhouse, in contrast, highlighted the communist links of EAM and stressed, "The EAM literature has a pro-Russian tinge and abuses the King, Tsouderos, and Kanellopoulos. I believe the Communists control EAM unknown to most members."[87] Myers further advocated the creation of a single command headquarters in the mountains for all the resistance groups. Neither Myers nor Woodhouse could have known that Lord Glenconnor, the head of the Cairo SOE, had proposed something similar and that the Foreign Office was in the process of agreeing that the direction of the Greek resistance, as long as it was strictly military in nature, should pass to the SOE representatives in Greece.

Myers also suggested that the British ensure a plebiscite after liberation to determine the fate of the Greek monarchy.[88] This proved to be too much for the Foreign Office, which "severely chastised" Myers and the SOE for meddling in politics.[89] It was one thing for the SOE to direct the military activities of the Greek resistance, but entirely different when it attempted to implement a political agenda. After this contretemps, Foreign Office officials in London and Cairo initiated a campaign to curtail the activities of the SOE in Greece. The Foreign Office now claimed that the SOE supported groups hostile to the Greek monarchy and those whose objectives were contrary to British policy.

They did not succeed and had to be content with the instructions given to members of the BMM to state: "While they don't mix in politics, they know that His Majesty's Government supports the King and his Government."[90] On 9 March 1943, on the advice of Woodhouse, Zervas proclaimed his loyalty to the Greek king,[91] which helped ease tensions between the Foreign Office and the SOE, but it was only a temporary truce.[92] Zervas' about-face on the issue of the monarchy, however, altered the political dynamic of the republican movement and set in motion the process that in less than a year would drive the resistance organizations into full-scale civil war.

In the period following the destruction of the Gorgopotamos viaduct, both EDES and ELAS had begun to expand their forces and to increase their operations against the Axis. Although during this time several new organizations took the field, from 1943 to 1944 ELAS and EDES dominated the guerrilla war in the mountains. The smaller bands usually confined their activities to the regions from which they recruited their personnel, but soon came under considerable pressure from ELAS to join that organization or disband. By the end of February, according to Myers' estimates, ELAS membership reached approximately 2,000 men and women, while EDES reached 2,420; the combined force of all the other bands did not exceed 550.[93] Myers reported confidently that the smaller ELAS ultimately had to accept the direction of a common headquarters guided by the BMM.[94]

Despite these optimistic assessments of the numerical superiority of the EDES forces, ELAS continued to expand at a greater rate. In March 1943, ELAS began to absorb by force or persuasion the smaller groups near its territory; by the summer, it had succeeded in establishing control over central and northern Greece as well as parts of the Peloponnese. By the end of the summer of 1943, ELAS had increased its forces to almost 12,000, with an additional force of 24,000 reserves. EDES, in contrast, did not fare as well; during the same period (January–May 1943) it increased to only 4,000.[95] One SOE report, however, argued that qualitatively, EDES possessed better-trained partisans and a greater proportion of former professional officers.[96]

The relationship of these numbers to the relative strength of ELAS and EDES was deceptive. Unlike EDES, ELAS could rely on the popular support from EAM that had been organized a year earlier in most cities and towns. In addition to a steady stream of recruits and supplies, EAM was able to provide for ELAS a network of support services based in villages and hamlets in the Greek mountains not under the control of EDES.[97] In the summer of 1943, ELAS also started to recruit considerable numbers of Greek officers, many of whom were attracted to that organization by its recent successes and by other senior officers associated with ELAS.[98]

Originally, the guerrilla bands had been unsuccessful in attracting professional officers. Most senior officers were averse to the idea of resistance because they were in awe of the German military machine or discouraged by the Greek government-in-exile. Many of the cashiered republican officers, however, saw the resistance as an opportunity for reinstatement in a post-liberation Greek army. At first, they provided large numbers of recruits for EDES, but as the resistance expanded in 1943, they were also drawn to republican organizations such as EKKA (National and Social Liberation). These new organizations diverted potential recruits from Zervas, and when ELAS or the Germans dispersed them, very few of their members went over to EDES.[99] In addition, when Zervas made his peace with the monarchy, it drove many EDES republican supporters away from resistance activity or into the arms of ELAS. This sharpened the difference between the two major guerrilla bands, as EDES became more and more associated with the monarchy.[100]

In the meantime, the BMM started to become more involved with political matters and was less able to steer the growth or direction of the Greek resistance movement. By the late spring of 1943, there were indications that relations among the guerrilla groups were heading toward a crisis. The BMM, although mandated to guide the guerrilla movement, was quickly losing control. Myers now began to send reports to Cairo indicating that EAM-ELAS was planning to dominate the resistance, but the SOE was reluctant to break with EAM-ELAS and there was still some suspicion in Cairo of Zervas.[101] The BMM nonetheless did manage to establish almost complete influence over EDES. According to D. J. Wallace, who had arrived in Greece at the end of June 1943 to act as Myers' political adviser: "Zervas is a British creation in the sense that we are responsible for his continued existence today and for all the consequences that may follow there from."[102]

In July 1943, after lengthy and difficulty negotiations, Myers convinced the EAM-ELAS leadership to accept coordination with the BMM and the other guerrilla bands. EAM-ELAS agreed, but on the condition that a joint headquarters should be set up in its territory and the role of the BMM relegated to that of liaison. In addition, Myers had to convince the SOE that ELAS should be recognized as a sovereign Allied force and that although it intended to accept general directions from the Middle East commander-in-chief, it should retain its freedom of action. In exchange, Myers was able to extract two major concessions from ELAS. The first permitted the BMM to raise new guerrilla bands in areas under the control of ELAS, and the second allowed Myers to coordinate a series of guerrilla operations that were part of a major Allied deception plan.[103] The SOE considered the National Bands Agreement, the name of this arrangement, as a major achievement in the development of the guerrilla war and even brought Myers the appreciation of the Foreign Office.[104] For the British, the advantage of a temporary pause in the clashes between ELAS and the other groups offset the recognition of ELAS as an Allied force, which gave that organization status and legitimacy.[105] In this context, the events that unfolded between August 1943 and January

1944 represent a critical stage of the Greek resistance and directly contributed to the outbreak of civil war in October 1943.

As the war swung in favor of the Allies, the leadership of EAM-ELAS was anticipating the liberation of Greece and the possibility that the Red Army would free all the Balkans. On 18 July 1943, the Greek communist newspaper, *Rizospastis,* announced the Soviet victory at the Battle of Kursk and two days later proclaimed that the Russians would soon reach the Balkans. A short while later the Allies invaded Sicily. Consequently, there was every indication that the liberation of Greece would take place in the very near future. These notions gathered additional credibility with the execution of Operation Animals, designed to deceive the Germans into believing that the Allies were about to invade Greece, whereas in reality it was to assist their landing in Sicily.[106] Part of the British strategy was to instigate considerable guerrilla activity in the respective regions of the Greek resistance groups, giving the impression of an imminent allied invasion.[107]

Operation Animals led to the immediate transfer of three German armored divisions to Greece and contributed to a speedy Allied victory in Sicily and later, the invasion of southern Italy.[108] In September, Mussolini was deposed and Italy surrendered unconditionally. For the Greek resistance these events not only created the perception of an allied landing in Greece; for EAM-ELAS and the republicans, they also raised the prospect of the return of the Greek government-in-exile and King George II. The failure of the British and the Greek government to come to terms with EAM-ELAS in August exacerbated further the climate of mutual suspicion. In August 1943, Myers had arranged for the transportation of a delegation from the main resistance organizations to Cairo.[109] The aim of the mission, at least as understood by Myers, was to improve coordination and organization among the guerrilla bands, the Greek general staff, and the Greek government-in-exile.[110]

Upon their arrival in Cairo, the delegation focused exclusively on political issues.[111] They demanded that the king remain outside Greece after liberation until the Greek people decided the fate of the monarchy by plebiscite and that the Greek government-in-exile had to include three representatives from the resistance organizations.[112] After consulting with both Churchill and Roosevelt, George II rejected all the demands of the resistance, and the Foreign Office instructed their officials in Cairo to terminate all discussions with the delegation concerning the Greek monarchy and the government-in-exile.

According to the Report on SOE Activities in Greece, in mid-September, the delegation "returned to Greece disgruntled at their treatment and in a most disappointed frame of mind."[113] The left-wing and republican leaders were now convinced that the British were bent on imposing the Greek king and the prewar political structure. For the KKE-led EAM, the only means of preventing this outcome while also achieving control of the postwar environment in Greece was to dominate the resistance. Civil war was now a necessity in order for ELAS to destroy all other resistance organizations and rival guerrilla bands. The only change that they managed to effect in Cairo was the acquisition of two American officers, which transformed the British Military Mission into the Allied Military Mission (AMM).

The two Americans were Captain Winston Ehrgott and Lieutenant Bob Ford. In November they were joined by Major Gerald K. Wines, who assumed command of the Office of Strategic Services (OSS) part of the AMM. Between August 1943 and November 1944, the OSS deployed over 400 men in various clandestine operations in Greece and provided the State Department with an independent source of information on the Greek situation. By the end of the occupation, the OSS maintained eight missions: five with EAM-ELAS and one with EDES, while the other two operated independently in several parts of Greece. For the most part, OSS personnel in Greece tended to support whichever organization they were attached to, but they had orders to use British communications under the control of a senior SOE officer. The Secret Intelligence group (the OSS intelligence units), however, maintained independent communications. In September 1943, relations among the SOE, MI6, and the OSS were formalized by a series of agreements that gave each organization certain geographic spheres of responsibility. Under the terms of these understandings, the SOE was given exclusive control over the Balkans and the Middle East.[114]

In Cairo, the failure by the British and the Greek government-in-exile to address the demands of the resistance delegation brought to the forefront the contradictory policies of the SOE and the Foreign Office toward Greece, which thus far had been cloaked in ambiguity. Equally relevant was that the Cairo crisis forced the British to choose between recognizing the resistance groups politically or continuing their unconditional support of the Greek monarch. In the final analysis, the choice had already been made by Churchill's conviction that after the defeat of the Axis, Europe had to return to the prewar political status quo. The presence of the delegation simply forced the British in Cairo to come to terms with that policy as far as the Greeks were concerned.

Fighting between ELAS and the other guerrilla forces broke out in Greece on 9 October 1943, and within one week had spread to parts of eastern Epirus under the control of EDES. By the end of November, Zervas had withdrawn his forces from the eastern side of the Arachtos River to defensive positions ranging from Ioannina to Arta. On 21 December, EDES units attacked the ELAS forces in the region of Amfilochia and Pramanda, approximately twenty-five miles from Arta, and pushed them back across the Arachtos. In January, Zervas began an offensive that forced ELAS to withdraw across the Akhelos. On 23 January, the EAM central committee authorized ELAS to discuss a truce, which lasted only until the 26th, when units of ELAS, commanded by Aris Veloukhiotis, launched a major counterattack that forced EDES back across the Akhelos. By 1 February, Zervas' situation was becoming desperate as ELAS forces were concentrating in the area of Flamburion, approximately twenty miles from Ioannina, which was EDES' base of operations.

German intervention saved Zervas at the last moment. Fearing that the destruction of EDES would mean that eastern Epirus, along with the essential Ioannina–Arta road, would come under the control of ELAS, the Germans attacked the northern flank of ELAS along the eastern bank of the Arachtos on 2 February 1944.[115] Although the Germans failed to destroy the ELAS forces in this region, they forced the guerrillas out of Epirus and saved Zervas. The Germans expected Zervas to take the offensive, but having suffered considerable casualties, he kept his forces west of the Arachtos; as long as he remained in this region, he no longer needed to fear ELAS, since the presence of strong Wehrmacht units guaranteed his safety.[116] Because of these maneuvers, the still-young civil war now stalemated, and both rival guerrilla organizations accepted the mediation of the AMM to end hostilities.[117] In addition, the civil war demonstrated that the Germans were slowly losing control of the mountain regions of Greece and did not have the resources or military forces to destroy the guerrilla bands. Instead they tried a strategy, somewhat like divide and rule, to keep both guerrilla forces in a state of play so that they would be busy killing each other and not German soldiers.

The civil war also renewed the conflict between the Foreign Office and the SOE; only this time it was Middle East command that was responsible for the latter. As mentioned earlier, the military was convinced that the Greek resistance was necessary in order to tie down as many German divisions as possible in the Balkans to support the Allied effort elsewhere in Europe. They disagreed with the Foreign Office policy of supporting George II, whom they viewed as an obstacle in continuing the expansion of the Greek guerrilla forces, particularly those of EAM-ELAS.[118] General Maitland Wilson, the commander of the Middle Eastern Theater of Operations, as well as the

chiefs-of-staff, still believed that it was possible to wean ELAS from the communist influence of EAM and reintroduced an earlier SOE proposal to bring
Plastiras from France to the Greek mountains to create a regency council
headed by Archbishop Damaskinos.[119]

The Foreign Office, although skeptical of the military value of ELAS, was
prepared to accept the council, providing that the military break with EAM-
ELAS. The latter provision was the price Leeper, the British ambassador,
demanded for accepting the Plastiras-Damaskinos compromise.[120] The War
Cabinet dealt with the matter on 22 November and authorized Churchill and
Foreign Secretary Anthony Eden to handle the issue in cooperation with the
Middle East Command. They further recommended that all supplies to
ELAS cease, and that the Greek army incorporate EDES as well as ELAS. To
ensure this settlement, the king had to agree to accept a regency council and
not return to Greece until the Greek people decided on the future of the
monarchy by plebiscite.[121] Churchill and Eden advised George II to accept
this proposal, but, after consulting with Roosevelt, he declined.[122] The most
that George II was prepared to do was to declare that he would reconsider the
timing of his return to Greece at liberation, in consultation with his government. Once again, the failure to resolve the constitutional issue remained
the major stumbling block to either reaching an accommodation with the
left or countering the influence of EAM-ELAS with those who opposed the
monarchy.

Although ELAS achieved considerable tactical success against Zervas'
forces, it failed to destroy EDES. ELAS was also beginning to lose popularity
because of the hardships endured by the mountain villages. Veloukhiotis, in
particular, exacted terrible vengeance upon any villager suspected of aiding
the enemies of ELAS—not just the Germans. Often, he even forced members
of the AMM to watch helplessly as he tortured a simple peasant for some
minor offense. In the village of Mavrolithary, ELAS arrested fourteen men
simply because they belonged to a rival band. The punishments, designed to
set an example for all the local inhabitants, usually took place in the village
square and set the pattern of death and degradation that continued until
1949. On this occasion, Veloukhiotis' henchmen grabbed the first prisoner
and stripped him of his clothes. Then in front of the villagers, they tied the
man to a table, spread eagle. The victim quickly realized what was in store and
vainly pleaded for mercy. In a few minutes, his shrill cries reverberated in the
village square as the executioner, splattered with blood, slowly proceeded to
hack away at the man's body, pausing enough for each blow to take effect and

prolong the process for as long as possible. The savagery went on until a British officer present pulled out his revolver and terminated the man's agony. Veloukhiotis, shaking with anger, had to be restrained from killing the officer.[123]

Regardless of their fear of the left, the British had come to terms with the Greek civil war and ELAS. The decision of the allies to implement Operation Overlord, taken at the Teheran Conference, meant continued support for Tito and the Greek resistance in order to keep the "Balkan pot boiling" for the Germans.[124] Because of this situation, the Foreign Office was not prepared to break with EAM-ELAS, but attempted to limit its strength and diminish its influence. To this end, it proposed "to restrain the more ruthless members of ELAS and to build an anti-KKE coalition around Damaskinos and the exiled government which was to be revived and strengthened by including fresh political moderates from Greece."[125] Furthermore, the Foreign Office, despite Churchill's objections, was prepared to accept EAM-ELAS representation in a new Greek coalition government.[126]

In January 1944, consequently, the Foreign Office proposed to initiate talks with EAM-ELAS for the purpose of ending the civil war, and although Tsouderos agreed, he insisted that any negotiations be limited to military matters. In turn, Tsouderos appealed to Archbishop Damaskinos to attempt reconciliation between the leaders of the traditional political parties and the Greek government-in-exile. In addition, if EAM-ELAS accepted an armistice, Damaskinos was to select a committee to negotiate the formation of a coalition government that would include representatives from the left. Tsouderos authorized Woodhouse to represent the Greek premier in the talks with EAM-ELAS, and after fourteen meetings, the civil war ended with the conclusion of the Plaka Agreement on 29 February 1944.[127] The signatories agreed to continue the armistice and maintain the territorial status quo in their respective regions, while accepting the principle to cooperate in the future. A secret clause was also included that the guerrilla organizations would participate in Operation Noah's Ark, designed to harass the German retreat from Greece.[128]

The Plaka Agreement was only a limited success because it essentially established a military truce but did not address any of the outstanding political issues. The absence of a political compromise now acted as a catalyst for EAM-ELAS to begin the process of forming its own government. Although most Greek politicians had rebuffed EAM's efforts to participate in the creation of a Greek government in the mountains, several liberals and republicans decided to work with EAM in order to moderate the KKE's influence and work toward achieving self-determination for postwar Greece. On 10 March 1944, EAM formally established the Political Committee of National Libera-tion (PEEA). The committee included not only members of EAM, but also Alexander Svolos, one of Greece's preeminent constitutional experts; Angelos Angelopoulos, another academic; Emmanuel Mandakas, the only senior Greek officer to lead a coup against the Metaxas regime (in 1938); and Eurip-ides Bakirdzis, who abandoned EKKA and joined PEEA.[129]

The formation of PEEA triggered a political crisis for the British and the Greek government-in-exile because it "presented . . . a real if not legal ri-val."[130] Many of the officers and men of the Greek armed forces in the Middle East viewed PEEA as the legitimate representative of the Greek people and resented the refusal of Tsouderos and the king to come to terms with PEEA's request for the establishment of a new Greek government.[131] On 26 March, the day after the celebration of Greece's Independence Day, PEEA made an-other appeal for a government of national unity, and this time it sparked a mutiny in the Greek armed forces in the Middle East. Tsouderos refused to deal with the demands of the mutineers to recognize PEEA as well as broaden the government. The British, particularly Churchill, who blamed the mutiny on extremists and communists, supported the decision of the Greek premier.

Meanwhile liberals and Venizelist politicians, who were in and out of the revolving door of the Greek government-in-exile, tried to convince Tsouderos to resign in favor of Sophocles Venizelos, the son of the great prime minister, who, they argued, was in a better position to deal with the rebellious Greek forces. Tsouderos at first resisted, but on 13 April he gave up his post and Venizelos took his place as premier.[132] The latter was equally unsuccessful in quelling the mutiny, and after thirteen days he also resigned. The British then took matters into their own hands and forced the appointment of Admiral Petros Voulgaris as commander-in-chief of the Greek navy to put down the rebels. After a short skirmish, Voulgaris, with the help of British military forces, restored order by the end of April.[133]

The end of the first civil war in February 1944 and the mutiny of the Greek armed forces in the Middle East left the Greek government-in-exile in tatters and with little credibility in occupied Greece. EAM-ELAS, on the other hand, emerged as a much stronger organization, increasing the prospect of conflict with the British. In early 1944, the allies decided that they would not launch an invasion of Greece and that liberation would follow in the wake of a German retreat, thus leaving most of the country under the control of EAM-ELAS. In the interim period, between the spring of 1944 and the German evacuation in October, the British had to plan for two possibilities. The first was to bring about the liberation of Greece with the cooperation of EAM-ELAS, at least long enough for the Greek government-in-exile to reassert its authority over the country. The second was to cooperate with the anticommunist elements linked to the puppet government and use them to maintain control of Greece until the British could bring sufficient forces to secure the country.

Both possibilities required at least a partial reform of the Greek government-in-exile, which had to include representatives from the resistance as well as deal with the question of the monarchy. Although these factors had come into play and had been summarily rejected when the resistance delegation had visited Cairo in August 1943, the new realities created by the civil war and the fact that no allied army would liberate Greece required an accommodation with the left, at least on British terms. Part of the means of addressing this problem required, at the very minimum, the semblance of a Greek coalition government and a premier who represented the liberal establishment and had some credibility in occupied Greece.

The man who had these qualities was George Papandreou. A follower of Venizelos, he had held three cabinet portfolios and had a reputation of supporting progressive legislation. In March 1942, he had signed the petition calling upon George II to remain outside Greece until a plebiscite determined the fate of the monarchy. During the occupation, Papandreou kept in touch with members of the resistance, but declined to join EAM-ELAS and later sent a series of dispatches to Cairo denouncing the left-wing organization, as well as warning the Greek government-in-exile and the British of the growing influence of the KKE. These communications had greatly impressed the Foreign Office—particularly Papandreou's analysis of the international political order, which he divided into pan-Slavist communism, which threatened to swallow Greece and Europe, and Anglo-Saxon liberalism, the only force able to oppose it.[134] Accordingly, the British and George II decided to bring Papandreou out of Greece, and, with Churchill's approval, he became acting premier on 26 April 1944.

Papandreou had many qualities and was sufficiently liberal, and like most Greek politicians was a liberal with a conservative bent, but he was no Charles de Gaulle. Unlike de Gaulle, a military man with the absolute loyalty of the Free French Army, who had imposed himself on the British and later the Americans (to the consternation of the latter), Papandreou was plucked out of obscurity in Greece by the British and foisted on the king, the government-in-exile, and the armed forces in the Middle East. To the left, at best he appeared to hold office through British favor and at worst he was seen as a puppet of a foreign power—effectively no different than the Quisling occupation prime ministers. Papandreou was a British solution dictated to accommodate their interests and those of George II. As head of the government-in-exile, he did not enjoy the whole-hearted support of the king, he was not the leader of a political party, and he did not command the confidence of the armed forces or even the non–left-wing resistance. He was a man destined to be a cipher for a variety of interests, foreign and domestic, and remain helpless as the country drifted to a second round of civil war two months after liberation. Greece needed a de Gaulle, but not one appointed by the British—a military man who stood above petty politics and who guaranteed bringing back stability but not the old order. Unfortunately for the Greeks, such a man did not exist.

Papandreou's first task was to chair an all-party conference in Lebanon on 17 May 1944, the purpose of which was to form a government of national unity that would also include representatives of the resistance organizations.[135] Papandreou skillfully isolated the EAM-ELAS delegates by accusing them of causing the civil war as well as the April mutiny.[136] Next, he sidestepped the constitutional problem by using a letter from George II (8 November), which declared that the king would reconsider his return to Greece in consultation with his government, as the guiding principle of the role of the monarchy in the immediate postliberation period.[137] The conference ended three days later on 20 May with the conclusion of the Lebanon Charter, whose eight points were accepted by all the participants including the EAM-ELAS and PEEA delegates.[138] Papandreou reported the results of the conference to the king and submitted his resignation. The king, in turn, accepted the Lebanon Charter and asked Papandreou to form a new government based on the principles agreed to at the conference.[139]

Papandreou's objective was to form a government of national unity that would include representation from the resistance organizations. This participation would force EAM-ELAS to act in concert with the new government and abandon PEEA. EAM-ELAS, however, upon receiving the terms of the Lebanon Charter, refused to endorse it or to join a government of national unity.[140] For the next several months, Papandreou and the British waged an overt and covert campaign to force EAM-ELAS into a coalition government. Papandreou, for his part, interpreted the king's letter of 8 November 1943 to mean that the Greek government-in-exile understood that George II would not return to Greece until a plebiscite decided the future of the monarchy, thus removing the most serious objection that was keeping EAM-ELAS from joining the government.[141] The British, in contrast, had been attempting even before the Lebanon agreement to contain the growing power of EAM-ELAS, and searched for new coalitions to form an anti-left front. Ironically, the Germans at this time were pursuing a similar policy.

After the outbreak of civil war in October 1943, it had become obvious to the British that the Venizelists and liberals were no match for the KKE. The republican forces, which the SOE had so carefully cultivated as the lesser of two evils, had lost their cohesion as a political organization. They still represented a considerable force, however, and a potential ally for the Germans, who in the fall of 1943 began to approach counterinsurgency from a political perspective, focusing on anticommunism. From the beginning of the occupation, the Germans concentrated on occupying and protecting key strategic positions straddling their lines of communication, effectively abandoning the countryside to the guerrillas except for limited and infrequent operations.[142] Until 1943, the Italians had responsibility for securing most of Greece as well as conducting antiguerrilla operations, and the Germans only took action in cases of specific sabotage in their zones of occupation.[143]

In the spring of 1943, Ioannis Rallis, a professional politician, agreed to head the third occupation government, with the proviso that his regime could establish a Greek security force. The German authorities agreed in principle, and on 7 April 1943, the Rallis government decreed the mobilization of four Evzone battalions.[144] At first, and in order to calm the fears of their Italian ally, the Germans armed the newly created battalions with rifles and machine guns only.[145] This policy changed with the surrender of Italy, and by October 1943 the first fully armed battalions came into service in Athens, followed by two more by the end of December.

Despite a persistent and aggressive recruitment campaign, the Rallis forces attracted just a handful of volunteers. The success of EAM-ELAS in the early stages of the civil war later drove many conservative officers to the Security Battalions. During the course of the civil war, some members of guerrilla bands dispersed by ELAS also sought refuge or revenge by enlisting in the battalions.[146] As a large proportion of these men were republicans, they were attracted to the units, which were advertised as anticommunist as well as antimonarchist forces. Moreover, after Zervas' reconciliation with the monarchy, EDES had ceased to represent the republican cause.

For the Germans, the battalions provided new forces to replace the Italian units stationed in Greece. Early in 1944, the Rallis government seized the opportunity offered by the willingness of the German authorities to expand the battalions and began an intensive campaign to attract new volunteers. In order to maintain a steady flow of recruits, the Rallis regime dismissed hundreds of men from local police forces without any pay or rations. To make recruitment palatable, the puppet regime spread rumors that the British and American governments secretly supported Rallis. In addition, on 19 March 1944, the puppet government enacted legislation that permitted all officers dismissed from the armed forces after 1927 to reenlist at their former rank provided they serve in the battalions.[147] This move, coupled with the propaganda that the battalions were to be used to combat communism, offered to many cashiered republican officers the possibility of reinstatement in a postwar Greek army.[148]

Ironically, officers loyal to the king faced a similar dilemma. In the spring of 1943, the monarchist faction of the officer corps had attempted to create an organization to represent and maintain the unity of the royalist officers. General Alexander Papagos, the commander-in-chief of the Greek army during the Albanian war, along with five other generals, established the Military Hierarchy. Very quickly, the new organization extended its influence among the professional officers in Athens and through them to those who resided in the military districts of the Greek army divisions before the war.[149] The aims of the Military Hierarchy were to support the organizations fighting the occupation forces by providing leadership and maintaining the established social and political order by gaining control of Athens after a German withdrawal.[150] Despite the prestige of Papagos, the generals were unable to solicit any interest from the British or from any of the guerrilla bands, and soon the German authorities arrested the six generals and sent them to a concentration camp. Although the Germans incarcerated the leadership of the Military Hierarchy, the organization survived and remained dormant until liberation. Then, many of its adherents resurfaced and were able to take advantage of the anti-left policies of the British and the Greek governments and to once again assume control of the armed forces and the security services.

The ambivalent attitude of the British toward these as well as the collaborationist forces carrying the label "anticommunist" contributed to the growth of the battalions. Even prior to the outbreak of the civil war, officers of the British intelligence services had come into indirect contact with the representatives of the Rallis government and with individuals associated with the battalions. In September 1943, Frank Macaskie, the *Telegraph* correspondent in Athens before the occupation and an officer in the SIS afterward, had attempted, with the assistance of Angelos Evert (the head of the Athens police force) and Archbishop Damaskinos, to form an anticommunist front as a counter to EAM-ELAS.[151] This coalition was to include several conservative republicans, but also certain members of the Athens EDES who were already working for the Germans or had been instrumental in organizing the Security Battalions.[152] EAM-ELAS was aware of efforts by British agents, whether authorized or not, to build a counter-organization to the left-wing resistance, which confirmed their suspicions of the British.[153]

The British and Greek government-in-exile initially avoided any outright denunciation of the Security Battalions, instead confining their comments to mild reprimands through the BBC broadcasts to Greece.[154] For example, one directive of 2 June 1944 stipulated that all those who joined the battalions were assisting the Germans but that they should not be denounced as traitors. Twenty days later, a second directive suspended all direct attacks against the Rallis forces until July 1944.[155] The Greek government-in-exile finally denounced these units publicly in September 1944.[156]

By the summer of 1944, the Greek political spectrum had shifted significantly, as the struggle between the left and right overshadowed the old royalist-republican schism. Within this spectrum the battalions assumed the position of intermediaries between the postwar "political revolution" represented by EAM-ELAS and the reestablishment of the old order identified with EDES and backed by the British. Inasmuch as the first round of the civil war spawned the Security Battalions, it also marginalized EDES and with it the republican cause, not only within the resistance movement but also as a potential player in postwar Greece.

In contrast, between the fall of 1943 and the summer of 1944 EAM-ELAS clearly emerged as a major political and military force that controlled most of the Greek countryside and had an established infrastructure within the major cities and towns. The collapse of Italy provided EAM-ELAS with an added bonus—one Italian division that managed to avoid internment by the Germans in Greece surrendered to the AMM, but in ELAS-held territory. Despite British efforts to keep the Italian force intact, logistical problems forced them to disperse the Italians, but in the process, the Italians had to abandon their weapons.[157] Most of these ended up in the hands of ELAS, giving that organization a considerable number of artillery and heavy machine guns and hence increasing its firepower and decreasing its dependence on British supplies.

Thus, with the exception of Zervas' numerically inferior EDES bands and the limited number of guerrillas controlled by right-wing groups, the only other force capable of containing ELAS was the Security Battalions. These circumstances forced Papandreou to consider incorporating the Security Battalions into the postwar Greek army.[158] Although this plan fell through, during the summer of 1944 the absence of any strong and outright denunciation of these forces served as indirect pressure for EAM-ELAS to join the Greek government.[159]

After many mutual denunciations between EAM-ELAS and the Greek government-in-exile, on 29 July EAM-ELAS informed Cairo that it was prepared to join the government providing that Papandreou stepped down as premier. Both Churchill and Eden, however, denounced EAM-ELAS' call for Papandreou's resignation. On 18 August, George Siantos, the acting secretary of the KKE and a member of the central committee of EAM, dropped all previous demands and accepted the admission of five EAM-ELAS representatives to the Greek government.[160] Some scholars have attributed this dramatic volte-face to the influence of a Soviet mission that had arrived in Greece on 26 July.[161] In the meantime, the British decided to send a small force to Greece to facilitate the transition from occupation to liberation, but primarily to prevent EAM-ELAS from seizing power.[162] In early September, the Greek government-in-exile moved to Caserta, Italy, and on 26 September, in conjunction with the British and representatives of the resistance, it concluded the Caserta Agreement to deal with the immediate problems of security after liberation. The main concern of the British and the Papandreou government, however, was the demobilization of the guerrilla bands and the transfer of the Government of National Unity (the name of the government-in-exile after May 1944) to Greece.

The agreement was signed by: Wilson, as the Supreme Allied Commander, Mediterranean Theater; Papandreou, on behalf of the Greek government; Harold Macmillan, representing the British government; and Zervas and Sarafis for EDES and ELAS, respectively. Remarkably, EAM-ELAS accepted these conditions, which after liberation effectively gave the British and the Greek government-in-exile control of key areas, thus enabling them to offset some of the strategic advantage held by ELAS. On 18 September 1944, almost a week before the Caserta Agreement, Macmillan, the resident minister of state, confided in his diary that Greece was "in grave danger of EAM seizing power whenever the Germans are leaving."[163] Nonetheless, despite the concessions given by EAM-ELAS, the British presumed that the communists would use the resistance to gain control of Greece. For the next several

months, this underlying principle guided British policy toward the Greek resistance and invariably contributed to the outbreak of the December Uprising
in 1944.

On 12 October 1944, the Germans pulled their forces out of Athens and
began their withdrawal from Greece. Six days later, the Greek government,
along with a small British force, arrived in the capital.[164] Despite the Hercu-
lean tasks facing the Greek government, the most pressing issue was the establishment of a new national army to replace the guerrilla bands and to participate
in the defeat of Nazi Germany. With the exception of the Greek navy and
small air force, the Greek government had under its control only the Third
Mountain Brigade and the Sacred Company, the latter made up of officers.
These forces were all that remained of the Greek units in the Middle East after
the mutinies and the subsequent purges. Their composition, following the
dismissal and court-martial of liberals and republicans who had participated
in the mutinies, was conservative and included many republicans such as
Vendiris, now transformed into a committed royalist. This made the government-controlled army unacceptable to EAM-ELAS, which feared that any
new army led by such officers would simply restore the prewar political establishment. For the time being, the Third Brigade was in Italy, and its future
disposition, at least officially, remained in question.

In the fall of 1944, consequently, the Greek government was dependent on
the small British force made up of logistical personnel, the goodwill of EAM-
ELAS, and the Security Battalions. It seems clear from the events that unfolded between November and December that the Papandreou government
had decided, in cooperation with the British, to quietly reinstate the officers
who had served in the battalions. At the same time, it had become British
policy to dissolve EAM and dismantle ELAS units while using collaborators
to support the Greek government. One SOE report of 8 September 1944 recommended that "a combination of secret and overt means [be used] to persuade the moderate majority to desert EAM-ELAS at an opportune moment
and join the supporters of the legal government. Details must vary slightly
according to local conditions but the two essential principles are that secrecy
must be maintained and that HMG [His Majesty's Government] must not
appear to be connected with this scheme." The same report also outlined British policy toward other groups, including collaborators: "By contrast with
EAM, the fragmentation of right wing groups Quisling and non-political
formations has less importance. Leaders and rank and file could easily be
made to support the legal Government of Greece when the time comes."[165]

After liberation, the British had incarcerated the majority of the Security Battalions in the Goudi barracks outside Athens and in other locations in Attica. In the middle of November, the British started releasing Security Battalion officers from Averoff prison, and soon some of them were freely walking the streets of Athens wearing new uniforms. The British and the Greek general staff assisted others in leaving Greece for Egypt, and placed those released in early November into regular army units.[166] On 23 November, the Ministry of Defense published a list of 250 officers designated to command the new National Guard units; of these, eight had served with the Security Battalions.[167] EAM-ELAS and the press were so outraged that the government had to revise the list and drop those associated with the battalions as well as having to replace the undersecretary of defense with an ELAS officer, General Ptolemaios Sarigiannis.[168]

The British army continued to provide protection and assist in the gradual rehabilitation of the former Quisling units into the Greek army and the police forces. They were guided in this policy, even before liberation, by the almost absolute conviction that EAM-ELAS, and through them the KKE, was determined to seize power.[169] On 9 August 1944, Foreign Secretary Eden outlined Britain's strategic interest in postwar Greece to the War Cabinet and stressed that it was imperative to avoid a communist coup in that country. Eden warned: "Were the Greek Communist forces, who were strongly armed, to seize power a massacre might follow. This would be very injurious to our prestige, and might even add Greece to the post-war Balkan Slav block which now showed signs of forming under Russian influence, and from which we were anxious to keep Greece detached."[170] The daily marches and protests by EAM-ELAS bolstered these fears, which ultimately created the conditions for a confrontation between the British and ELAS.

CHAPTER 4

Bloody December

THE SECOND ROUND OF THE CIVIL WAR

Democracy is no harlot to be picked up in the street
by a man with a tommy gun.

—Winston Churchill

Usually December is a mercurial month in Greece. The weather ranges from the soft warmth of the winter sunlight in the middle of the day to brisk evenings and damp, cold mornings. Sunday, 3 December 1944, marked a tragic day for Athens, a city on the verge of chaos. It had rained the previous day, and most Athenians were driven indoors by the chill and dampness. At dawn, the rays of the sun pierced the darkness and the light blended with the morning dew making the city sparkle and gleam. People slowly began their daily ritual of scrounging for scarce supplies and bits of wood so they could keep warm during the frosty nights.

December was made even colder by severe shortages of food and heating fuel that had taken bloom out of liberation two months earlier. During those early heady days, the gloom of occupation was shattered by parades of soldiers and resistance fighters along with the frivolity of round-the-clock celebrations, but by December, Athens had once again descended into darkness. The sudden exhilaration of freedom was replaced by recriminations and charges of collaboration or treason. Accusation, in fact, became the national discourse. Fear stalked every corner of Athens, grinding down what little trust that remained and diminishing any hope for the future.

On the morning of 3 December 1944, several processions of Greek communists, socialists, republicans, and antimonarchists were advancing to Constitution Square, the center of Athens and the heart of Greek political life. All

were members of the wartime National Liberation Front (EAM), a coalition
of communist, socialist, and agrarian parties that had developed into a mass
resistance organization during the occupation. The ranks of demonstrators
were filled with a disproportionate number of young women, teenagers, old
men, and even children. Some came as unwilling participants, because the
day before, bands of young men had gone through most of the streets of the
city and, armed with paper megaphones, issued orders to all citizens to come
and show their support for EAM by participating in the demonstration.

FIG. 3. Athenians celebrate the liberation from Nazi occupation on 12 October 1944.
The celebration was short-lived; two months later, the resistance was fighting the
British in the December Uprising. Greek Ministry of Foreign Affairs:
Photo Exhibition of the Diplomatic and Historical Archive Department.

During the first six weeks of liberation, Athenians had grown accustomed to the daily cacophony of slogans and rants, grievances paraded by the left. This time, however, it was different. Anyone who stayed away, the young men with the megaphones warned, would be considered an enemy of the people and dealt with accordingly.[1] Most residents had little reason to doubt the urgency of the exhortations or the veracity of the threats and the next day they made their way to the center of Athens. Threats aside, EAM enjoyed a mass following that had greater faith in the wartime resistance organization than in the provisional government. Many had walked from the outskirts of Athens, others from the suburbs and nearby villages, while a lucky few were brought to the city by a hastily established EAM transportation system, which was composed of a motley collection of dilapidated trucks and automobiles.

The demonstrators were descending on Athens to protest the decision of the Greek government to demobilize the resistance bands that had fought the Axis and to replace them with a new army. During the three and a half years of brutal occupation, the allies had hailed the resistance fighters as the torchbearers of freedom in Nazi-dominated Europe. Yet by December 1944, the resistance had become the unwanted guest of the exigencies of war and now was a threat to the Greek government and an embarrassment to its British patrons. The realities of peace could not fulfill the promises, or at least insinuations, during the occupation, and the demonstrators believed that their grievances had to be addressed before Greece could truly be liberated. They suspected that a new Greek army would simply force the return of the unpopular King George II and enable the provisional Greek government to reinstate the prewar political status quo, with its legacy of authoritarianism and repression.

In the view of the large number of Greeks who subscribed to the left, the resistance bands had to remain in order to ensure an equitable balance of power; the communist leadership, however, had other ambitions, as well as fears. Despite the fact that the membership of EAM was close to 750,000, the KKE did not have faith that this mass support would remain steadfast. Certainly, they could not rely on broad endorsement of a communist platform in a future election, thus the KKE continued to operate behind front organizations such as EAM. Preserving the military options provided by ELAS was the best chance the communists had of exerting influence in postwar Greece and nursing any hope of achieving control over the country. The decision of the provisional government to order the demobilization of the guerrilla forces meant that the KKE would lose the only effective leverage with which to impose its agenda on events.

The fate of the resistance bands and the issue of a new army, however, were symptoms of much deeper divisions that imposed themselves on the political process in postliberation Greece. Fundamentally, two visions of the country's future had come to the forefront: a radical Greece ruled by the "will of the people," the so-called popular democracy, promised by the rhetoric of EAM-ELAS; and the return of the prewar political establishment. Both political concepts had antecedents whose roots reached back to the Greek war of independence, but by December 1944 they were on a collision course. Supporters of each side suspected the other of hidden agendas and duplicity. The right believed that behind the promise of a liberal, socialist, and democratic Greece loomed the KKE and the prospect of a Soviet-style state, while the left was convinced that references to stability and order implied the specter of monarchy and authoritarianism.

Despite the suspicions of the left, the resurrection of a political system dominated by military and reactionary cliques was not necessarily a fait accompli—at least in the immediate postliberation period. The power and influence of the traditional elites and political factions became dissipated by war and occupation, as well as challenged by the phenomenon of a mass-based resistance. Unfortunately, the hasty and precipitous actions of the left practically guaranteed the return of the stifling rule of the prewar traditional elites, who would impose a new authoritarianism with a vengeance. On that morning in December, those thousands of demonstrators were marching to regain the political initiative that the war and occupation had created for the left and that they believed was about to be hijacked by the Government of National Unity.

Police cordons blocked off all streets leading to the center of Athens, but approximately one hundred demonstrators broke through from Sygrou Street and advanced toward the police station located on the edge of Constitution Square near the Grande Bretagne Hotel. As the columns of demonstrators snaked through the streets, converging on the center of the city, they were incited by the men with the megaphones and every so often the crowd stopped and chanted: "Down with Papandreou!" "Down with intervention!" "Try the collaborators!" "Down with George Glucksberg [George II]!" "Death to Traitors!" The police had set up barricades to block off the streets leading to the square, but these were overwhelmed by the sheer weight of people. In particular, angry young women, caught up in the excitement of the moment, screamed unrelentingly at the police, and some even left the columns and ran out into the street to shake their fists at the muzzles of the rifles.[2]

At approximately 10:00 A.M., a large group of demonstrators made its way to the apartment building of George Papandreou. A torrent of threats accompanied the chants of "Down with Papandreou!" Trapped inside his apartment, Papandreou watched anxiously as his police guard struggled to hold back the protestors. Suddenly, someone threw two grenades, killing one passerby and severely wounding another.[3] The sight of blood further enraged the demonstrators, and they attempted to force their way into the lobby of the apartment building. Fortunately, Papandreou's guards (with the aid of automatic weapons) succeeded in dispersing the angry crowd.[4]

According to Panagiotis Kanellopoulos, then minister of marine in the government, the day's events had almost unhinged Papandreou. Earlier in the morning, when Kanellopoulos first went to see the premier to discuss the pending demonstration, he was told that Papandreou was sleeping and could not be disturbed. A little later, Kanellopoulos tried once again to see the premier and reached his fifth-floor apartment just a few minutes after the police had beaten back the demonstrators. Once inside, he saw five or six ministers huddled in a corner; despite the circumstances, they remained unfazed, but the premier had withdrawn alone into his bedroom. Half an hour later, Papandreou finally emerged from his isolation, recalls Kanellopoulos, but "he appeared confused, nervous and incapable of making decisions."[5]

The crisis that followed liberation had taken its toll on the Greek premier and his family. Papandreou's stepdaughter, Miranda, was a communist who took part in the EAM parades and demonstrations, and the premier's son, Andreas, was serving in the United States Navy. Staring from his window, Papandreou may have mused that one face in that crowd could just as easily have been his own stepdaughter screaming for his blood. Later on, during the thirty-three days of the December crisis, Miranda went completely over to the other side and gave stage performances for ELAS. She further tried to raise the morale of the insurgents by drawing sketches that lampooned her parents. In the meantime, while the premier was trying to grapple with a country on the brink of civil war (as well as the future of his own family), Sunday's events were acquiring their own relentless momentum.

By approximately 10:45 A.M., one column of demonstrators was spilling into Constitution Square. They quickly formed ranks of eight to ten abreast, while every fourth person carried either a British, Greek, American, or Soviet flag. Others waved banners on which slogans were emblazoned in red print.[6] W. Byford-Jones, who witnessed the event, writes:

The ages of those who were taking part ranged from ten to twelve years of age to sixty and more. A few of the children were without shoes, most of the people without overcoats, but there were many who were well dressed. As before, there were a predominant number of girls between eighteen and thirty years of age. There was nothing sullen or menacing about the procession. Some of the men shouted fanatically towards the police station and the hotel, but there was a good deal of humorous banter, and many jokes were exchanged between demonstrators and those who watched from the curbs.[7]

Between the demonstrators and the police station were approximately twenty terrified policemen, who had taken position between the palace and the corner of the Grande Bretagne Hotel that faced the square. Armed with little more than Italian carbines loaded with blank ammunition, the police had no illusions as to their fate if the crowd got out of control.

The policemen had every reason to fear for their lives: as they had served under the jurisdiction of the occupation authorities, the majority of Athenians had, rightly or wrongly, labeled them collaborators. Although many Greek police officials had covertly assisted the resistance and the allies, not enough time had passed since liberation to permit a clear distinction between absolute traitor and patriot. Indeed, some had had to wear the mask of the former in order to assist the latter.

Making matters worse, the Greek government failed to purge the security establishments and civil service of collaborators, whose continued presence now tainted every state official. The government had argued that time was required to conduct a meticulous and judicious purge, but such reasoning was lost on the crowds advancing toward the center of the city in the morning of 3 December 1944. To the half-starved population of Greece, symbols truly mattered, and the gray uniforms of the police invoked the fear and agony of the occupation.

The handful of policemen positioned a few yards beyond their station were aware of this reality, and for the previous several hours they had witnessed dozens of wounded fellow officers being carried off on stretchers into the station following clashes with groups of demonstrators. As the crowd got closer and closer, the policemen's fears turned to panic, and some began to replace their blank rounds with live ammunition.

When the crowd advanced to less than one hundred yards from the police cordon, suddenly a man in military uniform ran out of the station and shouted, "Shoot the bastards!" He then dropped to one knee and began firing his gun.[8] A few seconds later the panic-stricken policemen followed suit. They did not fire in unison like a disciplined unit, but discharged their weapons sporadically. Some of the officers hesitated for a few seconds; others had remained transfixed by the spectacle before them, but one after another they began to return fire. The first ranks of the crowd fell forward; the fortunate ones found protection behind trees or nearby walls, but most simply lay flat on the ground.

The shooting continued for approximately half an hour, and when it was over twenty-two of the demonstrators remained still, twelve of them dead.[9] A couple of brave souls gingerly darted out onto the square to drag back the bodies of their comrades, while others attempted to cover the wounded with their own bodies. Once the firing ceased, fear of the police and anguish over the casualties were instantly replaced by rage. The metamorphosis from a disciplined crowd into a frenzied mob took place almost instantly. Hatred replaced terror and, according to Byford-Jones: "the demonstrators went mad. Thousands of people roared their threats and defiance at the police. It was the ugliest scene I had ever witnessed. . . . The demonstrators stood screaming and shouting, tearing open their shirts and crying, 'Shoot me, you cowards, you Papandreou hirelings.' "[10]

By noon, a second wave of demonstrators broke through the police cordons and was soon joined by thousands more, until the square was jammed with almost 60,000 people.[11] The police retreated to their station and locked themselves inside. Over the next thirty minutes, the remaining police barricades disintegrated as most of the officers discreetly left the scene and sought refuge in nearby private homes or managed to reach the safety of the police headquarters. A few police stragglers near the square, however, were not as fortunate. They were seized by dozens of hands, punched, kicked. and spat upon. Their protestations of innocence were drowned out by a torrent of verbal abuse. The lucky ones were dragged off to the nearest lamppost and lynched; some, however, could not be pried away from the clutches of the mob, which, intoxicated by raw animal savagery, tore the men literally from limb to limb.[12]

The crowd in the square continued to shout slogans and to wave banners, remarkably also carrying Greek, American, British, and Russian flags. Regardless of the chaos and commotion, every effort was made to display EAM's affection for the United States and its president. The masses repeatedly shouted "Roosevelt, Roosevelt" and carried numerous large flags of the Stars and Stripes. An American officer passing by was immediately pounced on by a group of boys, who raised him on their shoulders and carried him over forty blocks until the man managed to kick himself free.[13]

In the midst of this angry mass of humanity, an old woman dressed in widow's black stood outside the police station and, like the furies from the ancient past, hurled threats and curses at the men inside the building. For some time she stubbornly stood leaning on her stick, her presence the incarnation of hatred, fear, and helplessness that had become a metaphor for Greece.

After several hours, the crowd quietly dispersed and a squadron of British paratroopers, advancing single file, easily pushed the remaining demonstrators across the square. Despite the bitter fighting that would later take place, most firsthand accounts agree that initially there was no perceptible hostility toward the British. For the time being, and as far as most of the demonstrators were concerned, the killings were blamed on the police and the Papandreou government. After the last groups of participants and spectators abandoned Constitution Square, a strange silence engulfed the place, interrupted briefly by a crisp wind that playfully chased the odd bits of paper and brownish leaves across the pavement. Soon after, the skies darkened and a heavy downpour lashed the bare streets of Athens, driving indoors the handful of lingering protestors and onlookers.

The police continued to remain within the confines of their station, while the man who initiated the shooting in the square disappeared. His identity remains a mystery and has become another strand in the folklore that eventually framed the story of the December Uprising. The questions still linger— was he an agent provocateur of the right, or even the left? Over the years, no one has ever come forward to take credit or provide evidence of this man's identity. Whoever he was, he almost single-handedly lit the fuse triggering a sequence of events that catapulted Athens into the brutality of the December Uprising.[14]

The next day, Monday, 4 December, a sea of demonstrators converged on the city center to protest the killings, and again held the streets of Athens hostage. In the morning, thousands of EAM supporters joined a long funeral procession led by several trucks carrying twenty-four makeshift coffins of Sunday's victims. Reactions to the funeral delineated the left- and right-wing cleavages of Athenian society that now radiated to all of Greece. Although some Athenians mourned the death of the victims, others seized on the occasion to denounce the tactics of EAM. EAM's detractors baldly stated that the display of twenty-four coffins was exaggerated and intentionally provocative. They also claimed that several of the coffins were filled with stones and that not all the corpses were the victims of Sunday's clash.

At the cemetery, leading members of the KKE and EAM eulogized the dead and condemned the Greek government for the murders.[15] The demonstrators then headed back to the center of the city. Three young women at the head of the procession carried a long banner proclaiming: "When the people are in danger from tyranny they choose either chains or arms." Those following chanted slogans inscribed on placards and carried them along with allied flags and bloodstained pieces of cloth as a testimony of Sunday's casualties. Once again, a disproportionate number of young women led the columns, rendered almost hysterical with rage, spitting curses and threats.[16]

The path for Monday's procession was carefully chosen to challenge the authority of the Papandreou government and, failing that, to provoke a reaction. The possibility of casualties was of little consideration to EAM or to the government—fresh killings would simply generate new martyrs for either side. Around noon, the demonstrators headed to Omonia Square, but before they could advance any further, they came under fire from the police and members of the right-wing EDES and X (pronounced Chi), organizations who had been positioned on the rooftops and in outlying rooms of several hotels that faced the main streets. The X organization included fervent anti-communists as well many who simply sought revenge for atrocities committed by the left against members of their families.

This time, the demonstrators, flanked by armed ELAS cadres, began firing back.[17] In a few minutes, pandemonium broke out as most of the demonstrators started to run away from the shooting and scrambled for protection in the nearest doorways, store entrances, or any other possible shelter from the gunfire. The main confrontation took place around the Metropolis Hotel, and by the afternoon, when British troops managed to restore order, forty more people had lost their lives and seventy were seriously wounded.[18]

These new shootings and killings almost coincided with the gunfire of the reserve ELAS units opening the preliminary round of the battle of Athens. Remarkably, despite the threats and claims by the left for a mass uprising against the Papandreou regime, the initial crisis was a slow burn rather than a sudden eruption, or even part of a carefully calculated strategy. The first choice of targets was the police, which the left identified with the provisional government and the last vestiges of the occupation. Over the next several hours, the reserve ELAS units mounted dozens of small sieges against the police stations in Athens and the port city of Piraeus. By 3:00 P.M., ELAS had captured twenty-one out of the twenty-four police stations in metropolitan Athens, and unraveled the tenuous compromises that had held the peace since liberation.

These attacks followed a familiar pattern in which dozens of small, heart-wrenching dramas were played out. After a police station was captured, those not killed during the fighting were accused of collaboration and other crimes against the people. The policemen would plead innocence but their entreaties fell on deaf ears. These exchanges seldom lasted for more than a few minutes, and afterward the unfortunate officers were shot outright or dragged to the nearest lamppost, tree, or telephone pole and hanged. In some instances British troops, still encountering little or no opposition from ELAS, managed to rescue the condemned. In others, the presence of British soldiers served to encourage the extreme elements to descend into even greater human depravity.

In Piraeus, a British unit attempted to interpose itself between a police station and ELAS, but faced overwhelming opposition. After a tense verbal exchange, the guerrillas dragged out several of their prisoners and in front of the British soldiers proceeded to gouge out the eyes of these hapless prisoners. The British soldiers gawked, transfixed by the horror unfolding before them and disgusted by their impotency to interfere. The screams of the policemen reverberated along the empty streets, and were quickly reduced to low guttural moans, but the ordeal was far from over. For a few minutes, the ELAS executioners just grinned while savoring the spectacle of torment and the vulnerability of the British. Then, they took out butcher's cleavers and began to hack off the forearms of the blind policemen and continued slashing until the bodies resembled heaps of human pulp. The agony, for victims and spectators, ended when the policemen were put out of their misery by bullets to their brains.[19] The tormentors exploited such sadistic brutality on several levels—by exercising of their total superiority over their victims, and by forcing the British to observe the atrocity they made them de facto participants.

Yet, collectively or individually, other members of ELAS were also capable of remarkable demonstrations of human dignity and courage. During the early days of the fighting and before General Ronald Scobie, the British commander of all forces in Greece, gave the order to commit fully his forces into battle, a British squadron, supported by one tank, moved against the EAM ELAS headquarters in Athens located on Constitution Square, across from the Grande Bretagne Hotel. After the unit captured the building and took a few prisoners, a lone ELAS guerrilla approached them and, ripping off his shirt, stood bare-chested in front of the tank, challenging the British tank to pass through him. In that brief moment, the conflict was no longer anonymous and for the British tank crew the enemy had a face, commitment, and determination. The intimacy of the moment proved too much, and the embarrassed crew turned the tank around and abandoned the street to the ELAS soldier.[20]

Civil war, with few exceptions, quickly degenerates into brutal slaughter because the violence and killing are localized and intimate. Athens in 1944 was a small city in which life revolved around equally small neighborhoods, where everyone knew just about everyone else. The killing or torture of one individual seldom remained isolated, but instead rippled across many lives. Under these conditions, the emotional involvement of the participants is supercharged and, as exemplified by the man standing in front of the tank in Athens, absolute. Fanaticism and revulsion dominated Athenian society during the December Uprising and continued throughout the next stage of the civil war from 1946 to 1949. In this jungle of extreme emotions, atrocities were commonplace and not exclusive to one side or the other.

Another immediate target, during the early days of the battle, was the extreme right-wing X organization. ELAS units, in the early afternoon of 4 December, advanced on the X headquarters near the Temple of Theseus, close to the Acropolis, and laid siege to several buildings. X included approximately one thousand members and was led by Colonel Grivas, a fierce anticommunist and committed royalist. The organization came into existence primarily in Athens during the last year of the occupation to counter the overwhelming influence of EAM and ELAS.

The left had almost immediately denounced all members of X as reactionaries and collaborators—lumping them with the notorious German-led Security Battalions. In a short time, a fierce firefight ensued and neither side expected nor was inclined to give quarter. The battle raged all day, and after several failed attempts to capture the X headquarters, ELAS began to bombard the buildings with mortars. Some structures caught on fire, and by late afternoon flames from the burning buildings darted upward, licking the low-hanging clouds. In the evening, the glow from the fires rested like a red crown over a dark and dreary Athens.

In another part of the city, a smaller base of X came under fire from ELAS, and innocent bystanders and local residents became trapped in the ensuing fight. On the afternoon of 4 December, Alexander Zaousis opened the door of his apartment at 85 Solonos Street, near the University of Athens. Before he could step outside, a crescendo of gunfire and the thud of grenades forced the young Athenian back inside. The shooting went on for hours, as thirty-five young members of X were trapped at 108 Solonos Street by a superior ELAS force. The ELAS fighters attempted to penetrate the building from the roof but failed to break through. For the next twenty-four hours, the two sides exchanged sniper fire, using the nearby building as cover. The local residents were caught in between and had no choice but to wait out the battle.

The situation seemed to take a turn for the worse for Zaousis and his family. One group of X snipers had positioned themselves on the roof of his apartment building, and by late night he heard angry voices outside calling on the X members to surrender. Otherwise, the voices said, ELAS would use mortars. Fortunately for Zaousis the bombardment did not take place, but his ordeal was not over. Over the next several hours, the night was punctured by the short bursts of automatic weapons, the loud pop of rifle fire, and the frantic shouts of neighbors yelling, "We are unarmed," as X or ELAS gunmen kicked down doors or came crashing through windows in a deadly game of hide and seek.

The next day the British troops, accompanied by armored cars, arrived on the scene and were able to rescue the X survivors, including Zaousis and his family, but not those who had been taken prisoner and were now held as trophies by ELAS. They were able to hear their colleagues being led to safety on British army trucks, but they had no doubt about what was to be their fate. When the last truck left clanking along the empty streets of Athens, each one of the prisoners was made to kneel down, some crossed themselves, others simply stared blankly, and then a man stood over each one and in sequence dispatched them with a single bullet to the back of the head.[21]

Over the next several days, the fighting in Athens was sporadic and ranged from intensive firefights between armed combatants to scenes of gut-wrenching individual trauma. Rigas Rigopoulos was a remarkable young man in his early twenties who witnessed one of several spectacles of violence and death. During the occupation, he and a group of close friends had established one of the most effective espionage cells in Athens and Piraeus. For two years, he led the double life of a spy and lived under the constant terror of arrest, torture, and execution at the hands of the Axis. By the summer of 1943, the Gestapo was closing in and Rigopoulos barely managed to escape to the Middle East.

By December 1944, Rigopoulos was back home, but before he could once again take up his life, Sunday's crisis hijacked the promises of liberation. On the fourth day of the uprising, he was walking along narrow Omiros Street that led to the much broader Panepistimiou Boulevard when he heard the characteristic gurgling sound of a mortar shell. "Incoming missiles," he yelled and took refuge beside an iron fence. A few seconds later two mortar shells exploded in the middle of Panepistimiou Boulevard in front of the Bank of Greece.

Almost six decades later, sitting in the comfortable living room of his Kolonaki apartment, Rigopoulos, with some difficulty, summoned the painful recollections of the first days of the crisis. He remembers that approximately ten people were hit. "Two British soldiers lay side-by-side, face down on the tramlines. Their brains were scattered all around. I tried to lift up a woman dressed in black. She did not appear to be wounded, but she was moaning slowly. She turned her head and died in my arms. From her open purse, a pension book fell out with pictures of her and her two small children." Rigopoulos closed the woman's eyes and, turning away, saw that "a young girl, dragging herself across the asphalt with her hands, was crying loudly and calling me by name. It was an acquaintance of mine from Mytilini Island. 'I can't stand up,' she was screaming. 'I can't breathe, I am going to die.' Her back was full of blood. Two other men helped me, and we carried her to the municipal hospital. She had a fragment in her spinal cord, but did not die immediately. She lived for quite some time, paralyzed and in horrible pain."[22]

Despite the passage of so many years, Rigopoulos cannot easily excuse the actions of ELAS. "The Germans and Italians had never hit Athens. They respected the city and its historic monuments that shed light on humanity. This was not the case with ELAS. During the course of the Uprising, machine gun fire chirped from the windows and street corners. Snipers fired from behind shutters. Shells embroidered most of the facades of the houses. Every so often you heard explosions as ELAS was blowing up houses, collapsing them to block the streets."[23]

On 5 December, General Scobie, the British commander, received orders from Churchill to commit British forces and prevent the left from taking control of Athens. Scobie issued orders to ELAS to withdraw all its units from Athens within seventy-two hours and cease attacking the police stations. The KKE and EAM ignored this demand, but beyond that, they were not certain on how to proceed. It may be that George Siantos, the acting head of the KKE and an influential member of EAM's central committee, was expecting that the government would collapse and Papandreou resign, opening the door to negotiations and the establishment of a new administration that would include a large number of EAM and KKE ministers. More important, the ELAS forces would then not be demobilized until a new army was established, which would be free from the influence of the right.

Papandreou did submit his resignation, but Churchill would not hear of it. He ordered Rex Leeper, the British ambassador to Greece, to "force Papandreou to stand to his duty, and assure him he will be supported by all our forces if he does so."[24] According to Nigel Clive, at the time working for the SIS in Athens, Churchill used even stronger language and demanded that Leeper keep Papandreou as prime minister even if it meant "tying him to a chair and placing him under arrest until he changed his mind."[25]

Leeper, however, was able to persuade Papandreou to change his mind without resorting to any drastic measures. This unexpected turn of events left the KKE and its partners in EAM in a quandary. The hard-liners were adamant about continuing the battle, even if this meant fighting the British. The socialist members of EAM were not convinced and argued for compromise. After hours of uncertainty and heated arguments, both sides agreed to continue the war against the government but not engage British forces. How they believed they could achieve this is not clear.

Vasilis Bartsiotas, the head of the Communist Party in Athens, claimed after the civil war that ELAS could have taken on the British as well as the Greek government forces: "Again we had all the people of Athens with us and we would have fought in the capital for the lives of our children and for our homes." Bartsiotas argues, "this was the most ideal moment . . . to strike immediately against the forces of the reaction and the British and seize power. . . . We had then for the third time—after 12 and 15 October 1944—the forces to seize power."[26]

Thanasis Hadzis, a prominent member of the KKE, was less sanguine about the prospects of a quick victory, however. He writes that the KKE faced two serious problems with respect to an armed confrontation. First, there were the reactions of EAM's followers to Sunday's bloodshed event; although the majority of EAM supporters had been reassured by the widespread outrage against the police and the Papandreou regime, the majority still considered the British as allies and friends. After the shooting was over on Sunday, thousands of demonstrators continued to wave allied flags and shout, "Long Live Churchill," "Long Live Roosevelt," and "Long Live Stalin." This open enthusiasm for the leaders of the major Allies, according to Hadzis, indicated that Athenians held the police alone responsible for the killings. Hadzis also states: "The other disappointing factor was the paralysis that took hold of the masses once British troops arrived on the scene and saved the murderers, which prevented any further action against the provocateurs and the police who were shooting at the demonstrators from the hotels in Omonia Plateia."[27]

Hadzis believed that the ELAS reserve units in Athens were not ready and that it would have taken some time to prepare them for war against the mighty British Empire. Hadzis also realized, he later wrote, "On 4 December the popular movement and its political and military leadership were not ready for a general armed revolt. It was imperative to allow for some time to pass and to acquire tangible evidence . . . in order to convince the masses, that it was necessary to fight the allies when they [the allies] violate their national independence."[28] The bravado of communists such as Bartsiotas and the tempered analysis provided by Hadzis are conveniently reflected in their memoirs, which were written years later, to explain or absolve them of their part in the ultimate failure of the uprising. Nevertheless, Hadzis' account, in particular, offers some insight into the reluctance of the KKE leadership to rely on the support of the Greek population for a civil war. More than anything else, this lack of confidence in EAM's followers to participate in an uprising that also included fighting the British delayed the KKE's ability to launch an all-out offensive in the first weeks of December.

For a short while, this peculiar situation placed the British troops in an awkward position of being simultaneously bystanders and participants. They were seldom fired upon, at least in the first days of the crisis, but had to confront ELAS units daily; in some instances they tried to disarm them, in others it was a matter of persuading them to hand over prisoners or to abandon captured buildings. Frequently British officers were obliged to take part in long-winded discussions with representatives of ELAS or with the neighborhood EAM and KKE bosses. Most of these men, especially junior officers or those recently arrived in Athens, often found themselves in a bizarre and surreal environment.

Richard O'Brien had studied law at Cambridge and in 1940 joined the army. For three years he fought in North Africa and Italy, and in early December he and his company were transferred to Athens. After the hard fighting in Italy, O'Brien was not quite certain why his unit might be forced to fight ELAS, an organization that ostensibly had been an ally only a few days earlier. In his unpublished, partially completed memoirs, O'Brien captures some of the frustration, confusion, and strain that these soldiers underwent during their stay in Athens and Greece. A few days before ELAS escalated the battle to include the British, O'Brien was ordered, despite his protests, to disarm an

ELAS unit in the Piraeus area. He arrived at the ELAS headquarters, located in a small house near the sea, with only an interpreter. According to his account:

We began by negotiating. Nothing is more of a strain when it is not certain whether the other side is going to shoot you or talk to you. . . . My interpreter and I were ushered into a small room and given seats around a table. The door was kept closed throughout, but during the meeting, it was regularly opened by a guard outside, who would pass in dirty pieces of paper, and mutter furtively to persons inside the room. This comic, if rather sinister, sideshow provided light relief throughout our somewhat tense and protracted discussion. The argument was not important. It followed the obvious lines and went round in circles. I said we did not wish to fight, the Greek people were our allies, not our enemies, for were we not both fighting the Germans? They admitted this; but said that they must keep their arms to defend themselves against their own fascists. They maintained that Britain had no right to interfere in Greek affairs. To begin with, I more than held my own. In the room were three or four elderly amiable civilians, who were ready to agree with me, and had not wished to fight us. There was one soldier, a smartly dressed officer in a blue turn-out, who obviously took no interest in politics but only enjoyed parading around in his uniform; he was ready to do what anyone told him. My defeat was caused by a civilian who came in later, a smallish mean-looking man with a sallow complexion and spectacles. He was a true Communist— narrow, fanatical, embittered; and he swayed over to his side many who before were in two minds. He made no attempt to argue but monopo- lized all attention by a stream of impassionate harangues, during which he banged on the table, glared feverishly about him, and uttered the usual fatuous clichés "death to the fascists," "freedom to the people," "liberty for the masses." He was so effective in turning everyone against me that I began to feel like a secret agent in a Hitchcock film who sud- denly realizes he is about to be found out. I lay back in my chair trying to appear cool but wondering if I was going to get out of the place alive. In the end, we concluded amiably enough, but they refused to hand over their arms, and so my efforts had failed.[29]

To many Athenians, the outbreak of hostilities was almost a relief from the atmosphere of gloom and tension that had gripped the capital for the last previous weeks. A great deal had taken place in Greece during the past three years, and feelings across the political spectrum had run very high. The Greeks had suffered occupation, famine, reprisals, and even a small genocide. These cataclysms had brutalized and desensitized Greek society—people became harder, almost pitiless, and too easily tolerant of killings and torture.

The infighting between EAM-ELAS on the one side and the right-wing resistance groups and paramilitaries on the other, assisted by the anticommunist Quisling formations, had spawned bitter hatred and even a degree of sadism. The early rhetoric of the resistance claiming liberation, popular rule, and appeals to patriotism had, over the course of the occupation, been dipped in blood, and the outrages committed by the left and right could not easily be forgotten or forgiven. These sentiments promised that the December Uprising would raise the threshold of cruelty in the upcoming battle.

The events that led to the second round of the civil war not only epitomized the mistrust and fear that permeated relations between the left-wing resistance and the Greek government-in-exile, but fundamentally reflected the collapse of civil society. The occupation had robbed Greece of the institutions that ameliorated political differences in place of vigilantism, leaving the raw power of the gun as the arbitrator to masquerade for legitimate authority.

In this environment, particularly in the countryside, what passed for justice seeped out of the politics of the occupation. Security was hostage to political affiliation, on the indulgence of one or another of the guerrilla bands, and at the mercy of the occupation forces. Neutrality was tantamount to collaboration. The anarchy of violence ruled the shambles of Greek society. There was little time in the six weeks following liberation to rebuild the political and economic infrastructure of the country and, more important, to start healing the trauma of hate and division inflicted by the occupation.

Amid the ruins of postwar Greece, people expected relief from hunger and a modicum of justice, especially punishment for the collaborators. When the provisional government failed to address these critical priorities, there were few avenues to challenge the decisions of the ramshackle state or to seek redress for past wrongs. The followers of the left-wing resistance and the KKE found recourse for their grievances in the street, and when that was denied to them, they resorted to violence as an alternative.

The government, for its part, daunted by almost insurmountable problems, could only rely on British troops to uphold its writ as a legitimate authority. In so doing, Papandreou contributed to the transformation of the British troops from liberators into an occupation army. Churchill's directive to General Scobie—"Do not however hesitate to act as if you were in a conquered city where a local rebellion is in progress"— underscored not only the preponderance of Britain's sway over Greek affairs, but also the helplessness and ultimately the irrelevance of the government.[30]

A contributing factor to the estrangement between the postliberation government and the rest of society was that the political regime that now represented the state had not shared the experience of occupation. Concurrently for three and a half years the puppet regimes, foisted by the Axis, had gutted the credibility of government. Although individual members of the government had lived in Greece during those dark days and later made their way to the Middle East, the government as an institution and the monarchy operated in exile and remained alienated from the Greek world. In addition, during the occupation, contact between the Greek government-in-exile and the resistance was sporadic at best and overshadowed by the British. The SOE maintained almost exclusive control over contact with the resistance groups, further marginalizing the official representatives of the Greek state.

For the most part, the resistance supplanted the role of the state. This was especially the case with the KKE-dominated EAM, which created a civil and military infrastructure wherever possible and assumed the traditional trappings of governmental institutions. In the mountain communities of central and northern Greece, away from the immediate reach of the Axis, the KKE, through EAM, had established a parastate that remained entrenched after liberation. As a result, in December 1944, Greece was shared by two societies: the small mountain villages that enjoyed a measure of freedom from the Axis, and the left-wing resistance underground groups in the larger cities. In contrast, large segments of urban dwellers, as well as parts of the Peloponnese, remained loyal to the notion of traditional authority and hostile to the KKE and its front organizations. These two faces of Greece effectively confronted each other over the next thirty-three days in December and early January and continued to remain segregated long after the end of the fighting.

Despite these cleavages and mistrust, the question remains—was the bloodletting of December inevitable? The spark that set off the chain of events that led to Sunday's demonstration and killings was the failure or inability of the Papandreou government to balance the problems of security and the strategic interests of the British against the suspicions of the left. The critical issue was control of the Greek army and police forces. The side that commanded the military and security apparatus would also dominate the state. The KKE and EAM had proposed that all the armed forces in Greece be demobilized and a new army be created by conscripting eligible men from the general population. In practical terms, this meant that the ELAS guerrillas, as well as any other resistance bands, would hand in their arms and return home. At the same time, the Greek government would order the Third Mountain Brigade and the Sacred Company to disband.

The Papandreou government, with the exception of the EAM and KKE ministers, was reluctant to lose the only two loyal military formations at its disposal. The British, for their part, were not prepared to surrender to the KKE and EAM any military or political advantage. Churchill and the British Foreign Office were suspicious of all resistance organizations in Greece and viewed these as radical and revolutionary groups that would undermine the traditional establishment of the country as well as threaten British interests in the region. For Churchill, only the return of the Greek monarchy would guarantee stability and restore legitimacy.

Although this claim is not substantiated by any official documentation, some historians and other postwar accounts of these events state that Papandreou at one point agreed to disband the Third Mountain Brigade and Sacred Company, but that he was prevented from doing so by the British.[31] There is no doubt that Churchill was opposed to this and had written to the Foreign Office that "the disbandment of the Greek Brigade would be a disaster of the first order."[32] The Foreign Office, in turn, had transmitted Churchill's view to Leeper, the British ambassador in Athens, who passed it on to the Greek premier. According to several accounts, Papandreou was inclined to accept the demobilization of all volunteer units but was able to convince neither the British nor the right-wing elements in or out of the government.[33]

On 28 November, the three EAM ministers (Zevgos, Svolos and Tsirimokos) in the Government of National Unity, at the suggestion of Papandreou, proposed another compromise in which the new army would consist of one brigade of ELAS and another of equal strength to be recruited from the Third Brigade, the Sacred Company, and EDES—and all other Greek forces would be disbanded by 10 December. The cabinet accepted the compromise, but twenty-four hours later, on 29 November, Zevgos, one of the KKE ministers, returned to Papandreou's office, accused him of bad faith, and withdrew the offer, demanding once again that all forces be disbanded, including the Third Brigade and Sacred Company. What caused this about-face is not clear. The explanation provided by the KKE and EAM is that they withdrew their consent because Papandreou was planning to trick them, by excluding the Third Mountain Brigade and Sacred Company from the total strength of the proposed new brigades. Papandreou rejected the KKE's demands outright.[34]

Another explanation for the December Uprising is that it was a show of strength organized by George Siantos, the acting general secretary of the KKE. Siantos gambled that the small number of British forces in Greece, as well as the Greek Mountain Brigade and the Sacred Company, would not have been sufficient to prevent ELAS from easily gaining control of Athens, which effectively meant securing all of Greece. If that was the case, it is not clear why the KKE leadership decided to handicap its effort by committing only the reserve elements of ELAS in Athens, while the most experienced and best-equipped units were kept away from the capital during the first critical weeks of the fighting. All accounts agree that the December Uprising was triggered by the clash between the demonstrators and the police on that fateful Sunday, but reasons for the recourse to a full-scale war, rather than just acts of retaliation by the left, are more complicated. The situation is all the more remarkable because the communists had accepted a compromise that had enabled the British to send forces into Greece after the German withdrawal, as well as the decision of the KKE and EAM to participate in a Government of National Unity led by George Papandreou.

On 26 September 1944, in Caserta, Italy, the Greek Government of National Unity, along with all the resistance organizations, had concluded an agreement to facilitate the transition from occupation to liberation. This agreement included the provision that all guerrilla bands and allied forces in Greece would be placed under General Scobie's command for the duration of the war or until a new Greek army was established. With the stroke of a pen, the KKE and the other left-wing organizations had surrendered their military advantage in Greece and handed over control of the country to their opponents.

In the summer of 1944, the KKE-dominated ELAS numbered over 50,000 well-armed men and women and could have easily opposed the landing of British troops in Greece. Under these circumstances, the British would have been obliged either to fight ELAS after the Germans withdrew, creating a public relations nightmare for Churchill as well as for the allies, or to accept the inevitable and leave the KKE in control of the country.[35] Both options presented serious difficulties, but ultimately the KKE, thanks to Soviet intervention, went along with the Caserta Agreement.

The Soviet contribution to the difficult negotiations between the British and the Greek Government of National Unity with the KKE and the left-wing resistance took place in the Middle East and culminated, according to some sources, with the sudden arrival of a Russian military mission, headed by Colonel Grigori Popov, to occupied Greece on the night of 25 July 1944.[36] For several months, following the winter of 1944, the Soviets and the British were working toward developing some type of compromise over their mutual interests in the Balkans, pending the German pullout from the region. The only drawback to a potential Soviet–British understanding was whether the United States would accept the division of the region into spheres of influence.

During the negotiations, the Soviet embassy in Cairo was gingerly trying to send a message to the KKE that the Russians preferred an amicable resolution of the Greek situation. In July 1944, Nikolai Novikov, the Soviet ambassador in Cairo, recommended to Svolos, the head of PEEA (Political Committee of National Liberation), that EAM should join the Greek Government of National Unity. The Soviet attaché conveyed the same message to the KKE representative in Cairo, Petros Rousos, who was told to make sure that the ambassador's view was transmitted to the left-wing resistance in Greece.

Peter Stavrakis concludes that once the Soviets received direct confirmation of American willingness to accept a British-Soviet agreement over the Balkans, it became essential for Stalin to make sure that the KKE did not disrupt the delicate horse-trading between the Allies. Stavrakis suggests: "A plausible hypothesis is that Stalin felt compliance would be guaranteed only by the dispatch of a military mission to the partisan strongholds in the mountains of Greece, to present the KKE with direct instructions to adopt a more conciliatory policy."[37]

At the very least, the Popov mission to the KKE and ELAS underscored the Russian ambivalence toward the Greek communists, while its presence in Greece alarmed and surprised the British. Previously, in a gesture of Allied solidarity, the British had invited the Soviets to join the Allied Military Mission against the Greek resistance, but the Russians declined. Despite earlier indications that the Soviets were prepared to reach an accommodation over the Greek issue, the arrival of the Popov mission came unexpectedly, catching the British unprepared. The Soviets had flown from Yugoslavia to an Anglo-American base in Bari, Italy, and then asked permission from the British authorities to make a test flight over the Adriatic. Instead, once in the air, the Russian plane proceeded to Greece and landed on a makeshift airfield in Neraida, western Thessaly, near the location of the ELAS GHQ and headquarters of the KKE. The Greek communists were jubilant, but after the initial celebrations and talks with Popov they quickly became downcast.

There are several accounts of the Soviet mission, one provided by Nicholas Hammond, the British liaison officer with ELAS, and the other by the Greek communists who were present in Neraida and Petrilia or participated in the subsequent meetings. According to Hammond, the Soviets were cordial, but refused to be drawn into a discussion over the purpose of their mission or on any political subject, and the same restrictions applied to Hammond and West, his American counterpart. Both parties were limited to exchanging pleasantries. On the second day of their arrival, Hammond organized a lunch in honor of the Russian visitors and afterward Popov reciprocated with an invitation to tea. "The tea," recollects Hammond,

> consisted of a saucer of tomato slices, a bottle of whiskey from Italy, a flask of vodka, another brandy from Russia, and the reserve, a demi-john of ouzo. Popov explained to me that it was the Russian practice to drink their tea "bottoms up," at one gulp. We sat down and he poured out a small tumbler of whiskey for me first, as I had been longest in the Greek mountains. Then he toasted, "long live Churchill!" We duly gulped it down. As I emerged from the shock, I heard "long live Roosevelt!," reached out to find my tumbler of Vodka, and gulped that down. From very far off I heard the cry, "long live Stalin!," groped blindly for my tumbler, and downed it like the others. I awoke in the grey light of dawn in a strange room. I went next door and there in the room of the tea party lay the three Russians flat on the floor, fully dressed with their boots on. In another room I discovered West who was lying fully clad on a bed with his boots off and his socks on. I had some difficulty in rousing him. He opened his eye, remarked, "Say boy, we said nothing," and he went to sleep again.[38]

It is evident that the attempt by the Russians, and undoubtedly Hammond and West, to use alcohol to pry information resulted in a draw. What transpired, however, between the Soviets and the KKE remains controversial and no first-hand account so far has been produced. If Popov's mission was to assess the fighting capability of ELAS and the extent of the KKE's sway over Greece, it is apparent from the few comments he did make to the British officers that he did not develop a high opinion of the capability of the left-wing resistance. C. M. Woodhouse, the head of the British Military Mission in Greece, writes that "ELAS, who had expected the Soviet Mission to bring mana from heaven, found Colonel Popov unable to supply his own party with vodka, let alone ELAS with gold, arms and ammunition. On the other hand, the Soviet Mission, which expected to find an army of at least the same kind, if not in magnitude, as Tito's partisans, found a rabble thinly veiled by an elaborate centralized command."[39]

The unwillingness or inability of the Soviets to replace the British as the arsenal of the left-wing resistance was a severe blow to the Greek communists. The KKE, through its newspaper, *Rizospastis,* had been exalting the success of the Red Army against the Germans and anticipating that it was only a matter of time until the Russians would liberate the Balkans and Greece. No doubt, for many of the KKE leadership, the arrival of the Soviet mission was a prelude to a Soviet advance in Greece, but Popov's cool reaction to their enthusiasm dashed any hopes of Soviet liberation.

Most of the KKE accounts, it should be noted, vary over the sequence of events and play down the influence of the Soviets. There are differences over the dates of the Popov mission and whether this visit influenced the KKE's decision to join the Government of National Unity and later accept the Caserta Agreement. Yiannis Ioannidis, a key member of the Politburo and second in command of the KKE, in a long interview, states that when he broached the subject of ELAS fighting the British with the political representative of the Soviet mission, Colonel Tschernichev, the Russian made a "face," making it clear that the Soviets would not endorse such a move.[40] Petros Rousos summarized the discussions with Popov more directly: "What we extracted from exchanging opinions with the Soviets—and from the subsequent course of events—was that, the Greek issue, because of Churchill's position, was a thorn in the alliance against Hitler and that, according to all indications, from a strategic point of perspective we would have a serious problem confronting the imperialism of the British (and American) 'allies.' "[41]

Indeed, all of the published accounts of the Greek communists who wrote about the Popov mission agree that the Russian delegation discouraged any notions of the KKE using ELAS to take over the country. Vasos Georgiou, the editor of *Rizospastis,* and a principal assistant to George Siantos, provided a more recent testimony of these events and, in a roundabout way, conveys the elation and eventual disappointment generated by the arrival of the Soviets.

> We waited for them [the Soviets] with great anticipation and we welcomed them very warmly in the early afternoon, as the real liberators. . . . We were all strong pro-Soviets because we understood the decisive contribution of the Soviet Union in the struggle to destroy Hitlerism and we linked our liberation to the advancement of the Red Army in the Balkans. However, the leadership of the resistance, even though it took care to hide this [the nature of the Soviet mission] did not calculate well. Because it became apparent very quickly that the

Soviet mission was not sent to PEEA—with which it would naturally have relations—but accredited to the General Headquarters of ELAS and that it was not independent [mission] but represented an echelon of the greater Soviet Military Mission of the Red Army to Tito's Popular Liberation Army.[42]

Georgiou, as is the case with some of the KKE published accounts, simply cannot bring himself to say that the Soviets made it known that the KKE had to cooperate with the British and the Greek government-in-exile. Instead, he writes that the Soviets were there in a narrow military capacity and, as such, the mission was only accredited to ELAS and not PEEA or any other political organization. The fact that the Popov mission did not propose a political role indicated how noncommittal the Soviet government was toward the Greek resistance, whereas in the case of Yugoslavia the Soviets backed Tito completely. What is certain, however, is that immediately following the arrival of the Soviets, the KKE and EAM suddenly decided to join the Government of National Unity and place ELAS under British command.

Until Soviet documents are released, the exact purpose of the Popov mission remains a partial mystery and an analysis of its impact must be based, to some extent, on speculation.[43] Either Stalin had decided to abandon any hope of including Greece within the Soviet system and sent Popov to discourage the KKE from any adventures that may have led to a clash with the British or, conversely, the Russian officer's report persuaded the Soviet dictator that the Greek communists were not in a position to take over and keep control of Greece after the Germans departed. Unknown to both the KKE and the British liaison officers in Greece were the negotiations between Stalin and Churchill over the division of the Balkans into Soviet and British spheres of influence.

These discussions between Churchill and Stalin culminated with the so-called Percentages Agreement between Britain and the Soviet Union, concluded in Moscow on 9 October 1944. The minutes of the meeting between the two leaders indicate that after dealing with the problem of Poland, Churchill turned to Stalin.

There were two countries in which the British had particular interest. One was Greece. He was not worrying about Rumania. That was very much a Russian affair and the terms, which the Soviet Government had proposed were reasonable and showed much statecraft in the interests of general peace in the future. But in Greece it was different.

Britain must be the leading Mediterranean Power and he hoped Marshal Stalin would let him have the first say about Greece in the same way as Marshal Stalin about Rumania. Of course, the British Government would keep in touch with the Soviet Government.[44]

According to the minutes, Stalin acknowledged Churchill's position with regard to Greece and said that it was a "serious matter for Britain, when the Mediterranean route was not in her hands." He agreed with the prime minister that "Britain should have the first say in Greece."[45] Following this amicable exchange, Churchill writes: "The moment was apt for business, so I said, 'let us settle about our affairs in the Balkans. Your armies are in Rumania and Bulgaria. We have interests, missions, and agents there. Don't let us get at cross-purposes in small ways. So far as Britain and Russia are concerned, how would it do for you to have ninety per cent predominance in Rumania, for us to have ninety per cent say in Greece, and go fifty-fifty about Yugoslavia?' "[46]

While this was being translated, Churchill produced what he called a "naughty document" showing a list of Balkan countries and the proportion of interest in them of the Great Powers.[47] Churchill then pushed this paper across the table to Stalin, who had by then heard the translation. After a brief pause, recalls Churchill, "he took his blue pencil and made a large tick upon it, and passed it back to us. After this there was a long silence. The penciled paper lay in the center of the table. At length I said, 'Might it not be thought rather cynical if it seemed we had disposed of these issues, so fateful to millions of people in such an offhand manner? Let us burn the paper.' 'No you keep it,' said Stalin."[48] The hopes, ambitions, sacrifices, and pain inflicted by the Greek communists on their compatriots were consigned to a scrap of paper in which the British prime minister had sealed the fate of the Balkans until almost the end of the twentieth century.

The fortunes of the Greek communists and the left-wing resistance with respect to the immediate postwar period, insofar as Stalin was concerned, took second place to the security and grand strategy of the Soviet Union. Beyond that, anything was possible after the Allied victory over Nazi Germany and imperial Japan. In early September 1949, Stalin confided to Zachariadis that he could not advance the Red Army into Greece in 1944 because he did not wish to clash with the British; besides, the Soviet Union did not have a navy for such an undertaking. It is not known, and unlikely, as to whether Stalin also told Zachariadis about the Percentages Agreement.[49]

FIG. 4. Winston Churchill was instrumental in keeping Greece within the British sphere of influence immediately after World War II with the conclusion of the Percentages Agreement with Joseph Stalin. Library of Congress.

Churchill had informed Roosevelt that the arrangements with Stalin did not amount to a permanent division of the Balkans into spheres of influence but were intended as a temporary war measure to facilitate the Russian and British presence in the region. Churchill had no illusions that he and Stalin had now determined the future for the region. At their historic meeting in Moscow, both men were anxious to avoid the appearance of dividing the spoils of war. Churchill suggested to Stalin that "it was better to express these things in diplomatic terms and not to use the phrase 'dividing into spheres,' because the Americans might be shocked. Nevertheless, as long as he and Marshal Stalin understood each other he could explain matters to the President."[50] This caution did not diminish Churchill's imperial moment, especially as Britain by 1944 was quickly becoming a junior partner in the Grand Alliance, nor Stalin's pragmatism in reaching an accommodation with an empire that was soon to be eclipsed by the United States.

The KKE learned about the Percentages Agreement in 1952, which raises the intriguing question that had they known earlier, would they have acted differently in December 1944? As devout communists and Stalinists, the KKE leadership had to conform its policies to those of the Soviet Union and accept them without knowing all the facts. The needs of the Soviet motherland superseded the immediate ambitions of the Greek communists, and the KKE had little choice but to toe the line blindly, even when the leadership could not even be certain what that line was.

Under the leadership of Nikos Zachariadis, the policies of the KKE were practically dictated by the Soviet Union via the Third Communist International. Zachariadis had been Moscow's choice to head the KKE in the 1930s and he managed to oversee the bolshevization of the party during this critical period. After he became general secretary of the central committee in 1934, he succeeded in terminating the internal divisions that had plagued the KKE almost from its inception. As a result, the senior leadership of the Communist Party identified exclusively with Moscow and any deviation resulted in purges.

The occupation, however, altered the dynamic of the KKE and shifted the direction of the party to other men. Zachariadis remained in prison and was subsequently transferred to Dachau concentration camp, and thus took no part in the events that followed. George Siantos, one of the senior cadres who had evaded capture, took over the direction of the KKE and thanks to his leadership, the communists established the mass-based EAM, which quickly dominated the resistance.

A tobacco worker by profession, Siantos, unlike Zachariadis, was a mainland Greek from a small village in Thessaly, in central Greece. To those who met him, he appeared less a fanatic communist leading a revolution than a kindly village elder. A self-made man with little formal education beyond grade four, he started working at the age of thirteen as a tobacco worker in Karditsa and at fifteen joined the Tobacco Workers' Union. Within a short time, he became an active member and took part in strikes, demonstrations, and riots. From 1911 to 1920, Siantos served in the Greek army and rose to the rank of sergeant. In the early 1920s, he joined the KKE and during this ideologically turbulent period he was a key player in the factionalism and infighting that plagued the party.

He survived the purges, but he was demoted in the party hierarchy and lost the post of general secretary. In 1934, he was downgraded to a substitute member of the politburo, but a year later he was reinstated as a full member. After 1936, he was one of the few KKE leaders to escape arrest and thus, by default, became part of the handful of senior KKE leaders in a position to rebuild the party during the early period of the occupation. Friends and enemies alike described him as a mild-mannered and soft-spoken individual. He was a dedicated workaholic, with simple tastes and few pleasures, who took comfort in chain-smoking an endless supply of cigarettes over strong cups of coffee.[51] C. M. Woodhouse, who spent three years in Greece trying to counter the influence of the KKE in the resistance, describes him: "Ruthless and ambitious though he was, Siantos had a simple bonhomie and good humour. He was a tobacco worker, like many other communists, but he seemed to have no bitterness about his hard life."[52]

To the party faithful he was known as "O Geros," the old man. According to Vasos Georgiou, who served for a time as Siantos' aide at KKE headquarters in the remote mountains, Siantos was monkish in his habits and endowed with almost limitless patience. In contrast to some of the other, more sophisticated KKE leaders, most of whom had grown up in cities and large towns, he had a better understanding of the Greek villager and an appreciation of the power of nationalist sentiment in Greece. Siantos understood that in order for the party to exploit the opportunities created by the war, it was necessary to drop the narrow and dogmatic communist rhetoric and replace it with moderate and nationalist slogans that appealed to mainstream society. The establishment of EAM as a patriotic and pan-Hellenic organization gave the KKE legitimacy and placed it on par with the mainstream political parties. Despite EAM's invitation for all to join a common front to fight the Axis, the traditional parties viewed EAM as a front for the KKE and had declined to participate—they failed, however, to offer an alternative. This omission enabled the KKE, through EAM, to establish a predominant and powerful influence over the armed resistance and to hijack the intellectual discourse during the occupation over the future political reorganization of Greece.

The KKE, under the direction of Siantos, saw the possibilities offered by the establishment of guerrilla forces—specifically, that they could be used to impose a political settlement in the aftermath of liberation. In October 1943, ELAS not only was fighting the Axis, but also was attempting to absorb all other partisan units in the field so that at the moment of liberation, the Allies (the British in particular) would be confronted by a unified resistance movement.

Later in the same year, Ioannidis had commissioned a military plan designed to take over Athens once the German army withdrew. Ioannidis afterward claimed that ELAS could have secured Athens and would have been in an advantageous position to oppose the arrival of the British. He had proposed this strategy to Siantos and the other KKE leaders, but at the time they were not interested.[53] Ioannidis' hindsight is obviously self-serving and a means of distancing himself from Siantos and from the KKE policies that ultimately led to failure and defeat. In the postmortems conducted by the KKE after the December Uprising, responsibility for the Caserta Agreement, participation in the Government of National Unity, the decision not to oppose the arrival of British troops, and the December Uprising itself were all consigned to Siantos and his closest associates. Sharing the grave with Siantos is the ghost idea that the KKE did not consider the possibility of taking over the country just after liberation. According to Ole Smith, "It is one of the KKE's cherished fairy tales that at the time of the country's liberation from the Germans there were no plans for a military takeover and that the party did not face squarely the question of political power."[54]

After Siantos' mysterious death in 1947, his opponents went so far as to accuse him not only of incompetence, but also of being an agent of the security services, which they argued explained why he went along with the Caserta Agreement and intentionally lost the Battle of Athens. In October 1950, at the Third Party Conference, he was denounced by Zachariadis as a "traitor and an agent of the class enemy." In the same year, Zachariadis wrote that the strategy of the KKE was "the strategy of Siantos, that is the strategy of capitulation to the English, the strategy which did not serve or speed up the victory of the peoples revolution in Greece, the strategy which delayed and finally shattered the revolution, the strategy which promoted the plans of the British, the restoration of the bourgeois-feudal power, the return to the regime of foreign dependence."[55]

Vassilis Bartziotas, at the same conference, added his own condemnation of Siantos, as well as invoking the theme of grave errors, betrayal, and treason: "On October 12, 1944 we could easily have seized power with the forces of the First Army Corps of ELAS alone (that is the 20,000 Elasites of Athens and Piraeus). We did not seize power because we did not have a correct line, because we all vacillated, including me. . . . Thus, although we had decided on armed insurrection, beginning in September 1944, instead of going ahead, instead of organizing the struggle for power, instead of seizing power, we capitulated and kept order."[56] These allegations, clearly, are far from the truth and are part and parcel of the ritual demonization of those purged from the KKE. Of course, there was more than one strategy contemplated by different members of the KKE leadership for achieving power.

The KKE, despite its reputation for organization and ideological cohesiveness, could not remain monolithic and survive as an organization during the occupation. The successful decentralization of the party also resulted in a certain degree of fragmentation at the top, which created several centers of decision-making. Siantos and Ioannidis informally shared the leadership of the KKE, but neither had the influence or the authority to impose his will on all aspects of policy. The two men represented different elements and strains within the party and by virtue of this duality attracted separate followings. Ioannidis is often described as the hard-liner and, along with Aris Velouchiotis, advocated a revolutionary approach in dealing with the period following liberation.

Siantos was equally committed to revolutionary means, but, as mentioned above, he was more sensitive to Greek nationalism and the peculiarities of the Greek peasant and worker. Most Greeks were small farmers, and those in the industrial sector were too few and too disorganized to be effectively mobilized. Peasants who had land or wanted land were not well disposed to the KKE's plans for collectivization. "In general," writes Woodhouse, "the devotion of the Greek people to their family and their Church made them poor material for ideological recruitment."[57] EAM had not only been a successful political organization, but a convenient mask for the KKE, which many Greeks continued to identify with the Soviet Union, atheism, and Slavism. A naked grab for power at the moment of liberation that resulted in a fight with the British would have made it difficult for the KKE to take over the country, particularly Athens.

Whether the Soviet intervention prevented this scheme will remain a contested issue among historians, but the military and political realities confronting the KKE and the British in the late summer and fall of 1944 perhaps played a decisive role in Siantos' plans. It does not seem likely that during the critical period (July–September 1944) Siantos was willing to hand over the country to the Greek government-in-exile just to accommodate the Soviets, nor was he prepared to fight the British on the beaches—at least not without external support. Once the Soviets declined to get involved in the politics of liberation and made that known to the KKE, an alternative strategy was necessary. What the precise aims of that strategy were accompanied Siantos to his grave. Unfortunately, the man who directed the KKE and the left-wing resistance during the December Uprising left no record of why he chose a showdown with the government and the British and, having done so, why he decided to confine it to Athens. Even after his strategy began to unravel and ELAS was hard-pressed to achieve control over all of Athens, Siantos refused to back away from his plan until it was too late.[58]

A decisive factor that, for better or for worse, contributed to the chain of events that led to the fighting was that the KKE-EAM still had to function under the challenging conditions created by the occupation, making travel and communications extremely difficult and dangerous. The politburo and the central committee met occasionally to consider new policies, but it was not always possible to adapt quickly to new situations. For example, in April 1944, the KKE sent delegates to a conference organized in Lebanon in order to replace the Greek government-in-exile with a Government of National Unity that would include representatives from all the resistance organizations. After torturous negotiations, the KKE-EAM representatives accepted the new government, based on Soviet advice, but when they returned to Greece the KKE leadership denounced their actions. Yet, a few months later, because of the Popov mission, the KKE agreed to join the Government of National Unity under the same conditions as in May.

In the postliberation period, the communists, as was the case with all other parties, had to overcome similar problems that resulted from the wretched condition of the country, which made it difficult to maintain party discipline over the KKE, EAM, and ELAS as well as all the other left-wing resistance organizations. This situation continued to play into Siantos' hands, because it left him and Ioannidis, along with a small group of trusted associates, in control of the party's tactics and strategy. Therefore, a great deal of what took place in December 1944 is partly the by-product of the fears, ambitions, and prejudices of this old-time communist.

In an ironic twist of fate during the late summer of 1944, both the British and Siantos were working to avoid a clash and to limit the number of Allied forces that would enter Greece. The British needed troops for the Italian front, and Siantos wanted to take advantage of the enemy's numerical weakness in a future attempt to take over the country. By early December, Siantos was in a position to exploit this exact scenario. The British had only approximately 20,000 troops, most of which were administrative and technical support units, concentrated in Athens, Thessaloniki, and in few other urban centers, which left the rest of the country under the control of ELAS. The KKE and EAM were enjoying tremendous popularity, while the Papandreou government was losing credibility, culminating in the botched handling of Sunday's demonstration.

It is clear that Siantos had decided that he would direct the forthcoming battle against only the forces of the provisional government and avoid striking at the British. There is every indication that Siantos believed that if ELAS were to seize control of Athens quickly, the British would have little choice except to recognize a new government dominated by the KKE. Consequently, to maintain this delicate balance and avoid provoking the British, the battle had to be confined to the capital and waged against government targets. The choice of tactics was also motivated by ideological as well as practical considerations.

Siantos was a committed Marxist who subscribed to the notion that the party could count on the proletariat alone. All his adult life he was steeped in the mantra of the workers' revolution and orthodox communist revolutionary tactics. Like most Greek communists, he did not have much faith in the Greek peasant, and since a large percentage of ELAS was recruited from the countryside, he may have had doubts about the commitment of the rank and file to a civil war. Siantos was also a pragmatist who understood that an all-out war was not necessary if the capital was quickly secured. Besides, lacking sufficient transport, the main ELAS units would have taken much longer to move on Athens, which would also have provoked the British.

Even at the beginning of the armed resistance against the Axis, Siantos was fond of saying, "He who ruled Athens ruled Greece"—a maxim understood by the leaders of every coup before and after the December Uprising. Siantos also added that "the Athenian workers would be organized into military formations so that at the moment of liberation they could seize the city."[59] Soviet intervention, however, had stayed that strategy. The KKE had to change its plans and develop a political approach to power, at least for the time being. A critical element in the KKE's ability to shape events, and vital to its future as a power broker in the Greek political scene, was ELAS. The guerrilla army enabled the KKE to control most of the countryside, and almost all the towns and villages, while the reserve units in Athens, neither as well trained nor as well equipped as the regular ELAS force, gave the communists a direct means to challenge the government and its British allies. As long as the KKE could fall back on ELAS, it could continue to negotiate from a position of strength.

During the crucial weeks before the uprising, the monarchy, which represented the most incendiary issue, was, at least for the immediate future, held in abeyance. George II had agreed to stay out of Greece until the future of the monarchy was decided by plebiscite. The other demands by the left, such as the punishment of the Security Battalions and of all collaborators, were more or less compatible with the government's policies. The KKE and EAM had respected the Caserta Agreement and kept ELAS formations outside of Athens. The KKE went so far as to call on its members to join the new National

Guard. In a cable to party organizations on 22 November, Siantos instructed that all KKE members "of the 1936 class must be the first to join the temporary National Guard . . . communists and Eamites must organize themselves securely with the National Guard."[60]

At the same time, Siantos told the potential volunteers that before enlisting they had to visit the nearest party headquarters and receive orders on the course of action to be adopted once they were in the National Guard.[61] Clearly, Siantos had settled on a policy of infiltration rather than military confrontation on the road to achieving power. Similarly, KKE ministers in the provisional government were attempting to place loyal communists in key positions. Miltiadis Porphyrogenis used his portfolio as minister of labor to consolidate KKE's base in the trade unions by setting up a provisional committee of the General Confederation of Greek Workers as a vote generator for the elections that were to take place on 1 December. Since the provisional committee was staffed entirely by members of EAM, which, in turn, was

FIG. 5. Building damaged with bullet holes in the December Uprising, 1944.
WikiCommons.

controlled by the KKE, the communists would be able to instigate a general strike at a time of their choosing.[62]

There is no agreement among historians or even the participants of these events as to when or what precisely forced the situation in Athens past the point of no return, but when Papandreou refused to resign over the bloodshed of 3 December, the KKE lost any immediate advantage it would have gained from the establishment of a new government. Regardless of the failure to bring about a change in regime at that time, the KKE leadership, particularly Siantos, chose force as a means of achieving the same end—the collapse of the government—while keeping the British from taking sides in a Greek civil war. Siantos, therefore, had to keep control of events and decided to resurrect the ELAS central committee, rather than operate through EAM or the KKE, in order to limit the battle against Greek government targets and to not attack the British. At the same time, he took appropriate measures to ensure that the ELAS committee would bow to his will by ensuring that the only other two members present (except himself) were Michaelis Hadjimichaelis and Mandakas. He was determined that no one would question his authority or any decisions he made and explained to Ioannidis that Hadjimichaelis had no opinions and that Mandakas did what he was told.[63]

Consequently, the general headquarters of ELAS, along with most of the experienced officers and battle-hardened troops, remained in Lamia in central Greece. When the battle commenced in Athens, the ELAS headquarters was ordered to launch an attack against the forces of Zervas in Epirus (this was the only ELAS action outside of Athens), thus diverting three well-equipped divisions that could have tipped the scales in Athens. Other ELAS units were sent to destroy the guerrilla bands of Anton Tsaous, the leader of an independent right-wing group operating in the Drama district in northern Greece. After fighting had broken out in Athens, Stephanos Saraphis, the military commander of ELAS, asked permission from Siantos to attack all British units throughout Greece, which would have been a relatively easy task, but his request was rejected outright. A little later, Saraphis pressed Siantos to allow him at least to disarm the British garrisons outside of Athens, but instead the ELAS central committee instructed him to notify the British garrisons that all movement on their part was forbidden. Before any action was taken on the part of ELAS, however, the British were able to withdraw their smaller garrisons into Athens and Thessaloniki.

Siantos' strategy was to confine the fighting to the capital and deploy the reserve ELAS units in Athens. Although he was subsequently severely criticized by the KKE for not committing the main body of ELAS forces, had he done so it would have undoubtedly brought immediate British intervention. Siantos, of course, did not know that Churchill had ordered General Scobie to intervene in Athens and that no matter how carefully the KKE leader planned to conduct the battle, it is unlikely that the outcome would have been any different.

In other words, Siantos planned not so much for an all-out military assault, but rather a series of rapid small engagements sufficient to eliminate all vestiges of the government but not enough to provoke the British. ELAS was already in control of most of Greece and once the capital was in the hands of the KKE, the British would be confronted with a new political reality that would oblige them to accept a government dominated by the KKE. If not, then the onus would have been on the British to fight a new communist-dominated regime but one that represented the Greek state, and appear as the aggressor. Despite the thinnest veneer of sovereignty, Greece in December 1944 was a British protectorate. Yet, for the sake of the grand alliance and to pay lip service to the principles of the newly founded United Nations, Churchill's government had to at least pretend to act the part of an interested bystander. Under such circumstances, it would have been very difficult for the British to fight against a Greek regime, even one under communist control. All the more reason for the British to defend the capital as allies of even a rump Greek government.

The issue came down to the force of arms imposing legitimacy. The occupation had swept away the old political establishment, brought new leaders to the forefront, and gutted the prewar institutions. King George II and his government had spent the occupation years in London and Egypt and had been sidelined to irrelevance. As far as most people in Greece were concerned, the monarchy and the government-in-exile were creatures of the British and part of the discredited Metaxas dictatorship. They had few followers in Greece and even fewer in the resistance movement. Indeed, the Greek body politic had been in a revolutionary state since Ioannis Metaxas had, with the connivance of the king, usurped power in August 1936. The constitutional status of the Metaxas regime and the monarchy was not resolved when Greece fell under the control of the Axis. In fact, the constitutional situation was further complicated by the Quisling regimes, especially that of Rallis, whose Security Battalions were never denounced by the king or the government-in-exile. In the wake of the December Uprising, occupation collaborators found rehabilitation, and resistance fighters, other than those on the right, were labeled traitors. The December crisis and the defeat of the left invalidated the legitimacy afforded to EAM-ELAS by the allies and the Greek government-in-exile.

During the war, EAM and ELAS had been recognized and supported as allied forces by the British, the Americans, and the Soviets. This recognition not only provided the left-wing resistance with moral and material support, but also created a legal framework for EAM to function as a valid political entity. Under the constitutional morass of the time, EAM could claim as much lawful relevance as the Greek government-in-exile. In the fall of 1944, the British cobbled together a Greek Government of National Unity, which included ministers from EAM and the KKE as well as from all the other major resistance organizations. This arrangement provided political as well as military recognition to EAM, giving it parity with the traditional ruling establishment.

In October, this broad coalition arrived in liberated Greece as a provisional government and attempted to run the country until circumstances permitted a general election. When the EAM and KKE ministers resigned on 1 December, the authority of the Papandreou government was invalidated and should have been replaced by a new provisional regime. How this was to be accomplished—whether by violent or peaceful means—as far as the left was concerned was a matter for the Greek people. The left had helped form the first postwar government and, by the same token, could now demand to have it replaced. Once such a new government was in place, how could the British intervene and escape the ire of world opinion in addition to that of their allies? Fundamentally, this was the rationale of the left and Siantos' strategy.

For a few hours on 4 December, Papandreou's resignation confirmed the reasoning of the KKE and EAM, but the Greek premier, after considerable pressure from the British, changed his mind. Technically, if not morally, the government could remain in power as long as King George II was prepared to acquiesce. As head of state, the king, in the absence of a general election, could lawfully extend the mandate of the provisional government despite the resignation of the EAM and KKE ministers. Suddenly, the issue of the discredited monarchy emerged, and until a plebiscite decided to the contrary, George II remained as the constitutional arbiter of the Greek state.

This legal sleight of hand, however, was lost on EAM and its multitude of followers and made little impression on world opinion. Matters were made worse for the British as well as the Papandreou government by the fact that just about all the foreign correspondents in Athens were living at the Grande

Bretagne Hotel located at the corner of Constitution Square and across from the central police station. When the crisis broke out on Sunday, the correspondents were afforded a spectacular view of the ensuing pandemonium.

The first account of the crisis was reported in *The Times* of London on 4 December; it was dramatic, inaccurate, and gave the impression that the demonstrators included mostly children who were mercilessly gunned down by the police. According to *The Times'* special correspondent in Athens:

> Seeds of civil war were well and truly sown by the Athens police this morning when they fired on a demonstration of children and youths. . . . About 10 o'clock crowds began to gather. One section of the demonstrators, mostly girls and boys, with a sprinkling of adults, started to leave the square, presumably en route for the Ministry of Foreign Affairs, where the Prime Minister has his office. Just as the procession was halfway across University Street . . . the police opened fire with rifles and tommy guns. The crowd immediately fell flat to escape the bullets, but the police continued firing. When they stopped, the demonstrators got to their feet and started to pick up the wounded and dead and the police then fired again.[64]

Despite the inaccuracies, the early newspaper articles set the tone for most of the reporting for the duration of the uprising. The American and British press, in particular, gave considerable credence to the grievances of the left and remained critical of Churchill and Papandreou's handling of the crisis.

On 6 December *The Times* apportioned part of the blame for Sunday's killings to the left by stating: "The action of the EAM and communist Ministers imperceptibly withdrawing from the Government on an issue which seemed to have been already amicably settled must be held partly responsible for the present crisis." The influential conservative paper still placed most of the responsibility on the Greek prime minister: "It was a misfortune that M. Papandreou should have failed to use the opportunity of his broadcast on Sunday night to disassociate himself from the senseless and unnecessary display of force by the Athens police." In the same article, *The Times* also cautioned against British intervention in Greece and underlined the right of the resistance to participate in governing the country. "In Greece, as in all other liberated countries, the allied military authorities have a direct and overriding interest in the preservation of order while military operations are in progress. . . . This interest, however, must not be allowed to imply any participation in the politics of Greece." The article went on to say that the resistance organizations had "won the confidence of and loyalty of the people in a measure not easily emulated by patriots who have not shared the experience of enemy rule."

The next day, 7 December 1944, the negative press reports continued, and even before British troops were fully committed in the battle *The Times* editorial commented: "The disagreeable truth revealed by the news of the past three days from Athens is that British armed forces, originally invoked in the desire to avoid bloodshed, have become involved in a Greek civil war." The same editorial warned the British government against getting involved in Greek affairs as well as echoing the sentiments of the Greek left:

> If M. Papandreou is now maintained in power by the ban of a foreign government on any alternative, his moral authority in Greece can hardly survive; and British lives sacrificed, fighting against Greeks on behalf of a Greek Government, which exists only in virtue of military force. Neither Greece nor Britain can afford such an issue of this tragic struggle. Grievous errors, some recent, some of longer date, have been committed. For the Greek parties the imperative task is to re-establish a Government fairly representative of both wings under a head acceptable to both, and thus bring about a situation in which desperately needed measures of relief and reconstruction can be undertaken. For the British Government the paramount duty, and the only one consonant with British tradition and British interest, is to seek to bring about such a reunion, and at all costs to avoid taking sides in a Greek conflict. For the British Army the only conceivable role, in the face of every difficulty and every provocation, is one of strict neutrality and favour to none.[65]

Drew Pearson, the influential *Washington Post* journalist with close links to the State Department and the White House, in his weekly column lashed out at Churchill's policy, accusing the British of being in league with Nazi collaborators. He claimed that they wanted to secure postwar economic advantages in the region and planned to force the Greeks to cede the island of Crete.[66] The British suspected that the American Office of Strategic Services (OSS), which was often critical of how the British dealt with the Greek left, inspired Pearson's article.

For almost the duration of the December Uprising, the left continued to enjoy the support of the British and American media, which undermined Churchill and Papandreou, but sustained the morale of the ELAS troops and the supporters of EAM and the KKE. Inadvertently and indirectly, the positive press coverage encouraged the KKE and EAM to stick to their demands and remain intransigent over a peaceful resolution of the crisis.

Initially, and for the wrong reasons, the slow reaction of the British forces seemed to prove Siantos right. During those crucial few days Scobie's units, except for the rescue of Greek police officers, remained on the defensive. From the perspective of the KKE leadership, and certainly from that of Siantos, it was evident that the British were reluctant to get involved in a Greek imbroglio.

General Ronald Scobie, the British commander of all Greek forces, was the wrong man in the wrong place and at the wrong time. Scobie had limited battlefield experience, and was ill equipped to participate in the intricate and convoluted labyrinth of Greek politics in the aftermath of liberation. He failed to understand or appreciate the impact on the Greek psyche of the resistance, whose popularity and increasing mythology was in inverse proportion to the rapid decline of the popularity of the government. Papandreou and his ministers had to confront the economic and food crises as well as a burgeoning black market, while the resistance basked in the glory of its heroic accomplishments during the occupation. Naturally it could not be held responsible for the current difficulties—that was the responsibility of the government and its British allies.

Mass unemployment, coupled with a black market that sucked up most relief supplies, and hunger devoured the initial enthusiasm and good will generated by liberation. Under these circumstances, the glory of resistance remained the only staple in an otherwise bleak environment. Scobie, however, chose to ignore the resistance and perfunctorily dismiss its leaders. Scobie was the quintessential British officer and had had little exposure to guerrilla warfare and the politics of resistance. The British general believed that, regardless of the contribution of the guerrilla fighters, liberation came to Greece because of the victories of regular forces over the German army. To conventional officers like Scobie, the achievements of the partisans and covert operations were merely an adjunct to the real war fought by the Allied armies in the field. Now that the resistance groups had completed their allotted task, it was time for them to go back to their homes and resume their civilian lives.

The relegation of guerrilla warfare as less than secondary in importance to the war effort, and the failure to appreciate the impact of the resistance, was prevalent among most British officers who had taken over Greek affairs from the men of the SOE. This was evident from almost the day of liberation up to and including the outbreak of hostilities in December. In the early days of jubilation that followed the withdrawal of the German army from Athens, Scobie's staff made preparations for a victory parade. Chris Woodhouse, the head of the Allied Military Mission in the Greek mountains and one of the few SOE officers left in Athens after liberation, was offered a seat in one of the automobiles that would take part in the victory celebrations. When Woodhouse inquired as to "where the guerrilla leaders were to be placed," Scobie's adjutant remarked, "The guerrilla leaders . . . what has it got to do with them?"[67] The rapid removal of most SOE personnel from the country took away the few people who had a thorough knowledge and understanding of the delicate political situation in Greece. Had they remained, however, the conventional British officers who arrived in Greece were not inclined to listen to them. Woodhouse discovered that "incoming officers had been advised to disregard us, because we had been too long in Greece and our judgment had become untrustworthy."[68]

Disdain for the military capabilities of guerrilla forces in general, and those of the Greek left in particular, created a false sense of security along with the overconfidence that an irregular force was no match for the British army. According to William McNeill, who in 1944 was stationed at the American embassy in Athens when fighting broke out in early December:

> British military circles seriously underestimated the resistance they had to deal with. Armoured cars and tanks were able to move freely through-out the streets, and no systematic resistance was made to British troops. Most Britishers thought that the leftists would yield after a few days, when they had seen British strength and determination.[69]

From early November, Scobie began receiving warnings from Churchill and General Maitland Wilson, the commander-in-chief in the Middle East, that a confrontation with EAM-ELAS was probable. On 8 November, Churchill had telegraphed General Wilson and the ambassador, Rex Leeper, requesting urgent reinforcements to be sent to Greece and instructed Leeper that "British troops should certainly be used to support law and order, even by shooting if necessary."[70] On 15 November, General Wilson instructed Scobie "to hold all troops already in Greece [and] to concentrate on Athens whose neighbour-hoods would be declared a military area" and to order ELAS to withdraw from the capital. Furthermore, Scobie was to disarm or if necessary imprison any ELAS forces that refused to leave Athens. In the event of attack, Scobie had orders to "use British and Greek forces to crush any opposition.[71] In addition to the warnings and in response to the escalating agitation by EAM and the KKE, Middle East Command increased British forces in Greece to 22,600 along with five squadrons of aircraft by the end of October.[72] Increasing the number of British troops further contributed to the climate of suspicion, recriminations, and mutual hostility that had infected relations between the left and the government. Matters almost reached the breaking point with the arrival in Athens of the Third Mountain Brigade and the Sacred Company on 9 November, and relations collapsed after the violence on Sunday, 3 December.

Remarkably, and despite the deterioration of the political situation, Scobie was ill prepared for a confrontation with ELAS. Throughout October and mid November, British forces were concentrated in Athens, Thessaloniki, Patras, and a few other cities. Little effort was made to maintain secure communications with Piraeus and the airfield outside Athens. To make matters worse, a great many of Scobie's troops were spread thin in the capital guarding government buildings and important installations. The rest of the country (with the exception of Epirus, the Drama district, a few islands, and the region around Athens) was under the control of ELAS. Because of this deployment, the British, even before the outbreak of hostilities, were virtually besieged.

ELAS, meanwhile, enjoyed the strategic advantage of controlling most of mainland Greece along with having active supporters in almost every corner of the country. By the end of November, the ELAS order of battle was based on approximately 49,000 men and women in eleven divisions, a regiment of cavalry, and a makeshift navy. ELAS also maintained a reserve of 45,000, of which 22,000–23,000 were based in Athens. In late November, the Athens reserve was designated as the 1st ELAS Army Corps. Most of the rank and file of these reserve forces was of uneven quality, of limited fighting experience, and poorly equipped, but at least 6,000 were armed with rifles and another 3,000 carried revolvers and pistols.[73] A few of the men and women had attained considerable experience in urban warfare during the last year of the occupation, but a large proportion had little or no combat experience and many had never fired their weapons. Despite ELAS' initial advantages, the insurgents were hampered by serious difficulties and liabilities.

As mentioned earlier, Siantos had decided to wage the battle through the ELAS central committee and essentially try to control the battle by himself. Bypassing the experienced ELAS general headquarters staff meant that Siantos had to fight a campaign without a proper command structure, communications, logistical organization, and a transportation plan to enable him to shift units quickly from one part of the battle to the other. Siantos himself had practically no command or military experience, and had taken no part in the ELAS campaigns during the occupation. He had fulfilled his military service as a noncommissioned officer in the Greek army, but that was hardly adequate and Theodoros Makridis, a former Greek officer and a senior commander in ELAS, often referred to Siantos as the "general of sergeants."[74]

The regular ELAS was a guerrilla army, albeit of uneven skill, armaments, and discipline, but had acquired considerable experience in irregular warfare. The ELAS reserve, in contrast, was a pale reflection and woefully inadequate as a military force, lacking experience as the rank and file had not had any opportunity to fight as a cohesive force until the December Uprising. Siantos made matters worse by a combination of indecisiveness and naiveté. In addition to dividing his forces by sending three ELAS divisions to destroy EDES in Epirus, he also hampered the coordination of his forces by dividing KKE headquarters between Athens and a small village, Hashia, in northern Attica. The senior KKE cadres who were critical in securing supplies, maintaining communications, providing intelligence, and conducting a host of other critical duties wasted valuable time moving back and forth between the two locations, while the situation in Athens slowly spun out of the control.

The British had kept a watchful eye on the movements of the regular ELAS units outside of the capital practically from the first day of liberation. The increasing agitation of EAM in the streets of Athens throughout October and November was seen as a barometer of angry leftist sentiment, but hardly a military threat. They assumed that if, or rather when, hostilities broke out, ELAS would attack Athens from the outside with help from KKE and EAM supporters in the city acting as a fifth column and not the primary force. As late as 6 December, Scobie's staff was still concerned about ELAS proper and reckoned that ELAS had concentrated approximately 20,000 troops in Attica and that a full-scale attack seemed imminent.[75]

The mistaken notion that an attack against the capital would come from outside partially explains why Scobie refrained from committing his troops in the street battles until after his army was besieged. In other words, both sides misunderstood each other's intentions. Scobie was husbanding his strength to meet the expected assault from outside the city, and until reinforcements arrived it was not prudent to provoke any street battles. Siantos, for his part, must have assumed that Scobie's restraint was an indication that the British were not yet committed to participating in a Greek civil war. Consequently, ELAS was thrown against Greek government forces and targets, while making a determined effort not to provoke the British.[76]

Formal hostilities began on 6 December, when Scobie's ultimatum for the withdrawal of all ELAS forces from Athens expired. In the early dawn, hundreds of grim ELAS men dressed in civilian clothes and armed with only rifles briskly advanced through the royal gardens and headed toward the side that led to Kifissias Boulevard (present-day Vassilisis Sohias Boulevard). An iron fence surrounded the gardens, and the drab-looking ELAS fighters bunched up, as they had to climb over the railing to reach the street. Kifissias is a broad avenue where the ministries of foreign affairs and war and other key government offices were located. The object of the attack was for ELAS to seize the physical symbols of the state and quickly replace the Papandreou government with their own administration. As the ELAS men approached the government buildings, the early light of day revealed that British sentries guarded the front entrances. The attackers paused—they had no instructions to fight the British, only orders to capture the buildings. Some of the more aggressive officers urged their men on, while others held back and some even began retreating. The assault proceeded unevenly, quickly stalled, and was easily repulsed by the police detachments assigned to protect the buildings.[77]

Within the week the fighting escalated, but for the most part it remained confined to Athens and it was not until after 14 December that ELAS launched any direct attacks against British units.[78] On 12 December, Siantos met with Scobie to discuss a negotiated settlement, but Scobie insisted on full compliance with his original demands—evacuation of Athens and the disarmament of ELAS. Siantos refused and the negotiations broke off.[79]

Despite the relatively small field of engagement, ELAS failed to overwhelm the limited forces available to the government, while the British were not able to drive the guerrillas from the city. As a result, the British government was forced to transfer thousands of troops from the Italian front to Greece during the final phase of World War II. These forces were committed in a battle to destroy a major part of the Greek resistance that the British had so desperately tried to create three years earlier in order to fight the Axis. It was a cycle of violence that had already caused the death of many Greeks and would continue to claim thousands more. For the KKE it was a major defeat because it set in motion the transformation of Greece into an authoritative state, the rehabilitation of most of the collaborators, and ultimately the marginalization of the left.

The December Uprising did not necessarily guarantee another round of civil war, but the fact that the KKE came so close to victory set the stage for Zachariadis to try and succeed where Siantos had failed. For the succession of governments that came after Papandreou, the December Uprising confirmed the suspicions of the right that the communists and all the left were bent on seizing power. As a result, they lost an opportunity for reconciliation and instead looked the other way while the White Terror killed, tortured, raped, and humiliated ELAS veterans as well as anyone on the left. Certainly, individual ELAS fighters and units committed excesses and horrific acts against their fellow Greeks—some acting on their own—but many atrocities were organized by the KKE and calculated to instill fear and exact vengeance. The killings and atrocities on both sides were further enhanced by exaggeration and mythologized for maximum effect, thus demonizing both sides. Ultimately, the December bloodletting and how it unfolded set the stage for the last and most deadly phase of the civil war, from 1946 to 1949.

ΗΛΙΑΣ ΗΛΙΑΣ ΤΕΛΩΝΙΑΚΟΣ ΜΑΚΕΔΟΝΙΑ
ΜΕΓΑΛΟΓΕΝΗΣ ΣΠΥΡΟΣ ΥΠΑΛΛΗΛΟΣ ΖΑΚΥΝΘΟΣ
ΠΕΤΡΙΤΗΣ ΓΡΗΓΟΡΙΟΣ ΕΡΓΑΤΗΣ ΠΑΤΡΑ
ΜΠΑΝΑΚΟΣ ΘΕΟΔΩΡΟΣ ΑΓΡΟΤΗΣ ΜΥΤΙΚΑΣ ΠΡΕΒΕΖΑ

ΑΝΤΑΡΤΟΕΠΟΝΙΤΕΣ

ΚΑΒΒΑΔΙΑΣ ΘΕΟΔΩΡΟΣ	ΜΑΘΗΤΗΣ	ΠΡΕΒΕΖΑ
ΚΟΝΤΟΣ ΝΙΚΟΛΑΟΣ	››	››
ΛΕΟΠΟΥΛΟΣ ΧΡΗΣΤΟΣ	››	››
ΣΑΜΙΩΤΗΣ ΝΙΚΟΛΑΟΣ	››	››
ΑΝΑΓΝΩΣΤΟΠΟΥΛΟΣ ΠΕΡΙΚΛΗΣ	››	ΙΩΑΝΝΙΝΑ
ΚΑΛΔΑΝΗΣ ΔΗΜΗΤΡΙΟΣ	››	ΚΑΜΑΡΙΝΑ
ΠΑΝΑΓΟΣ ΓΕΩΡΓΙΟΣ	››	››
ΠΕΠΟΝΗΣ ΑΛΕΞΑΝΔΡΟΣ	ΜΑΘΗΤΗΣ	ΒΡΥΣ. ΠΡΕΒΕΖΑΣ
ΓΚΟΓΚΑΣ ΘΕΟΧΑΡΗΣ ››	ΩΡΩΠΟΣ	››
ΔΙΑΜΑΝΤΗΣ ΧΑΡΑΛΑΜΠΟΣ ››		››
ΔΡΟΣΟΣ ΑΠΟΣΤΟΛΟΣ ››		››
ΚΥΡΛΑΣ ΣΙΔΕΡΗΣ ››		››
ΠΕΤΡΗΣ ΔΗΜΗΤΡΙΟΣ ››		››
ΤΣΟΥΚΗΣ ΒΑΣΙΛΕΙΟΣ ››		››
ΤΡΟΜΠΕΤΑΣ ΔΗΜΗΤΡΙΟΣ	ΑΞΙΩΜΑΤΙΚΟΣ	ΠΑΡΓΑ

FIG. 6. A partial list from a monument in Parginoskala, Preveza, giving the names of individuals executed by the Greek government in 1944. The KKE holds an event every year to commemorate these deaths. WikiCommons.

CHAPTER 5

The Pogrom of the Left

THE PRELUDE TO WHITE TERROR

A revolutionary movement is first betrayed by its means,
second, by its people, and third by its purpose.

—Theophilos Frangopoulos, "Betrayals"

"You are lucky to be going to Greece," ran the opening sentence of the pamphlet issued to each member of the 11th Battalion of the King's Royal Rifle Corps. They were embarking for Greece after a protracted period of inactivity in Egypt. Lt. Ron McAdam, one of the battalion's young officers, leapt with joy at the news that the unit was finally on the move: any action was preferable to enforced idleness. Like most of the men in his battalion, McAdam could no longer stand the tedium and vast emptiness of the desert, where each day bled into the next without form or variation.

McAdam had volunteered to join the British army from his home in Rhodesia to defend a country he hardly knew in a war that had engulfed the entire world.[1] For almost seventy years he had not thought about his experiences in Greece nor has he had occasion to visit the country, but in 1944 this young man found himself in a vortex of a battle far removed from the simplicity and monotony of the desert, and even farther yet from the vast expanse and lush countryside of southern Africa.

On 12 October 1944, McAdam, along with most of the men of the 11th Battalion, embarked the Royal Navy cruiser, the *Black Prince*, in Alexandria, Egypt, and steamed north toward Piraeus. For the voyage, the young lieutenant had decided to deploy his platoon on the deck near the bow, to avoid the stifling interior of the ship. The autumn day was sunny but on the cool side, and McAdam recalled:

The sea was clear and we could see the German mines bobbing in the water. We amused ourselves watching the ship's machine guns firing at the mines and the great showers of water cascading when one them exploded. . . . As we were nearing Piraeus, it became obvious that we were in the midst of a very large minefield and we had lost ships. The person in charge of the flotilla wisely turned it about and another set of minesweepers moved in and we eventually docked on 15 October 1944.[2]

According to the *Eleventh Battalion War Diary*, a German noncommissioned officer, for fifty gold sovereigns, had given the British directions to a gap in the minefield covering Piraeus harbor. Unfortunately, the information proved false and the flotilla lost five ships. By 16 October the troops had disembarked and were proceeding to their objectives, passing through a dilapidated landscape stripped bare by the retreating Germans. The population greeted the British with applause and pelted them with flowers. After such a welcome, very few had any notion that they had traded a war in which the enemy was easily identifiable for one where death lurked behind doorways, in sewers, and on balconies and rooftops. A smiling face was no guarantee of welcome; at times it was rather a mask to lure the unsuspecting soldier into a trap. McAdam remembered, "On arrival in Athens we were welcomed by the civilians, some of who obviously remembered the 9th Battalion that had been there in 1941. We spent most of the 16th to the 29th of October reorganizing the city. I was impressed, as we moved into Piraeus, that first day with the lack of any animals and that there were not enough men around."[3] McAdam's impression of the Greek interior was even grimmer:

> On the 21 November our company was ordered to Lamia, this was a small provincial town which actually when we got there, we found out was the headquarters of ELAS. Our job was to take supplies to the countryside as they were very short of food and short of transport, the villages had been badly damaged by the Germans who as they left destroyed bridges and in fact had burnt down many houses. People were short of clothes, they had malaria and were without any drugs, they also had typhoid and it was a very difficult job to get the food out to them.[4]

Like most British forces in Greece, the 11th Battalion was spread out, with each of its six companies trying to distribute relief supplies over a large area. Reports from the company commanders mirrored McAdam's observations. An extract from one patrol typifies the conditions the British encountered in the Greek interior and the obstacles they had to overcome in order to provide some assistance to the local population:

> Visited Karpenisi—population approximately 2,100. Only fourteen houses left standing out of an original 204. Remainder burnt by Germans. Supply center for 25,000 people in the surrounding villages. These can only be reached on foot—many three days journey—and mules are short. . . . Food situation very bad—beans being the main diet. Last distribution of food early last October. This consisted of rice milk powder and macaroni. Clothes urgently needed. No single person possesses anything but what he stands up in. Children looked miserably cold. Clothes were sent up recently by Red Cross, but unfortunately had not been inspected. They turned out to be light summer frocks and useless articles such as handbags. Eighty percent of the population have malaria. No quinine or atebrine. Twenty-five people have typhoid. More serum needed. There is no doctor in the whole area, the only medical officers being two Greek Red Cross Sisters.

The difficult conditions that prevailed in Karpanisi, with few exceptions, reflected the plight of the population in the rest of Greece. Little would change for large segments of the country over the next five years. Greece seamlessly passed from the harsh grip of the Axis occupation to the agony of civil war that dragged on until the summer of 1949. Even afterward, parts of the countryside continued to suffer deprivations for another two decades or more.

On 1 December, McAdam, as well as the other men in the company, became aware that ELAS troops were heading south toward the Athens area. A day or two later, they spotted large numbers of civilians streaming out of Athens to the north and northwest of Greece. Unsurprisingly, on the first day of the uprising (4 December) the relationship between the British and local EAM-ELAS in Lamia started to unravel and got progressively worse as the violence in Athens escalated. On 9 December, the 11th Battalion received orders to decamp for Athens, and by the evening was fighting its way to the center of the capital. The diary of the battalion describes a city desolate and shrouded in darkness:

> At Athens things were very different from what we had expected. There were no lights and not a sign of anyone about. Broken tram wires festooned the deserted streets, and these nearly accounted for more than one rifleman perched on the cab of each vehicle. Automatic

fire and sniper's bullets whipped across practically every crossroads. There was nothing for it but to put the foot and the head down at the same time and run for it. Somehow we arrived without casualty. Firing and heavy explosions were going on all over the city, but in the immediate neighbourhood of Constitution Square all was fairly quiet.[5]

During the battalion's first night in Athens, ELAS had dynamited the front door of the house occupied by one of the battalion's platoons (number 9) and in two separate attacks penetrated as far as the hall before the British unit drove them back with heavy casualties. Similar assaults erupted throughout the night, engaging elements of the 11th Battalion in a series of firefights, but at different times, enabling the British to defeat the ELAS forces piecemeal. In the morning most of the houses around the battalion's positions were burning, but the British took 150 prisoners, including some women, looking "quite respectable until a grenade fell . . . from one of the ladies' handbag."[6]

From 8 to 12 December, the scale of the ELAS offensive intensified, as ELAS regulars gradually reinforced the reserve units and joined in the fighting. ELAS also placed mines on the principal streets in addition to deploying artillery and heavy machine guns. ELAS demolition teams easily moved about the city via sewers, rooftops, and back alleys, blowing up houses and police stations. In a desperate attempt to break through the lines, ELAS squads also packed dynamite into tramcars and hurled them against British defense positions.

In the face of these reinforcements and firepower, General Scobie, the commander of all British and Greek forces in the country, withdrew most of the isolated British units into the center of Athens, but inevitably had to abandon several supply dumps, which provided additional food and ammunition for ELAS. The Greek Third Mountain Brigade, however, located on the outskirts of Athens (before the outbreak of fighting), remained exposed and was forced to hold its ground for the duration of the hostilities. ELAS surrounded the brigade and subjected it to mortar bombardment and a steady stream of small arms fire for almost a month. The British could supply the brigade with food and ammunition, but only at night and with convoys of armored cars.

Initially, the battle swung in favor of ELAS; the British forces were quickly forced back into three small pockets. The first included a small group of soldiers who had managed to retreat to the tip of the peninsula in Piraeus. They were immediately isolated from the main British force in the center of

Athens, but managed to keep contact with the Royal Navy flotilla anchored in the harbor. A second British unit defended the main airfield at Hassani and a sliver of the shore leading to Phaliron Bay. Remarkably, ELAS did not make any serious efforts to capture the airport and paid for this blunder when later the British airlifted an entire army division from Italy to Athens, which turned the tide of battle. The third and largest concentration of British forces was in the center of Athens. Within this narrow perimeter, the British and the few Greek government units were compressed into an area just two miles long and five or six blocks wide, which included Constitution Square, the main government buildings, part of the business quarter, the district of Kolonaki, and the Grande Bretagne Hotel. The rest of the capital, as well as most of Greece, fell under the grip of the KKE-ELAS-EAM.

After 12 December, both sides settled into a deadly pattern. The British, under siege, had to repel attacks day and night as well as contend with sniper fire and ambushes in the unfamiliar streets of the capital. ELAS, with far superior numbers, sustained an almost constant offensive with waves of infantry, shifting from one part of the British position to the other, while maintaining round-the-clock sniping and ambushes. In some respect, the Battle of Athens was a mix of conventional firefights, but with streets and buildings as the primary targets, accompanied by the uglier side of urban warfare that blurred the line between civilian and soldier. A good number of the ELAS troops did not wear an identifiable uniform. Snipers, in particular, dressed in civilian clothes and operated from rooftops and balconies. They would fire at the British and quickly retreat within a house or apartment building and hide their rifle, making detection almost impossible.

Very often, ELAS overstepped even these bounds in order to gain an advantage over the British. This is not surprising considering the fact that just two months earlier, the ELAS reserve units in Athens and, to a lesser degree, the regular ELAS in the mountains, had been fighting the Germans in a conflict in which the rules of war did not apply and allowed no quarter for guerrillas or civilians. The occupation forces did not hesitate to employ torture, killing of hostages, burning of villages, and other reprisal tactics against the resistance groups.

Consequently, the mixed units of ELAS reserves and regulars could hardly fall within the strict definition of a conventional military force. At the same time, the British had condoned and applauded the use of guile and subterfuge by the guerrillas against the Axis. Indeed, the British, during the course of World War II, pioneered the use of deception tactics and strategy, some of which took place in Greece.[7] The ELAS-EAM had learned quickly from the British liaison officers attached to the various guerrilla bands. In addition to picking up British techniques, they could fall back on a long tradition of covert skills honed by Greek partisans in the struggle for independence against the Ottoman Empire. Although this may explain the use of deception tactics, it does not dampen the odious impression caused by the ELAS "dirty tricks" campaign.

For example, ELAS troops occupied hospitals and disguised themselves as patients (going so far as to wear mock bandages) and attacked unsuspecting British patrols while lying in bed with their rifles concealed. On 10 December, a British patrol of armored cars in the southwest area of the Likavitos district came under fire from an ELAS hospital, where nurses in Red Cross uniforms threw hand grenades from the windows at the passing British unit. The patrol responded with heavy machine gun fire, and after a while the ELAS troops inside the hospital raised a white flag. Despite this, when a British officer approached, he was gunned down by a sniper firing from the same window from which the white flag was hanging. In frustration, the commander of the unit forced two of the ELAS nurses from the hospital to stand on top of one of the armored cars to ensure the safe withdrawal of his men. Later, the same unit secured the perimeter of their position with booby-trapped barbed wire, which killed three ELAS troops, two of them women, trying to cut the wire.[8] "I did not fear the frontal ELAS attacks, but the sniping was another matter," McAdam recalled from his time in Athens. "Snipers were used a fair bit by ELAS and they were very effective. They caused an awful lot of fear in the troops because we never knew when we might expect them to be active."[9]

The British deplored the ELAS tactic of using women and, occasionally, children to lure their soldiers into a trap. In a typical ambush, a young woman would call to soldiers from a balcony, and when one approached (for what he assumed would be a chat with a pretty girl), a sniper, hiding behind the girl's skirts, would open fire. In one incident, an armored car passing a street came across the same girl five times; like the sirens of old, she beckoned the occupants of the vehicle to approach, and each time they did, a machine gun around the corner would open fire with deadly consequences. The sixth time, the British were forced to shoot the girl.[10] On other occasions, a little boy would stand on a balcony waving a Union Jack, while a sniper fired between his legs. Often battle-hardened British troops refused to fire at women and children, until circumstances forced them to reconsider. According to the War Diary of the 11th Battalion, Lieutenant B. E. D. Collier ordered a rifleman to fire at a young woman approaching his house with a tray of food and wine. The rifleman obeyed, and then begged not to be given such an order again. He quickly changed his view when the German stick grenade in her right hand was pointed out to him.[11]

Nevertheless, shooting at women and children was demoralizing for British soldiers, who, over and over again, had to keep coming to terms with this new twist in the inhumanity of war. Regrettably, the exploitation of women and children did not end with the Battle of Athens, but assumed a greater role in the next round of the Greek civil war, eventually becoming a feature in all the dirty little wars of the twentieth century and beyond.

Another disconcerting factor for British soldiers was the inability to separate friend from foe, in addition to the language barrier. A few days before Christmas 1944, McAdam received instructions for his platoon to guard a bridge on Sygrou Boulevard straddling the road between the capital and Piraeus, over which Winston Churchill was to travel to Athens from the airport. Churchill was coming to Greece to negotiate an end to the civil war with EAM-ELAS, and McAdam's job was to make sure that no one booby-trapped the bridge. The young officer had his doubts about securing the position, and even more so when local Greeks warned him that he would be eradicated during the night. "I will never know if those people had my welfare in mind or the warning was simply a trick to chase me away," McAdam continued to speculate on that incident over half a century after the event.

In this environment of subterfuge and deadly games of hide and seek between snipers, McAdam recalled,

> We devised a simple technique for conducting patrols. We moved along a district and after securing one street, we fired a flare so that machine gunners and mortar bombers, behind us, could set their sights to cover us to the next block. On some patrols we had the assistance of a tank. The infantry would travel along on either side of the tank. Each soldier carried a rifle with tracer bullets to indicate the direction of a shot and its target. The gunner on the tank would then be able to locate the spot at which the enemy was firing from and would then remove the side of the house with an eighty-millimeter shell.[12]

During the December Uprising, the Greek government was practically a bystander and watched helplessly as the British and EAM-ELAS fought for control of the streets of Athens. The prime minister and the other members of the government, accompanied by their wives and children, as well as most of the foreign notables, withdrew to the Grande Bretagne Hotel. The hotel, one of the largest and most luxurious buildings in southeastern Europe, was constructed in the early nineteenth century under the supervision of Otto I, the first king of Greece. It was one of the few structures in Athens that offered state-of-the-art conveniences such as electric door locks (operated from above the headboards), light signals, house and city telephones in every room, and individual safes.[13] For the besieged government ministers, however, the hotel's most important feature was its thick exterior stone walls.

For the duration of the battle, the Grande Bretagne accommodated well over one thousand people, with rooms set apart for cabinet meetings; offices for the premier as well as for the other ministers, former Greek generals, and well-known writers; space for war correspondents; rooms for UNRA and for senior British officers. When the city center was cut off, the hotel bar was transformed into a hospital for wounded civilians and military personnel, whose awful groans filtered throughout the main floor. A makeshift bar was created from one of the small rooms, although refreshments were limited to Samos wine, retsina, and ouzo.[14]

In addition to Scobie and his staff, the six members of the former Soviet mission had—tellingly—decided to take their chances in the hotel rather than trust the hospitality of the KKE. Colonel Popov, the former head of the Soviet mission, spent his time sitting at a table in one of the main rooms of the hotel saying very little except to lament the quality of British rations. Yet culinary disappointments did not deter the Russian colonel from insisting that General Scobie provide him with a British armed guard.[15]

In the early days of the siege, everyone had to accept minor inconveniences and adjustments. Because of the scarcity of servants (some had joined ELAS, many more were just too frightened to ignore EAM's call for a general strike), all the guests, regardless of rank or status, had to line up outside the kitchen for their meal of "bully beef" with biscuits, a second course of cheese, and a cup of tea. All the guests had to make their own beds and clean their rooms with the communal brooms (leaving the garbage in the corridors). In some instances, ingenuity often overcame adversity, with unexpected results. For example, old military maps from the Italian campaign replaced the stained and dirty tablecloths in the dining room. As one British historian has written, "This had its consolations. Many officers were able during meal-times to discuss their battle experiences, to point out which particular valley or mountain had been the scene of their feats of daring."[16]

As the fighting crept closer, conditions in the hotel deteriorated accordingly. When ELAS cut off the water supply to central Athens, the ration was strictly limited to half a gallon per person each day for drinking and washing. This did not dampen the spirits of the guests, who had to join yet another line in order to collect their half gallon in empty gin, brandy, or whiskey bottles. Despite the deprivations, Byford-Jones' account of the December events offers a nostalgic description of the Grande Bretagne, including images of the two pianos in the hotel being played daily and often well into the night, accompanied by the din of battle raging in the streets. The bonding experience was further enhanced by the sure knowledge that the hotel (as well as its occupants), or the "Royal Kingdom of Greece" as it was called by the KKE and EAM, was one of the primary targets of ELAS.

For the men and women trying to storm the British defenses outside the walls of the Grande Bretagne, the battle held a different legacy. Despite notions to the contrary, ELAS-EAM did not represent homogeneous organizations. The degree of commitment, loyalty, fighting ability, and even fanaticism within the ranks was uneven and varied in each unit. The ELAS formations included recruits from the countryside and mountain villages, from the working districts as well as from the upper and middle classes of the cities and towns. Some of the volunteers were naive young men and women who had rarely left their villages and could hardly differentiate between Marxism and monarchy—they fought because they trusted the leadership of EAM-ELAS in their communities. Village priests often accompanied units raised in their parishes, thus lending another layer of credibility.

Others, especially recruits from the urban centers, discovered the appeal of EAM and ELAS in the first stages of occupation and flocked to its banner because they came of age when the influence of the left, for the first time in Greece, dominated most of the country. Even for the sons and daughters of the largely right-wing upper- and middle-class Athenian families, membership in EAM-ELAS became fashionable. During the harsh winter of 1942, when most Greeks were trying to survive the famine, some of the upscale homes in Kolonaki hosted parties for the newly established EAM. The parties, explains Petros Makris-Staikos in a recent study of the period, provided a curious link between the mass-based EAM and the privileged classes in Athens. In one such event,

> The mistress of the house, one of the daughters of the Papastratou (the owner of a major tobacco company), was open and "sympathetic" to

every ideological current that appeared progressive. This particular party attracted the "reactionaries"—the children of the major right-wing families of Athens, who did not go hungry and the occupation had not interfered with their preoccupations. Now, however, that they saw that their class offered approval, the road to EAM was open. For many it was a way out of their tedious and stifling environment or a means of escaping the suffocating grip of their parents. In a short while, accordingly, EAM became a fad. Kolonaki, Psychiko as well as other wealthy districts became filled with male and female EAM members.[17]

With the assistance of these new recruits, EAM succeeded in seizing control over most of the relief work in Athens and permeated all the professional guilds and student organizations. Invariably, for many of the sons and daughters of the Athenian establishment, EAM served as a transitional step to the KKE. EAM also attracted a large number of professionals, particularly among the ranks of university professors, who used their influence with the student body to secure the election of EAM candidates in the various university societies.[18]

The fad quickly turned into a mass movement and spawned the revolution that exploded into the streets of Athens after liberation. The leadership of the KKE may have planned to use the December Uprising as a means of increasing their representatives in the government of national unity, or influencing the formation of a new army, or even as part of a strategy of getting control of the Greek state in stages, but after the fighting erupted, they progressively lost control of events. In effect, the movement created through EAM and its subsidiary organizations became larger than the sum of its parts and represented a wide variety of liberal desiderata. Some individuals and groups exploited the fighting to pursue their own ends.

Between 1943 and 1944, EAM and the anti-left groups fought bitterly over control of the student societies in the Greek institutions of higher learning, particularly over the student bodies of the University of Athens and the Polytechnic School. Other battles took place in the streets, in coffee houses, and in back alleys of Athens and in other cities. The various anti-left forces could count on the indirect support of the German authorities and the puppet government, and some did not hesitate to collaborate with the occupation security services in their common struggle against communism. Occasionally, the Athens Security Battalions raided the university, arresting dozens of students. Some of the unfortunate young men and women underwent extensive interrogation and torture in the dungeons of the Greek Special Security Service, and a lucky few escaped, but only after their parents used bribes to secure their release.

At other times, the battles between left- and right-wing organizations revolved around revenge and counter-revenge killing. For example, in 1944, a few months before liberation, the KKE assassinated a member of the far right-wing X organization just as he was about to board a bus. In retaliation, X dispatched six teams of five men each to terrorize EAM-ELAS and KKE groups. In early December 1944 the teams broke into the usual haunts of the left, shouting "hands up in the air," and proceeded to search all those present, severely beating anyone caught with weapons. In one place they found a couple of groups with red paint in their possession for writing slogans on walls. The X team forced them to drink the red paint and then went on to dynamite two KKE offices in the neighborhood. Afterward, they dragged ten of the communists to the square, forced them against a wall, and went through the motions of a mock execution.[19]

In response to the arrest of its followers and those of EAM, the KKE expanded the mission of OPLA (Units for the Protection of the People's Struggle), originally established as an intelligence unit in the winter of 1942–43, to carry out assassinations. After liberation, the mandate of OPLA was further modified to include torture and executions of KKE rivals, collaborators, and "reactionaries." In the countryside and some neighborhoods of Athens, OPLA henchmen served as officers in the KKE's National Civil Guard (Ethniki Politophilaki). Although former police and gendarmes filled the ranks of OPLA, the communists also preferred to employ local cadres who were from the area or neighborhood of a designated assassination. This had the advantage of making identification of the prospective victim easier, as well as binding the newer members of the KKE closer to the party by implicating them in the killing. As the day of liberation approached and the grip of the German occupiers weakened, Athens was quickly becoming a killing zone.

In this context, the KKE pursued narrow goals dictated by Stalinist principles such as purging of collaborators, rivals, potential rivals, and particularly members guilty of apostasy—even at the expense of the party's broader interests. One such example was the ill-fated Kitsos Maltezos, a young Athenian poet, representative of the intellectual and cultural elite, and the last living relative of Yiannis Makriyiannis, one of the heroes of the Greek War of Independence. Although Maltezos fell victim to the KKE's assassination units in the last months of the occupation, how he was killed was typical of the murder of other KKE targets during the December Uprising and provides a rare insight into the tactics of the communists.

When Maltezos joined the youth wing of the KKE, he was more than just a trophy convert, as his connection to the legendary Makriyiannis gave the KKE another avenue for associating the EAM movement with the Greek War of Independence. Consequently, when Maltezos decided to leave the Young communists in 1943, it constituted not only betrayal of the movement but also a dangerous precedent. Making matters worse, Maltezos openly condemned the communists and went over to the anti-KKE forces that had sprung up in reaction to the EAM-ELAS.

In early 1943, the KKE held a secret trial for Maltezos in absentia and condemned him to death; the execution was to take place at first opportunity. On 1 February 1944 at 9:30 A.M., Maltezos left his apartment and was making his way to Panepistimiou Street to the nearest tram stop. When he walked across Sygrou Boulevard to Amalias, four men came up behind him and followed discreetly. As he passed the statue of Lord Byron and was about to board the tram, two of the men pulled out their guns and yelled "now." One of the men then called out "Kitsos," and when Maltezos turned the first bullet struck him on the right temple followed by several more in the chest.[20] In the midst of so much killing, the death of Maltezos, albeit cold-blooded, hardly seemed unusual in a city where killing had become commonplace.

Yet this talented young man became a tragic symbol of his generation and a metaphor for the fratricide that had infected Athens, that would, in a short time, consume Greek society. Although the KKE ordered his execution, it did so with the cognizance and even urging of classmates and even friends of Maltezos who had grown up in the same neighborhood and who, up until the occupation, had shared the same values. Adonis Kyrou, the son of the publisher of *Estia* (one of the oldest conservative Greek newspapers) and the scion of a powerful Athenian family, was a member of the KKE. In 1943, Kyrou was instrumental in the KKE's decision to condemn Maltezos to death. The primary executioner, Mikes Kouroniotis, had been Maltezos' close friend in university and was also a classmate of Andreas Papandreou (Greece prime minister in the 1980s) when they both attended the American College before the war. Like Kyrou, Kouroniotis came from an established and prosperous family and had also joined the KKE while in university during the occupation.

In the eyes of his family, Kouroniotis had betrayed his class and they were anxious to avoid a scandal. The old establishment quickly sprung into action to protect one of their own. The Greek Special Security Service, who had apprehended Kouroniotis and conducted extensive interrogations that had revealed the names of the others connected to Maltezos' death, received orders to hand the young man over to the Germans. Kouroniotis' family preferred that he be executed by the Germans for carrying a weapon (an offense punishable by death), than going through the motions of a trial that would have revealed his membership in the KKE and, in turn, implicate sons and daughters of other prominent Athenian families.

Despite the assassination of a high-profile man of Greek letters, the censored press did not report the killing until two days later and omitted the name of his assassin and any accomplices. On 21 March 1944, Kouroniotis, along with eleven others, was executed by firing squad. He died in obscurity, which suited everyone concerned. His family was spared further scandal, and the occupation regime escaped the embarrassment of appearing helpless by failing to protect a prominent Athenian. The KKE and OPLA were also relieved by the quick elimination of Kouroniotis, which avoided exposing their secrets in the course of a public trial.

Not all the men and women from the Athenian elite succumbed to murder and assassination. The father of the former prime minister of Greece, Kostas Simitis, at the time a popular professor in the business school, was one of those who endeavored to get EAM students elected to the boards of student societies at the universities. Later he joined PEEA, established by EAM in the Greek mountains as a rival to the Greek government-in-exile in London and Cairo, and struggled against George Papandreou, the premier in 1944 and the father of Andreas Papandreou who led the Greek Socialist Party (which claims EAM's ideological mantel) to victory in 1981.

Men like Simitis, who came from well-to-do middle- and upper-class families, did not join ELAS and subsequently lost the opportunity to fight the Axis. As members of EAM they waged a passive battle against the occupation by distributing pamphlets, writing on walls, and by performing a variety of other nonviolent activities, all of which had its dangers, but lacked the romanticism of guerrilla warfare. Many became members of the reserve ELAS and in December 1944 got the opportunity to fight for the lofty ideals that had motivated them to join EAM during the occupation. Others, such as the young men who murdered Maltezos, went a step further and became followers of the KKE. As educated individuals, they made the intellectual link to the communist party, although whether they bought into the ideology because of guilt or conviction is difficult to ascertain.

For most Athenians, however, the terror of the December Uprising was not an issue of ideology, but of fear exacerbated by the misery of a general strike that paralyzed the city for thirty-three days. The KKE and EAM organized the strike as a means of placing additional pressure on the Papandreou government and used organized labor as a tactic of urban warfare. Electricity, water, and gas supplies ceased, and only a few telephones remained in operation. Once all workers went on strike, theaters, stores, hotels, and restaurants closed. Transportation came to a halt, as did the work on the docks, which prevented, for the duration of the fighting, the unloading of ships that carried foodstuffs, medicines, and other critical supplies needed by a desperate and hungry population. The strike spread to Attica and Thessaloniki, thwarting the first attempts to revive the economy, and more important, to feed the starving Athenians.[21]

During the occupation, daily hardship and violence unfolded in a constant and predictable pattern, but people learned to adapt to the new realities and adjusted accordingly. Now, though, the random nature and intensity of urban warfare compounded the chaos and street-to-street gun battles of December. Firefights erupted suddenly, and then just as quickly the streets came under long periods of sniper fire, forcing people to remain indoors. The enforced confinement created an atmosphere of claustrophobia that Athenians suffered along with hunger and fear.

Like many Athenians, Dione Dodis was trapped by the outbreak of hostilities. In December 1944, she was a resident of the fashionable Kolonaki district and although at the time she was only a young girl of fifteen, the deprivations caused by the national strike are still etched in her memory. After almost sixty years she recalled: "We suffered during the occupation and had little food, but during the Uprising we got to know real hunger. On some days it was impossible to go out, but regardless of the danger it was necessary to dispose of the garbage and waste in nearby makeshift dumps."[22] Dodis added, "During the curfew, which started by allowing us out for only two hours (12–2 p.m. and later until 6 p.m.), our main concern was to get water from the nearest wells. Another great concern was how to cook our limited amount of stored food without electricity or gas. We resorted to chopping down and burning our kitchen chairs."[23] During the occupation, the small trees that lined the streets of Kolonaki as well as those of other Athenian districts vanished, along with the nearby forests.

As was the case with all the areas within the British zone, an influx of people from other parts of the city displaced by the fighting streamed into the upscale district. The refugees added a new burden to the besieged residents whose spare rooms were liable to be temporarily requisitioned by the government to accommodate those fleeing the communist forces. Local residents knew only too well that once rooms were commandeered, they would become protected quarters long after the end of the crisis. If the Kolonaki residents had to play host to anyone, British officers and soldiers were preferable to the uncertainty of visitors imposed by the government. The British could be counted on to pay a small, but regular rent, and they would eventually leave; at the same time their presence would forestall any imposed guest.[24]

The Athenians endured the December Uprising, isolated in their homes, hungry, cold, and in the dark. For most people, the Battle of Athens was not a terrible spectacle of war, but short vignettes of bitter street fighting and long hours of sniper fire. Many were also mindful that a knock on the door could come from the police searching for communists or a visit by the KKE security forces searching for suspected collaborators. In either case, the issue of guilt or innocence was hostage to the whims of the grim visitors. For the most part, accusation was tantamount to condemnation, and nondescript men anxious to take vengeance in the name of ideology, nationalism, God, king, or country, or simply to settle old scores, often delivered justice in a seedy basement or back alley.

For weeks following the liberation, some Athenians indulged in an exorcism of guilt by distributing blame on each other. It became common practice to denounce individuals for collaboration, and those singled out were then summoned by the authorities to give an account of their activities. At best it was a long process often leading to arrest and extended periods of detention. Michael Ward, an SOE officer who took part in vetting people accused of collaboration, relates that "All these accusations had to be investigated, which in the nature of things involved long delays, and until a victim had at length cleared himself, he became a file number in the records of the Greek and British security services, forbidden to leave the country and unable to find work in a wide range of jobs. Denunciation, therefore, became the ideal means of settling many irrelevant private grudges and vendettas."[25]

As Ward points out, the poison tongue of the informer could be aimed at followers of both the right and the left, with less regard for political susceptibilities than for private motives. During the course of the December Uprising the consequences for those denounced were often lethal. OPLA, the KKE secret police, generated lists of names of current and potential enemies as well as those accused of collaboration with the Germans or, for that matter, with the British. On the whole, OPLA agents were concerned less with accuracy than with simply purging large numbers of suspects. Similar conditions applied in the Greek and British security services, but they had more flexibility, and as Ward states, "while the civil war in Athens was raging . . . it was decided to ship away all detainees, as and when they were arrested, to Tobruk where they could be interrogated at leisure and out of the way."[26]

On both sides, self-serving individuals exploited the chaos to satisfy greed and ambition, or to cover up their own crimes. Kaiti Economou fell into this category. Economou was a young actress in the Greek National Theater and during the occupation had lost little time coming to terms with the new order. In the fall of 1941, she married Kostas Petrotsopoulos, a notorious traitor and agent of the German secret police. Petrotsopoulos served his German masters by posing as an enthusiastic anglophile anxious to render assistance to the allies, but in reality he was working to betray Athenians hiding British soldiers. Occasionally, Economou also played the role of informant for the Axis at the expense of her countrymen, all the while pretending she was a patriot. In time, Athenians saw through the charade spun by the couple, and used every opportunity to heap scorn and abuse during Economou's performances. Theater audiences often assailed her with verbal abuse and obscene gestures, and even by sending her threats.[27]

At the end of the occupation in October 1944, Petrotsopoulos left with the Germans, but Economou remained in Athens, and to squelch the stigma of collaboration became an enthusiastic supporter of EAM. She took part in demonstrations against the monarchy and the Papandreou government and styled herself as a leftist liberal as well as anti-British. It was not enough, however, to dispel completely the aura of traitor and, like others of her ilk, Economou chose to mask her past by denouncing Eleni Papadaki, another actress, as a collaborator. Papadaki had emerged in the 1930s, and particularly during the occupation, as one of the best actresses in Greece and is an example of the tragic convergence of fear, greed, and professional jealousy exacerbated by the occupation and resistance.

In the charged atmosphere following the liberation of Athens, the National Theater mirrored the divisions of Greek society, and some of the actors carelessly flung accusations of treachery and betrayal against each other with little regard for the consequences. The actors, managers, and even the stagehands had to distance themselves from the potential charge of entertaining the enemy during the occupation. Indeed, the maxim that "the show must go on" regardless of circumstances was often lost on a population coping with conditions of hunger, disease, and reprisals.

Although few could criticize those in essential services such as sanitation, medical, fire, and ordinary police work, performers, especially high-profile entertainers in occupied Europe as well as Greece, were vulnerable to charges of collaboration since quite often their audiences included German and Italian officers as well as officials of the local puppet regime.[28] After the war, many flocked to radical and anti-establishment organizations partly because the puppet governments had sprung from the right-wing spectrum of society and partly to retroactively acquire bona fide resistance credentials. Most chose the mass-based EAM.

Economou joined the other EAM members of the National Theater Actors Guild in purging from the organization a number of actors, including Papadaki, suspected of collaboration and treason during the occupation. During the course of the general assembly of the Actors Guild on 20 November 1944, Papadaki was formally expelled to a chorus of "death to the whore."[29] The actors, however, were hardly in a position to differentiate between traitor and patriot—they did not conduct even a cursory investigation, and some exploited the chaos and cacophony of accusations to eliminate competitors. Katina Paxinou, Papadaki's older rival, allegedly played a key role in the arrest and subsequent execution of the younger actress. Paxinou, according to this claim, had been the leading actress in the theater until Papadaki surpassed her during the occupation.

Papadaki's crime was twofold; she had a relationship with Ioannis Rallis, the last puppet premier, and she had quickly emerged as the most popular and successful actress in the theater. Rallis was a friend of Papadaki's father before the war and it had continued during the occupation. Furthermore, she was an easy target. As a high-profile actress, she was readily identified when in the company of German officers, but it was her affair with Rallis and his obsession with her that dogged Papadaki until her death.

During the last year of the occupation, Rallis showered her with gifts and provided protection and patronage. The puppet premier was smitten despite the twenty-five-year age difference. Kenneth Matthews, a friend and an admirer of Papadaki, in his personal memoir of the Greek civil war, reflected on this unusual relationship.

Of the fatal friendship with Rallis, I heard a little and shut my ears. There was no need to think it love. Prime minister and young actress complemented each other; he with his powers could offer advancement, she with her glamour, flattery. I knew Rallis too. Born into a ruling family, he had the patrician's values and manners: with a monocle at his eye and a gardenia in his buttonhole, he could have strayed out of the courts or council chambers of the nineteenth century. He was fond of women: by a strange accident, I came into the possession of a letter he wrote in French, which portrayed him as a wooer, at great pains to charm and to please. Vanity, perhaps, destroyed him—vanity, fogged principles, faulty judgment in that he did not foresee who was going to win.[30]

Years later, his son, George, declared that Rallis was convinced of an Axis victory, but during the first years of the occupation he did little else than express this point of view. In 1941, the Axis had first offered Rallis the opportunity to form a government and only turned to General Tsolakoglou when he refused. Ironically, Ioannis Rallis slid into the quagmire of occupational politics and collaboration in the spring of 1943 when it had become obvious, even to the most obtuse sympathizers of the Third Reich, that the Germans were facing defeat. Yet, according to his son, Rallis believed he could save Greece from the clutches of the left and ensure that the country passed from Axis rule to liberation with little upheaval.[31]

Nevertheless, the relationship between the naïve actress and the love-struck premier caused a sensation in Athens and drew considerable fire from the left-wing underground press.[32] On 15 October 1943, the newspaper *Ellinikon Ema* (Greek Blood) condemned Rallis with considerable sarcasm: "The puppet government of Athens does not take any measures to . . . protect the people but is focused on the amorous fixation of its president, Ioannis Rallis, towards the well-known actress (Papadaki). It should be noted that Rallis has given the object of his attention a platinum belt, worth hundreds of millions. Meanwhile, the premier plays the potent lover while the nation is dying of hunger."[33]

Two months later, the paper reported that Rallis was in the process of proclaiming a new law to facilitate his third divorce in order to marry Papadaki.[34] The rumor of a pending wedding was baseless, but the speculation persisted, and after liberation some people even believed that Rallis and Papadaki had married secretly; most took it for granted that the two had carried on a love affair. Papadaki, at the same time, had little regard for the perception that her relationship with Rallis was aiding her enemies. She was usually conveyed to the theater by Rallis' automobile, and the chauffeur would formally step out and open the door for her, causing further resentment among her rivals.

Papadaki nonetheless exploited her relationship with Rallis and her German admirers to save hundreds of resistance members from execution. She tried to save the life of one of the theater's seamstresses, who had been arrested by the Gestapo because her two sons were in the resistance and wanted by the Germans. Despite her efforts, Papadaki was not able to facilitate the woman's release because the Gestapo insisted that the sons surrender and only then their mother would be spared. When Papadaki brought the bad news back to the theater, the information was intentionally misrepresented to mean that Papadaki herself had insisted that the woman's sons surrender in exchange for their mother's freedom. The seamstress was executed and her sons assumed that Papadaki was responsible. During the December Uprising they, as well as several actors of the theater, were instrumental in having Papadaki arrested by the KKE civil guard.[35]

After the outbreak of hostilities in December, despite her close association with Rallis, and faced with the label of collaborator, Papadaki refused to leave her home in Patisia, at that time a relatively upscale Athenian neighborhood, for the safety of the British zone in Kolonaki. In the early afternoon of 21 December, Kostas Bilirakis, a medical student, and two other men from the EAM chapter of Patisia came to pick her up for questioning at the apartment of a friend. According to witnesses, Papadaki remained unconcerned even when her interrogators, addressing her as Mrs. Rallis, pressed her to confess her marriage to Rallis, slapping her across the face when she repeatedly denied the accusation.[36]

At midnight two men transported the actress in a black Ford taxi to Galatsi, a modest settlement nestled on the outskirts of Athens that served as one of the KKE slaughter centers. The few who survived recalled that a water distillery scarred this otherwise bucolic setting of pine trees and rolling hills. Fresh victims came almost every hour and at all times of the day and night. The communist leadership served makeshift justice from a cluster of ramshackle houses, unfettered by legal procedure or rules of evidence. A typical trial consisted of a brief interrogation, usually taking less than a quarter of an hour, and those found guilty of an ever-growing list of crimes were sent to the grounds of the oil refinery less than a hundred yards from the "court." There, hundreds of luckless people, including a large number of police and gendarme officers, in some cases including their wives, were executed after being tortured.

The standard means of execution was the ax or meat cleaver. In addition to the terror that such means of execution inspired, it was also quieter, aside from the screams of the victims, than the use of a pistol or a rifle.[37] Each victim had to undress and kneel with the head resting on a large stone. The executioner could decapitate the condemned man or woman (occasionally also children), slice their throat, or hack away with the ax or meat cleaver, reducing the individual to a heap of flesh and bone. Gendarmes and police officers usually suffered ghastly and extensive torture just prior to execution, but exceptions were made for well-known members of the right or collaborators.

Upon arrival in Galatsi, Papadaki was taken to one of the houses expropriated by the KKE that served as a holding area for the accused. The commander of the unit, Captain Orestes, was a twenty-two-year-old sadistic killer who was less interested in Papadaki's guilt or innocence than in her fur coat, or at least this is how he was later portrayed by the KKE.[38] An investigation by Nikos Andrikidis, a senior commander of the KKE civil guard, accused Orestes of not sharing the valuables of the victims with the party and instead giving them to his girlfriends.[39] Orestes was a nom de guerre; his actual name was Andreas Moundrichas. Before the occupation he was a student in the Faculty of Law at the University of Athens during which time he joined the KKE. Orestes came from a middle- to upper-middle-class family, most likely from Kimi in Eubea, and was typical of the young intellectuals attracted to the communist cause. It is not certain if he had joined the KKE during the occupation or he had been a member before 1941.

The "trial" of Papadaki, along with that of seven officers of the gendarmerie, was quick and decisive. Captain Orestes, followed by two of his henchmen, approached the accused and brusquely, in the name of the people, collected all their valuables, jewelry, watches, and money. At first, he decreed that Papadaki be held as a hostage and then moved on to the next batch of prisoners. A little later he remembered Papadaki and turning to one of his colleagues inquired, "what did she say her name was" and "isn't she the one denounced by the Actors Union?" After these queries, Orestes changed his mind and condemned Papadaki to death, specifying the use of the ax for the execution.[40]

Once again, she was hustled into the same black Ford taxi and in a few minutes covered the hundred yards to the oil refinery. Vases Makaronis, a former grocer and the one charged with killing the actress, recalled at his trial a few months later: "She arrived in a car squeezed between two members of the Civil Guard. She was clutching her fur coat to ward off a devil's of a cold day." Orestes showed up in another car and ordered her to hand over the fur coat. She meekly complied, but when he demanded all her clothes, Papadaki finally realized that the end was near, broke down, and started to scream.

The guards then seized her and dragged her a few yards away to the side of an open pit. There, they tore off the rest of her garments and for a few minutes left Papadaki shivering and whimpering, waiting for the inevitable blows from the ax. At his trial, Makaronis testified that he felt sorry for the actress and decided not to use the ax. Instead, he sat her down at the edge of the open grave and fired one bullet into her right temple. Seconds after the shot rang out, Papadaki's body slid into the improvised tomb.[41]

Whether this version of Papadaki's demise is true, or just the killer playing up for the court's sympathy, is not certain, just as it is not completely clear which person or persons were in fact ultimately responsible for her death. It is plausible, however, that the individuals who caused her arrest were the EAM theater actors who had denounced her as a collaborator and expelled her from the actors' guild.

Over a month later, on 26 January, Papadaki's remains were uncovered along with four other victims in a series of shallow graves, not too far from the place of execution in the garden of a small villa. All her clothes were gone, except for a silk slip that was raised to her chest and a garter belt still fastened about her waist, suggesting sexual assault. According to the autopsy report, in addition to extensive trauma, large parts of her skin had been ripped off, before or after decapitation.[42] News of the discovery, as well as the dreadful condition of Papadaki's body, spread rapidly. Dozens of students from the School of Drama rushed to the gravesite and attempted to guard her modesty by covering what was left of Papadaki with branches from nearby cypress trees.[43]

They were not the only ones to visit these gravesites left by the KKE. North of Athens, in the suburb of Peristeraki, clusters of people hung about the edge of a mass burial site that stretched across an empty field etched along a rocky hillside. A desperate few strayed onto the field to pick through the decomposing human fragments in a valiant effort to identify fathers, mothers, brothers, sisters, husbands, wives, and children and at least spare them the indignity of a common grave. Approximately 1,500 victims of the KKE's pogrom were discovered there. The victims, according to witnesses, had been executed mostly with axes and knives. Some of the women and girls had been sexually violated and most had been mutilated. The bodies were dumped in trenches two hundred yards long, and, during the course of the exhumations, the coroners and their workers came across an extraordinarily grisly sight—a bucket filled with gouged out human eyes.[44]

Many of the dead were military and police officers, but the Peristeraki mass burial site also included a cross-section of Athenian society and members of the intelligentsia.[45] "If there ever was a scene straight from hell, this was it," wrote Kenneth Matthews, the BBC correspondent in Athens. "The bodies were being exhumed from a series of parallel trenches in which the diggers were still working. As each was uncovered, it was laid out on the lip of the trench, naked or half naked, just as it had been buried. Scattered in small groups on the hillside, the women folk of the victims kept up a low wailing which rose from time to time to a blood-chilling shriek of lamentation. Over all a charnel smell making the air sick, and the bright January sunlight, which picked out every detail in dreadful clarity."[46]

Evidence of further atrocities materialized when the British, joined by newly recruited Greek National Guard forces, drove ELAS away from the sections of Athens they had controlled. Each new discovery of executions and mass burial sites underscored the indiscriminate nature of the killings. Many of the KKE's victims were ordinary people who had, at one time or another, made disparaging comments about EAM, or a neighbor who had simply exploited the circumstances to settle a vendetta. In many such instances, the accused were apprehended late at night, dispatched with machine guns, and their bodies thrown down the nearest well. Hundreds of wells and cisterns had provided water to Athens and the surrounding districts for millennia, but after the construction of the Marathon Dam they had fallen in abeyance. In the course of the fighting, the wells became makeshift burial sites and a convenient place to leave corpses of murdered and executed Athenians.

One such victim was a twenty-seven-year-old gardener, Charilaos Karlis, who remarkably survived execution and entombment in a well. The knock on the door for Karlis came at 3:00 A.M. on 25 December 1944; when he answered, a group of men burst into his home, dragging him outside along with his two sisters and a brother. Out in the street, more people were being rounded up from the neighborhood. The ELAS detachment finally led thirty-five men and women first to the bank of the Ilisus River and from there to a partially built church in the area. The ELAS men found a small house beside the church and decided to use it for the interrogations. They forced the occupants, a family of four, to leave and proceeded to interrogate the prisoners. According to Karlis,

First, they took our clothes and after some perfunctory questioning they marched us in single file for about fifteen minutes to the edge of a large well. At that moment, they fired on us with automatic weapons. A few jumped into the well to avoid the gunfire, most, however were killed or wounded. My brother and I survived because we played dead. I had thick and long hair, which made my head appear larger, so that when an ELAS fired three shots in the direction of my head he missed and I was only grazed by one bullet. I continued to pretend I was dead. The executioners dragged the bodies to the edge of the well, stripped them and tossed them into the hole. When my turn came I could hear them saying "take off his shoes they are new and should not go to waste." I was thrown ten or twelve meters down into the well, my body and face hitting its sides but the corpses of those tossed earlier broke my fall. For a few minutes I kept being struck by the other bodies they were throwing into the well. Not all of them were dead and I could hear a few still moaning. When the ELAS men finished, they tossed stones, pieces of wood, empty cans and other trash in order to fill and cover the well. I was fortunate because I found a curved piece of metal that I held over my head to protect me. After two hours I managed to climb to the top and with considerable effort I moved one of the large stones that had covered the top of the well.[47]

The KKE leadership was appalled by Papadaki's death, but remained silent and made no apologies for the other killings and atrocities. A few days later, Orestes, the commandant of the Galati execution center, was arrested and incarcerated in Averof prison. It is not certain if he paid with his life for the atrocities he committed in the name of the KKE, and as late as 1948 he was still in prison.[48] A firing squad, however, dealt with some of his close associates not too far from the oil refinery, where he had arbitrarily and casually dispensed pain and death often for no other reason than to claim the clothes or jewelry of the accused. Nikos Zachariadis later denounced the execution of Papadaki, and in the decades following the civil war the KKE absolved itself of all responsibility for Papadaki's execution by continuing to blame the entire episode on Orestes.

Some of the senior communist leaders who had led the KKE during the December Uprising even tried to spin the outrageous tale that Orestes was an agent of the British secret service and he killed Papadaki at their behest in order to discredit the Greek communists. Others claimed that Orestes came from a good family with solid communist credentials and was the dupe of a manipulative mistress who drove him to commit excesses.[49] In a lucid letter to his aunt and uncle, Orestes gave no indication of remorse and, aware that he might be soon facing the firing squad, he wrote an upbeat letter. Maybe he believed, despite the reality of his situation, that ultimately he would be spared the death penalty at the last minute. The letter is revealing in that it also suggests that Orestes was not a crazed killer or that he had any regrets, but that he was simply a soldier doing his duty. He wrote: "I am incarcerated in Averof prison, because I have done my duty towards my country, humanity, and history."[50]

Orestes was not a victim of circumstance and not transformed into a pitiless and sadistic killer because of the exigencies of war, but was guided in his actions by KKE policy. The burden of guilt remains with the KKE. The communist party orchestrated the arrests and mass executions and thus created an environment that desensitized young men and women in its ranks and enabled them to commit atrocities. Phoibos Grigoriadis, an officer in ELAS and one of the early left-wing historians of the Greek civil war, however, admitted "that murders such as those of Papadaki could not be covered up under any circumstances."[51] Grigoriadis' bold admission of KKE responsibility for the atrocities also strongly suggests that killers such as Orestes were not acting on their own initiative or out of some sadistic impulse, but under the order of the KKE leadership. Perhaps not the entire leadership, however, some senior KKE commanders directed men like Orestes to instill fear in order to intimidate the population and are equally responsible for the reign of red terror that held sway when Athens was under communist control. In so doing they gave the fanatics on the right an excuse later to persecute and inflict death and torture against those on the left.

While the KKE condemned Orestes, it did not, however, disown Makaronis, the man who either tortured Papadaki to death or, moved by pity, simply shot her. He, along with all the executioners from the oil refinery, was arrested a few months after the end of the December Uprising and eventually condemned to death. Remarkably, following the cessation of the city's hostilities, they resumed their civilian vocations. One of these men, employed as a ticket collector, was wearing the sweater of one his victims and a relative of the victim identified the garment.

Makaronis was a humble grocer, typical of the thousands of loyal communist cadres who followed the KKE's directives to the letter and one of the functionaries who undertook the party's dirty work. In this respect, he was little different from some of the men who filled the ranks of the Security Battalions and practically identical with those who later tortured confessions and declarations of repentance out of suspected communists. Men like Makaronis, who had resented being at the beck and call of wealthy neighbors or prosperous farmers, or who harbored a grudge against civic officials, or had been awed by the expertise of professionals, suddenly were in a position to humble, humiliate, and destroy their betters.

Such individuals, for the first time in their lives, could exercise power by exploiting the chaotic conditions that prevailed in Athens, but others only did so at the behest of the KKE, which instituted a reign of terror against the wartime collaborators that quickly expanded into a general purge of all vestiges of the political, economic, educational, professional, and cultural establishment of Athens. Astonishingly, the KKE took the decision to implement such a radical and brutal course of action after the tide of battle had turned against ELAS. Part of the motive was revenge; the KKE was striving to punish collaborators and opponents while it still had the ability to do so. The executions also indicated the outline of a clumsy attempt at social and political engineering by trying to decapitate the old order through the elimination of its current and prospective leaders.

In addition, the KKE made a concerted effort to destroy all rival Marxist organizations, and during the course of the December Uprising, OPLA hit squads killed dozens of members of the rival Archive Marxists organization as well as followers of Trotsky. The Archive Marxists originally formed a secret group within the Socialist Labor Party, which later became the Greek Communist Party. In 1924, the KKE expelled the Archive Marxists, who, in turn, went on to establish their own political party. Their membership, during the interwar period, often surpassed that of the KKE.[52] The KKE murdered any Archive Marxists who were unlucky enough to be captured to settle old scores and eliminate their closest rival. Another consideration is that such vicious policies were born out of fear. By the third week of December, even the most optimistic Greek communist must have realized that it was no longer possible to overcome the British defenses in the center of Athens and it was only a matter of time before ELAS would concede defeat.

The high point of the ELAS advance against the British and Greek forces in Athens came on the night of 15–16 December 1944. After the collapse of any prospect for a diplomatic settlement with the British and the Papandreou government, ELAS prepared for an all-out offensive against the British positions in the center of Athens. The objective was to overwhelm the enemy by striking simultaneously against the British defenses from three different directions. Coordinated assaults are a difficult feat for well-trained and disciplined armies, but next to impossible for the haphazardly organized ELAS forces. When ELAS launched the attacks on the night of 15–16 December, the assaults were not synchronized and the British were able to defeat them piecemeal. During the course of the battle, British armored cars and tanks easily shifted from one sector to another, giving the hard-pressed infantry additional firepower at critical moments in the fighting.

ELAS troops, on the other hand, did manage to break through on the east flank of the British lines. In the late night of 13 December (two days ahead of the main ELAS offensive), about 1,000 ELAS troops stormed the area of the Infantry Barracks, which were the quarters of the British armored brigade and a few other units. The ELAS unit succeeded in penetrating very close to the barracks by using troops dressed in British and Greek police uniforms. By the time the defenders realized the ruse, ELAS had captured half the barracks, but instead of trying to capture the British artillery and mortars, they diverted their attention to burning and looting the supply dump as well as killing the civilian radio operators. In the morning the 2nd Battalion (King's Royal Rifle Corps), supported by armor, cleared the barracks, inflicting heavy losses on ELAS.

Once again, however, rumors of ELAS atrocities were further chipping away at the self-styled moral superiority that the left-wing forces had enjoyed from the beginning of the battle. This time a story was circulating among the soldiers of the 4th Division that the body of a noncommissioned officer of the Parachute Brigade attached to them was found in a horrible state. The man had his legs and arms cut off and then was buried alive. The paratroopers became outraged and, although they had taken over 120 ELAS prisoners in the previous engagement, after this alleged atrocity the number of prisoners captured fell off considerably. Despite the determination of ELAS to seize the barracks and the high casualties this engagement inflicted on both sides, the attack failed. As long as ELAS had engaged in hit-and-run, sniping, sabotage, and other irregular tactics, it could inflict significant losses against the British and perhaps bring about a political outcome to the December Uprising. Although ELAS enjoyed numerical superiority and was fighting on familiar ground, it could not successfully make the transition from guerrilla warfare to conventional battle.

The failure of the ELAS offensive spelled the end of any prospects for a military victory in Athens and hence the collapse of the left's effort to influence events in Greece. From this point, Scobie's forces grew stronger, with the increasing flow of reinforcements, while that of ELAS grew progressively weaker each passing day. Toward the third week of December, two British divisions as well as a brigade of the 4th Indian Division and several miscellaneous units arrived in Phaliron Bay and began the process of relieving the beleaguered British forces in Athens. A new officer, General John Hawkesworth, took operational control of all the British and Greek government units. Except for rushing to the rescue of a sector under immediate threat and slowly opening a link with the center of Athens, Hawkesworth's Corps did not launch an all-out offensive.

The storm of criticism in Britain as well as in the international community over British intervention in Greece had forced Churchill to attempt a compromise resolution of the crisis with EAM-ELAS. Churchill, joined by Foreign Secretary Anthony Eden, made the difficult journey to Athens on Christmas Day to preside over a conference that included representatives of the Papandreou government, the KKE, EAM, and ELAS. The meeting took place at the Greek Foreign Ministry on 26–27 December, in a bleak room with no heat and lit by hurricane lamps. All the while, sporadic gunfire accompanied the proceedings.

Unfortunately, none of the parties saw any reason to make serious concessions and reach an agreement to end the fighting. The British terms remained the same—ELAS had to disarm and evacuate Athens and the surrounding area. For their part, the KKE-EAM-ELAS delegates remained intransigent and, refusing to concede defeat, declined to accept the British terms. Furthermore, they insisted on a predominant role in any coalition Greek government. It may be that they did not appreciate the scale of British reinforcements, or that they were counting on international pressure, especially from the Americans and Soviets, to force Churchill to accept a compromise that left them with ELAS intact and in control of Athens.

The conservative politicians, especially the royalists and the ultra-right-wing cabals that had emerged during the uprising, were not in a hurry to see the British stop demolishing EAM-ELAS. When the conference began, some of them tried to walk out rather than sit with the "bandits," and were only prevented from doing so by the British. They were not to be disappointed. After two days of fruitless negotiations, the meeting broke down. The only point of agreement was the future appointment of Archbishop Demaskinos as regent, pending the outcome of a referendum on the future of the Greek monarchy. It fell on Churchill, after his return to London on

29 December, to convince a very reluctant George II to accept the Greek cleric as regent. It was not a pleasant task for Churchill who, according to Roy Jenkins, "had to spend half the night (with Eden) bludgeoning the stubborn Greek King into accepting a regency."[53] Eventually, Churchill had to tell George II that "if he did not agree the matter would be settled without him and that we would recognize the new Government instead of him."[54]

In the meantime, some of the communist political leadership chose to grapple with the inevitable consequences of military defeat by a means so terrible that afterward even the most stalwart defenders of EAM-ELAS were hard-pressed to find excuses. In a fit of shortsightedness, the KKE decided to take hostages in order to guarantee that the right would not seek retribution against members of the left. This fateful decision was made around the middle of December, in a secret meeting of senior communist leaders at the home of Mitsos Partsalidis, secretary of the EAM's central committee. Partsalidis' house was out of the way and set within a large garden, an ideal location for confidential discussions. Only a few of those present opposed this drastic action, and afterward orders were given to EAM-ELAS as well as the various organs of the KKE, such as OPLA and the National Civil Guard, to round up hostages. A quarter of a century later, Kaiti Zevgou, who had taken part in the decision, wrote in her memoirs: "Instead of sitting down and analyzing which people should be taken and under what conditions, some of our members, at times, simply set an artificial number and filled it. Many mistakes were made, which considerably damaged our reputation. We are still paying today for these consequences."

A little later, Zevgou had an opportunity to see the significant cost of her decision as well as that of her colleagues:

> One day I was on the road to the party headquarters at Chasia and shared a ride with Chrysa (a member of the KKE's Central Committee). I could see something in the distance moving like a snake on the ground. A few moments later we understood it was a column of hostages, which was coming from the direction we were going. Both Chrysa and I were shocked. We turned our heads the other way and remained silent. The spectacle was unsettling. A column of people exhausted and worn out by fatigue with despair on their faces, herded by armed guards on the other side of the column. I still remember that the head of the column was a very old man who was barely dragging his feet. As I said above, it was one of the mistakes of the movement.

The reaction (the Right) exploited such mistakes to cover up the orgy of terror that spilled out after December and continues, whenever it can, until today and will not allow the national schism to end.[55]

The voices of the victims, however, are rarely heard above the din of re-criminations and finger pointing over the atrocities of the December Upris-ing. Despina Makka-Photiadi was a proud woman devoted to her family, her friends, and her part of Athenian society. She came from a family of well-to-do professionals, who ensured she received an excellent liberal education and that she could speak German, English, French, and some Italian. In the great de-bate over monarchy, she remained for the rest of her life a committed Venizel-ist and opposed the return of the king. In 1940–1941, she was a volunteer nurse and during the occupation she labored in the soup kitchens of the Greek Red Cross.[56] Effectively, Makka-Photiadi's liberalism and antimonarchism did not set her too far apart from the general goals of EAM. Her daughter had been a member of the left-wing organization for one year. Her reward for surviving the famine and the exigencies of foreign occupation was to be taken as a hos-tage by the KKE. Toward the end of her life she decided to compile her expe-riences as an attempt to make sense of that terrible ordeal.[57]

Makka-Photiadi's poignant account begins with the joy of liberation, which was all too brief, and the outbreak of the December Uprising. From her home in Psychiko, a suburb of Athens (without radio, telephone, and limited travel to the city), she and her friends could only get snippets of news of events in Athens. In the first week of December, she noticed that some ac-quaintances who were members of EAM started acting strangely, and one of them warned her daughters to leave as soon as possible. After 20 December, Makka-Photiadi, to her horror, watched as the Communist National Civil Guard start rounding up men and a little later also women as hostages. Her turn came a few days later. A group of ELAS men came to her, and when she inquired what they wanted they replied, "You and your two daughters." One man then said, "You have five minutes to get ready, bring two blankets and if you have food ready bring it along."[58] From this point on, life, as Makka-Photiadi and her family understood it, vanished as she and her daughters became hostages at the mercy of the KKE.

> They organized us in a column of three across, the men were placed ahead of the women and we proceeded along Kiphisias Boulevard. The sky darkened and a light rain began to fall. As we headed towards the mountains a strong wind began to flail our faces but the guards

yelled at us to move faster. We passed the suburbs of Galatsi and Kypseli and only when we reached a small town in the late evening, they stopped and allowed us to rest on the sidewalks and on the ground. There we sat in the cold December night. Eventually, they led us to an abandoned community center where we spent the night.[59]

Makka-Photiadi and her daughters, along with dozens of other women whose names had been placed on a list of suspect reactionaries, were forced to walk for days. At first they left behind well-known suburbs northwest of Athens and then headed further north into unknown parts of the hinterland, past small villages in the mountains. In some places, the locals were kind and offered the hostages what little food or milk they could spare. As they moved from place to place the column grew longer. The guards had little sympathy for the hostages, and regardless of whether they were old, young, pregnant, handicapped, or sick, those who could not join the column were shot, stabbed, or on some occasions beaten to death.

A group of RAF prisoners, who fared little better under ELAS captivity, witnessed one of these wretched civilian columns: "Mostly old and elderly men, women and children, they were all scantily clad and most without shoes. Some were leaving bloody footprints in the snow. Like drunken cowboys urging on a herd of cattle, their guards repeatedly fired shots over their heads. When an old man collapsed, moaning, "He was shot and thrown into a ditch." Nicoloidis Fortis, an architect at the Athens town hall and one of the hostages, remembers: "We were compelled to march thirty miles a day. Children were taken from their mothers because they were unable to keep up." He saw two women murdered, the first because she had hidden thirty gold sovereigns in her clothing and the second because she failed to make that known to the guards.[60]

For Makka-Photiadi and her daughters, the ordeal came to an end in the first week of January after both sides began negotiating a truce, but for some of the others the agony went on until the end of the month. After the collapse of the talks on 26–27 December, General Hawkesworth launched a major offensive on 3 January 1945 that drove ELAS from Athens in just two weeks. On 11 January 1945, delegates from ELAS met with General Scobie and asked for an armistice. ELAS agreed to evacuate Athens and Boiotia as well as fall back twenty-five miles from Thessalonica. Although Scobie and Hawkesworth preferred to push their offensive until ELAS was completely destroyed, political considerations and events beyond their control spared the left the humiliation of total defeat.

FIG. 7. Arms surrendered by ELAS following the Varkiza Agreement, 12 February 1945. Greek Ministry of Foreign Affairs: Photo Exhibition of the Diplomatic and Historical Archive Department.

Meanwhile, the German Ardennes offensive had threatened to break through the allied lines and, even though it failed, the British needed to reinforce their armies on the northwestern European front. They could not afford the public relations nightmare of continuing to fight EAM-ELAS, which, for most of the world, represented the Greek resistance. After protracted negotiations the British, the Greek government, and the KKE-EAM-ELAS formally ended the Battle of Athens with the conclusion of the Varkiza Agreement on

12 February 1945. The agreement ultimately achieved little in the long run, except to end the fighting in Athens. Both sides could claim victory—the British and the Greek government because they actually won the battle, and the KKE-EAM-ELAS because they did not lose the war, but merely one campaign.

The December Uprising left Athens in shambles with thousands of people homeless and a large number of its citizens permanently scarred and its population bitterly divided. Despina Makka-Photiadi begins her unpublished memoir by lamenting: "As long as I live (she passed away in 1990) I will never forget December of 1944. I, along with thousands of other Greeks who suffered a great deal, believe that Greece should not forget that cursed month, which unleashed a great storm that was brewing for years."[61]

During the thirty-three days of fighting, the once proud neighborhoods of Kolonaki, which had been synonymous with upper-class privilege, were squeezed from all quarters by the fighting and reduced to a beleaguered enclave. The ELAS attacks against the fashionable districts also symbolized the assault of the left against the political hegemony of the traditional political and economic establishment.

In 1944, however, the authority of this elite was in tatters. The ravages of the occupation along with the chaos of liberation and civil war had humbled and distorted the once affluent and influential Athenian families. The powerful groups and individuals who had reigned over Greece before the war, and whose imprint was stamped on all aspects of Greek political (whether republican or royalist), economic, and cultural life, had been decimated by the occupation and rendered almost irrelevant by the resistance. During the crisis, the village peasants and the humble folk of the working-class districts fighting with ELAS were ever so briefly the masters of Greece and Athens. Astonishingly, for the first time in the Greek political dynamic, the village ruled the city.

The survivors of the middle and upper classes clung to whatever represented the old political authority, whether this meant following the monarchy, the government, the British, or even the ultra-right-wing paramilitary bands that had sprouted just prior to liberation. Still others sought another alternative by trying to leave the country. However, there were few places in the world that were accessible, except for the very wealthy. Just about all of the Greek shipping magnates, for example, had escaped to London and New York—they were first on the death lists of the KKE, perhaps even ahead of the collaborators.

Young women discovered that marriage to foreigners offered one of the few practical avenues of escaping from the prospect of a grim economic future in war-torn Greece. To these women, British officers and even ordinary soldiers were their passport to a fresh start, especially since many wrongly assumed that any man from the United Kingdom was wealthy and a member of the British aristocracy. Later, in the case of Americans, the equally mistaken notion was that they were all fabulously rich. After liberation, during and after the December Uprising, just about every social occasion in Athens included its share of what Michael Ward, one of the few SOE officers in Athens at the time, described as "Kolonaki girls, almost all known to each other and encountered repeatedly at party after party . . . gyrating on the floor with their British boyfriends. There was something exotic about going out with a foreigner and escaping in the mildest way the strict control exercised by many middle class parents, and to be frank, there was the chance of marriage to an Englezaki (Englishman)."[62]

At first dozens, then hundreds of these young, mostly middle-class women managed to walk down the aisle with their trophy Englishman and later were transported to Britain to begin their new lives. Dodis also recalls that language was not a barrier:

> In the spring after the Dekemvriana I went to work (after school) at a British Officers' Mess as an interpreter. By then I was sixteen years old. Few people knew English then in Greece. At the canteen my main occupation turned out to be interpreting for couples who were planning to get married. The Greek girls didn't know any English and, of course, the British soldiers didn't know a word of Greek. Yet, they were intending to get married. The girls wanted to know where the men lived and how well off they were. The British soldiers presented a rosy picture. In other words, they told them a bunch of lies and that is why most of the girls returned within a year or two. As it was natural the girls were hoping for a better life in England. The only girl I know who didn't return to Greece was my husband's sister. She braved it in Flixton, outside Manchester, in quite poor conditions until her family was able to send her financial help. She stayed married and still is with Frank.[63]

According to Ward, who also acquired a Greek bride, most of these unions did not survive more than "a year or two and the majority of these women decamped back to Greece."[64]

Individually and collectively, the Greek war brides were symptomatic of the social distortions that buffeted Greek society in the postwar period. They may be viewed as a metaphor for the relationship between the British and the Greek right—destined for disappointment. Eventually, and to some extent because of the December Uprising, the conservative element of Greek society, including that of Athens, was reconstituted and reinvigorated after 1945 as the "new right." By the end of 1944, the old monarchist–Venizelist schism had mutated beyond recognition and its adherents melted into the forces of either the left or the right.

Prior to the occupation, the Venizelist-republican and royalist factions had monopolized the Greek political scene. Although Greek liberalism and antimonarchism had become synonymous with the Venizelists, it did not necessarily mean that all the members of the Venizelos faction subscribed to liberal convictions and loathed the monarchy or that every royalist rejected liberal ideas. Rather, personal rivalry and competition for power often blurred their ideological differences and, on occasion, they easily shifted from one group to the other. The parties and factions of the left, in contrast, were small and marginal in prewar Greek society. During the period of the resistance, however, the roles were reversed and the influence of the left overshadowed that of the traditional political parties.

At the same time, membership in the left or right did not necessarily emanate from defined constituencies of liberals, socialists, communists, royalists, or conservatives. In this context, it is difficult to determine the ideological proclivities of those who joined EAM as well as those who fought for ELAS. Yet, it is evident from the extant sources that many who followed EAM-ELAS did so out of patriotic and nationalist motives. The same can be said for those who supported the other resistance organizations. For example, ELAS and EDES included a large number of professional and monarchist officers, while approximately another thousand, many of them republicans, joined the notorious Security Battalions. After liberation, thousands of resistance fighters, regardless of their ideological proclivities, were labeled leftists simply because they had fought with ELAS or participated in EAM. Ironically, this stigma included the professional officers in ELAS, most of whom had been loyal to the crown, just as thousands of republicans decided that the monarchy was the best guarantee against communism and went over to the royalist camp. Hence, the fear of communism and professional opportunism converged in the emergence of the new right and contributed to the establishment of the anti-communist Greek state.

The breakdown of most marriages between British servicemen and Greek wives was also indicative of the changing nature of Greece's foreign policy. For over a century, Greece had relied upon Great Britain as its primary external patron. Great Britain's triumph in World War II had come at the cost of its position as a preeminent global power. As the war came to an end, Britain's commitment to Greece steadily decreased, and was eventually replaced by that of America. U.S. support, however, came with a significant price. American largess saved Greece from collapse, but U.S. political patronage extended to the right—more specifically to the very conservative right—and propped up a conservative and, in the words of Talleyrand commenting on the Bourbons after the fall of Napoleon, "They learned nothing and forgot nothing." The chasm in Greek society that had been exacerbated by the Axis occupation and the first and second rounds of the Greek civil war solidified and, aggravated by the atrocities inflicted, was, perhaps, beyond hope of reconciliation.

Furthermore, the unwillingness of the British, because of political considerations, to inflict total destruction on ELAS meant that the left could count on a large number of men and women, brutalized by the White Terror, to join ranks of the Democratic Army and inflict the third round on the devastated country. Arguably a large number of ELAS and EAM followers accepted defeat and attempted to reintegrate in society, but a great many could not avoid persecution by their political opponents. The failure of the succession of governments in the aftermath of the December Uprising to effect even a modicum of compromise between the adherents of the left and right, and their inability to control the lawlessness of the right-wing gangs roaming the countryside, practically guaranteed another confrontation. The next, and final, round of the civil war (1946–1949) was the most destructive and left deeper wounds and divisions in Greek society that continue to linger into the twenty-first century.

CHAPTER 6

Balkan Machinations

KKE, CPY, AND THE MACEDONIAN CONUNDRUM

The Greeks have acted foolishly.

—Joseph Stalin

In the early hours of Friday 14 February 1992 a cold wind swept through the streets of Thessaloniki. Although a working day, schools, universities, government offices, and most private businesses were closed. At first hundreds, then thousands, then hundreds of thousands of Greek citizens converged onto the main square of Greece's second largest city. Soon the protesters flooded Thessaloniki's vast Plataea Dikastirion as the human tidal wave clogged the streets, avenues, and boulevards that led to the square.[1] This tremendous sea of humanity thundered over and over again, "Macedonia is Greece."

Dignitaries included the mayor, bishop, and politicians from Athens who stood at the newly built stand and with impassioned speeches tried to raise the emotions of the crowd. The speeches struck chords of shared historical memories and fears. The chants of "Macedonia is Greece" reached an ear-piercing crescendo, echoing accelerated by Thessaloniki's concrete buildings. Some bystanders feared that the authorities would lose control of the demonstration. Frenzied human waves almost cascaded over one another and pressed against the uneven lines of those in front. Remarkably, there were neither fatalities nor serious injuries, and after several hours of cheers, chants, and speeches the demonstration came to a peaceful end with the crowds slowly dissipating from the square and adjoining streets.

Rarely (if ever) in European history have so many people assembled to scream their lungs out over the name of a country. The crisis unfolded after the former Socialist Republic of Macedonia declared its independence in 1991 from Tito's rapidly disintegrating Federal Yugoslavia and immediately assumed the name "Republic of Macedonia" for its new sovereign state. Reactions in Greece were immediate and consisted of a mélange of indignation, anger, and fear. The event caught the attention of the world media, which attempted to explain why the Greeks had become unhinged over the use of the name "Macedonia" by one of Yugoslavia's breakaway republics. At the same time, newspaper, television, and radio reports tried to fathom why the contagion of nationalism had also spread to Greek communities in Europe, Australia, and North America. Demonstrations were televised worldwide showing thousands of protesters carrying flags of Greece and placards demanding that the new Yugoslav republic cease using Macedonia as its name.

What caused these powerful emotions that moved hundreds of thousands of Greeks to protest worldwide? The fact that Bulgaria and Turkey, Greece's traditional rivals and enemies, recognized the new republic on 15 January and 5 February 1992, respectively, fed the frenzy of the masses as they imagined a new enemy bordering Greece's northern frontier with the intention of incorporating the Greek region of Macedonia. Greek indignation and fear spoke to memories of war, famine, and slaughter, tragic events shrouded in history and legend. The dramatic changes that ushered the death knell of the Yugoslav federation raised the specter of a grim war spilling over its boundaries into northern Greece. The images in the media of mass killing, torture, rape, and systematic destruction sweeping some of the former Yugoslav republics were proof that the past ethnic enmities and territorial ambitions had returned.

For many it was also the long shadow of the civil war that mixed fears of the past with memories of the events of the 1940s. Because so much of the civil war was fought in northern Greece, the memories of the conflict were fresher. Macedonia had been the primary battlefield with respect to the fighting, but also the prize that the KKE was willing to offer first to the Yugoslavs and in 1949 to the Bulgarians. For many people in northern Greece the competition for Macedonia had been the catalyst for violence and wars in the Balkans since the nineteenth century. An irrational segment, egged on by ambitious politicians, suggested that conflict was going to resume and that Macedonia would degenerate into a battlefield.[2] The key to why the independence of a former Yugoslav republic with the assumed name of Macedonia should have caused such an emotional upheaval in Greece can be found by understanding how the history of Macedonia is intertwined with the Greek civil war of 1946–1949.

The struggle for Ottoman Macedonia had dominated the strategies and politics of the newly established Balkan states in the later part of the 1800s. Indeed, nineteenth-century Ottoman Macedonia offered a buffet of ethnic and religious minorities—many of Macedonia's residents were Greek, Slav, or Muslim, with smaller communities of Vlachs and Roma, and a significant number of Thessaloniki's residents included Sephardic Jews. In effect, this diverse population was a microcosm of Balkan societies and minorities. The new Balkan states were anxious to claim their coreligionists still living in Ottoman territory. Accordingly, Greece, Serbia, Bulgaria, and to a lesser extent Romania concentrated their energies and limited resources on territorial expansion. Each of these countries found historical, linguistic, or ethnic grounds with which to claim the territory and inhabitants of Ottoman Macedonia. To the Greeks, history was the handmaiden of irredentism and they could boast that the region was a part of their heritage and culture from ancient times. Indeed, this was the case not just in Ottoman Macedonia. Almost from the inception of the Greek nation in 1830, ambitious politicians and dreamers called for the expansion of the new state to incorporate the territories of the Byzantine Empire. In the imagination of the nineteenth-century Greeks it meant Macedonia, the Aegean and its islands, Crete, and Asia Minor.

The Bulgarians argued that they and the inhabitants of Macedonia shared kinship of ethnicity and language. The Serbs had the weakest case and could only make vague references to Serbia's medieval empire, which for a short time included the territory of Ottoman Macedonia. Complicating matters even more was the inability of the decaying Ottoman Empire to stem the violence occasionally plaguing the unfortunate region at the end of the nineteenth century.[3] Hostilities, of course, were instigated by the competing Balkan powers, whose agents and armed bands waged an unrelenting struggle for control of Macedonia's population, either through fear or with the promise of a better future.

The origin of the "Macedonian Question," which later bedeviled the policies of the Greek communists in the twentieth century, was rooted in the diplomatic arrangements that settled the Great Eastern Crisis of 1876–1878. The crisis was the result of the victories of the armies of Tsar Alexander II over the Ottomans and had threatened to destroy the Turkish Empire, thus creating a power vacuum that favored Russian ambitions in the Balkans and Near East. To contain Russian expansion, Britain, France, and Germany assembled the Congress of Berlin and by aligning against Russia succeeded in preserving the Ottoman Empire with only some loss of its territory in the Balkans.

Macedonia's potential to explode had been exacerbated even further by the creation of an autonomous Bulgaria. The decision of the Great Powers to revise the Treaty of San Stefano (3 March 1878) at the Congress of Berlin (which under Russian pressure had created a large Bulgaria), into two autonomous "mini-states" under nominal Ottoman tutelage, caused much bitterness among Bulgarian nationalists. The Great Powers' decision to exclude Macedonia from the new state had convinced Bulgarian irredentist circles in Sofia to work toward overturning the provisions of the treaty and fulfilling their dream of a "Greater Bulgaria that included Macedonia." Predictably, it was not long before Bulgaria's aggressive designs on Macedonia came into conflict with Greek and Serbian aspirations and laid the foundations for a protracted and violent competition.[4]

The Congress of Berlin, the subsequent Treaty of Berlin (13 June–13 July 1878), and the Treaty of Constantinople (1881) altered the geopolitical dynamics of the Balkans. The Treaty of Constantinople awarded Greece the regions of Thessaly and southern Epirus at the expense of the Ottoman Empire. The acquisition of the new territories brought the Greek frontier alongside that of Ottoman Macedonia. This redistribution of Ottoman territory stipulated by the treaties transferred to Greece and Serbia areas that bordered on the three Ottoman *vilayets* (provinces) that constituted Ottoman Macedonia. This development practically ensured that Macedonia was the next cause célèbre for the nationalists in both countries and, a little later, in Bulgaria. For the next four decades, attempts to acquire the region for their respective states became the primary focus of the Balkan states.

The first phase of the struggle, from the late 1870s to the mid-1890s, was relatively mild, at least when compared to what would follow. The majority of Macedonia's population defined identity on the basis of religious affiliation rather than ethnicity. Greece and Serbia focused their endeavors on winning the "hearts and minds" of the locals through a vigorous campaign of nationalist and secular propaganda. Both countries officially were Eastern Orthodox, so appealing to religious sentiment under these circumstances offered little advantage. Ethnicity, language, and history underscored the propaganda efforts of these Balkan states. Bulgaria, in contrast, separated from the Ecumenical Patriarchate unilaterally and on 23 May 1872 established the Bulgarian Exarchate as a national church. Subsequently, the Bulgarians used religion in combination with nationalism to win over the Christians of Ottoman Macedonia.[5]

By 1895, hundreds of Greek, Serbian, and Bulgarian schools, funded by associations such as the Greek Association of Hellenic Letters, the National

Society, the Serbian Society of Saint Sava, and the Bulgarian National Committee, sprouted throughout Macedonia. These organizations and schools aggressively competed with one another in an effort to convert their pupils to the respective national causes of the three countries.[6] Considerable propaganda material was also disseminated from the consulates, which the three governments had established in Ottoman Macedonia's major cities in the 1880s.[7]

The Macedonian struggle underwent a dramatic shift in 1893, when a group of young intellectuals established the Internal Macedonian Revolutionary Organization (IMRO) in Thessaloniki. The organization's leadership rejected the Greek, Serb, and Bulgarian identities and countered them with a vision of an autonomous Macedonia within the Ottoman Empire.[8] To fulfill this goal, IMRO dedicated itself to creating conditions that would compel the Ottoman government to enact the provisions of Article 23 of the Treaty of Berlin, which obliged the Ottoman government to implement a series of internal reforms in its European provinces.

Violence and terrorism constituted the core of IMRO's tactics. The leaders of the movement assumed that the Ottoman government (often referred to as the Sublime Porte[9]) would implement Article 23 only if pressured to do so by the Great Powers. In order to attract the attention of the Europeans to Macedonia and persuade them to intervene with the Sublime Porte, the IMRO intended to unleash a campaign of revolutionary terror. IMRO planned an urban terrorist activity combined with a mass, peasant-based, uprising in the countryside. This strategy, the leaders of IMRO believed, would reduce Macedonia to a state of political and economic chaos, rendering the region unsafe for foreign investment and provoking Ottoman reprisals against the local population. In turn, they hoped that these developments would thrust Macedonia to the forefront of the European powers' agenda and force the Ottomans to grant the region the autonomy demanded by the revolutionaries.[10]

In 1903, IMRO launched the long-awaited insurrection.[11] The Illinden Uprising, named for Saint Elijah, on the night of 2 August of the same year prompted the Ottoman government eventually to deploy 175,000 soldiers to Ottoman Macedonia in an effort to crush the rebellion.[12] The course of the uprising exposed IMRO's limits. So long as the bands restricted their activities to cutting communications, fighting small-scale engagements against isolated Ottoman units, or burning Muslim settlements and massacring their populations, they were able to hold their own, or at least survive to fight another day. As soon as they challenged the Ottoman forces to conventional combat, however, as was the case at Krushevo (12 August), the result was catastrophic defeat.[13] Without external support from a nearby state, IMRO guerrillas could not stand up to even poorly trained, but numerically superior Ottoman forces. The Greek communist insurgents would fare little better in the Greek civil war whenever they abandoned guerrilla tactics and tried to hold a town or fight a conventional battle.

By late October 1903, the Ottomans brutally suppressed the uprising, and IMRO suffered extensive losses.[14] Yet the revolt had at least fulfilled the purpose of attracting the Great Powers to the issue of Macedonia. Consequently, the Ottoman government agreed to the implementation of reforms specified in the Muerzsteg Agreement concluded between Austria-Hungary and Russia on 30 September. The most novel feature of the reforms was the stipulation for the reorganization of the Ottoman gendarmerie under the guidance of foreign military and police personnel.[15]

This provision for what can be loosely defined as the first "peacekeeping" operation in history, however, did not substantially contribute to the restoration of order in Macedonia. On the contrary, the weakening of IMRO escalated guerrilla warfare in the region that had been instigated by the competing Balkan states. Beginning in early 1904, Greek, Serb, Bulgarian, and even Romanian bands poured into Macedonia in order to take advantage of IMRO's decline. By 1907, as many as 110 Bulgarian, 80 Greek, 30 Serbian, and 8 Romanian bands may have been operating in the region, fighting each other and the Ottomans in an effort to uphold their countries' claims to the area.[16] Regardless of the exertions of the bands and the reform efforts of the Great Powers and the Ottomans, the Macedonian problem did not find complete resolution until the early twentieth century as a result of the two Balkan Wars of 1912–1913.[17] In these wars Greece and Serbia acquired most of Ottoman Macedonia, with the Greeks securing 51 percent of the territory. The Balkan and Ottoman armies and the irregular bands that accompanied them committed atrocities that shocked the West and made the word "Balkans" in the eyes of Europeans synonymous with barbarism and ethnic hatred.[18]

Not just Greeks inhabited Greece's new province, despite government propaganda. The new territorial acquisition also now included large numbers of Muslims, Sephardic Jews, Slavs, and Vlachs. The government in Athens made a determined effort to Hellenize the minorities, but only when an influx of over 600,000 Greek Orthodox refugees—victims of the population exchange between Greece and Turkey—were resettled in the new province did the Orthodox Greeks represent 88 percent of Macedonia's population. The refugees were the by-product of Greece's unsuccessful attempt to annex Asia Minor in Turkey (1919–1922) and the victims of brutal Turkish revenge. They brought with them memories of mass killings, death marches, and mass rape and they passed on the memory of these atrocities to their descendants. Equally significant, many filled the ranks of the Greek Communist Party and its leadership. In the 1920s and 1930s, the communists achieved modest electoral victories at the polls, in part, thanks to the votes of the Asia Minor Greeks. Ultimately, war and occupation in the 1940s propelled the communists to a dominant position in Greece and set in motion the events that led to civil war.

The Axis invasion and occupation of Greece also added a new chapter to the Macedonian history of violence and destruction. The Bulgarian army attacked Greece on 20 April 1941 without declaring war. As a member of the Axis, Bulgaria was awarded Eastern Macedonia and Western Thrace by Germany. Almost immediately, a regional genocide by the Bulgarians exterminated over 15,000 Greeks and expelled another 100,000.[19] Bulgarian policy dictated either conversion to Bulgarian identity or, for those who refused, execution, torture, death by famine, or for the lucky few, expulsion. Many local Slavs were quick to shed their Greek citizenship and instantly transform into Bulgarians. Because they identified as Macedonians, they subsequently tainted Slavophones in Greece as collaborators and foreigners.

During the course of the occupation, northern Greece underwent yet another twist as the Yugoslav communists took advantage of their superior numbers and organization to force their Greek communist counterparts to serve the interests of a greater postwar Yugoslavia. This action underscored the notion in Greek society that Slavophones were dangerous aliens. As a harassed minority, some Slavophones looked to the KKE for protection because the Greek communists had recognized Macedonian self-determination in the 1920s. The Greek communists, however, were not the only alternative for Slavophones in Greek Macedonia. Many looked to the north and Tito's partisans for support and even assistance to create an independent Macedonia. The Macedonian issue, as a result, played a critical role in the relationship between the Greek and Yugoslav communists.

The Comintern in the 1920s forced the Greek communists to accept autonomy of Macedonia within a Balkan Federation operating under the principles of self-determination. This would weaken Yugoslavia and Greece while strengthening the position of the Bulgarian communists, since they could claim to be finally realizing the territories awarded to Bulgaria under the Treaty of San Stefano—albeit in a modified form. This decision undermined the KKE's efforts in attracting Greeks to their communist cause and alienating many of their supporters among the Asia Minor residents of Macedonia. The impact of the KKE's decision to accept Macedonian autonomy resonated during the occupation and the civil war and continues to reverberate in the twenty-first century. The fixation of the Former Yugoslav Republic of Macedonia (FYROM) on Macedonian identity, and the paraphernalia of an imagined link with Alexander the Great as well as allusions that the Greek province belongs to the former Yugoslav republic, are relics of Balkan mythology and the Greek civil war. For the residents of northern Greece, the references to Macedonia by the government in Skopje conjure memories of death and destruction—memories that have been passed on from one generation to another. The establishment of FYROM in 1992 resurrected the Macedonian issue and remains a thorn in the side of Greece's foreign relations with the new Balkan republic. To some extent, the Macedonian issue, with all its manifestations, is a metaphor for the failure of the KKE to understand Greek nationalism.

The Yugoslav and Greek communist parties rose to political significance in the first half of the twentieth century, and both achieved prominence by their success in establishing effective resistance organizations during the Axis occupation. Surprisingly, and despite the proximity of their respective countries, the Greek and Yugoslav communists only made contact in 1943. This was because the CPY and the KKE, as was the case of all communist parties, were at the mercy of the divide-and-rule policies of the Comintern— effectively the arm of the Communist Party of the Soviet Union (CPSU). In theory the Comintern was supposed to encourage, along with international revolution, solidarity among the world's communist parties, but Stalin's paranoia and ambition precluded any such effort.[20] In practice the Comintern became the mechanism by which Stalin could advance his international agenda, with the interests of local communist parties subordinated to those of his CPSU.

The Macedonian issue exemplified the Comintern's interference in the affairs of communist parties for the benefit of the USSR. The Soviets, in an effort to secure the loyalty of the powerful Bulgarian Communist Party (BCP), had the Comintern rule in favor of the establishment of a Macedonian and a Thracian state and compelled the KKE and CPY to adopt this policy, which the KKE did in 1924.[21] This was a public relations nightmare for the Yugoslav and Greek communists, but it proved especially damaging for the KKE, which, unlike the CPY at the time, was a legal political party and had to account for its pro-Soviet policies in a public forum. In the intensely nationalist atmosphere within Greece in the 1920s, the KKE's political position on the Macedonian issue caused a sharp downturn in the party's electoral prospects and popular support, which reached a nadir of 1.41 percent in the 1928 general election.[22] This was the price that Greek communists paid to belong to the international communist brotherhood. It would prove to be a millstone around the neck of every Greek communist and deny the party mass support.

The Comintern imposed its policies on other communist parties by managing their internal affairs. By the 1930s the Comintern was able to remove the leaders of other communist parties at its own discretion, particularly in the weaker Eastern European communist organizations. It was the Comintern that appointed Nikolaos Zachariadis secretary general of the KKE in 1931 because the Greek communist leader had demonstrated his loyalty to Stalinist principles.[23] Tito was placed in charge of the CPY in 1937 after the previous secretary general of the party, Milan Gorkić, fell victim to the Great Purges and was executed.[24] The Great Purges within the USSR forced communist parties to remain insular and discouraged relations between them, lest they be associated with individuals whom Stalin considered disloyal to him and the USSR. Furthermore, the CPY and KKE's fluctuating membership, and frequent purging of leadership, provided an additional barrier that inhibited close ties between the two communist parties.[25]

World War II proved to be the catalyst for the two organizations to establish a closer relationship. Two years after the Axis invasion of Greece and Yugoslavia, the KKE and CPY found common ground through the exigencies of occupation and resistance. Both organizations, in the early years of the Axis occupation, were more concerned with survival than with making contact with foreign resistance groups.[26] Another consideration was that while the CPY had managed to maintain contact with the Comintern during the war through the Comintern's regional transmitter in Zagreb, the KKE lacked such equipment or access via a third party. Subsequently, the KKE leadership was not able to contact any part of the communist world, including the CPY.[27] Although the exact date when the KKE lost contact is unavailable, most likely it was sometime in the spring of 1941.[28]

At the beginning of the occupation, however, the CPY was not a unified organization and its regional committees remained relatively independent.

Under these circumstances, the regional committee of the Yugoslav Communist Party of Macedonia did not receive directives from the CPY central committee until 1943. As a result, in 1941 the regional committee of Yugoslav Macedonia, under the leadership of Metodi Shatarov (1941–1943), had detached itself from the CPY and was taking its orders from the Communist Party of Bulgaria (CPB).[29]

Unlike the CPY, the Bulgarian communists did not organize an active resistance against the Axis. Two considerations guided the policy of the regional committee of Yugoslav Macedonia: the first and the official reason, stated by Tito in a 4 September 1941 dispatch to the Comintern, was that Shatarov had "adopted a position in favour of a Soviet Macedonia and of awaiting the coming of the Red Army."[30] To ensure that Macedonia resisted passively, Shatarov "refused to distribute the proclamation of the CPY Central Committee calling for military actions [and] issued a directive that all arms should be surrendered to the authorities."[31] The other reason, proposed by Tito in 1948 at the Fifth Party Congress of the Communist Party of Yugoslavia, was that leaders of the regional committee for Macedonia had "sabotaged the uprising in Macedonia, for, in their opinion, Macedonia was not occupied but liberated by the troops of Tsar Boris while the German troops played a 'positive role' because they helped 'liberate' Macedonia."[32]

Until the CPY was able to reassert control over Yugoslav Macedonia and weaken the authority of the occupation forces by active resistance, contact between the Greek and Yugoslav communists remained difficult. Greek and Yugoslav Macedonia was the nearest point of contact between the two communist organizations. After the Germans successfully eliminated the short-lived CPY-run Republic of Užice, based in western Serbia (November–December 1941), the central committee of the CPY was forced to flee to eastern Bosnia. This turn of events increased the distance between the central committee of the CPY and Vardar Macedonia and made it difficult for the CPY to assert its control over the communist Yugoslav Macedonians. In a 26 February 1942 telegram the executive committee of the Communist Party of Bulgaria, as part of their argument for increased influence in Vardar Macedonia, noted, "for about three months the Macedonian comrades have had no ties with the CPY."[33]

This was an unacceptable state of affairs for the CPY. As a result, the central committee of the CPY decided that in order to reassert its authority over the Vardar Macedonian communists, it had to dispatch a special envoy to represent the interests of the Yugoslav communists in the region. Tito chose Dobrivoje Radosavljević who, because of the difficulties in mobility imposed by the occupation forces, did not arrive in Vardar Macedonia until six months later.[34] As the special representative of the central committee, Radosavljević laid the foundation for much of Yugoslavia's later success in dealing with the Macedonian issue.[35] The CPY had begun its struggle to regain control over the Yugoslav Macedonians, which provided the motivation for contacting the KKE.

Svetozar Vukmanović-Tempo's arrival in Macedonia accelerated Radosavljević's previous efforts to bring the Vardar Macedonian communists into alignment with the CPY. He arrived in Skopje in February 1943 with two immediate duties: developing the partisan resistance and asserting CPY's control over the Macedonian party.[36] For the CPY, these tasks were interrelated. Tito explained the CPY's goals in a 16 January 1943 letter to Radosavljević, the substance of which would have been familiar to Vukmanović: "With the correct stand in the national question . . . with organization and participation in this [National Liberation War] . . . our Party can raise all of the Yugoslav peoples to an armed uprising . . . preparing the conditions for the solution to other problems."[37] Vukmanović's description of his mission parrots this formal letter. As Tito's representative he stated that his mission was "to implement, together with Macedonian communists, the CPY line in the conditions of war and the occupation of the country."[38]

In effect, Vukmanović planned to initiate an armed uprising that would provide the foundation to solve the Macedonian issue in favor of Yugoslavia. One of the means by which Vukmanović sought to ensure control over the Vardar communist Macedonians was by upgrading the regional committee to the newly named Communist Party of Macedonia that would operate within the framework of a communist Yugoslavia. He and Tito believed that such a measure would appeal to Vardar Macedonian nationalists, although it had the potential to backfire, a possibility that haunted Vukmanović. His fears were confirmed in June 1943 when the central committee of the Communist Party of Macedonia issued a document stating that its goal was "the unity of all Macedonians, without regard to whether they were earlier 'Burgophiles,' 'Serbomans,' or 'Grecomans.' "[39] Vukmanović, realizing that such a statement would undermine Yugoslav control over the region, quickly corrected this "tremendous political mistake," and by 2 August 1943 the Macedonian Communist Party central committee released a new document that emphasized the role of the Yugoslavs in the struggle for Macedonian independence.[40] It was while Vukmanović was attempting to stabilize the Vardar Macedonia

Communist Party in the face of overwhelming nationalist sentiments that contact and negotiations between the KKE and CPY were established. Unfortunately for the KKE, when the CPY and KKE finally made contact, Tito's primary objectives were to extend his control over Vardar Macedonia and keep his options open with respect to acquiring Greek and Bulgarian Macedonias. Toward these ends, the Yugoslav communist leader adjusted his policy and was ready to seize any opportunity to secure a greater postwar federation.

For its part, the KKE could only negotiate with Tito from a position of weakness. The KKE, even before the war, had been devastated under Metaxas. The regime had left the Greek communists in tatters and racked with suspicion over who collaborated with the Metaxas authorities. As a result, KKE prospects at the beginning of the war were not great. The KKE's situation improved after the Axis occupation of Greece and particularly with the German invasion of the USSR in 1941. The German attack against the Soviets transformed the war into a struggle between Nazism and communism, thus enabling all Greek communists to take up the struggle against the Axis with the blessing of Moscow.

The KKE had succeeded in leading a large resistance movement by setting up EAM-ELAS, a political and armed resistance, respectively, and had managed to convince most people that these were separate from the Greek Communist Party. Although the KKE emerged from the sidelines as a substantial organization during the occupation, it was at a disadvantage in its relations with the Yugoslav communists because of its prewar commitment to the future disposition of Greek Macedonia. The KKE recognized this weakness and adopted the only possible tactic—to avoid discussing the Macedonian issue for as long as possible. When forced to take a position in 1943, likely as a result of Bulgarian and Yugoslav pressure, the KKE pleaded ignorance and tried to hide behind meek denials that an actual issue existed in the first place.[41]

The KKE's policy of evasion over Macedonia continued into 1944, when Zevgos again noted, "The minorities which live in other countries will acquire full national, economic, social and political equality of rights [after the war]."[42] But it was an issue that the Yugoslavs would not concede, regardless of the cost to their Greek communist allies. Fundamentally, CPY pressure on the future of Greek Macedonia and KKE efforts to avoid dealing with it characterized the relationship between the Greek and Yugoslav communist organizations during the occupation and throughout the course of the Greek civil war.

The desire of both communist parties to cooperate and establish direct contact was genuine, but with different motives. The minuet of the Yugoslavs and the Greek communists over Macedonian independence, nevertheless, went on during the occupation and until the final year of the civil war. It took many forms, and in June 1943 the pretext was the organization of a joint Balkan headquarters for the Greek, Yugoslav, and Albanian partisans. Toward this end, on a blistering hot June day, three die-hard communist partisans met in one of those nondescript villages somewhere in the mountains in northwestern Greece. Prior to the Axis occupation, the three individuals and the communist parties they represented had been marginally relevant in the rough-and-tumble world of Balkan politics. Yet, the three insignificant communists were meeting to redress the land boundaries of the Balkans, at best a volatile and toxic exercise. The participants: Vukmanović, a Yugoslav communist and Tito's henchman for Macedonian affairs; Enver Hoxha, a cold-blooded killer and the head of the Albanian Communist Party (ACP), who after 1945 would isolate Albania from the world and impose a harsh communist regime; and Grigoriadis, perhaps the least significant participant, representing the KKE.

FIG. 8. Tito at the Bolshoi in 1945. Three years later, Tito and Stalin would become archenemies. WikiCommons.

Ostensibly, Vukmanović had summoned the Greek and Albanian communists to meet about establishing a joint Balkan headquarters to coordinate the activities of their respective resistance organizations. Vukmanović, however, had a hidden agenda and with the connivance of Hoxha tried to force Grigoriadis into a discussion about the future fate of Greek Macedonia. The KKE leadership had some suspicions that the meeting was a trap to satisfy Tito's appetite for a greater postwar Yugoslavia at the expense of Greece. Accordingly, Grigoriadis admitted, when pressed, that he did not have the authority to sign on behalf of the Greek Communist Party.[43] The Greek communist, however, had another agenda and the KKE had sent him with the purpose of contacting Moscow through the Yugoslav channel.[44] Communist solidarity notwithstanding, the relationship among the Yugoslavs, Greeks, Bulgarians, and Albanians operated on two tracks: a common goal of promoting communism and the aim of gaining regional advantage in advancing their respective national agendas.

The crafty Vukmanović later offered an idealized version of why he proposed a Balkan resistance headquarters, stating that he was "convinced that the idea of forming a Balkan HQ was realisable and would contribute to the strengthening of the struggle against occupation."[45] After the discussions concluded, on 20 June 1943, Vukmanović and Hoxha produced a document: "Conclusions of a Meeting of Delegates from the Central Committees of the Greek, Yugoslav and Albanian Communist parties, held on 20 June 1943."[46] The document included generalities about cooperation among the communist organizations as well as the future fate of Macedonia. Vukmanović and Hoxha signed it as members of their respective central committees, but not Grigoriades. Despite the KKE's attempt to sidestep the Macedonian issue, the agreement signed by two out of the three communist representatives revealed Tito's plans for interfering in Greek Macedonia.

Grigoriadis quickly realized the implications that this document would have for the KKE and demanded the removal of any references to Greek Macedonia. He insisted that his objections be included in the following statement: "[The KKE delegate] considers [the] (Macedonian) question sensitive and that it must be looked into by the KKE Central Committee."[47] Vukmanović, however, was not to be denied. Immediately following Grigoriadis' protest he had Hoxha add: "The other delegates do not share the view of the KKE delegate and consider it necessary and beneficial to give the Macedonian people the opportunity to conduct their own national liberation struggle."[48] The Yugoslavs were prepared to pursue a policy with respect to Greek Macedonia regardless of the protestations of the KKE.

Two additional meetings between Vukmanović and the KKE followed later in the summer of 1943. The first took place at ELAS headquarters in Kastania at the end of June and went on until 9 or 10 July.[49] The main participants were Vukmanović, Koci Xoxe representing the ACP, and Stephanos Sarafis, Andreas Tzimas, and Aris Velouchiotis from ELAS.[50] Although Vukmanović once again attempted to impose his vision of a Balkan headquarters, the Greeks resisted, claiming that because they carried out operations in accordance with the allied command of the Middle Eastern Theater of Operations, they could not join any organization that would subordinate those obligations.[51] Ultimately, they only agreed to the exchange of liaison officers and shared information, pending approval from the EAM central committee. Nevertheless, despite failing to establish a Balkan headquarters, Vukmanović managed to get the Greek delegation to accept the formation of Slavophone units within ELAS.[52] This agreement would later provide the foundation for the Slav National Liberation Front (SNOF) in October 1943, and further aggravate KKE-CPY relations.

The final meeting took place on 8–10 August 1943. On this occasion representatives from ELAS and the KKE central committee, accompanied by Georgios Siantos, the acting secretary general of the Greek Communist Party, came to negotiate with the Yugoslav and Albanian communists. The arrival of such high-profile KKE leaders bolstered the confidence of Vukmanović, who claimed that after his personal meetings with Tzimas he held great hopes that the Greek Communist Party would change its position with respect to the Balkan headquarters.[53] But Vukmanović was again to be disappointed. Saraphis writes in his memoirs that Siantos denied ELAS the right to participate in a Balkan headquarters.[54]

Although Vukmanović failed on this count, and was in fact later admonished by Tito for overstepping his mission, he did secure part of his objectives in achieving the admission of Slavophone Macedonians into ELAS.[55] When contact was reestablished with the CPY, Tito reprimanded Vukmanović for having fallen for a British ruse. It was later determined that Djilas had actually composed the admonishment, and Tito signed it, for "It was a practice of the Central Committee—though not a frequent one—to have a letter written by the Central Committee member most involved with the relevant question, and then have Tito sign it." It also proved effective in diverting criticism from Tito. Elizabeth Barker noted that at the meeting, Siantos "agreed that the Yugoslav Partisans should cross into Greek territory and encourage the local Slavophone population to join EAM/ELAS, under guarantee of national freedom and equal rights; Slavophone-Macedonian units could be formed, though they must be under ELAS; Macedonians should be told that they would win the right to self-determination only through armed struggle."[56]

The Slav National Liberation Front was organized in October 1943 and almost immediately created friction between the KKE and CPY. The KKE made matters worse by choosing Ilias Dimikis, known in Greece as Gotsis, to command SNOF forces. Unfortunately, for the KKE, Dimikis was more committed to Macedonian autonomy than to the Greek Communist Party.[57] At first, SNOF was a valuable asset to ELAS, Sarafis observed; "they were well disciplined, repeatedly took part in actions against the invader and showed patriotic spirit."[58] Slavophone Macedonian particularism, however, quickly trumpeted military considerations. In May 1944 the remnants of the Axis-trained Slavophone gendarmerie surrendered and joined SNOF, further heightening tensions between SNOF and ELAS. The addition of the former expanded the manpower and weaponry of SNOF and increased its units from the battalion to divisional level.[59] Yet now ELAS included collaborationists with blood on their hands, exposing the left-wing and communist-dominated resistance to charges of treason as well as ethnic betrayal. Although the SNOF created a public relations nightmare for the Greek communists, the KKE took little action to check the growing strength of the Slavophone Macedonians in ELAS until the end of the occupation.[60]

Adding to its difficulties, the KKE could not change Allied perceptions that it was a junior partner of the Yugoslav partisans. John S. Koliopoulos argues that by 1944, the KKE realized that "Tito had the unqualified and very public support of the Allies and was expected to play a decisive role in the Balkans after the war."[61] There was some consolation for the Greek communist leadership. According to an OSS report (24 June 1944), the KKE had obtained Tito's assurances that "his independent Macedonia does not include Greek Macedonia."[62]

The KKE, for its part, attempted to control and contain the potential damage by the SNOF units and incorporated them individually into ELAS. This ploy backfired and the Yugoslavs, in a thinly veiled threat in June 1944, stated that the CPY "thought that the Greeks should accept the formation of one such brigade, if not, we ourselves shall start to form one. In that case, we shall inevitably come into controversy with the Greeks."[63] Although the KKE's response to this communiqué is unavailable, the aggressive tone of the CPY message reflected the evolving client-patron relationship between the Greek and the Yugoslav communists.

The Yugoslavs were angered by the Greek attempts to break up the Slavophone-Macedonian units because by the summer of 1944 Tito had decided to deal with his problem of Vardar Macedonia by exporting Yugoslav Macedonian nationalists to the Greek communists. Although the CPY had used Macedonian nationalism as a means of gaining control over Yugoslav Macedonia, Tito was exploiting the Macedonian issue as a means of downgrading the influence of the Vardar Macedonians and the radicals within his own party.[64]

Nevertheless, the Vardar Macedonians proved to be the most difficult for Tito to dominate. The CPY included many prominent Macedonian nationalists rather than dedicated communists in the central committee of the Macedonian Communist Party. Most prominent among these was Dimitar Vlahov, later the first premier of the People's Republic of Macedonia in 1946,[65] who had formerly been a member of the United Internal Macedonian Revolutionary Organization.[66] He was also born and raised in Aegean (Greek) Macedonia.[67] It is plausible that Tito would have seized Aegean Macedonia if he had had the opportunity, but maintaining order within Vardar Macedonia was ultimately far more important. Despite the rhetoric of a united Macedonia, political expediency and opportunism guided Tito's policy until his break with Stalin.

Macedonian self-determination and independence were not the only issues over which the CPY criticized the KKE, but these were issues with which it had the most at stake. In a meeting between Tito and a member of the KKE in late 1944, Tito censured the KKE for its policy toward Macedonia and the British.[68] The KKE representative maintained that they were forced to make concessions because of pressure from the British. Tito responded that the British "tried to do the same with us, but we were ready to suffer for three more years. We declined help."[69] When the KKE representative claimed that they had "managed to liberate our own country," Tito tersely replied that the KKE representative "should thank your liberation to the Red Army because their actions had forced the whole German army to relocate to Yugoslavia."[70] Unfortunately for the KKE, the Germans withdrew from Greece and a small number of British units, instead of the Red Army, arrived to help with relief.

When liberation came in October 1944, the KKE nonetheless controlled the largest guerrilla force (ELAS) in the country with a resistance organization (EAM) of over one million active and passive members. Yet unlike the Yugoslav partisans, the KKE and the left-wing resistance lacked a singular leader such as Tito. Zachariadis could have fulfilled that role, but he was an inmate at Dachau and had no impact on events in Greece during the occupation. In the absence of a strong and charismatic leader, Stalin was indifferent to the fate of the Greek communists. As mentioned earlier, following instructions from the Soviet Union, the Greek communists acquiesced when British forces landed in Greece in October 1944. The communist-controlled EAM-ELAS would have easily gained control of Greece and imposed their own government; instead, they compromised and accepted the British-backed government of George Papandreou. For almost two months the country enjoyed relative peace, but events quickly degenerated into an urban conflict after 3 December 1944. The December Uprising certainly set the stage for the last round of the civil war, while becoming a symbol of protest for Greek radicals into the twenty-first century.

In the period after the December Uprising and during the course of the White Terror, the Greek communists found it exceedingly difficult to navigate the fine line between revolutionary action and legitimate political pressure. Compounding this difficulty was the fact that the White Terror forced many ELAS fighters to seek shelter in the mountains. Some estimates suggest that as many as 3,000 ELAS fighters, operating in groups of ten, had taken to the mountains in the Peloponnese and northern Greece.[71] The persecution of the former resistance guerrillas by right-wing groups forced the ELAS cadres to rearm and fight in self-defense. Zachariadis and the Politburo decided to prepare for an organized military response and sought help from the Soviet Union. Their entreaties to Stalin for diplomatic recognition, let alone military support (at least for most of 1945), however, fell on deaf ears. Peter Stavrakis writes, "The Soviets seemed to be content with probing the British influence in the Balkans, most likely knowing that it was coming to an end."[72] Stalin, meanwhile, was determined to avoid a breach with the British over Greece. Immediately after the outbreak of the December Uprising, Stalin had even forbidden Georgi Dimitrov, his faithful Bulgarian satrap, to grant asylum to the defeated ELAS fighters. Although a storm of protest from British and American newspapers castigated Churchill's government for pitting the British army against ELAS during the uprising, the Soviet media remained silent.

In 1945–1946, however, the White Terror had alienated a sizable segment of the Greek public; many of them had been members of EAM, and this, as well as the failure of the Greek government to contain the economic crisis and the black market, created excellent conditions for a communist insurgency. Zachariadis was aware of these circumstances and could not miss such an

FIG. 9. Joseph Stalin and Vyacheslav Molotov at the Yalta Conference, 1945, during
which Stalin assured Churchill that he would uphold the Percentages Agreement. U.S.
National Archives and Records Administration.

opportunity. An interview Zachariadis gave to Springe of the *Manchester
Guardian* on 25 August 1945 in Thessaloniki sheds some light on his thinking
and reveals, partly, why the communist leader believed he could achieve
success in a civil war. In the course of the interview, the journalist asked

Zachariadis why he gave an anti-British speech to a crowd of 50,000 left-wing Greeks in Thessaloniki: "Is it because you want the British to leave Greece?" Zachariadis replied, "Yes," and Springe commented: "Are you aware of the consequences?" To which the communist leader said: "I am aware that a civil war, to which we are aspiring, shall follow. It will be a question of two months. After that everything will be alright."[73]

Despite the conditions in Greece in the summer of 1945, Zachariadis' optimism was undaunted. The odds, however, were against him. The White Terror was running its course; the economy near-collapse, mass unemployment, poverty, and a revolving door of successive Greek governments offered little prospect for improvement. More significantly, the Greek government had to rely almost exclusively on the British army for internal security. By excising the British, Zachariadis and the communists would improve their chances of a successful government takeover.

The anti-British theme of the KKE's propaganda as a cause for an armed struggle against a foreign enemy is reflected both in the new name of the communist forces—the Democratic Army of Greece (DAG)—and in the oath of allegiance taken by recruits and conscripts. On 27 December 1946, the KKE adopted the name Democratic Army of Greece instead of continuing with ELAS (Greek Popular Liberation Army). Zachariadis believed that the word "popular" in ELAS was a code word for class struggle, while "democratic" was sufficiently bourgeois to appeal to all Greeks.[74] The DAG's oath of allegiance also aimed to steer away from allusions to civil war and to remind the recruit that the struggle was against a foreign occupation and fascism.[75]

The KKE and the supporters of the EAM found common cause in the British presence, which could easily be construed as a foreign occupation. The Greek government was reorganizing and expanding its own military, but the chaotic situation within Greece was making this a painfully slow process. In February 1945, at the end of the December Uprising, the Greek army numbered 30,000 men and by December 1945 it only reached the strength of 75,000. Under these circumstances, Zachariadis was optimistic about defeating a small army using mostly inexperienced conscripts. The conflict, Zachariadis believed, would last only a short while and would sidestep Stalin's policy of gradualism. A quick communist victory would leave little time for Soviet recriminations. It would even give him a military reputation (denied earlier owing to his incarceration in Dachau).[76]

A delegation of Greek communists led by Mitsos Partsalidis visited Moscow in the middle of January 1946 to sound out the Soviet leadership for their immediate assistance, but failed to secure an audience with Stalin. The only tangible response Partsalidis could bring back to Greece was a message from the central committee of the Soviet Communist Party that the KKE was to "take part in the elections now. Later, review the situation. In accordance with the way it develops the center of gravity may move as necessary, either to legal methods or to armed struggle."[77] Further indication of Soviet disinterest in providing military support for the KKE came in November 1946, when Andrei Zhdanov, the head of the Information Bureau of the Communist Parties, the Cominform, did not mention Greece in his address on the anniversary of the Bolshevik Revolution.[78] It was a deliberate snub and a clear sign that the Soviets were not prepared to sanction the KKE's call for an armed struggle. Yet Zachariadis was planning some form of armed response against the Greek government.

One can extrapolate Zachariadis' intentions from the decisions of the KKE in early 1946, which called for a military response to the White Terror. At the party meeting in February 1946, Zachariadis stated that "since our enemies are continuing the one-sided civil war, we will answer with the same means—weapons. Now has come the time for us to make the historic decision for armed struggle."[79] Ole Smith concludes: 'The partisan movement was to be regarded as a defensive weapon first; if the government did not give in, and a democratic development should prove impossible, then the partisan groups should play a more active and offensive role. . . . The KKE should wait and see, use both parliamentary and legal methods, and armed action depending on circumstances and opportunity."[80]

After the meeting, the KKE dispatched a number of well-known ELAS officers to organize the disparate bands of resistance fighters who had sought the protection of the mountains. When the shift from uncoordinated raids to full-scale civil war took place is not clear; but what is certain is that by fall of 1946 the KKE leadership was bringing all the various guerrilla bands operating in the mountains under its control and into an organized force. Even at this point, the KKE still held back from committing its fighters to a full-scale conflict, because throughout 1946 the KKE leadership remained uncertain about how to secure Soviet support.

In 1947, Stalin decided, with strong encouragement from the Yugoslavs, at least to allow the KKE to obtain aid from nearby communist states. Stalin's change of mind was partly in response to Tito's support of the Greek communists, and partly in reaction to the Truman Doctrine the U.S. president presented to the joint session of Congress in requesting aid for Greece and Turkey on 12 March 1947. In effect, the escalation of full-scale civil war in

Greece was in part a by-product of Soviet and American rivalry and the development of regional factors linked to Tito's machinations for territorial expansion. Stalin's fear that American intervention in Greece could lead to U.S. aggression against the Soviet satellites in the Balkans was one possible consideration. It remains an open question whether Zachariadis would have confined his activities to the political arena, had Stalin not given the KKE the green light to launch an armed conflict. The Greek communist leader was loyal to Stalin, yet he could not have remained indifferent as former ELAS fighters headed to the mountains and organized into loose bands to protect themselves from the practitioners of the White Terror.

The destabilization of the Greek state served Tito's regional ambitions well. The Yugoslav leader was planning to incorporate the Greek province of Macedonia as part of a Yugoslav-dominated Balkan federation that included Bulgaria and, of course, a communist Greece and Stalin's blessing. This would not have been possible without a sympathetic government in Athens. Although Tito did not think very highly of the Greek communists, they provided him with the means to reshape the Balkans and establish Yugoslav hegemony. In 1950, Zachariadis claimed that the KKE had decided for military action after "Tito and his clique promised us the most substantial aid. This played a decisive role in our decision because in Yugoslavia, the main factor in the Balkans at that time, our new revolutionary movement did not have an opponent who could pose insurmountable obstacles."[81]

Furthermore, when Zachariadis arrived in Moscow in May 1947, two months after Truman had made his pivotal speech, Stalin was ready to help the Greek communist insurgency. According to declassified Soviet documents, Moscow's policy with respect to the Greek question was, at this point, a reaction to the Truman Doctrine, and was viewed by the Kremlin as a direct threat to the USSR from the south.[82] Stalin, however, was careful not to display openly his support of the Greek communists. Aid had to come from Soviet satellites and be distributed by Yugoslavia, Albania, and Bulgaria, but none of these countries, including the USSR, ever afforded diplomatic recognition to the rebel government established by the KKE. As a result, Zachariadis and the KKE became hostage to their Balkan neighbors' good will, which only endured as long as Stalin was in a position to exercise his influence over his Balkan vassals. It was Zachariadis' misfortune that Tito was the most effective of these with respect to sustaining the DAG in the field; he was apostatized from Soviet communism in 1948 because the Yugoslav leader became too independent from Moscow.

Tito's fall from Stalin's favor created an almost impossible dilemma for the KKE. The Greek communist leaders, led by Zachariadis, despite their material dependence on Yugoslavia, secretly decided to side with the Soviet Union against Yugoslavia after Stalin cast out Tito from the Cominform—the postwar organization that replaced the defunct Comintern.[83] Ideology, not for the first time in the history of the Greek Communist Party, had trumped local tactical advantage and political common sense. At least this was the perspective from the Soviet Union, the Yugoslav leadership, and Zachariadis' detractors. Regardless, Zachariadis had to choose between the Soviet Union and Stalin—a loyalty that he had cherished all of his life—and Tito, another Balkan leader, who without the backing of the USSR offered the Greek communist leader no guarantee of success. Perhaps Zachariadis was unwilling to submit to another Balkan communist and saw this as an opportunity to rise above the Yugoslav leader, providing he would be successful in establishing a Greek communist state.

For centuries Balkan people competed for territory and legitimacy and did not acknowledge any of their neighbors as superiors. Instead, it was more common for the Balkan peoples to view one another as competitors. In the complex world of the Balkans, loyalties are layered by religion, history, tradition, and equally important claims to lost territory. Zachariadis, despite his commitment to international communism, could not fail to see that Tito was not committed to the historic affinity between Greeks and Serbs. He was not Eastern Orthodox or Serb, but a Catholic Slovene-Croatian with little connection to the Greek-Serbian alliance, which fostered trust and close relationships between the two peoples.

The Greek communist leader was also aware of Tito's ambition to acquire the Bulgarian provinces of Macedonia and to dominate the Balkans—an ambition shared by a succession of Balkan leaders. The mantle of communism hardly disguised Tito's appetite for Balkan territorial expansion. In contrast, Stalin was a larger-than-life figure who transcended regional attachments and prejudices and, as it turned out, one who opposed Tito's plans to acquire Greek territory (at least as perceived at the time). The Soviet leader could barely tolerate Tito's rapid rise to the top of the communist world pyramid and was not inclined to allow the Yugoslav upstart to achieve any further successes at his or Greece's expense. Stalin adopted a position that maintained Greek territorial integrity. Ironically it was Zachariadis who ultimately prepared to surrender Greek territory by agreeing to give Greek Macedonia to Bulgaria.

At the same time, Macedonia was one of the main battlefields of the Greek civil war. The initial strategy of the KKE was to isolate Macedonia, Greece's northern province, and use it as a staging ground to expand the war to the rest of the country. The other part of the KKE's grand strategy was to secure a large town and hold it as the capital of a provisional Greek communist government. To accomplish these ends, the KKE leadership had to rely on Yugoslavia, Bulgaria, and Albania for logistical support as well as for bases and safe havens for the DAG to fall back on after engaging the Greek army. To a great extent, Yugoslavia carried the main burden of supplying the insurgents as well as providing staging areas for the hit-and-run tactics of the Greek communist forces. A critical element of the KKE's strategy was exploitation of Greek Macedonia as a resource region to sustain the DAG units in the field. The insurgents often requisitioned food and livestock at the expense of the villagers. The expropriations and the forced recruitment of young men and women caused severe shortages of both foodstuffs and workers in the region.[84] These actions, combined with the negative accounts of deserters and government propaganda, eventually eroded support for the KKE in the region.

The choice of Macedonia as a staging ground for the Democratic Army had the advantage of securing easy access to supplies from Yugoslavia and Bulgaria as well as a steady stream of Slavophone Macedonian recruits for the communists. The KKE could also count on moral and material support from many of the residents of the region who had settled as refugees from Asia Minor and were sympathetic to the Greek communists. The refugees were the backbone of the KKE voters since many had ended up as low paid tobacco workers with considerable grievances. The Slavophones in northern Greece were generally hostile to the Greek authorities that had historically employed heavy-handed policies in order to assimilate the minority. The KKE led many Greek Slavophones to believe that they could establish an independent state by separating the Greek province of Macedonia and merging it with the People's Republic of Macedonia in Yugoslavia, if the KKE emerged victorious in the civil war. The high proportion of Slavophone Macedonians in the Democratic Army gave credibility to the claims of the Greek government that not only did the KKE represent external interests, but also it was made up of foreigners.

The number of Slavophone Macedonians was a critical factor to the DAG, but it is open to considerable debate. One difficulty in determining how many Slavophone Macedonians served with the communist forces is that their numbers fluctuated in each year of the conflict and increased significantly by the end of the civil war.[85] The dependence of the DAG on Slavophone

Macedonian recruits left the KKE leadership with little choice but to support first Macedonian self-determination and eventually independence. Ultimately, the calculation paid off. The Slavophone Macedonians provided a steady stream of recruits, volunteers, or pressgang, and their numbers sustained the DAG as a viable force, particularly in the final year of the civil war.

At first, Stalin's refusal to directly support the KKE's armed struggle had left them with one option: guerrilla warfare. Irregular fighting gave the Greek communists early successes but in and of itself could not achieve victory. A guerrilla campaign can sustain an insurgency for a considerable period of time, as long as there is ongoing logistical support, but victory can be achieved only if the guerrillas evolve into a conventional army to defeat the government forces.[86] Generally, the insurgents must bring a third party into the conflict that will provide them with military assistance. These preconditions also depend on the failure of the state to maintain and supply its forces in the field. None of these key ingredients was available to the Greek communists. The KKE eventually received support from communist countries, but it was Yugoslavia that provided material aid and training camps as well as a place of refuge for the communist insurgents. Unfortunately, for the KKE, Tito had a price—Greek Macedonia.

After the KKE had lost the first round of the Greek civil war in 1943, the CPY had become even more aggressive over Greek Macedonia. Vukmanović, not known for his subtlety, was particularly blunt in his assessment of the situation in Greek Macedonia. On 2 August 1945, in a speech in Skopje, Vukmanović declared: "Comrades, you know very well that there is a part of the Macedonian people, which is still enslaved. . . . There are tens of thousands of Macedonian men and women who suffer today under the yoke of the Greek monarcho-fascist bands."[87] Tito, during the course of a speech, on 11 October 1945 in Skopje, was even more emphatic about the right of Slavophone Macedonians within Greek Macedonia to independence and unification with the Yugoslav and Bulgarian Macedonians. He proclaimed: "We will never renounce the right of the Macedonian people to be united. . . . We are not indifferent to the fate of our brothers in Aegean Macedonia and our thoughts are with them."[88]

Most likely these comments were intended for domestic consumption, but the KKE as well as the Greek government took them at face value. Compounding the challenges confronting the Greek communists, by the end of World War II the relationship between the CPY and the KKE had become completely lopsided. Unlike the Greek communists, the Yugoslav communists dominated the postwar Yugoslav government and by 1945 were in the process of taking outright control, which further enhanced their regional power and increased their prestige within the communist world.[89]

In the late summer of 1946 when Zachariadis launched the third round of the civil war, one of the reasons he did so was because the Yugoslavs had promised substantial military aid.[90] The Yugoslavs allegedly made these guarantees during a meeting among representatives of the Bulgarian, Greek, and Yugoslav communist parties in the town of Petrich along the Greek-Bulgarian border on 15 December 1945.[91] At this meeting the Yugoslavs promised to underwrite the KKE's armed struggle and committed to "co-ordinated plans [with them] for active war [against the Greek government]."[92] Tito made one of his close associates, Alexandar Ranković, responsible for coordinating logistics among the communist parties.[93] Ranković's significance within the CPY—he was head of the secret police as well as a member of the CPY Politburo—underscored the Yugoslav's level of commitment to the KKE's armed struggle in Greece. Meanwhile, the Yugoslavs became increasingly vocal in their support of the Macedonian Slavophones in Greek Macedonia. Although the CPY directed its attacks at the Greek government, it created pressure on the KKE to accommodate the Macedonian Slavophones.

Tito continued to face his own problems with the Macedonians in Yugoslavia. As early as January 1945, Vukmanović, the most vocal proponent of the Macedonian cause within Tito's inner circle, noted that not only was there resistance to the new regime in Yugoslavia, but one of the most significant dangers was of "regionalist" tendencies.[94] In a 6 June 1946 cable from Belgrade, George Clutton, the first secretary of the British embassy, reported that "Macedonia still remains a problem to the Yugoslav Government. . . . The present measure of control by Belgrade is . . . intensely resented and this is somewhat confirmed by the complaints of the Bulgarian Opposition parties."[95]

The CPY also used Macedonian nationalism as an excuse for domestic shortcomings. In 1946, Vardar Macedonia was one of the least developed regions in Yugoslavia, as a result of interwar policies of the Yugoslav governments.[96] The CPY attempted to attribute the economic problems to the "unnatural" boundaries between the Macedonian regions. According to *Borba,* the publication of the Yugoslav Communist Party, the true cause of the region's economic backwardness was the artificial division of Macedonia, which separated the port of Thessaloniki from its hinterland.[97] Dimitar Vlahov, who by 1948 was vice president of the Yugoslav Presidium, embraced this point as another reason for incorporating Greek Macedonia into the Yugoslav Federation."[98]

FIG. 10. Dimitar Vlahov, an influential Bulgarian Slavophone politician, member of
IMRO, and later a member of the Macedonian Communist Party. WikiCommons.

The KKE's postwar position on the future of Macedonia at the Twelfth
Plenum of the Central Committee of the KKE on 25–27 June 1945 continued
to reflect the Greek Communist Party's prewar policies. The KKE had reluctantly accepted, to some degree, the decisions of the Fifth Congress of the
Comintern in June and July 1924, for an autonomous Macedonia and
Thrace.[99] Although the Greek communists remained steadfast to the Comintern, advocating the surrender of Greek territory was anathema to most

Greeks. The KKE temporized and made references to self-determination for Macedonians, but tried to shy away from proclaiming outright indepen- dence. After the occupation, this policy became impossible to sustain.

Throughout 1945, however, Zachariadis continued to avoid committing to Macedonian autonomy and stated: "We are against any forced change of the boundaries of 1939 from any side. The only democratic solution we rec- ognize is the principle of the self-determination of peoples."[100] But this was a classic example of doublespeak in which the KKE seemingly promised a great deal while essentially offering little in return. The 1939 boundaries were to remain intact, albeit only against forced changes. The KKE recognized the right of self-determination, but Zachariadis did not define what he meant by the term. The Yugoslavs, for example, interpreted self-determination as a means of peacefully changing the border between Greece and Yugoslavia. At the Seventh Party Congress of the KKE, Zachariadis explained that respect- ing Slavophone Macedonian rights was "to avoid conflicts, misunderstand- ings and discussions over Greek Macedonia, which is inhabited by 90 percent Greeks, a fact which renders it an inseparable part of the Hellenic land."[101]

Despite the exertions by the Yugoslavs to secure Greek Macedonia, after June 1947 Tito began to scale back the rhetoric on Macedonia, ending it com- pletely by January 1948.[102] There was no official reason from Belgrade as to why Greek Macedonia was no longer important. One consideration is that the Bled Agreement, concluded on 1 August 1947, implied that the Bulgarians were prepared to hand over Pirin Macedonia (Bulgarian Macedonia) to Yugoslavia. Although there was no formal settlement, the Bulgarians decided to permit Macedonian cultural workers from Yugoslavia access to Pirin Macedonia.[103] The CPY now had an effective outlet for Macedonian reclamation of territory, a place to relocate recalcitrant Macedonian nationalists, and no need to relo- cate them in Greek Macedonia. Furthermore, certain groups within Pirin Macedonia had genuine enthusiasm for unification within Yugoslav Macedo- nia. A British cable describing the Pirin representative at the first Macedonian People's Front Congress in Skopje in 1946 declared: "The people [of Pirin Macedonia] wished to be united with their brothers within Yugoslavia."[104]

Another reason for the shift in Yugoslav policy toward Greek Macedonia was that it was no longer necessary to fight for annexation because of the declining influence of Yugoslav Macedonian nationalism. Vardar Macedonia continued to remain a troublesome republic, but it had achieved significant political improvement by 1947. A contributing factor to Macedonian stability was that the purges of the Yugoslav Communist Party during the same year, conducted by the secret police, had eliminated Macedonian nationalists who refused to accept Yugoslav tutelage and identity.[105] Another reason that Tito gave up on Greek Macedonia may have been that he did not have much confidence in a Greek communist victory, especially after the proclamation of the Truman Doctrine brought significant U.S. military and economic assistance to the Greek government.

Under these circumstances, for Tito the annexation of Greek Macedonia was becoming less important and would soon be eclipsed by dramatic developments in the communist world. On 28 June 1948, the Comiform expelled Yugoslavia from the community of communist states. The grounds were that the Yugoslavs had slandered the USSR and that the CPY was no longer a true Marxist organization. In fact, Stalin had grown weary of Tito's territorial ambitions, particularly the Yugoslav's designs on Bulgaria and Albania. The Yugoslavs became anathema to all communists and lost their Balkan allies and with them all the agreements with respect to territorial changes. For a few months, the position of the KKE regarding the Tito-Stalin split remained inscrutable, but there were indications in Belgrade that the Greek communists were siding with Moscow.

On 8 August 1948, the plenum of the executive council of the NOF, the Slavophone-Macedonian organization, removed Michael Keramidijev from the secretariat. Superficial reasons for his expulsion were spun, but Zachariadis ousted him, according to a secret report in the Greek Foreign Ministry, because he remained loyal to Tito.[106] The Greek communist leadership had taken immediate action to secure the support of the NOF, fearing that the Slavophone Macedonian organization would remain loyal to Tito. Slavophone Macedonians by this time represented almost half of the DAG's rank and file. In a secret telegram on 28 July 1948, a Yugoslav agent noted that the Macedonian Slavophones were threatening "to confront [the Greek Communist Party (KKE)] and even organize their own Macedonian units."[107] If a Yugoslav informer was cognizant of the questionable loyalty of NOF forces, the KKE was certainly aware. This is why the policy of purging the NOF, whether by imprisonment or execution, continued unabated throughout the fall and winter of 1948–1949. Evangelos Kofos writes: "By December the Cominformists appeared to have won, as evidenced by the fact that pro-Yugoslav elements had fled en masse to Yugoslavia. Safely at Skopje, they accused the leadership of the KKE of lacking 'love' and 'trust' for the 'Slav-Macedonians.' "[108]

Zachariadis did not limit the purges to NOF. They extended to the highest levels of the KKE leadership. The most prominent example was the removal of Markos Vaphiadis as commander of the DAG. The Tito-Stalin split magnified the tensions between the two Greek communist leaders and reached a breaking point in November 1948 when Vaphiadis presented his "platform" to the KKE Politburo, which was critical of Zachariadis' military direction. Vaphiadis emphasized the necessity of returning to "intensive, guerrilla-type activity, by small, mobile lightly armed contingents, saboteurs and snipers, able to choose where and when to fight."[109]

This alternative strategy failed to impress the KKE leadership. On 15 November 1948, Zachariadis succeeded in securing Politburo support in denouncing Vaphiadis as a defeatist.[110] To maintain morale, the Politburo announced that the party "sent him away to recover" from a mysterious ailment.[111] The fact that Vaphiadis went to the Soviet Union for medical treatment rather than Yugoslavia underscores the point that Tito was not the primary cause for the rift between him and Zachariadis. Even so, the Yugoslavs had lost their most powerful ally in the KKE and the DAG and, through him, their principal means of influencing the Greek Communist Party. Almost immediately after Vaphiadis' "sick leave," General Popović, his Yugoslav liaison, was removed from the DAG headquarters.[112]

The CPY's reaction to the KKE's purges of all pro-Titoists was remarkably cautious. The Tito-Stalin split had caused an existential crisis within the Yugoslav Communist Party itself. Yugoslav portrayals of the rift typically depict the CPY resolutely convinced of the righteousness of its cause and confident of ultimate triumph.[113] The reality, however, was starkly different. The CPY was divided and key members actually defected, or attempted to defect, to the Soviet Union for many of the same reasons that the KKE ultimately chose to support the CPSU.[114] This change in allegiance made it difficult for the Yugoslavs to continue to influence the KKE. Further compounding the difficulties of the Yugoslavs, the communist parties of Bulgaria and Albania denounced the CPY.

On 12 July 1948 at the Sixteenth Plenum of the central committee, the Bulgarian Communist Party declared that "the federation of South Slavs and the eventual annexation of the Pirin region to the Macedonian People's Republic are possible only on the supposition that Yugoslavia remains faithful to the common front of socialism."[115] In December 1948 at the Fifth BCP Congress, Dimitrov argued, "Our party has always advocated and continues to advocate that Macedonia belongs to Macedonians . . . within the framework of a federation of South Slavs."[116] The Yugoslav response was through Ranković, who on 12 January 1949 stated: "How can one enter a federation, when the Bulgarian Central Committee has joined from the very outset in the slanderous campaign against our party and country? . . . The Yugoslav Communist Party have always been, and remain, advocates of the unification of the South Slavs."[117]

The CPY leadership was concerned about the negative impact of Bulgarian propaganda on their ranks, but ultimately it had little consequence. The Communist Party of Yugoslav Macedonia had the lowest expulsion rate and fewest supporters of the Cominform in the aftermath of the Tito-Stalin split.[118] A British cable at the time noted, "The Ministers who were removed in Governmental reshuffles in October 1948 and March of this year paid the penalty for inefficiency rather than political error."[119] It would not be until the summer of 1949 that the CPY discovered the benefits of the purges. In the interim, the CPY had to remain on its guard against Bulgarian chauvinism, and this to a large extent minimized its interaction with the KKE.

The CPY also lost its Albanian ally. The entire communist world, except the KKE, directly attacked the Yugoslavs. It is possible that the CPY was not yet completely certain of the KKE's response to the Tito-Stalin split. The urgent report by a Yugoslav agent, codenamed Bitolan, to the central committee of the CPY on 28 July 1948 about the potential of the Macedonians forming their own units was contingent upon the KKE remaining loyal to Tito or siding with the Cominform, as the party had "not yet transfer[ed] its attitude to the ranks."[120] Until there was a clear indication of the KKE's position, the CPY leadership decided to wait. In effect, it had little choice since it was now ostracized by the other Balkan communist parties.

By the summer of 1948, the CPY had become aware of the KKE purges of pro-Tito Greek communists. Furthermore, many of the lower-ranking members of the KKE did not keep silent about their opposition to Tito. British journalist Kenneth Matthews, who was kidnapped by the DAG in mid-October 1948, noted that a DAG brigade commander, Stathakis, openly declared, "Tito was in the wrong and would have to give way or go under, perhaps both."[121] By November 1948, the central committee of the CPY received reports that the KKE leadership had remained loyal to the Cominform.[122] Regardless of this information, and considering the tension between the Greek and Yugoslav leadership that had developed, neither party took any definitive action until January 1949.

The official falling out between the Greek and Yugoslav communists came about on 31 January 1949 with the resolutions of the Fifth Plenum of the central committee of the KKE, which made it clear that the Greek communists decided to remain loyal to the Cominform and Stalin. Officially, it was on 1 April 1949 when Zachariadis, on behalf of the central committee of the KKE, notified the Yugoslavs that the KKE sided with the Cominform, but surprisingly the Greek communist leader appealed to the CPY to continue supporting the Greek communist forces.[123]

The Fifth Plenum also conceded almost everything that the Yugoslavs had demanded with respect to Macedonia, as the resolution stated that "the Macedonian people will realize their full national restitution, as they themselves want it, [with them] offering today their blood to win it."[124] Free Greek Radio, after the Second Plenum of NOF in 1949, parroted the KKE resolution and called for the "union of Macedonia in a complete, independent, and equal Macedonian nation within the framework of a People's Republican Federation of Balkan peoples."[125] This statement directly echoed the Bulgarian policy on the future of Macedonia.

On July 1949, the Greek and Yugoslav communist parties finalized the motions of mutual demonization that was the communist practice of terminating ties between states, organizations, or individuals. On 23 July, Yugoslavia closed its borders with Greece.[126] Edvard Kardelj, a central figure in the CPY Politburo, told a press conference of Yugoslav journalists that the leaders of the KKE now considered "participation in the struggle against Yugoslavia more important than the fight against Greek reactionaries and foreign intervention in Greece."[127] Naturally, the reporters had no questions; they had become accustomed to accepting the pabulum of information fed to them by the party functionaries without comment or dissent. Tito and his partisans had waged a savage resistance against the Axis occupation under the slogans of justice and liberty only to banish these ideals in a communist Yugoslavia.

A month after the Yugoslavs closed the border with Greece, the Greek National Army crushed the DAG at Grammos and Vitsi. Stalin decided to abandon the cause of the Greek communists. The Soviet leader was convinced that Britain and the United States would not accept a communist Greek state, and he faced the additional problem that the USSR lacked a significant battle fleet with which to challenge the Anglo-Americans in the Aegean.[128] From the beginning, Stalin had been skeptical about the chances of the DAG to achieve victory and he had refused to recognize the provisional Greek communist government. Stalin's sentiments about the situation in Greece had manifested in a tirade against Yugoslav delegates in February 1948. After railing at them over the proposed Balkan Federation of Yugoslavia and Bulgaria, Stalin turned to the civil war in Greece: "No, they have no prospect of success at all. What, do you think Great Britain and the United States—the United States, the most powerful state in the world—will permit you to break their line of communication in the Mediterranean? Nonsense. And we have no navy. The uprising in Greece must be stopped, as quickly as possible."[129]

The debate on whether Zachariadis should have stayed with Tito continues, and there are several theories as to why the Greek communist leader remained loyal to Stalin. It is plausible that Zachariadis' allegiance to Stalin was a life-long commitment that he could not discard. The Soviet Union was the apex of communism, and denying it and Stalin for Tito would have been a rejection of everything Zachariadis had fought and sacrificed for all his life. Siding with Tito, in addition to kowtowing to a fellow Balkan communist, also held the prospect to reverting to guerrilla warfare for the foreseeable future. Certainly, the landscape of northern Greece was conducive to irregular warfare and forbidding ground for conventional forces. But a guerrilla war without an end in sight in the inhospitable mountains of Greece held few prospects for victory and would, at best, result in a protracted struggle. Besides, the Greek National Army was becoming well trained and well led and would soon confine the communist insurgents to a war of hit-and-run tactics over remote mountain ranges. It would also mean the return of Vaphiadis, the acknowledged master of guerrilla warfare, along with a loss of face and influence for Zachariadis over the KKE.

The issue of Macedonia is more difficult to explain. Although in the 1920s the Comintern forced the KKE to accept, at the very least, Macedonian self-determination, Stalin was, at most, indifferent to Macedonian aspirations—more so if they expanded Tito's Yugoslavia. In addition to the consequences linking the KKE with Macedonian independence and the odium of surrendering Greek territory, Zachariadis guaranteed the KKE's marginalization in Greece for the foreseeable future. The Athens government could convincingly argue that support for the Greek communists was tantamount to rolling back the Greek victories in the 1912–1913 Balkan Wars. Yet Zachariadis at the pivotal point in the Greek civil war embraced Macedonian independence, knowing full well the negative impact this would have on most Greeks. The question remains, why did Zachariadis chart such a course? Did he believe that the Greeks would choose communism over Macedonia? Not likely. Perhaps, he had little choice: a large percentage of the DAG included Slavophone Macedonians, and the price of their loyalty was independence.

CHAPTER 7

The Politics of Hate and Retribution

Cry "Havoc!" and let slip the dogs of war.
—Mark Antony, *Julius Caesar*

Major Nicholas Mouskoundis, the head of the Greek General Security Service in northern Greece, kept his office spare. The plain desk, chair, and file cabinet underscored the solitude of the room. It was a space devoid of any personal items, with the exception of a large icon of Jesus Christ hanging on the wall directly behind the major's chair. A God-fearing man, he attended church services every Sunday, regardless of circumstance. Major Mouskoundis was Spartan in his habits, taciturn in his demeanor. He was overweight and bald, and known as a man who got things done. Perhaps most important, he also had a reputation as a fierce nationalist and a fanatical anticommunist.[1]

On a blazing hot afternoon in August 1948, a man in his early thirties was sitting on a hard, straight-backed chair in the director's office of the Thessaloniki General Security Service, which was the branch of the government that was responsible for combating the internal threat of communism. Grigoris Staktopoulos, the man sitting in the chair facing Mouskoundis, had been a journalist up until the moment he became a pawn of the General Security Service. In 1948, before the Security Service picked him up, Staktopoulos was making a modest living as a stringer for the British wire service Reuters and as a reporter for the Greek newspaper *Macedonia*. He had achieved little in his personal and professional life to distinguish himself. According to some accounts, he was "an unpretentious run-of-the-mill journalist, conscientious as a reporter but only modestly ambitious and not very imaginative, gentle to a fault, a bachelor much tied to his mother and sisters, for whom he was the principal means of the support."[2] Individuals less well disposed to Staktopoulos described him as "restless, egotistical at times, something of a show off . . . [who] always pretended to know everybody and everything and was ready to tell you so, especially if you were a foreigner."[3]

Staktopoulos had been educated at the elite American-run Anatolia College, where he became fluent in English. His education enabled him to work as a translator and interpreter.[4] During the occupation, he was one of the hundreds of thousands of EAM followers, and like some of them he had drifted to the KKE; not an ideologue or a committed Marxist, he had joined in order to secure employment as a journalist. Edmund Keeley, who wrote one of the few accounts in English of the Polk affair, writes of Staktopoulos: "To ensure the family's sustenance he was apparently ready to work for almost anybody of whatever political persuasion who would use his special qualifications as an English-speaking newspaperman."[5]

In this respect he was similar to many Greeks trying to survive in a bankrupt country. Some parts of Greece would come under communist control for a brief period and then revert back to government authority. Accordingly, for many of the poor and desperate, adopting the label of communist or nationalist was another type of currency no different than bartering for cigarettes or black market goods. Absolute ideology was a luxury for those with means on the right and for devout communists, who had paid too high a price in prison, abused at the hands of the authorities, to give up their Marxist beliefs. For ordinary people, survival was the only priority that mattered. Although Staktopoulos' past was not remarkable, he became the prime suspect for the assassination of the American George Polk, the CBS Middle East correspondent in Greece.

There are several versions of Polk's last hours in Thessaloniki, but none provide a satisfactory explanation of why the American journalist disappeared and was not seen again until his lifeless body was found floating in the Thessaloniki harbor. One theory has it that Polk had arrived in Thessaloniki on 7 March 1948 after his plane had been diverted from the Kavalla airport, his original destination, because of heavy rain. He proceeded to make some indiscreet inquiries about establishing contact with representatives of the KKE, who could secure for him an interview with Markos Vaphiadis, the commander of the Democratic Army of Greece, whose successful guerrilla tactics had garnered him an international reputation.

Polk paid a visit to the American consul, who warned him against making any attempts to contact the insurgents or travel to territory controlled by them. Next, he contacted Randall Coat, the British information officer reputed to have links with the rebels; Coat, again depending on conflicting accounts, either demanded that Polk leave his office or encouraged him by offering to help.[6] A few days later Polk vanished, and Coat was transferred to Oslo, Norway, and his secretary to Australia, a fact lending some credence to the subsequent conspiracy theories that have continued for more than half a century after the Polk murder.[7]

One theory blamed the communists, arguing that they killed Polk to embarrass the Greek government. Another accused the right, who could have had Polk killed because of the negative articles and reports on the corrupt practices of government officials or had him murdered in order to blame the KKE. Another theory placed the responsibility on the British, who may have had Polk assassinated in order to stop his negative reports, thus keeping the Americans from pulling out of Greece. Yet another theory points the finger at a British mole working for the Soviets who wanted Polk dead to blame the right wing. Elias Vladas and Zak Mettger posit that Polk was killed by Americans or Greeks to prevent the journalist from exposing their participation in a criminal organization involved in drugs, guns, and U.S. aid dollars. They also argue that Mouskoundis knew the identity of the criminals and the nature of their illicit activities, but looked the other way because he needed them for information and preferred to blame the murder on the communists to spare the government any embarrassment.[8]

In the course of his inquiries, Polk met with several other journalists as well as British, American consular, and UN officials. On one occasion, at the bar in the Mediterranean Hotel, Helen Mamas, a Greek-American and stringer for the Associated Press, introduced Polk to Staktopoulos and a Greek liaison officer with the United Nations Special Committee of the Balkans (UNSCOB). After a few drinks, Polk, Mamas, and a few others went on to dinner. Later Staktopoulos called Mamas to get the exact spelling of Polk's name as well as the names of the other American correspondents. Staktopoulos did so in order to report the visit of the foreigners in the newspaper *Macedonia,* a professional courtesy common among journalists in Thessaloniki.[9]

At 11:00 P.M. on Saturday 7 May, Polk and the others left the restaurant, at which point Polk headed down a street toward his hotel. Later, the hotel porters testified that they had seen Polk return at 1:00 A.M. Leaving his room very early the next day (Saturday), Polk dropped in on an acquaintance at the

American consulate and went on to visit Randall Coat at the British information office. In the afternoon he telegraphed his wife, Rhea, and told her to expect him in Kavalla on Monday or Tuesday. At 7:00 P.M. he had a drink at his hotel bar with Gerald Drew, the American delegate to UNSCOB, and his wife. The hotel staff noticed that Polk left the hotel at 11:00 that night, returned fifteen minutes later, and departed again at 12:45 A.M.

That was the last time anyone ever saw Polk alive. A week later, the American's bloated body surfaced in Thessaloniki Bay, plunging the Greek authorities into a fruitless search for the culprit or culprits responsible for killing Polk. The list of suspects who, directly or indirectly, may have had some link to delivering Polk to his murderers was a long one. From the outset, however, the Greek authorities as well as the American officials in Greece and in Washington preferred communist culprits. Any other conclusion placed U.S. policy in Greece in jeopardy or at the very least would have caused considerable embarrassment to the Truman administration. It would have been difficult for Washington to explain to the American public that the Greek government, the beneficiary of U.S. largess, was responsible for or even indirectly associated with the death of an American journalist.

The news of George Polk's death also brought the distant Greek civil war directly to America. The impact of radio news, which had emerged in its own right as a new form of media during World War II, added considerable intensity and drama to an otherwise obscure event. The killing of this American journalist put a face to the conflict, which for most people in the United States was as impersonal as it was remote. Americans became outraged. Howard K. Smith, from CBS, reported that Polk's death was "deliberate execution . . . planned to be spectacular, planned to intimidate. If the murderers are not discovered, an invisible but inevitable pressure of intimidation will rest on every American correspondent abroad."[10] The Greek government quickly attributed Polk's murder to the communists, and thus absolved itself of any responsibility. Greek officials, however, underestimated the public outcry in the United States, and the failure to produce the killers provoked accusations of cover-up.

The American Overseas Writers' Association, led by Walter Lippmann, offered a $10,000 reward for any information on Polk's murder and acquired the services of William Donovan, the former head of the wartime OSS, to undertake a separate investigation. Donovan, with much aplomb, traveled to Greece and intimidated, cajoled, and flattered the representatives of the Greek security services as well as the police. Afterward, he announced that they were "handling the case satisfactorily."[11] It was only when George Marshall announced that he was going to Greece to look into the situation himself that the Greek authorities produced Staktopoulos.

On 14 August 1948 at 2:30 in the afternoon, two nondescript men approached Staktopoulos while he was waiting to board the trolley. One of them tapped him on the shoulder and demanded, "Your identity card." Staktopoulos, realizing that the men were plainclothes police, complied instantly. After scrutinizing the document, one policeman said, "Come to the Security Service for an identification [check]."[12] Staktopoulos could hardly refuse. He was held and questioned for months, and in addition, the Security Service arrested his mother and his two sisters—their crime was suspicion by association.

Almost six weeks later Staktopoulos was sitting tied to a chair in Mouskoundis' office and staring into a blinding light. He could barely follow the major as the policeman slowly circled him like an animal closing in on its prey. He kept repeating, "You are involved, you are involved"; then in a soft voice the major intoned, "I will save you." Ignoring his prisoner's denials, the major continued to hover, resuming the chant, "You are involved, you are involved," and then in a hush he whispered in Staktopoulos' ear, "I will save you. I could have had you disappear any time when you were returning home late at night, but you are fortunate that your mother has had a son killed in the war."[13]

Staktopoulos, the victim, and Mouskoundis, the tormentor, performed this ritual for weeks. Afterward, the major's assistants subjected Staktopoulos to further interrogation, which in the parlance of the General Security Service meant torture. The "interrogation" varied from day to day and was inflicted according to the whim of each inquisitor. Staktopoulos was compelled to stand for hours and then made to suffer sleep deprivation. Subsequently, he was tormented with hunger and thirst, followed by severe beatings with truncheons and knuckledusters. Occasionally, Mouskoundis got physical with Staktopoulos, forcing him to stand with his back against a wall and then grinding down on his toes or kneeing him in the groin. On other days, Staktopoulos would be hung upside down in his cell; later he was subjected to electric shocks applied to the soles of his feet.[14]

Astonishingly, the tormentor knew that Staktopoulos was innocent. Mouskoundis had fabricated the evidence that implicated the unfortunate journalist. Yet in the turbulent and brutal environment of the Greek civil war, which had begun its third phase two years earlier, guilt or innocence was not germane.

The word *ethnikophron,* which translates as "nationalist-minded," encapsulated how the right labeled itself; more precisely, it defined people in black-and-white terms as either godless communists or *ethnikrophrons*. In this politically charged climate, individuals, when challenged by the authorities, had to prove that they were not communists and to demonstrate their "nationalist-minded" credentials. If individuals were lacking "nationalist-mindedness" they could face prison, and if exposed as communists, they faced prison and possibly execution. The communists were equally adamant in punishing those refusing to accept a Marxist alternative and inflicted torture or death on those refusing to embrace the dictates of the KKE, since they did not have the ability to maintain prisons. Whenever the insurgents captured soldiers or civilians the KKE gave them the option of joining the communist forces or execution.

Staktopoulos could establish he was nationalist-minded by admitting to the murder and serving the interests of the Greek state. "You have an obligation to the fatherland to confess," demanded Constantine Rendis, minister of public order.[15] Sacrifice for the fatherland was the relevant issue. During the course of the civil war, the ultra-Greek right usurped patriotism as an absolute virtue exclusive to itself. The minister, anxious to see a speedy end to the Polk affair, had made a snap visit to Thessaloniki to confront Staktopoulos. Unfortunately, the victim refused to spare the fatherland further difficulties by confessing to a crime he did not commit. For his impudence, Mouskoundis and his aides devised new, and more imaginative, techniques of persuasion. They forced him to strip and proceeded to yank slowly the hair on his chest and back, one at a time. This painful exercise was only a prelude to another, and much more excruciating, torment. Using wire, they tied his wrists to his elbows and his knees to his ankles, then his arms to his legs.

Afterward he was laid out on the floor his cell. In a short time, Staktopoulos began to struggle against the binding in response to intense pain, but the movement only made it worse, and soon his cries reverberated in the corridor.[16] He passed out, and when he finally came around, disoriented and terrified, his lost his courage. He agreed to confess that he had lured Polk to a secret meeting with two communist assassins who shot the American on a small boat in the harbor. The investigation, confession, and subsequent trial did little credit to the Greeks, the Americans, or the cause of justice. On 21 April 1949, a jury that deliberated for less than three hours found Staktopoulos guilty as an accessory to murder after the fact. He was sentenced to life imprisonment, although he received a pardon twelve years later.[17]

Someone had to answer for the death of George Polk, and the Greek state had to be absolved of any and all responsibility at all costs. Polk had challenged the veracity and integrity of the Greek government at a time when American-Greek relations were still fragile but of paramount importance to Greece. By 1948, U.S. military and economic aid was all that stood between victory and defeat for the Greek government forces in the ongoing civil war. To the coterie of old royalist politicians and former republican-Venizelists, each time George Polk produced an exposé of the corruption and the heavy-handed policies of the Greek government, he negated the cause of anticommunism that often served as a mask for otherwise incompetent and self-serving politicians.

Ultimately, the publicity swirling around Polk's murder, the Donovan investigation, and the direct interest of the Truman administration compelled the Greek authorities to force a confession from Staktopoulos in order to link the death of the American journalist to the struggle against the communist insurgency. In the summer of 1946, the third round of the Greek civil war had broken out and by 1947 was turning Greece into a zone of confrontation between the USSR and the United States—at least that was the perception in Washington. In that context, Polk's murder at the hands of the rebels was convenient as it was symbolic of the communist threat to Greece as well as to the United States. The actual circumstances surrounding the murder of American journalist George Polk may never come to light.

Nevertheless, the wider background—the conflict that fueled the civil war in Greece and set the stage for his death—was the onset of the East-West confrontation that was reshaping the postwar world in 1948. In this respect, Polk was one of the first American casualties of the Cold War. Yet Polk was not a soldier. He was a journalist and a civilian, underscoring the fact that the Greek government was incapable of protecting Americans in Greece. This circumstance demonstrated the weakness of the Greek state and the ability of the communists to strike anywhere and kill anyone.

A critical factor that made the third round of the Greek civil war almost inevitable was the failure of the right-wing governments, which became increasingly conservative after 1945, to deal, in a nonpartisan manner, with ordinary people labeled as left wing. In the aftermath of the December Uprising, these regimes could not, or would not, differentiate between the leadership and the hard-core elements of the left-wing resistance organizations led by the KKE, on the one hand, and ordinary Greeks who did not subscribe to any particular ideological agenda, on the other. Moreover, the leaders of the right, by their actions and their failure to contain the ultra-right extremists, compounded this error by driving home the point that anyone not with them was automatically against them. In so doing, they had to invalidate the left-wing resistance as a factor in the war against the Axis.

The right needed to negate the efforts of EAM-ELAS in order to discard the success of the left in fighting the Axis and obscure the role of the collaborators, particularly the Security Battalions, during the occupation. The officers of the armed forces, police, gendarmerie, judges, prosecutors, district prefects, mayors, civil servants, journalists, and others who (willingly or under duress) had served the Axis were vulnerable to charges of collaboration, if not treason, and had been hunted down by the left during the December Uprising. Consequently, for these men and women, recognition and eventual institutionalization of the resistance meant that the proverbial sword of Damocles would continue to hang over their heads for the foreseeable future. Hence, while the rest of Europe celebrated the contributions of the groups and individuals who had opposed the German and Italian occupation, the Greek state refused to acknowledge the contribution of the resistance until 1982.[18]

The persecution of the left during the period of the White Terror (1945–1946) consequently affected a large segment of Greek society and forced many to seek refuge in the communist-led bands forming in the mountains. Rex Leeper, the British ambassador to Athens, understood this and in his 1945 annual report on Greek affairs warned Ernest Bevin, the new British secretary of state for foreign affairs, that Greece was becoming dangerously polarized:

> The Right, in a vengeful mood, urged on the police, who were only too willing, to arrest thousands of the Left-wing supporters, many of them innocent of anything but socialist sentiments expressed in somewhat intemperate language, others, no doubt, guilty of murders, though even in these cases, owing to the circumstances of the civil war, it often proved difficult to produce conclusive evidence.... A favourite charge, on which many respectable citizens were arrested, was "moral responsibility" for murders, i.e. in most cases membership, under the occupation, of EAM resistance and local government committees, or of People's Courts, which had condemned to death people described by EAM as "traitors" and by their opponents as "peaceful citizens opposed to communism." The courts were not able to deal with the rush of work, and thousands of EAM supporters remained in the overcrowded jails awaiting trial, often for much more than the statutory six months.[19]

On 25 August 1945, under British pressure, the Greek government introduced a partial amnesty to release those not accused of murder, but it had
made little impact. Three weeks later, on 17 September, Vasilios Kiriakopoulos, the minister of justice, reported that 16,700 were still in prison, of which
14,252 were awaiting trial, and only 1,949 had actually been set free by the
amnesty.[20] Remarkably, although not so for the times, out of the 16,700 inmates only 2,896 were ever convicted of collaboration. In 1952, the number of
collaborators still incarcerated was 1,275 out of a prison population of 28,000.
Over the course of 1945, 80,000 adherents or suspected sympathizers as well
as members of left-wing organizations faced prosecution.[21] In contrast, members of ultra-right-wing groups, collaborators, and officers who had served in
the Security Battalions were infiltrating the security apparatus of the state, the
police, and the armed forces. After the March 1946 general election, the drift
to the extreme right was further accelerated by the election in parliament of
men who had openly supported the puppet occupation governments. This
turn of events facilitated the transition of the Security Battalions from collaborators to anticommunist warriors.

The officers and men of these notorious forces were a living symbol of
everything that had gone wrong with the political establishment in the course
of the occupation. After liberation, most of the junior officers and men of the
Security Battalions were placed in a detention camp in Goudi (outside Athens) and the more senior officers in Averoff prison. In November, the British
had begun to release some of the officers from Averoff prison and brought
others to Egypt. According to an OSS report, former members of the Security
Battalions were slowly being integrated into regular Greek army units. An
American intelligence report added: "EAM's fear, and it is a real one, is that
not only will ELAS be dissolved and disintegrated but that there will be
no popular national army in the true sense. Not only are the ex-Tsoliadhes
[Gestapo-controlled Greek secret police] and members of the Security
Battalions being trained as units but there is a strong tendency to place
Royalist and ex-Metaxist officers in high-ranking positions."[22]

It was the December Uprising in 1944 that created the circumstances for
the mass release and employment of almost all the incarcerated collaborationists as well as the officers and ordinary ranks of the Security Battalions.
Ultimately, 12,000 of those who had served in the Security Battalions
were enrolled in the National Guard that was formed during the December
Uprising. In one act the Greek government destroyed its credibility with
most moderate Greeks. At the same time, releasing the Security Battalions

convinced many who had fought in the left-wing resistance that the intent of the Papandreaou government was to restore the prewar political establishment, many of whose members had collaborated. The Greek right was able to succeed because communism was emerging as a new threat.

The geopolitical dynamic in Europe, Asia, and the Middle East created the distinct possibility that the Soviet Union intended to continue to expand or export the communist revolution to almost every corner of the globe. Eastern Europe had fallen under communist control, as had most of the Balkans with the exception of Greece.

Just two years after the December Uprising, consequently, the United States inherited not only Britain's responsibilities in the Mediterranean and a little later in the Middle East, but also its role as the patrons of the Greek right. The withdrawal of the British from Greece in early 1947, and the proclamation of the Truman Doctrine a few weeks later, meant that the Americans officially assumed Britain's international responsibilities in these regions; therefore, U.S. intervention in Greece was not only new, but unpredictable. Greek politicians, after a century of accommodating and ingratiating themselves to the British, were not accustomed to the new "superpower," and they were unfamiliar with the quirks and peculiarities of their new protectors. The murder of an American journalist, however, did not portend well for the new relationship. George Polk may have been disagreeable and a thorn in the right-wing Greek politicians—but he was an American just the same. Thus, the Greek regime felt compelled to force a confession from Grigoris Staktopoulos that put the blame squarely on the communists.

The Staktopoulos family, like hundreds of thousands of other families, had been swept up in the conflagration of the Greek civil war. This latest round of fratricide was part of the cycle of violence and retribution that had hijacked the lives of Greeks since the occupation. After liberation, a combination of fear, mistrust, desperation, and competition for political control between the left and the right had ignited into the Battle of Athens in December 1944. The toll on the Greek state was high. The fighting stymied efforts to rehabilitate the economy of the country and retarded most attempts at providing a modicum of subsistence for the thousands left homeless and destitute by the earlier ravages of the war. The wreckage (even by the industrial-scale standards of World War II) was overwhelming.

In 1948, almost four years after liberation, the economic plight of the country and the hardships confronting the population were staggering. Over 2,000 villages that had been destroyed by Axis reprisals and the additional ones devastated by the civil war remained in ruins. One quarter of all the structures in the country—400,000 buildings—were totally demolished. Over one million people in Greece were struggling as refugees or displaced persons. The Athens sprawl, characteristic of the congested capital today, is one of the civil war's legacies, triggered by the influx of hundreds of thousands of homeless villagers and refugees from the interior of the country to the capital.[23] The state had to support 700,000 people—the families of soldiers in the army and those who had been killed in battle. Thirty-four percent of the Greek population depended on appropriations from the national budget.[24]

Simultaneously, a combination of uncontrolled forest fires and foraging for wood to use as fuel in some areas decimated 75 percent of Greece's forests. State finances were practically nonexistent, and Greece was drowning in an avalanche of worthless paper currency generated by the inflationary policies of the occupation authorities.[25] Sadly, liberation had little impact, and the Greek currency continued to plummet unabated. In March 1948, the drachma traded at the rate of 170 quadrillion drachmas to a single American dollar.[26] The cost of living by the end of the Greek civil war in 1949 would be almost 254 times higher than it was before the occupation. During the same period, according to a report from the British embassy in Athens, "two million and four hundred thousand people were said to be one step from starvation."[27]

The cost in human losses was equally appalling. A conservative estimate places the number killed, as a result of the war, at approximately 500,000 and another 880,000 disabled by disease. In other words, out of a population of just over seven million, approximately 19 percent suffered a violent death or incurred chronic disabilities.[28]

The third round of fighting that had broken out in the summer of 1946 was partly a response to the reign of terror that cascaded across the country in retaliation for the atrocities committed by EAM, KKE, ELAS, and OPLA during the December Uprising and partly because of the ambitions of the KKE to achieve power. Effectively, the period of White Terror from February 1945 to September 1946 created the momentum for the last phase of the civil war because it left the adherents of EAM-ELAS and the KKE with little choice except to fight or face heavy-handed persecution for an indefinite period of time at the hands of former collaborators. The scale of retaliation by ultra-right-wing gangs against the partisans of the left was widespread and remained unchecked, especially outside of Athens and the other major urban centers. The authorities could not, or would not, intervene in thousands of situations where fanatics of both political extremes indulged in beatings, looting, rape, and murder.

The story of Andreas Patrikios is one example of how the vicissitudes of occupation and the politics of the resistance impacted one family. Patrikios was born and raised in the provincial town of Patras. He graduated from university a short time before the outbreak of World War II. In 1942, like many young men, he went to the mountains to join ELAS and fight against the Axis. His legal training, however, was more valuable to the left-wing and communist-controlled organization, and Patrikios was made a judge. In this capacity, he had the task of determining the guilt or innocence of collaborators and those accused of treason against EAM-ELAS. According to one of his relatives, Patrikios tried very hard to dispense even-handed justice, but often the local ELAS leadership overruled him and executed innocent men and women.[29]

In the meantime, the Germans and the Security Battalions constantly harassed Patrikios' family. Soon after the occupation, members of the local right-wing X organization paid a visit to Angeliki, his older sister, on her farm. A couple of them punched and kicked her in the stomach, thighs, and head. They tormented her for hours, until she was unconscious. In the months following the outbreak of the 1946 civil war, while Patrikios was still in hiding, the ultra-right-wing group also went after Kratitira, his younger sister. This time, they hauled the young girl to the town plaza of Lower Achaia and beat her publicly and then tossed the almost lifeless body to the side of the street. Witnesses to the spectacle cheered and egged on the girl's tormentors; however, some sympathetic bystander afterward provided first aid, thereby saving her life.[30]

Patrikios hid in his cousin's house (spending most of the time on the roof), and when it became too dangerous to stay in Patras, he joined his sisters in Athens. They had moved to the capital to escape the persecutions meted out to the families of ELAS veterans and members of the KKE. In addition, Patrikios had blood on his hands, because whether he condemned actual collaborators to death or remained helpless as the ELAS leadership executed men and women he had found innocent, the relatives and friends of the victims were prepared to exact their own brand of justice if they got their hands on him before the authorities. The KKE, whether through ELAS, EAM, or OPLA, drafted professional men and women and exploited their expertise, but also ensured that they committed or participated in extrajudicial murder, assassination, or torture so that they had little choice but to remain loyal to the KKE as outlaw enemies of the government. Many of the men Patrikios judged were members of rival right-wing bands who had refused to join ELAS and, as a result, were accused and convicted as collaborators.

For months, Patrikios, tired and suffering from tuberculosis, wandered from place to place in Athens. He managed to evade capture by remaining indoors and using the small laundry room in his sister's house as a hiding place. Eventually, due to either betrayal or carelessness, he was arrested. First, he was imprisoned on the island of Zakynthos and then transferred to Averoff prison in Athens. He had to be hospitalized for a few months because of the tuberculosis. He tried to defend himself, and despite his own difficulties he provided legal help to other inmates. Ultimately, it was all to no avail. The military court found him guilty and he was executed a few months before the end of the civil war in 1949.[31] Judging by similar cases, the Patrikios' trial itself would have been a mere formality and mirrored identical tribunals across Greece in order to bring communists and traitors to justice. Certainly many were innocent, yet a large number of those arrested were guilty of terrible crimes during the occupation and in the December Uprising.

What had passed for justice in the small mountain villages that had the misfortune of coming under communist control was at best outright murder and guilt by association. Executions were often accomplished in the most horrific manner. An example of this was the small Albanian villages of Limnes and Gerbesi in the region of Argolida. The Germans had occupied these communities in August and had executed a number of people, including some who were members of EAM. When the Germans left, ELAS units swept into Gerbesi and immediately murdered twenty-three people, including several children. Their crime was that some villagers, sick of the KKE's rule of torture and death, had joined the Security Battalions, but since they had left with these forces, ELAS took its revenge against members of their families. In the nearby village of Limnes, EAM and OPLA representatives tortured and killed twenty-four people. Stylianos Perrakis, in his account of the murder of members of his family at the hands of the communists, writes:

> The Limnes executions were a carefully staged affair, a macabre theatrical performance . . . directed by Gavros (a senior communist) with the assistance of several other KKE politicals [*sic*]. It started with a meeting in front of the village church during which Papasotiriou and the Cross-Eyed One delivered short but violent speeches, likening to a field full of thorns that needed to be pulled out before being ready for cultivation.

This murderous metaphor, showing the schoolteacher antecedents of both Gavros and Papasotiriou, was prelude to the arrests and executions that were to follow. The show started with a lynching . . . the victim was a shepherd accused of having betrayed the executed relatives of village people to the Germans, and the crowd was urged by the political leaders who were present in the proceedings to punish him as he deserved. A . . . mob started hitting the unfortunate man, who was finally shot in the end by a KKE official. . . . The single killing was only an appetizer for the main performance that took place a couple of days later, following show trials in front of a forcibly convened village assembly. A group of victims was escorted to some fields outside the village by an OPLA group . . . and nineteen of them had their throats cut with a butcher's knife, the familiar OPLA trademark. The two executioners were actually professional butchers in civilian life.[32]

To some extent, the butchers, grocers, schoolteachers, and university students had filled the ranks of EAM, the KKE, and OPLA. No doubt Patrikios had served as a judge on similar occasions and willingly or unwillingly stood by and watched innocent men, women, and children executed under terrible conditions and by the most brutal means. During and after the civil war, the perpetrators of these atrocities were arrested, tried, and convicted sometimes through due process that included written evidence and the testimony of eyewitnesses.

The stage trials, the notion of collective punishment, and the use of butchers that guaranteed a horrific killing aimed at instilling fear were not the individual actions of men deranged by war but KKE policy. In forcing the villagers to engage in stage trials as well as participate in executions, the communists aimed to make the villagers co-conspirators, thus ensuring their loyalty. Another factor was that the reign of terror inaugurated with the arrival of ELAS or implemented by EAM and the KKE's OPLA murder squads in many of the villages throughout Greece forced the local inhabitants to seek protection from the Germans and the Security Battalions. Under these circumstances the Germans or Security Battalions arrived to liberate a village from the clutches of the communists. When the occupation forces left they often armed the villagers so that they could fight off the ELAS and EAM. Under the perverse circumstances, the villagers sought salvation from the communists often by summoning the hated Germans and Security Battalions and informing them who were the local EAM and KKE individuals in their village. Consequently, after liberation it was difficult to sort out collaborator and traitor from desperate villager. The KKE and EAM insisted that anyone who worked with the Germans or informed for them had to be arrested and tried as a traitor, while the victims of the communist abuse insisted that members of EAM, KKE, ELAS, or OPLA had to answer for the atrocities they conducted during the occupation and the December Uprising. In the absence of swift justice both right and left took matters into their own hands and dispensed with judicial niceties.

A few weeks after the Polk murder, Kenneth Matthews, the BBC correspondent in Greece, witnessed a military tribunal sitting at a women's detention center and by reconstructing the proceedings offers rare insight into the absurd and crude attempts at what passed for justice in northern Greece during the civil war. Matthews recalled:

> The general presiding [asks the accused]:
>   "Where do you come from?"
> The woman witness: "From Thessalonica."
>   "What is your work?"
>   "I am a doctor."
>   "How long have you practiced in Thessalonica?"
>   "Twenty years.'
>   "Then since you have some experience and are besides a qualified scientist: you will be able to tell us: is Thessalonica a Greek or a Bulgarian City?"
>   The question, like those devised by the inquisitors of the Holy Office, was framed to disclose whether the witness preserved a Greek and Christian soul or whether she was given over to the abomination of Communism. She replied:
>   "I don't know."
> The Bishop of Volos (a member of the tribunal):
>   "Kill her, my general! In the name of the religion, kill her where she stands!"[33]

Denying or merely questioning the Hellenic identity of Greece's second largest city was tantamount to treason. Another consideration is that the authorities in this region—exposed to frequent DAG intrusions—were less inclined to conduct trials at leisure.

A large number of women in Thessaloniki and Athens as well as in dozens of small cities and towns went through a similar experience because they were members of the KKE or their male family members were in hiding or had joined the communist forces. Many of them also suffered imprisonment or execution because of accusations from malicious neighbors or duplicitous spouses. Mary Henderson, who served as a Red Cross nurse and had occasion to visit the women prisoners, writes:

> As we were leaving the camp a pretty little woman called Fotini— Greek for light—grabbed my arm and begged for help. "I am only here," she blurted out, "Because my husband wanted to be rid of me. He wanted to be free to marry his mistress, Vromokoritso the dirty girl—so he told the police that I was a Communist. I am no Communist, just a broken-hearted woman. What should I do?" Her big, black eyes veiled with tears searched for mine—for help. "How can I prove that I am not a Communist now that I am in prison?" . . . As I looked back at Fotini's black, imploring eyes I longed to be able to help—but how?[34]

A great many of the women in prison, especially those from the villages, had no understanding or commitment to Marxism, but had participated in the fighting just the same. In another of Henderson's experiences as a nurse visiting the women's detention center, she recalls how Ekaterina, a young peasant girl, "after an incoherent explanation of her symptoms and how she did not want anyone to know—ran into the toilet and a few minutes later gave birth to a premature baby on the pink ladies' cloakroom floor."[35]

The baby did not survive, and Ekaterina, who had been arrested for hiding a gun under her skirt, most likely languished in a prison for months before being formally charged with a crime. Thousands of young women, like Ekaterina and Fotini, were trapped by the tumultuous events sweeping over Greece in the 1940s and uprooted from the security of the traditional village life. For them the resistance had been an opportunity to escape the asphyxiating role prescribed for women in both the rural communities of Greece and the large urban centers. They had fought the Axis and afterward the British; some of them, like Ekaterina, had smuggled weapons or had volunteered to act as decoys during the December Uprising so that ELAS snipers could pick off British and Greek soldiers.

They paid a heavy price for participating in EAM-ELAS because with the defeat of the left in December 1944 many of these women became displaced within their own country. After breaking the bonds of tradition and religion by abandoning their families, they could not return to their villages; at any rate, it is doubtful that the small and tightly knit communities would have taken them back. In some cases, the shame of prison, suspicion of unacceptable sexual behavior, and pregnancy out of wedlock meant that most of these women were doomed to remain unmarried and thus constituted an unacceptable economic and social burden to their families. Consequently, the third round of civil war in 1946 had offered a large number of these women an avenue of escape from the uncertainties of attempting to reintegrate into mainstream society, this time by joining the communist bands assembling in the mountains.

Young men also faced stringent social and economic liabilities as well as the stigma of antinationalism and anti-Greek behavior for participating in ELAS. In a society as small as Greece's in which citizens were categorized and catalogued by the police and security services so that their "file" followed them the rest of their lives, the labels of communist, anarchist, Slav, Arvanitis (Greek-speaking Orthodox Albanian), traitor, atheist, or any combination of the above had economic as well as political consequences. A bad file barred an individual from employment in the civil service, large companies, and even domestic work. Later on, such files prevented people from emigrating. In the 1950s, and until the collapse of the military junta in 1974, emigration was only possible after a prospective candidate obtained a certificate of "nationally correct views" from the police. Without this certificate, obtaining employment was difficult; marriage, baptism of children, and church-sanctioned burials were denied unless an individual produced the document of political and national correctness.

In the heat of the moment, thousands of young men, inspired by the prospect of a better future advertised by EAM, had fought the British in the streets of Athens to prevent the return of the prewar political and economic establishment. For ELAS veterans who had battled the German occupiers, the fighting in December was an extension of the resistance; for others, particularly the younger and less battle-experienced men of the ELAS reserve units in the capital, the Battle of Athens represented a watershed in the political future of Greece. Almost all the younger men came from the working-class districts of Athens. Some of these foot soldiers of the December Uprising may have fought for a new and better way of life, some because they were communists, but many others simply joined to take advantage of an opportunity to improve their present circumstances. Rex Leeper, the British ambassador, lost his housemaid when she went off to find her son "who was with ELAS, a mere boy who had gone because he was offered food, pay and a uniform."[36]

Ultimately, the EAM-ELAS supporters not only advocated the establishment of a socialist or communist state; rather, many insisted on justice—particularly the arrest, trial, and punishment of the collaborators—and a level playing field in addressing the constitutional problem. The KKE's accusation of treason against Greek officials was made plausible by the presence of high-profile collaborators frequently spotted in the streets of Athens. For the most part, they got nothing with respect to the former and very little with respect to the latter. The young men and women who had joined ELAS were not party to the KKE's strategy of using terror to secure the loyalty of the villagers or trying to eliminate rivals by accusing them of collaboration. They trusted their superiors and followed them to battle in December, and afterward many had little choice but to flee to the mountains of northern Greece to escape the White Terror.

In 1945, the Plastiras government established military committees to select officers for the new army, which went on to appoint 228 who had served with the Security Battalions and 221 ELAS veterans. Despite the apparent impartiality of this selection, succeeding governments between 1945 and 1949 tended to discriminate in favor of officers from the Security Battalions rather than ELAS. In fact, the Greek general staff, with a few exceptions, placed officers with service in ELAS on the inactive list, even those who had held commissions in the Greek army before the occupation.[37]

After the end of hostilities in January, the Greek government continued to use former Security Battalion forces to maintain security in the countryside. The cruel absurdity of this situation was that the personnel of the Security Battalions, in the guise of national guard units, now had responsibility for establishing law and order in large areas of Greece that had supported their enemy combatants, EAM-ELAS. Effectively, the former collaborationist forces were simply given license to settle scores against the left. In September 1945, however, the national guard was withdrawn from active service and replaced by the reorganized gendarmerie, leaving the former Security Battalion officers unemployed, with the exception of the two hundred and twenty-eight already appointed in the new army. This professional setback was only temporary; the outbreak of hostilities in 1946 and the radical changes taking place within the new armed forces created a fresh opportunity for them to gain readmission.

During this period (1945–1946), secret leagues and associations honeycombed the officer corps. The structure and membership of most of these groups were shadowy, and some represented only a loose collection of officers with common professional interests. To a great extent, the development of these factions was a reaction against constant political intervention in the armed forces before and after the occupation. The parade of short-term governments in the post–December Uprising period only intensified the insecurity of the officers as each regime promoted its favorites. It was a matter not just of professional ego but also of economic survival. Unemployment for officers with a meager pension (a by-product of inflation) would leave them practically destitute. Former Venizelist officers who had accepted the monarchy and had been readmitted into the armed forces were the most vulnerable group. The Plastiras government had reinstated many former Venizelist-republicans at the expense of royalists, but the limited tenure of this regime left them professionally exposed. Meanwhile, many in the royalist faction lost their posts to former republicans, and they responded by creating their own organizations to protect themselves from forced retirement or dismissal.

Beginning early in 1946, ultra-right-wing royalist officers, who favored the king because they believed that monarchy was a safeguard against communism, were gaining control of the military. To enforce their brand of nationalism, these conservative officers created a secret organization, which came to be known by its acronym as IDEA (Sacred Association of Nationalist Officers). IDEA quickly spread its tentacles within the officer corps and infiltrated the general staff as well as the headquarters of the new army divisions. In the summer of 1946, representatives of IDEA took the initiative and persuaded the minister of defense to admit into the army officers who had served with the Security Battalions. The reason, according to George Karayiannis, the unofficial biographer of IDEA, was that these officers were not only capable professionals, but also fanatical anticommunists. In addition, they had considerable experience in counterinsurgency warfare, first under the Germans and later under the British during the December Uprising.[38]

Many officers, however, who had fought with ELAS, were now excluded from the armed forces and bore the brunt of the White Terror, and a year later many of them took up arms and eventually helped to create the Democratic Army of Greece. In response, the Popular Party government of Dimitrios Maximos, in collaboration with the military, established three detention camps on the islands of Makronisos, Gioura, and Trikeri in 1947. There were supplementary detention centers on other small islands, but the first three camps were set up to deal with three categories of leftists and suspected communists: Makronisos for military personnel, usually officers and men who had served with ELAS; Gioura for politicians; and Trikeri for men and women from areas under the control of the communist bands. Makronisos achieved considerably more notoriety than the other two prison islands and became linked with some of the most savage treatment inflicted on leftists or suspected leftist prisoners during the civil war. From 1947 to 1950, 1,110 officers along with 27,000 soldiers passed through Makronisos, labeled "the new Dachau" by the left.[39]

Perhaps more galling for the professional officers, who by fighting for ELAS had compromised their careers in the postwar army, was that in many cases the men who condemned them to these horrible islands had either actively collaborated with or passively acquiesced to the Axis. In 1947, over 10,000 suspected leftists and communists were rounded up in the larger urban centers and placed in the detention centers and prisons on the mainland as well as on the islands. Many men who could have filled positions of responsibility in the armed forces and police services instead were forced to languish in prison or submit to a process of political rehabilitation on Makronisos. According to Artemis Leontis,

> Greek Government officials nicknamed it the "National Baptismal Front" because they imagined this to be the place where prisoners of the Greek Civil War would wash themselves into more conservative citizens. Philosopher and politician Panayiotis Kanellopoulos called Makronisos the place where Greeks could build new Parthenons, because there, on an island best suited for grazing, prisoners were forced to build out of local materials in a span of three or four years not only administrative buildings, villas, and a club for their persecutors but also a factory for non-alcoholic beverages, a radio station, a convalescence area, kitchens, water, reservoirs, roads, six chuches, four theaters—where their ideological rehabilitation was to take place—arches, statues, bas-reliefs, monuments with shells and mosaics, as well as miniature versions of the Parthenon and Hagia Sophia.[40]

The treatment of the inmates, because they had been officers and soldiers, was harsh and designed to break their spirit. The object of the torture, random beatings, mock executions, and mindless daily drudgery was to force the inmates to sign a declaration of repentance, followed by public denunciations of communism. The prisoners who agreed to be saved from the clutches of "atheist-Marxism" could also demonstrate their sincerity by joining in the beatings and torture of fellow inmates who had held out against embracing "love of country and religion" by rejecting godless communism.

Before all of this came to pass, a number of veteran ELAS officers (the precise figure is impossible to determine) recognized the direction that the 1945–46 governments were taking and joined approximately 5,000 men and some women whom the KKE had sent to safety in communist Yugoslavia, Bulgaria, and Albania. During the winter of 1946, small groups infiltrated back into northern Greece and, linking up with bands of leftist guerrillas hiding in the mountains, conducted occasional raids either to secure supplies or to exact revenge against ultra-right-wing gangs.

The problem of lawlessness was further compounded as increasing numbers of ELAS veterans left their homes throughout 1945 and 1946 for the protection of the rugged terrain in parts of northern Greece, in the Peloponnese, and on some of the Aegean islands. Although ELAS had surrendered an impressive number of weapons as part of the Varkiza Agreement, an almost equal number were hidden and being used by the leftist bands forming in the mountains for self-defense and for attacking police stations, villages, and other targets of opportunity.[41]

Initially, the KKE had not sanctioned the increasing and widespread banditry or encouraged its members to join the bands operating in the mountains. Although the communist press made references to the guerrilla activity of former ELAS members, the leftist publications suggested that the people who had taken to the hills did so to escape the White Terror in the cities. According to Ole Smith, an expert on the KKE, "There is no doubt that the KKE, throughout 1945 and early 1946, held the view that the struggle was political, and thus had to be fought in the cities, by mass organizations, trade unions, and agrarian cooperatives."[42]

Certainly, the defeat of ELAS in the December Uprising left the KKE leadership in disarray and the party organization in shambles. According to some estimates, at the time of liberation in October 1944, membership in the KKE had peaked at 400,000, but dropped off to 200,000 after the debacle in December.[43] The critical political problem confronting the KKE in 1945, however, was the first postwar parliamentary election planned for early 1946. The parties of the left as well as the KKE demanded a thorough revision of the electoral lists as a precondition for taking part in the elections. According to Smith's analysis: "They did not wish to create the impression abroad that elections could be held in the existing anarchical situation. Since there were no indications that the government would carry out a revision or establish law and order, the Center and the Left were inclined to boycott the elections."[44]

The decision not to take part in the March election, ultimately, proved a serious mistake for the KKE, which in tandem with the increasing scale of violence in the Greek countryside as well as the transformation of the international environment generated the momentum for civil war in Greece. Certainly it played into the hands of Zachariadis, as mentioned above, since the communist leader was inclined toward a violent resolution of Greece's political future.

Indeed, 1945 had been a defining year for Greece and the rest of the world. At the Yalta Conference of 4–11 February 1945, Stalin quietly reaffirmed to Churchill the so-called Percentage Agreement with respect to the British and Soviet spheres of influence in the Balkans. Although during the meeting the Big Three discussed the shape of postwar Europe and Asia, Churchill and Stalin disagreed over Poland, but not over Greece, which the Soviet leader continued to accept as part of the British sphere. In a matter of months, all that changed. Roosevelt died in April and Churchill was swept from office in July, leaving Stalin, the only remaining member of the original wartime Allied leadership, to enjoy the fruits of victory as head of his country.

Furthermore, when World War II ended with the defeat of Germany in May and Japan in August, the international relations dynamic, forged out of the necessity of war, gradually shifted and deteriorated. The United States and the Soviet Union were rapidly undergoing metamorphoses into superpowers; the Grand Alliance that had achieved so much in the war was quickly unraveling in peacetime, susceptible to new fears and suspicions. By the time Truman and Prime Minister Clement Atlee met with the Soviet leader in Potsdam (17 July–1 August 1945), Stalin had become less conciliatory and chided the British over the Greek government's breaches of the Varkiza Agreement, the document that had ended the December Uprising.

During the course of the meeting, Stalin surprised the British and Americans by demanding a Soviet presence in the Aegean, with a naval base at either Thessaloniki or Alexandroupolis or in the Dodecanese Islands. Stalin then pressed for a revision of the 1936 Montreux Convention on the Dardanelles and the Bosphorus Straits to facilitate Soviet access to the Mediterranean, arguing that it was no less unreasonable than Britain's control of the Suez Canal. He also demanded that Turkey surrender the frontier provinces of Kars and Ardahan to the Soviet republics of Armenia and Georgia. Meanwhile, throughout Eastern Europe and the Balkans, the Soviets were already imposing communist regimes.

Yet, despite Stalin's advantage of position, the fact that the Red Army occupied large parts of Eastern Europe and the Balkans, he would just as quickly retract these claims in the face of opposition from his Anglo-American allies. Stalin agreed to withdraw the Red Army from Vienna as well as Iran, while failing to force the British out of Syria.[45] Regardless of these compromises, the perception of the Soviet juggernaut gobbling up the rest of postwar Europe was beginning to take hold. After George Kennan's famous "long telegram" from Moscow in 1946, the notion that the West must contain communism—and therefore stop Stalin in Greece and Turkey—was the policy consensus of both the Democrats and Republicans in Washington. Greece became a concern because the anticommunists in Washington could point to an actual communist insurgency taking place; Turkey was seen as another domino, one that could set off a cascade of Middle East petroleum-producing countries coming under Soviet influence and eventual control. The domino theory—if one country in a region fell under communism then the surrounding states would also succumb—assumed considerable clout in U.S. government circles in the 1950s.

In the meantime, the boycott of the elections had marginalized the KKE politically, leaving the initiative to right-wing factions to dominate the makeup of the postwar governments and in the process destroy the influence of EAM in Greek society. The increasing lawlessness, moreover, provided the excuse for those regimes to restructure Greece as a centralized and authoritarian state. In addition to reviving Metaxas' instruments of repression, such as the use of internal exile and the infamous declarations of repentance extorted from prisoners, they established extraordinary court-martials throughout Greece. These tribunals by summary procedures condemned thousands of people to prison or to the firing squads for crimes against public security. David Close calculates that over the three years of the civil war, these bodies "sentence[ed] over 2,000 people to be executed, and several thousand more to be jailed for offenses as trivial as the reported slandering of prominent public officials."[46] Other scholars have estimated that the number of those condemned to death during this period reached as high as 7,500, with 3,000–5,000 political prisoners being executed.[47]

The legal framework that facilitated the imprisonment and execution of captured communist insurgents, as well as their supporters in the cities or those suspected of sympathizing with the guerrillas, was established by the newly elected Populist Party government on 18 June 1946, a few months after the elections. The first article of Resolution C "on extraordinary measures concerning the public order and security," passed by the Greek parliament, imposed the death penalty for those who intended to "detach a part of Greece from the whole of the country."[48] This was clearly directed at communists because of the KKE support for an autonomous Macedonia. On 27 December 1947, the government put forward Compulsory Law 509 to address "security measures of the state, the regime, and the social order, and the protection of citizens' liberties."[49] Effectively, this legislation banned all leftist parties and organizations and imposed the death penalty on those who were "seeking to apply ideas, which overtly aim to overthrow the regime or the established social system by violent means, or aim to detach a part from the whole of the country."[50]

The consequences for ordinary Greeks trapped in the maelstrom of the civil war could be catastrophic. The police used their new authority to hunt down anyone suspected of supporting the rebels and established a wide-range network of informants. The owners of newspaper kiosks, who by law had to be disabled military veterans (or their offspring), were a good source of local intelligence and could categorize individuals simply by indicating if they purchased left- or right-wing publications. The authorities could also coerce the proprietors of coffeehouses to inform on their customers or lose their license. The burden of arrest and punishment fell primarily on the KKE members and left sympathizers in the cities and towns, who could easily be identified by the kiosk and coffee shop owners, by malicious neighbors, or by those who had suffered at the hands of the left during the occupation and the December Uprising. Proof of guilt or innocence was at the discretion of the local extraordinary court.

For example, Koula Eleftheriou was accused of recruiting guerrillas under the pseudonym of Maria. The only evidence against her was the accusation of a member of the gendarmerie who was alleged to have collaborated with the Axis forces during the occupation. The court found Eleftheriou guilty and sentenced her to death on 1 May 1947. Five days later, she was executed. Although the twenty-four-year-old Eleftheriou was a member of the KKE, her complicity in aiding the insurgency is not certain. Accusation was sufficient if it was aimed at a member of the KKE.

Others were catapulted into the chaos of postwar Greece not because of ideology, but through happenstance. Three such examples were Leo, Kostas, and Andreas Katsuris from the small village of Lidouri in the Peloponnesus. The lives of the three brothers were indelibly changed by occupation and civil war. By the economic standards of the times, the Katsuris family was prosperous. Their father had followed the well-trodden path of many Greeks at the turn of the century and migrated to the United States to seek his fortune. He eventually ended up in Vancouver, Canada, and his monthly remittances enabled the family to live comfortably and build a large house. The boys received their primary and secondary education, but their studies came to an end with the Axis occupation.

In the winter of 1942–1943, Andreas and Kostas left the village, along with other young men, to take part in the resistance. Kostas joined ELAS and Andreas was trained by EAM to be a teacher. Leo, four years younger than Kostas, remained behind: "I didn't join the partisans, I was young, slim, I didn't have the stamina to go there (to the mountains). While Kostas was crazy already from high school."[51] Leo, however, often risked his life taking food and water to the local ELAS units hiding in the nearby mountains. Kostas took part in numerous firefights against the Germans and was wounded in August 1944.

Four months later, Leo was conscripted for military service and was assigned to the 9th Infantry Division. Kostas was studying law while recovering from his wound in Athens. After the outbreak of the White Terror he could not bear the prospect of arrest, the accompanying beatings, and internal exile so decided to make his way to the communist bands in the mountains. Andreas was caught and sent to the infamous Markonisos prison island. Thanks to a sympathetic officer, Andreas was quickly released from captivity. After reaching the mainland, he was seized by a right-wing gang and shot. For over a year the family did not know Andreas' fate. They received letters from acquaintances claiming to have spotted Andreas, but the young man had been buried in an unmarked grave by the side of the road.

For the duration of the civil war, Leo and Kostas were fighting on opposite sides and under different conditions. Kostas was made an officer in the DAG and given responsibility for recruitment and training. Leo, along with six hundred other men, was assigned to a special battalion for suspected leftists. They were often given the thankless task of walking over suspected minefields or were committed to particularly dangerous missions. "One time they sent us to the Albanian border," recounts Leo. "Our battalion incinerated a village and killed a bunch of Albanians in a guardhouse. Then we built some defenses on high ground in order to outflank the partisans returning to their hideouts in Albania. But we failed and we couldn't go any further and the Albanians attacked us. Four hundred out of six hundred were killed."

During this time, Leo was fully aware that Kostas was across the line, high up in the rugged mountains intersecting Albania and Greece. "When we reached the Albanian border, you could see a lot of people: partisans walking on the Albania side. But I knew from my mother that Kostas had joined the Democratic Army of Greece and where he was located. Every now and then, our mother received a letter from Kostas which was sent from the front to Yugoslavia, then to my father in Vancouver, and finally to my mother in Athens." While Leo, Kostas, and Andreas were caught up in the politics of civil war, their destinies were increasingly shaped by circumstances unfolding in London, Washington, and finally Moscow.

By 1948 Greek society was divided into distinct political fault lines. A minority of the population were staunch supporters of the KKE, and another minority were the followers of the extreme right.[52] Most people identified with the moderate left or right, although their political sympathies shifted according to the hardships faced or the acts of the government authorities and those of the communists. The aftermath of the death of George Polk revealed that no one was safe. The arrest, torture, and imprisonment of Staktopoulos made a mockery of law and signaled that anyone with a left-wing affiliation during the occupation was vulnerable to persecution and in some cases death at the hands of the state or by a right-wing paramilitary group. Arrest, trial, imprisonment, and execution were at the whim of local authorities. Justice was meted out and determined by political attachment—often mere accusation was tantamount to indictment and led to summary punishment. In this respect, the communists and the Greek government officials shared a fanaticism that allowed little room for collective or individual ambiguity. Neither side, accordingly, held the moral high ground—at least until the KKE decided to commit to Macedonian self-determination and subsequently was censured for agreeing to surrender Greek national territory.

CHAPTER 8

From Insurgency to Civil War

In times of peace, sons bury their fathers. In times of war,
fathers bury their sons.

—Croesus to Cyrus

At the higher elevations the mountains of northern Greece and the Peloponnese, deep ravines and jagged cliffs scar the landscape, leaving an impression of desolation and loneliness. This inhospitable landscape has for
generations hosted bandits, rebels, and revolutionaries, offering them shelter
from conventional forces seeking their destruction. The safety of the mountains, however, is not enough. The barren peaks and dank caves provide protection but little else—survival depends on sources of food and supplies and
the ability to replenish weapons and ammunition. Historically, outlaws have
preyed on the small hamlets and tiny villages that dot the foothills, extorting
or taking whatever supplies they could pilfer from the hapless villagers.

The period of the 1940s was not an exception to these activities, whether
carried out by guerrilla bands fighting the Axis during the occupation or desperate men escaping the White Terror that engulfed Greece after liberation.
Between the winter of 1945 and spring of 1946, sporadic clashes between small
bands of ELAS and the gendarmes expanded the reign of lawlessness that
plagued the Greek countryside and imposed greater misery on the local inhabitants. By the summer of 1946, the increasing scale of violence outside of
Athens and the other large urban centers caused the country to drift toward
civil war.

The traditional date for the outbreak of the 1946–1949 civil war is 30–31
March 1946, the night before the national election, when a communist band

descended from their mountain hideout into the small town of Litochoro on the eastern slopes of Mount Olympus. Thirty-three ELAS men carried out the raid. These rebels had sought refuge on Mount Olympus to escape the persecution of the White Terror. A large number of them were from Litochoro and knew the lay of the land so they were able to slip into the town unnoticed. During the course of the attack several buildings were razed, including the police station, and nine people were killed—six soldiers and a gendarme, along with two civilians. The communists captured another seven soldiers and gendarmes but shortly afterward they let them go.[1] Perhaps this was a message that the communist leadership sent to the government in Athens in response to the general election scheduled on the same day. The raid was meant to frighten the Greek government into making concessions.[2]

By the spring and summer of 1946, communist guerrilla bands began crossing the Yugoslav border back into Greece and raided isolated Greek army and gendarme outposts as well as small villages. Food was their primary objective, yet over the summer the raids penetrated deeper into Greek territory, bypassing the Greek national guard detachments deployed to protect northern Greece and the countryside of the Peloponnese.

Under the best of circumstances, it was a difficult task to patrol northern Greece. Even the most ruthless efforts of Greece's recent occupiers, the Italians and Germans, had failed to contain the resistance fighters. The guerrilla bands would attack government positions and then quickly withdraw to their mountain hideouts. The frontiers of northern Greece extended over six hundred miles of rugged terrain, most of which were unguarded and, to a great extent, unguardable. Even during the Ottoman period, it was impossible for the sultan's armies to maintain security over this region, and the authorities could provide safe passage for mule trains and other commercial travelers only by essentially coopting the local bandits to serve as a regional militia.[3]

Initially, the communist bands that infiltrated into the mountainous regions of Greece, like the Greek bandits of the Ottoman period, were independent of a central command and their success relied on the skill and daring of the men who led the insurgents. Testament to the unique role of the leaders was that most independent guerrilla units were known by the name of the commander. Right-wing groups persecuting communists outside the large cities and towns also followed this custom. In August 1946, however, the central committee of the KKE appointed Markos Vaphiadis to command the guerrilla forces that were forming into various bands and to bring them under the control of a single command.[4]

FIG. II. ELAS guerrillas. Greek Ministry of Foreign Affairs: Photo Exhibition of the
Diplomatic and Historical Archive Department.

Like Zachariadis, Vaphiadis came from Asia Minor as a refugee in 1923. In
his teens, as was the case with many young Asia Minor refugees, he joined the
KKE and ended up in prison because of his communist activities. During the
occupation he served with ELAS as a representative of the National Liberation Front. Although not a soldier by training but a political commissar,
Vaphiadis was a gifted amateur and learned a great deal from Euripides
Bakirdzis as well as from actual combat operations.[5] He gained valuable
experience in guerrilla warfare operations in which he displayed remarkable
ability. This experience served him well when he took over as head of the
Democratic Army of Greece (DAG), as the guerrillas were renamed as they
came together under the KKE in 1946.

August was late in the season to organize and implement insurgency operations in the arid mountainous regions of northern Greece. Vaphiadis had
limited time to secure sufficient food supplies and ammunition to sustain a
guerrilla campaign throughout fall and winter. Food shortages would remain
a serious challenge for Vaphiadis' guerrilla bands, as in order to maintain their

Map 3. Greece 1946–1947: Democratic Operational Areas. Map by Costa Dedegikas.

mobility they either had to live off the land or extort supplies from the local villagers.[6]

Zachariadis and most of the KKE leadership remained in Athens, and only joined the communist forces in the mountains sometime during October 1947—possibly anticipating or vainly believing in a mass urban uprising leading to an orthodox communist revolution. At the very least, Zachariadis believed that a sufficient upheaval would occur to enhance the KKE's influence in a new government, which would include a significant number of communists.[7]

Vaphiadis, meanwhile, arrived in Bulkes in September 1946 and assumed command of the communist forces with the rank of general. Vaphiadis acted very quickly to establish his authority over the various guerrilla bands. He overhauled the KKE's intelligence network deployed throughout Greece and organized political and insurgent training for both officers and other ranks.

Clandestine cells called *Yiafka* were a critical asset for the insurgents, supplying intelligence, recruits, and logistical support as well as funds, depending on their location. The *Aftoamyna* (meaning self-defense) was an extensive network outside the main urban centers that provided the regional communist bands with information, coordinated supplies, identified recruits, and served as couriers to both the guerrillas and DAG units.[8] Each Yiafka cell ranged from six to eight men and women and operated directly under a particular DAG regional headquarters.[9]

The members of the Yiafka represented the hard-core support base of the KKE in Greece and served as its primary intelligence organization. Individual Yiafka cells were responsible for specific areas that included several villages. They responded to requests for supplies and information from communist bands or DAG units prior to attacks in a particular region. The Yiafka coordinated the DAG static formations of fifty to sixty lightly armed men of the local Popular Civil Guard. Units of the civil guard occasionally accompanied larger DAG formations and manned, for example, field kitchens as well as carrying bulky supplies. The Yiafka also took over the tax collection that in the period of resistance was the task of ELAS and the ETA and during the civil war handled the disbursement of funds to DAG and other KKE units. The cells operated in cities and towns in addition to the villages of northern, central, and southern Greece and in some of the islands of the Aegean.[10]

The Yiafka and Aftoamyna were the intelligence and logistic backbone of the communist insurgency and crucial to the success of the insurgents' hit-and-run tactics.[11] A major responsibility of the Yiafka cells was to liaise and coordinate the self-defense or Aftoamyna in each region under communist control. At its peak, the Aftoamyna included approximately 50,000 active participants and approximately another 250,000 sympathizers.[12] Some of the Aftoamyna members also worked for OPLA, a secret KKE organization of assassins that murdered individuals condemned by the KKE. Later, the DAG continued to expand intelligence gathering locally and nationally and, after 1948, established a centralized intelligence organization.[13] The KKE military leadership created and attached intelligence units to battalions and larger formations that conducted reconnaissance and interrogation of prisoners in the field.

Remarkably, the DAG forces also developed the ability to intercept the signals communication of the government army units. From 1947 onward the communist intelligence units had been able to intercept Greek national army communications by taking advantage of frequent security lapses by careless government army operators. From 1947 to 1949, the communist forces succeeded in the Peloponnese to a great extent because they had advance information of the location of government army formations and gendarmes as well as tactics and deployments. This advantage in intelligence enabled the DAG bands to ambush the GNA, while avoiding disastrous pitched battles with superior Greek army units.[14] The communists enjoyed additional support from a significant part of the Greek population but they, beyond endorsing the left in private, feared taking part in any public demonstrations and were reluctant to become directly involved with the insurgency.

On 27 December 1946, the KKE decided to rename the guerrilla bands the Democratic Army of Greece and to arrange these forces into a formal military organization. This was a deliberate move to abandon Stalin's policy of gradualism or simply to bring further control over the disparate bands operating in northern Greece and the Peloponnese by imposing command and control and military discipline. By establishing the DAG and appointing a commander in August 1946 the KKE wanted to place the disparate bands operating in and out of Greece under the direct control of party authority. Although Zachariadis, like most communists of the period, believed that revolution would take place in the cities, the establishment of the DAG underscored the KKE leader's shift in strategy to a mountain war.

Over the late summer and early fall of 1946, the KKE formally established the general command headquarters of the DAG at Bulkes, under Vaphiadis, which later oversaw the regional commands in the Peloponnese, Roumeli, Epiros, Thessaly, central and western Macedonia, eastern Macedonia, and western Thrace. In October, Vaphiadis announced the creation of a mobile headquarters in the field. The larger part of the command center remained in Bulkes, but Vaphiadis required an operations headquarters nearby, and when possible, in Greece to coordinate the DAG units.[15] When Vaphiadis assumed command in the late summer of 1946, however, the KKE forces had a complement of only 4,000 men and some women. The new commander, accordingly, confined the activities of the guerrilla bands to eastern Macedonia.

Zachariadis soon directed the Yiafka cells to begin recruiting former ELAS members, and by October 2,000 new recruits arrived. The addition of reinforcements over the course of the autumn enabled Vaphiadis to extend the

FIG. 12. ELAS, the left-wing resistance, encouraged young women to join its ranks. During the civil war, many young women were press-ganged into the Democratic Army of Greece or volunteered because of their association with ELAS. Greek Ministry of Foreign Affairs: Photo Exhibition of the Diplomatic and Historical Archive Department.

activities of his forces and to initiate hit-and-run tactics striking from eastern Macedonia to targets across northern Greece. Small, mobile guerrilla units began attacking unguarded villages for supplies and, in a short time, he expanded their area of operations as far south as Larissa. One large raid against Deskati (near Mount Khasia, in Thessaly) and other villages resulted in the death of 120 people, forcing the Greek government to declare martial law throughout northern Greece. In late fall Vaphiadis intensified the pressure and increased the number of raids both to impose the will of the KKE and, more important, to secure food for the winter.[16]

The food problem plagued the communist forces throughout the civil war and was a factor in Vaphiadis' strategy. Lack of adequate supplies often left guerrilla units starving for days. When they could not find villages from which to requisition essential foodstuffs, they resorted to eating rations abandoned by the Greek National Army, which often had been exposed to the elements for days and led to many cases of food poisoning. In one extreme case, in March 1947 in Thasos, guerrillas were forced to find sustenance from their dead comrades.[17] Vassilios Bartziotas admitted his concern as to what effect hunger had upon the fighters, and that during the course of battles the government forces, using megaphones, often called out to the DAG fighters: "Come to us. We have white bread and you are hungry."[18]

Food was not the only scarcity, for as late as July 1949 a report by KKE to their communist allies claimed that over 50 percent of the DAG soldiers lacked uniforms and footwear. The problem by 1949 had been compounded by the transition of the KKE guerrilla units into a conventional army. Charles Shrader points out: "Larger conventional units were less able to sustain themselves off the countryside, which in any event was so devoid of resources as to constitute a desert in many of the mountainous areas of Greece."[19] During the first two years of the civil war, the KKE was able to sustain, to some degree, the DAG guerrilla units. Through a combination of extorting, looting, even purchasing supplies the insurgents had enough food, ammunition, and other necessary provisions. Once the KKE transformed the guerrilla forces into a conventional army, logistical support became an acute problem. The concentration of some units did not make it easier to supply the DAG since the communists, when operating in Greece, lacked a secure line of communications with their bases in Yugoslavia, Bulgaria, and Albania. The small villages in northern and central Greece could not supply large insurgent forces but only small communist bands. Despite the efforts of the Yiafka and Aftoamyna, supply and manpower shortages dogged the DAG units throughout the civil war.[20]

In some cases the DAG bands could count on the support from friendly villagers, and this was one of the reasons why the government decided to adopt a program of forced resettlement of these villagers to cities in 1946. The objective of the policy was to deprive the DAG from securing food, clothing, fuel, and medical supplies and, most important, deny them access to manpower from the villages within the range and influence of the insurgents. The government implemented the resettlement in areas most exposed to recruitment by the DAG, particularly northwest Greece and including parts of Epiros, Macedonia, and Roumeli as well as central Greece. In effect, people became passive weapons of the civil war, because these small communities were a manpower resource for the guerrilla bands and losing this asset worsened the logistical problems of the communist forces. By the middle of February 1948 the combination of refugees and displaced persons reached over 485,000 and in January 1949 exceeded 666,374.[21] Many of these individuals begrudgingly accepted leaving their homes and way of life, while some joined the guerrillas.

The government authorities relocated many of the refugees to Athens and Thessaloniki. In a country of limited resources and devastated by war, these cities had the resources to provide some support for them. The new refugees added to the urban sprawl set in motion by the million and a half Asia Minor refugees dumped on the urban centers in 1922–1924 that eventually made Athens home to over half of the population of Greece. While the resettlement inflicted hardships on the uprooted villagers, the program did have an effect and further limited the DAG's supply chain. Dimitrios Vladas, a senior DAG commander and part of the KKE leadership, lamented that by 1949, "the greatest difficulty which our troops faced during enemy operations was hunger, as a result of the evacuation of the peasants and their concentrations in towns."[22]

In addition to foraging for food, Vaphiadis' guerrillas frequently took hostages, executed the local village police as well as pro-government individuals, and in a short time cast a pall of fear throughout northern Greece and the Peloponnese. For those who supported the insurgency and the KKE, the arrival and departure of the guerrilla bands in a village exposed them to certain persecution by their neighbors and more than likely arrest by the authorities. In October 1946, in one of the largest raids of the insurgency at the time, four hundred communist guerrillas took Naoussa with the help of a fifth column of communists from inside the town. Communist strategy throughout the fall of 1946 was for the insurgents to quietly infiltrate or capture a village by surprise attack, kill the gendarmes and locals identified with the government, and then quickly withdraw after looting supplies of food. They also took hostages and encouraged young men and women to "volunteer" in the DAG, and if encouragement failed they press-ganged the hapless recruits.

Until the fall of 1947, the communist forces restricted their campaign to essentially a series of guerrilla raids. This may have been the case because Zachariadis believed there was hope for a political settlement with the regimes in Athens or because Stalin had declined to authorize the KKE to launch a full-scale offensive.[23] Certainly the lack of significant logistical support and manpower precluded any overly ambitious military operation.

By the early fall of 1947, the KKE had ascertained that it was no longer possible to reintegrate the left within the legal framework of the Greek political system.[24] On 11–12 September 1947, the Third Plenum of the central committee of the KKE decided to abandon all attempts at a negotiated end to hostilities.[25] The KKE leadership declared in an October edition of *Rizospastis*:

> The armed struggle of the Democratic Army of Greece constitutes the only imperative response that the people and Greece have to give to the foreign occupiers and their local underlings. Outside this struggle there is no life and no honor for Greece and the people. This is why the primary obligation for each Greek patriot is to give all his might so that the work of the DAG succeeds, with the solid conviction that the more strong and determined and victorious the people and the DAG in their struggle against the sacrilegious occupiers and their local slaves, so much the more will they force them to accept the democratic solution for the Greek issue that EAM suggests.[26]

The KKE leadership during the course of this meeting adopted Operation Limnes (Lakes), which proposed that the DAG "liberate" Macedonia and Thrace with Thessaloniki as the main base and capital of the communist region in northern Greece.[27] The KKE imagined that to accomplish these aims they would organize a fully equipped army of 60,000, along with an air force and navy. They assumed or hoped that the Soviet Union and its communist allies would provide the weapons, heavy artillery, warplanes, and naval vessels.[28]

Indeed, as early as February 1947, the KKE had made the decision to develop offensive operations for the newly established Democratic Army.[29] On 20 May 1947, Zachariadis had met with Stalin in Moscow, and subsequently the Soviet dictator gave the KKE permission to proceed with the civil war. More important, Stalin authorized the communist states in the Balkans and Eastern Europe to provide material support to the DAG.[30]

Prior to 1947 the Greek communists had to keep faith with Stalin's policy of gradualism, and without substantial military aid from the communist bloc they had enough resources only for sporadic raids and small skirmishes. Although Stalin had given his blessing to Zachariadis' pleas for authorization to advance the insurgency to full-scale civil war in May 1947, he did so strictly unofficially. The Soviet dictator refused to recognize the KKE's provisional government, established in December 1947, and did not allow the KKE to join the Communist Information Bureau created in September 1947 in

response to the Truman Doctrine and the Marshall Plan. Stalin was only prepared to request that Albania, Yugoslavia, and Bulgaria covertly supply and
support the Greek communists. Yugoslavia alone, however, provided immediate support as well as bases and medical assistance to the DAG: 35,000
rifles, 3,500 light machine-guns, 2,000 German heavy machine-guns, 7,000
antitank guns, 10,000 mines, and clothing for 12,000 men and women, in
addition to medical supplies, medical care, and access to bases.[31] The basic
uniform of the DAG was British battle dress, great coats, and boots. Some
DAG fighters wore British uniforms, and many were also carrying British
weapons and equipment.[32]

After the Varkiza Agreement, the Yugoslavs permitted the KKE to use an
army camp outside the village of Bulkes to settle communists fleeing from
Greece and later for training and as a rearguard home base.[33] Initially, Bulkes
was a refuge for hardline ELAS fighters from the frontier areas; it also included
a large number of Slavophone Macedonians who refused to accept demobilization and return to their homes as stipulated by the Varkiza Agreement. During the course of the civil war, the camp was more than a training center; it
became an autonomous, extraterritorial mini-Greece, with language schools,
media, police, hospitals, and even its own currency. In effect, it included DAG
troops but also families and community infrastructure.[34] The administrative
board declared itself an autonomous government and went so far as to print
its own money.

The village afforded training facilities for medical personnel as well as
other professionals. In 1946, there were fourteen professors, forty-three teachers, thirty-two agricultural engineers, six physicians, eighteen officers, twenty-
five musicians, three hundred cooks and waiters, and three hundred and
twenty shepherds. Equally important, the KKE operated an educational facil-
ity for officers under the guise of a School for General Education. The school
offered a variety of military courses and as early as 1947 about six hundred
individuals had completed training and went on to join the DAG forces in
the field.[35] The KKE also operated a separate school for communist party
members in which thirty to forty students attended courses in semiannual
cycles.[36] The Yugoslavs, however, were careful to downplay the role of Bulkes
as a military training center for the Greek communists and in general did not
permit journalists access to the village.[37]

Bulkes offered the Greek communists and ELAS refugees a communal life
and the opportunity to practice collectivization, yet one that kept them segregated from ordinary Yugoslavs. The inhabitants of Bulkes were not permitted to

leave the village, and any who slipped out were arrested and returned or con-signed to prison. Kenneth Matthews, a BBC reporter who had visited Bulkes, accused the KKE leadership who ran the commune of corruption and claimed that they lived quite comfortably while most of the inhabitants were overworked and barely had enough to eat. Many KKE leaders had cellars that held scarce supplies of sugar, chocolate, tobacco, and other luxuries intended for general distribution but instead reserved for their own personal consumption and the black market trade.[38]

The official explanation by the Yugoslavs for the termination of the Greek communist Bulkes commune was announced in the editorial in Belgrade's *Borba* on 5 September 1949. The publication offered a history of the Bulkes community and exposed, with embarrassing details, the fraud of the KKE leadership uncovered by the inspection of a state commission. The commis-sion based its exposé on the testimonies of dissatisfied and harassed inhabit-ants who had disagreed with the policies of Zachariadis and the KKE. Although eight hundred Greeks remained at Bulkes, presumably because they had supported Tito, the commune experiment came to an end.[39]

Bulkes was a small and revealing insight into how the KKE would orga-nize a future Greek communist state. In the meantime, the communist insur-gency had brought little besides death and misery to Greece. The civil war not only pitted Greek against Greek but also distorted the geographical distribu-tion of Greek society. Hundreds of thousands, communists and noncommu-nists, fled or were forced by the authorities from the countryside and exposed village communities to the larger urban centers. Overnight shantytowns, rem-iniscent of the Asia Minor refugee dwellings, sprung up in Athens and other cities. Many other displaced people built shacks with bits of wood and old iron along the side of roads and railway lines, barely "surviving on a meager government dole waiting on the promise of better times."[40] Many towns dou-bled in size and the authorities could not keep up with the arrival of so many desperate refugees.

When the wealth that came with American aid flowed into Athens to mitigate the problem, much of it lined the pockets of unscrupulous politi-cians and seedy businessmen. After 1947, the new money transformed the capital into a city of taverns, bars, and dancehalls catering to the nouveau riche while creating a much greater chasm between the fortunate wealthy and the poor. Initially, this atmosphere proved a boon to the KKE since these shady practices proved that communism was a proper antidote to capi-talist corruption. The opulence and excesses of one part of the population encouraged many to join the KKE underground. Occasionally, in the out-skirts of Athens, grim reminders of the war came with the appearance of sev-ered heads left on the local square—the perpetrators alternated between right-wing bands and communist guerrillas—seeking vengeance or exacting punishment to terrorize their enemy.

By the middle of November 1947, the Greek government had to admit that it only had intermittent control of the region north of Mount Olympus. For his part, in January 1947, Vaphiadis claimed the DAG held one hundred villages. Later in the year, he established his Greek headquarters in an area that was adjacent to a spot near Lake Prespa where Albania and Yugoslavia converged—a section of territory that included the Grammos and Vitsi as well as other mountain ranges. It was a wild terrain, craggy, desolate, easy to defend, and extremely difficult to assault. The communists held this ground, except for a few short intervals, until the end of the civil war.[41]

Vaphiadis maintained these raids throughout the winter, and his guerrillas displayed remarkable mobility despite the adversity of cold, snow, and limited supplies. In the process, the communists secured the loyalty of the local villag-ers, by intimidation if necessary. In a war of hit-and-run tactics, the guerrillas had the ability to make their presence felt in the remote villages of northern Greece—a constant reminder that the communists would return while the Greek army remained in static defense of larger towns and cities with the oc-casional sweep by the national guard. Many of the rank and file of the recon-stituted national guard included a significant number of former members of the collaborationist Security Battalions, who often escalated the savagery of the fighting. During the occupation the Security Battalions, armed and trained by the Germans, set out to destroy the left-wing resistance represented by ELAS, which led to mutually inflicted atrocities.[42] After liberation the officers and men of the collaborationist forces were imprisoned. During the course of the December Uprising most were placed in the reconstituted national guard.

The use of former collaborators in the national guard units, in addition to brutalizing the fighting, further undermined the government's credibility and increased the draw of the communists. The former Security Battalion officers and men cloaked in the uniform of the national guard exacted vengeance and inflicted extensive hardship on those who had served with ELAS as well as their relatives, particularly in the countryside. Not only did the national guard units consequently fail to check the raids of the insurgents, but their very presence drove many of the former left-wing resistance fighters or their relatives to join the rapidly expanding communist bands.

By March 1947, through a combination of volunteers and press-ganged conscripts, Vaphiadis was able to field an army of 13,000, which included a number of women with some degree of training.[43] The fate of women in the guerrilla bands and the DAG was particularly tragic. Some endured sexual exploitation; many more could never go back to their villages since these very conservative communities did not welcome the return of those who had strayed from traditional society. A diary of Major Kronos, an officer in the Democratic Army, indicated that his battalion of 212 included fourteen women.[44]

In April 1947, the Greek National Army (GNA) launched its first major counteroffensive. The plan called for several divisions to sweep through central Greece to the Yugoslav-Albanian border.[45] Afterward, Greek government forces were to secure the border and intercept future guerrilla infiltration from their bases in Yugoslavia and Albania into Greek territory. The offensive lasted for several months, but it lost momentum and eventually fizzled out. Because of superior DAG intelligence and mobility, the communists were able to evade and, on occasion, counterattack the incursions of the government forces. Field marshal Papagos, who eventually was given command of the Greek armed forces, writes:

> Despite their losses and numerous defections, the communist bands succeeded in refilling their ranks through compulsory recruiting of peasants. They also retained their fighting spirit. In June [1947] they actually attacked a significant urban center with large forces. That attack failed but it was another proof that the numerous military operations undertaken against them had neither destroyed their fighting ability nor curbed the warlike disposition of their leaders. . . . The result of the 1947 operations was disheartening.[46]

A major problem of the GNA was that the army commanders had to acquiesce to the demands of the politicians and keep substantial forces in place to guard areas important to their supporters. Under these circumstances it was difficult and often too late to move GNA units and use them against communist incursions. During the Axis occupation, the resistance and Britain's SOE had destroyed most of Greece's transportation infrastructure. Another factor was the rigid command and control of the Greek general staff. The high command was often under considerable political pressure, rigid, and overcentralized. Divisional commanders could not move any of their formations without permission from the general staff, which further undermined initiative and curtailed mobility.[47]

The GNA leadership at all levels lacked leadership experience in commanding battlefield units. The British military observers commented in a report that: "There is practically no training on the bn [battalion], coy [company] or pl [platoon] level and no attempt is made to rehearse or practice an operation which may be contemplated. . . . The result is that units usually blunder into battle without taking the most elementary precautions."[48]

As a result GNA officers lacked confidence and assumed that simply repulsing a communist attack was sufficient; rarely did they seize the initiative and pursue the defeated insurgents. Compounding these drawbacks, most senior officers had little confidence in their units and the men commanding them. As a British report mentioned: "Few commanders will order any form of deep patrolling because they feel that a patrol . . . would be incapable of looking after itself once it had made contact with the bandits or had arrived in the vicinity of a band. More than one commander maintained that, even in broken, wooded and hilly country, the infantry were unable to draw up to less than 2,000 yards of a band without artillery support."[49]

In addition to these shortcomings, the GNA intelligence on the guerrillas was woefully inadequate, usually six to twenty-four hours late. In regions exposed to the communist incursions, it was impossible for the Greek army units to obtain any information from the frightened villagers and shepherds.[50] They knew only too well that once the GNA forces left the area the communist bands would return and punish those who offered information. The villagers, instead, focused on survival; they often collaborated with the guerrillas or, when not afraid of KKE retaliation, with the GNA and exploited circumstances for their benefit. In some villages the guerrilla bands paid the locals to plant mines, who conveniently reported the location of the mines to the Greek army for reward.[51] Until the GNA was able to hold the terrain after expelling the communists, the cautious locals refused to openly take sides.

After the dismal results of the 1947 offensive, the Greek National Army established static defense perimeters adjacent to the major population centers and awaited the arrival of American military aid. In addition to serious morale problems and the lack of mobility, the GNA faced a major geographical challenge in containing (let alone defeating) the communist guerrilla bands. The communists themselves, according to Kousoulas, best described the problem in an article that appeared in the May 1947 issue of *Komep*: "Greece has approximately 25 mountain ranges on the mainland, exclusive of the islands. If we visualize a radius of 20 kilometers from the centre of each mountain complex, we have a periphery of approximately 120 kilometers. Thus we have a total front-line of 3,000 kilometers. This will require huge forces on the part of the enemy."[52]

In the summer of 1947, the writ of the Greek government was limited to Athens and its surroundings. Northern and central Greece and extensive parts of the Peloponnese were exposed to frequent incursions by DAG forces, resulting in the communists retaining control over much of these regions. The Greek army lacked the manpower and firepower to defend Greece's frontiers, let alone protect the inhabitants of the countryside.

Before the arrival of the Americans, British advisers to the Greek army treated the problem of communist guerrilla bands as an internal police matter and refused to authorize the use of regular troops against what they described as bandits.[53] The British preferred to leave the counterinsurgency operations to the national guard and the gendarmes. The frequency and intensity of the communist raids, however, eventually forced the British advisers to concede that the insurgency was no longer a matter of banditry, but a full-scale civil war that required the commitment of the regular Greek army.[54]

One reason for the British failure to treat the conflict as a civil war was poor intelligence. Most of the SOE officers who had served in Greece with the resistance bands, and had a thorough knowledge of the dynamics of the left-wing forces, had been rotated out of Greece immediately after liberation. The officers who replaced them had little knowledge of the country and its people—certainly they had only sparse information on ELAS and the self-contained societies of the small mountain villages where in the DAG drew its recruits. The British officers who replaced the SOE did not understand the political schism in Greek society and the inability or unwillingness of the Athens political establishment to compromise with the center-left that represented a substantial percentage of Greeks. Making matters worse, the limited number of troops forced the British to keep their forces in and around the major cities and towns, thus inhibiting their ability to collect tactical information.

As mentioned above, Woodhouse, the head of the Allied Military Mission in the Greek mountains, cited an instance of British amnesia regarding the resistance and revealing the ignorance of the British with respect to the situation of occupied Greece. Accordingly, the confluence of events led to the outbreak of violence two months later. He cites that when the Greek government of national unity arrived in Athens in 1944, Scobie's adjutant invited Woodhouse to participate in the victory parade. When Woodhouse inquired where the guerrilla leaders were to be placed in the parade procession, the response was "The guerrilla leaders? … What it got to do with them?"[55] As a result of this attitude, the British initially assumed that the civil war was only banditry. The question is, would it have made any difference had the Greek army been ordered to fight the communist bands earlier? Certainly, in 1946 and early 1947, the Greek army lacked the manpower and was poorly trained and equipped to combat the insurgents. The problem was the inability of the Greek government to deal with the political crisis in 1944.

The Greek National Army in 1947 was in a poor state of affairs. A short while after liberation, the Greek government of national unity, with British cooperation, brought to Greece the Rimi Brigade and the Sacred Company from the Italian front.[56] The former was a mountain infantry brigade and the latter was an independent battalion—an elite formation that consisted of officers that had fought alongside the British Special Air Service (SAS) in North Africa. Both units had seen action during the December Uprising, and their arrival in Greece in part precipitated the outbreak of the 1944 crisis. Most of the officers in these units had little empathy with the resistance fighters, and considered just about all members of ELAS to be communists, despite the fact that many ELAS commanders had been commissioned in the Greek army as junior officers prior to and during the Greek-Italian war and some volunteers had come from the ranks of senior officers cashiered during the purges of the Greek officer corps in the 1930s.

Because of ideological polarization, relations between the officers of the GNA and the conscripts, who represented a wide spectrum of political allegiances, remained uneasy in the first couple of years of the conflict. The conservative officer corps had links with and often collaborated with clandestine right-wing organizations that terrorized individuals and groups suspected of communist or even of republican leanings. Officers who had contacts with left-wing organizations or the KKE, however, faced summary court-martial and internal exile.[57] For example, General Euripides Bakirdzis, who at the beginning of the occupation agreed to work for the SOE as Prometheus I, was exiled to Ikaria, a small island in the Aegean, and in 1947 his body was discovered in a remote part of the island shot in the heart. He was one of those who had made a significant contribution to the Greek resistance, but Bakirdzis had also been a commander in ELAS, and later was chairman of PEEA. For these actions, he was condemned to internal exile.

The officers of the Rimi Brigade and the Sacred Company had contempt for men like Bakirtzis as well as for guerrilla warfare. Both units had experienced war in North Africa, and the Sacred Company also fought as special forces; their war was one of commando-style raids against specific military targets. The campaign waged by the DAG units was, instead, a guerrilla war that offered few unique targets. The larger communist forces struck quickly and then retreated into safe havens of Yugoslav or Albanian territories, while the smaller bands fell back to their mountain hideouts.

Fundamentally, both guerrilla bands and special forces rely on surprise and hit-and-run tactics. Accordingly, they are not equipped to capture and hold territory. For the insurgents, this meant the inability to establish a foothold in Greece, consequently forcing them to operate from Yugoslavia, Bulgaria, and Albania or from remote hideouts in the Greek mountains. Special forces faced the same problem. They could strike quickly and effectively against the communist bands, but afterward they had to retreat and thus could not afford the villages permanent protection. Ironically, both sides faced the same dilemma.

If the GNA commandos could have attacked the DAG in their Yugoslav and Albanian strongholds then they could have inflicted serious damage against stationary and significant targets. The fluidity of the fighting in the first two years of the civil war obviated the advantage of the elite Greek units, while the poor training and weapons relegated to the regular army made that force ineffectual against the hit-and-run tactics of the communist forces. Meanwhile, the superior KKE intelligence network was able to give advance warning to the DAG units, who simply melted away before the GNA commandos could get close.

In the post–World War II era the British, in organizing the new Greek army, predominately drew its officers from the elite Sacred Battalion and Rimi Brigade. This decision ensured that the commanders of the new divisions would have strong links to the crown and ideological leanings far from left of center. These officers had survived the purges of the Greek armed forces in the Middle East in April 1944, but regardless of their royalist credentials, they had little or no experience in irregular warfare, with the exception of commando raids. The lack of mobility, furthermore, made it very difficult for the Greek army to enforce the draft in rural areas, and political interference excluded the sons from well-connected families. As a result, the GNA lost the opportunity to include in its ranks hardy young men from the rural areas of Greece who were familiar with the terrain of the rugged northern regions. Furthermore, the low number of conscripted educated men made it difficult for the Greek army to fill critical technical positions.[58]

Initially, the GNA was organized in three field divisions, five mountain divisions, twenty-four commando companies, and three independent brigades.

All the units were grouped in three corps and distributed within seven military districts, which in 1945–1946 included approximately 75,000 troops. For the first two years of the conflict, however, the communist forces retained the initiative. GNA military doctrine, even after the arrival of American advisers, favored a static defense and relied on special forces and commando units (LOK) to carry the war to the communists by striking behind enemy lines. The raids inflicted some casualties and damage on the DAG, but failed to inhibit the ability of the communist guerrillas to attack villages and even larger towns. The high number of special forces was partly due to the influence of the British and the fact (as mentioned earlier) that a large number of middle-level and senior commanders came from the Sacred Company (later expanded to battalion strength) who were influenced by the tactics of the SAS in the Middle East.

Successes for the GNA were few and rarely decisive. One of the reasons was the inability of Greek army commanders to deal with fighting guerrillas, even when on the defensive. According to one British report,

> When attacked a commander is usually satisfied if the bandits are repulsed. It does not seem to be realized that a band which attacks or merely opens fire on a defended locality provides the GNA with a valuable chance of destroying it. One defensive lay-out which was inspected bore a marked similarity to dispositions common in 1915–1917. Troops were entrenched in a long continuous line behind barbed wire. There was no mobile reserve and little patrolling beyond the wire. A feature within sight of the position was said to be held by the bandits but it was admitted that no patrol had been there.[59]

British accounts during the first two years of the civil war were unflinching in their criticism of the conduct of GNA commanders. Although cronyism and incompetence were rife in the Greek officer corps and low morale infected the soldiers, the British were at a loss on how to retrain the Greek forces in antiguerrilla operations. The most recent experience of the British army in dealing with insurgencies had been in colonial policing, and the situation in Greece was not an uprising against an occupying power, but was metastasizing into a civil war.[60]

Perhaps a better comparison is the first phase of the Vietnam conflict (1956–1960). After the Geneva Accords (20 July 1954),[61] Indochina was divided and the Vietnamese communists, like the KKE, organized an insurgency partly in response to the persecution and disruption of the communists and the urgency to save the communist party apparatus in South Vietnam.[62]

Over a short period of time, sporadic guerrilla raids implemented by the Viet-cong escalated into a full-scale insurgency that spread outside the large urban centers. Like the Greek communists who fell back to Yugoslav and Albanian safe havens, the Vietcong could strike and then fall back to the safe haven of North Vietnam.[63] Ultimately, the United States was dragged into both con-flicts, except that in Greece the Americans did not commit ground troops. American advisers in Vietnam faced the same problems with the South Viet-namese military as the British had with the Greek National Army. A major difference was that the U.S. government had at its disposal considerable eco-nomic support for the war in Vietnam, while the British had emerged victori-ous from World War II but faced serious financial constraints.

By early 1947, the British, after expending their economic resources to defeat Nazi Germany and imperial Japan, were financially exhausted and could barely maintain their rapidly dwindling colonial commitments. The Labour government of Clement Atlee that had replaced Churchill's in 1945 could not resuscitate the British economy as well as wage a new struggle against Soviet encroachment in Europe and the Middle East. The specter of a long, drawn-out competition with the USSR was simply beyond Britain's capabilities in economic or military terms. As a result, a message was sent by the British embassy to the American State Department on 21 February 1947, dramatically altering America's role in Greece. The message announced the end of British aid to Greece and Turkey and expressed the hope that the United States would step into the ensuing vacuum. This, and subsequent messages from the British, conveyed the impression that if the United States did not assume Britain's place, the entire Middle East and Greece would shortly fall to the Soviets.[64]

President Truman, already profoundly concerned by the escalating civil war in Greece, agreed that urgent action was necessary. The Truman admin-istration, consequently, formulated an intricate and far-reaching aid scheme for Greece and Turkey. Although this plan included military assistance, Tru-man's vision of aid to Greece and Turkey was based on economic and finan-cial support, which he saw as fundamental pillars of democracy. Truman's legislation covered "authorization for the President to transfer to Greece mili-tary and other supplies . . . to procure for Greece military and other supplies, to detail military and civilian personnel of the United States Government, and to train Greek personnel." A mission was to be sent to Greece to oversee the expenditure of American funds and, in addition, to "assist the Greeks in the planning and execution of reconstruction projects, improvements of

FIG. 13. President Truman sent the battleship USS *Franklin D. Roosevelt* to Greece and
Turkey as a representation of American power and an indirect warning to the Soviets.
U.S. Navy National Museum of Naval Aviation.

public administration and agricultural recovery, control of wages and prices
and programming the sale or other disposition of government purchased supplies." Although the initial financial allotment was to cover the period up to
30 June 1948, the "authority granted with respect to the foregoing is not
limited as to time and may, therefore, continue in effect after the date."[65]

Such a massive peacetime aid program was unprecedented and represented
a fundamental change in American foreign policy. As Truman put it, should
Greece and Turkey fall to communist and totalitarian forces, it would "undermine the foundations of international peace and hence the security of the
United States."[66] Truman recognized this critical turning point in America's

foreign policy. "It means," he said, "the United States is going into European politics."[67] Secretary of State George Marshall echoed the significance of this new responsibility to students at Princeton University in 1948:

> You should fully understand the special position that the United States occupies in the world geographically, financially, militarily, and scientifically; and the implications involved. The development of a sense of responsibility for world order and security, the development of a sense of overwhelming importance of the country's acts, and failures to act in relation to world order and security—these, in my opinion, are great "musts" for your generation.[68]

The Truman Doctrine was described in broad terms as a remedy to problems created by the withdrawal of Britain from the international stage. In this respect it could be applied to countries other than Greece and Turkey in the future. Greece and Turkey represented, in the Balkans and the Middle East, respectively, key spheres of Western and American influence, which were now vulnerable to communist pressures. As a result, these countries were the focus of the Truman plan at its outset.

The Truman administration expressed various motivations for altering its international policies and forming the new doctrine. These included: a new policy in support of self-determination; fears that increased communist influence in the Balkans could shift the international balance of power; and, strategically, the need to take a more interventionist role internationally, and to protect American interests in the Middle East. In essence, Truman was putting into practice George Kennan's idea of "containment," to stop communism from spreading regionally. The Truman administration's internal papers prior to the announcement of the doctrine primarily focused on the communist threat as the mitigating factor in extending aid to Greece and Turkey. Some members of the government recommended stressing this threat to Congress and the public to gain their support, but in the end much of the anticommunist rhetoric, which had been written into drafts of Truman's public announcement, was removed from the final speech.[69]

Having conceived of a line of action, the Truman administration was faced with the challenge of convincing the Congress and the American public that aid to the remote countries of Greece and Turkey was necessary to American security. In 1947, Congress had a Republican majority and was antagonistic toward the Truman administration in general, and toward excessive expenditure in particular. On 27 February 1947, Truman called a meeting with several senators and members of the House to announce his plans. Secretary of State Marshall spoke first and was followed by Undersecretary Dean Acheson, who felt Marshall had not made a strong enough impression. Acheson described the situation as being at a point "where a highly possible Soviet breakthrough might open three continents to Soviet penetrations. Like apples in a barrel affected by one rotten one, the corruption of Greece would affect Iran and all to the East."[70] The impact of these speeches was powerful enough to sway the group, which urged the president to address Congress with the same frankness they had heard from Marshall and Acheson.[71]

Once Truman and his advisers had gained the support of these influential congressmen and senators, the group made a combined effort at concocting a persuasive argument with which to win over all of Congress and the public. It was decided that an appeal from Greece would be key in engaging the humanitarian and charitable instincts of Congress and the American people. Such an appeal was indeed presented, but it was written by the State Department, in tones most likely to charm American citizens, and then given to the Greek chargé d'affaires, Paul Economou-Gouras, to be signed by the Greek government and returned to America.[72]

A complex campaign was launched to engineer the perfect speech with which to approach Congress. For this address, Truman and his advisers decided to stress the preservation of democracy as the primary motivation for the aid plan (even though neither Greece nor Turkey had in place what could be considered a strictly democratic government). The Truman administration wanted to avoid underlining the threat to petroleum in the Middle East, to avoid seeming cynical, and to avoid belaboring an anti-Soviet message, to avoid instigating war with the Soviet Union.[73] Thus, the focus was on "freedom," "democracy," and "self-determination," and the appeal, ostensibly from the Greek government, was cited as the motivation for Truman's plan to provide aid.[74]

On 12 March 1947, Truman made his historic speech to Congress, announcing: "I believe that it must be the policy of the United States to support free peoples who are resisting attempted subjugation by armed minorities or by outside pressures."[75] Such ambiguous references to "armed minorities" (communist guerrillas) and "outside pressures" (the Soviet Union) were code terms that framed the situation for Congress without explicitly antagonizing the Soviets. Initial congressional reaction was influenced by frugality and caution. Some members accused Truman of attempting to divide the world into spheres of influence, others of being aggressive, and still others of being intemperate and reactionary.[76] Truman's legislation finally passed three months later.

Ultimately, the American perception of the Greek and Turkish situation centered on the notion of the domino effect, in which Greece and Turkey's fall to the communists would cause a chain reaction of Soviet expansion throughout the Middle East. Marshall had poignantly expressed this fear in his 27 February 1947 presentation to Truman and his advisers:

> Our interest in Greece is by no means restricted to humanitarian or friendly impulses. . . . If Greece should dissolve into civil war it is altogether probable that it would emerge as a communist state under Soviet control. Turkey would be surrounded and the Turkish situation . . . would in turn become still more critical. Soviet domination might thus extend over the entire Middle East to the borders of India. The effect of this upon Hungary, Austria, Italy and France cannot be overestimated. It is not alarmist to say that we are faced with the first crisis of a series which might extend Soviet domination to Europe, the Middle East, and Asia.[77]

The petroleum motive, mentioned above, must also have preoccupied the Truman White House. Military demands for oil had vastly increased during the war, and America was undergoing a general shift toward the use of oil and natural gas. In response to the threat of oil shortages, Secretary of the Interior Harold Ickes urged that "nothing must be left undone" in the effort to secure overseas oil for the United States.[78]

In 1947, after congressional approval of Truman's request, the administration had to decide exactly how they were to step into Britain's place—how deeply involved to be, and through what methods. The policy the president outlined, which became known as the Truman Doctrine, resulted in committing millions of dollars to be sent as financial aid, as well as American advisers, to Greece. On 27 May, the first group of American military advisers arrived in Greece as part of the U.S. Army Group Greece (USAGG). It was their responsibility to make recommendations regarding the management of the Greek general staff, the Greek army, and the gendarmerie. The Truman administration considered but decided against direct American military involvement, fearing that such a presence would "give substance to the communist charges of American aggression."[79]

The official U.S. line was that American military advisers were not to engage in fighting or actively command Greek troops. Their position, like that of the OSS in Athens before them, remained ambiguous, despite the clarification of American policy toward Greece. When General William

Livesay, director of USAGG, briefed the first twenty American officers going into the field, he told them: "Go out among the troops and see what is going on. You are not armed and you take the best cover you can and see what you can but don't get involved in the combat."[80]

Regardless of careful instructions and stringent intentions, stories of Americans participating in the fighting soon seeped into the U.S. media.[81] In February 1948, United Press correspondent Dan Thrapp reported from Thessaloniki that Colonel Augustus Regnier, the commanding officer of a U.S. army detachment, "personally led a Greek platoon up a mountain slope under heavy machine fire." Regnier apparently said that he "took the lead when the Greek major commanding the battalion was hesitant about pushing his troops forward in the face of heavy fire." Regnier reportedly asked the Greek major, "Will you go forward if I do?" to which the major responded, "Sure, pal." Regnier then "led one platoon to the topmost mountain peak south of the lake, though [he] had to hit the dirt often."[82]

Before CBS correspondent George Polk was murdered, he reported to the U.S. embassy in Athens that he had been told by an American colonel in Thessaloniki that U.S. military advisers were leading Greek troops because "their commanders from the brigade level up were not worth a damn.' " Response to this allegation was described by journalist Constantine Poulos as "half a dozen feeble denials, a brief flurry of censorship on the part of the American Mission for Aid to Greece, and Colonel Regnier's transfer out of Thessalonica."[83]

Even with the largesse of U.S. military assistance, the Greek army was unable to crush the insurgents quickly, while the communist forces, by their very survival and presence, could claim victory. The new Greek army and its commanders could not match the mobility and coordination achieved by the smaller communist units. This problem was further compounded by the low morale of the conscripts, many of whom deserted at the first opportunity. In fairness to the general staff, the Greek National Army, with the exceptions of the Rimi Brigade, Sacred Company, and the national guard, existed solely on paper in January 1946, and the few units that could be organized were hastily deployed in July of that year. According to the official history of the Greek army (which was only made available after 1998), most of the new recruits were considered communists or sympathetic to the left; also, many of the new units had been infiltrated by KKE cadres and could not be trusted.[84] As a result, most of these soldiers lacked the will to fight, and when in combat they did not trust their officers. Communist control of the countryside meant that the conscripts in the new national army came from the poorer areas of Greece's cities and towns and resented that the sons of professionals and wealthy Greeks managed to avoid military service.

The U.S. advisers, commented Larry Cable, found that the GNA in 1948 "consisted of a bewildering hodgepodge of six different types of infantry: field and mountain divisions, commando groups, the territorial static defense formations of the National Defense Corps, paramilitary gendarmerie, and local irregulars."[85]

While reorganizing and training the Greek army, however, the Americans had little choice but to employ at first the British-trained special forces to maintain some semblance of offensive operations. The units, as was the case under British supervision, undertook long-range patrols and raids, but could do little against the DAG in its mountain strongholds.[86] A postwar assessment was critical of the development and the use of Britain's special forces: "It is doubtful if the functions assigned to the commandos were of such a nature as to warrant the maintenance of special units, with the concentration of effort and dislocation of morale that such a course of action entails. To a degree, the effectiveness of the commando was achieved at the expense of the infantry units."[87]

Larry Cable contended that the analysis overlooks that commando units undertook limited offensive operations until the Greek army was trained and ready to commit to battle. Although effective at raiding enemy territory and achieving limited successes, the Greek commando units were less effective against the DAG's mountain strongholds.[88] The communist bands, when hiding in their mountain redoubts, were well entrenched and almost impossible to surprise. The GNA commando units were lightly armed, in contrast to the DAG defenders who could deploy some artillery, heavy machine guns, and mines to defend their positions.

Equally relevant is that the officers of the Greek special forces had acquired their military experience in North Africa—a region with vast expanses and few mountains and towns, while taking part in battles against conventional forces. Regardless, even when successful, the commandos, lacking the numbers and lightly armed, had to withdraw, and the communists reestablished their forces in a region after the GNA commandos abandoned it. The Rimi Brigade, the one unit in the Greek army with considerable expertise in mountain warfare, lost many officers to the new divisions organized in 1946–1947.

The U.S. army developed an antipathy toward elite units during the Greek civil war because American military leaders believed that commandos and other special forces used up considerable logistical support in proportion to the results they achieved.[89] The large number of commando units in the Greek army also meant that these forces included the best junior and non-commissioned officers. This concentration deprived the regular army of experienced and motivated commanders.

Another possible consideration for the American bias against commando units was the failure of the predominately British special forces to capture some of the Dodecanese Islands in the fall of 1943. During the course of the ill-fated campaign—about which the Americans had serious reservations—the British forces were accompanied by commando units that liberated some of the islands, but fared little better than the regular British troops against the German counterattack. A critical factor was local German air superiority and their ability to react very quickly after the Italian surrender on 8 September 1943.[90]

Commandos were skilled in hit-and-run operations, reconnaissance, and sabotage behind enemy lines, but were ill prepared to hold the territory they had captured. Raids by Greek commando units provided the Greek government and its American advisers with short bursts of small offensive operations, yet did little to offer ongoing security for the inhabitants of the countryside and mountain villages that remained vulnerable to communist attack after the commandos withdrew. Resolving this issue was part of the key to winning the war. Unlike the British, the U.S. military had limited experience with commando operations during World War II.

For the British, until America and the Soviet Union took part in the global conflict, commando raids were one of the few avenues for offensive action against the Germans. Overall the military strategy of the United States in the war, in contrast, focused on engaging the Axis in large battles in order to effect maximum destruction of the enemy's forces. Complementing that strategy was mass bombing aimed at obliterating Germany's industry. The few American experiences in the use of special forces, as in the stalled Anzio operation in Italy, had limited and disappointing results.[91]

Until the Americans retrained the Greek military, the order of battle of the Greek army was based on traditionally organized divisions, in three corps along with the independent commando units. The field army was under the tactical control of the Greek general staff, which, in turn, received its orders from the Greek Supreme Council of National Defense, a body that included political as well as military membership. The political leadership was less inclined to commit the Greek army in a full-scale offensive against the elusive DAG than to protect the large cities, towns, and harbors. As a result, the static deployment of the Greek forces, and its cumbersome command structure, made it difficult to respond quickly to DAG incursions. In order to respond to or take initiative against communist attacks, local commanders had to wait for orders, and by the time they received instructions, the enemy had vanished behind the Yugoslav or Albanian borders.

Ironically, the organization of the DAG, like the Greek National Army, eventually abandoned small commando-style guerrilla units in favor of conventional-sized forces in response to political events in the Balkans and as a last-ditch effort to achieve a decisive military victory. According to D. G. Kousoulas, the DAG went through three stages of evolution.[92] During the first phase (March–September 1946), the KKE forces consisted of small groups of 7–10 men armed with older weapons and a limited supply of ammunition. The bands were instructed to move quickly, strike at small targets, and group together before a major offensive operation. In the second phase (October 1946–March 1947), the guerrilla bands were increased to 70–100 men and some women and led by a military commander as well as a political officer (commissar). They were armed with rifles and some automatic weapons, and the detachment in each area was placed under the supervision of the regional KKE party organization. In the final period of the Greek civil war (1948–1949), the DAG units reached brigade strength of 700–1,300 men and women, battalions of 200–400, platoons of 20–60, and battle groups of 10–30. In September 1948, the brigades were increased to divisions.[93]

The three phases indicate a progression of organization culminating with the transformation of the DAG by 1948 into a conventional army. It remains an open question if that had been the intention of Zachariadis from the beginning or a response to events beyond his control. There has been considerable debate over the disagreement between Zachariadis and Vaphiadis regarding the strategy of the DAG. According to some scholars, Vaphiadis advocated an ongoing guerrilla war, while Zachariadis and his followers preferred an escalation from guerrilla to conventional battles.[94] The abandonment of the hit-and-run tactics by the DAG and the Tito-Stalin split have been the traditional explanations for the defeat of the communists in the late summer of 1949. The same scholars blame Zachariadis for the change in tactics and the subsequent defeat of the DAG.[95]

Ole Smith, one of the few scholars who had access to the KKE archives, did not reach the same conclusion. Smith argued that Zachariadis had intended to mobilize fully all the human resources of EAM and ELAS and commit them to full-scale battle as early as 1946. The KKE still had control over the members of EAM and ELAS, in Smith's view, while the Greek government was in disarray and lacking a substantial military force. According to Smith, Zachariadis ordered Vaphiadis to bring 20,000 former members of ELAS to Yugoslavia where they were to be armed. In July 1946 the KKE had at its disposal around 30,000 weapons hidden in Greece, which, in addition to the 20,000 that could be procured from Yugoslavia, could have armed a force of 50,000 men.[96] Smith goes on to hypothesize: "Thus there can be no doubt that in the summer of 1946 Zachariadis gave orders to raise an army of a strength never actually attained by the DSE (DAG), and moreover of a size that would have settled the outcome of the Civil War in favour of the left in 1946. The weak Government Army would have been unable to cope with a virtually resurrected ELAS in 1946."[97]

Smith posits an intriguing argument. The Yugoslavs had the resources to arm 20,000 men, but even with contributions from Bulgaria and Albania they could not supply an army of 50,000 men without significant support from the rest of the communist block. It was not only a matter of rifles, bullets, and rations, but maintaining the flow of supplies for an indefinite period. To be effective, an army of 50,000 would have also required heavy weapons, as well as transportation, medical support, and a well-trained officer corps. Nevertheless, it will remain an open question since the KKE failed to come close to fielding a force of such size. The reality is that Zachariadis and Vaphiadis, regardless of their differences over tactics and strategy, oversaw a guerrilla campaign that was transformed into conventional warfare, but without the necessary number of troops or firepower to win.

It may be that after the KKE sided with Stalin, Zachariadis correctly deduced that it was only a matter of time before the Yugoslavs would terminate their support, but the KKE could still count on aid from Bulgaria and Albania. Throughout 1948, Zachariadis expounded his view on guerrilla warfare in a series of pamphlets, speeches, and articles claiming his ideas were in sync with Mao Tse-Tung's.[98] The theory is that a guerrilla war of attrition made sense only if the communist insurgency spread to the towns and cities.

The DAG, however, with the exception of raiding and holding for short periods a significant number of villages in northern Greece, was not able to extend the civil war to Greece's urban centers. The one possibility was external intervention, but Zachariadis must have come to the conclusion that the Soviets would never intervene directly to aid the DAG. Stalin was not willing to permit any of the communist bloc countries to recognize the KKE's provisional government. In addition, the inability of the DAG to capture and hold a large town was a major setback for the KKE. The failure of the KKE to secure a place on Greek soil to establish a government guaranteed that neither the Soviet nor any other communist regime would ever have recognized what was effectively only an insurgency.

The alternative was an indefinite guerrilla war, but that was not possible because the United States was pumping military supplies into the country and helping to expand and train the Greek army so that it would contain and eventually destroy the communist forces. The Vaphiadis strategy of an ongoing guerrilla war, consequently, was not a long-term option—at least once the United States intervened. Guerrilla warfare was an effective strategy insofar as it could have forced the parade of Greek governments before the spring of 1947 to seek a political accommodation with the KKE. Unfortunately for the KKE, the British kept supporting the Greek state until the Americans stepped in, and the communists could not achieve early decisive victories such as the capture of a major town that would have given them considerable leverage in opening negotiations with the regime in Athens.

The only viable option for the communists in 1948 was either to give up the struggle or to risk everything in a conventional battle, which if victorious may have forced the Americans to abandon Greece. As unlikely as this latter scenario was, it would not have brought about a complete victory, but one in which the government in Athens would have been forced to come to some terms with the KKE—at the Soviets' insistence because they were not ready to confront the Americans. The United States, however, had too much invested in Greece, and a defeat in that country would have undermined American interests around the world.

Until 1948, the communists held the upper hand in a conflict that had spread throughout the countryside and in many of the Aegean islands. In the Peloponnese, the communist bands controlled not only the villages and mountain areas but also an extensive web of clandestine networks that could influence or intimidate the residents of the region. Despite being hampered by logistical difficulties, the DAG forces could attack when and where they chose, while the Greek National Army units failed to leave their defensive positions and counterattack the communists. Yet the war had reached a stalemate. The communist forces could not capture a large town and the GNA was not able to defeat the Democratic Army or defend the Greek countryside from communist incursions. Time, however, was on the side of the government forces. American intervention provided the Greek National Army with considerable firepower and training, in the process raising morale and bringing a younger generation of senior officers to command the new divisions.

The communists, for their part, were in the process of completing the transformation of their guerrilla bands into a traditional military force and committing them to a conventional battle. The KKE leadership had come to believe that such a strategy would bring the war to a conclusion. In that respect both sides had the same goal.

CHAPTER 9

The Cauldron of Battle

GRAMMOS AND VITSI

God is high above, and Russia is far away.

—Serb proverb

Three years of civil war devastated Greece and gutted the country's economy. Greek society could ill afford a new conflict, having suffered mass destruction in World War II during the Axis occupation. The impact of the civil war on most of the population was catastrophic. Entire rural communities were the targets of raids by the Democratic Army of Greece and as a result their inhabitants lived in a constant state of trepidation. Other villagers had fallen victim to the government policy of resettlement and joined the hundreds of thousands of internal refugees and displaced persons in the large cities and towns. For the vast majority of Greeks there did not seem to be an end to the war in sight.

Everyone was directly or indirectly affected by one facet of the conflict or another. For those on the left, the ever-present potential of arrest and languishing in prison or in camps was constant. For the unfortunates in the isolated rural communities, the arrival of the insurgents held a different set of horrors. When a DAG unit took a village, after the initial fighting, the village mayor, gendarmes, or police not lucky enough to have escaped faced summary execution. The locals not only lost part of their supplies, but the able-bodied young men were rounded up and taken as "volunteers" in the DAG. Some fortunate few could surrender to government forces at the first opportunity, and those not able to escape faced seemingly endless treks across mountains and every kind of deprivation.

During the course of 1948, Markos Vaphiadis' strategy of raids on towns, conducted by insurgents now mostly wearing uniforms, had proven successful but not decisive. They were a reminder, however, that the civil war was not over and underscored the inability of the Greek National Army to maintain security as well as law and order. Although the GNA, with massive American material support, was quickly becoming an effective fighting force, it remained handicapped by an officer corps of uneven quality and by inept political leadership. The strategy of the GNA was to advance from south to north and in the process destroy the bulk of the DAG forces. Toward this end, the Greek general staff had launched a series of operations, which so far had achieved some success but failed to achieve decisive results.

Meanwhile, over the same period, the DAG managed to strike at towns with ease and quickly vanish in the mountains, demonstrating that it remained a formidable enemy. Hit-and-run tactics achieved minor victories and sustained the morale of the insurgents; however, they were not instrumental in securing ultimate victory. After 1947 Nikos Zachariadis' strategy was to try to capture a town in the hope of securing a permanent foothold in Greece and use it as the capital of the KKE's provisional government. The most significant such effort was the attack on Karditsa, a town on the plain of Thessaly. Under normal circumstances Karditsa had a small number of inhabitants, but by December 1948, it had swollen to 50,000 with the arrival of thousands of refugees from nearby regions.[1]

The operation was the responsibility of General Kosta Karagiorgis, a former journalist and a gifted commander in the DAG. Karagiorgis established his headquarters in the upland plain of Nevroupolis, a location that had served ELAS during the occupation.[2] Karagiorgis' forces included two divisions, each consisting of two brigades (3,000 men and women), a cavalry brigade, a battery of three mountain artillery, and a unit of the DAG's officers' school. Karagiorgis' command totaled 6,000 combatants, and by the limited resources of the DAG the force represented a significant commitment of manpower and weapons. In contrast, only one GNA battalion and one company with a complement of 915 officers and other ranks defended the Karditsa garrison. Twenty posts, manned by units of five to seven men and located five to six miles from the center of the community, ringed the town; the defenders could also count on support from two battalions stationed nearby at Trikkala and Sophades (in Thessaly), respectively, and another from Larisa.[3]

Karagiorgis' plan was to isolate and destroy or simply bypass the outposts. The DAG force was to advance against Karditsa from the northwest and south, where the foothills of the Agrapha (the southernmost part of the Pindus range) offered cover for the first wave of attackers. On the evening of 11 December 1948, the first wave of insurgents advanced, and by the morning they were on the outskirts of the town. During the day of 12 December DAG units pinned down the garrison in a few fortified buildings. Other communist forces collected supplies and press-ganged recruits—in effect the only practical outcome of the operation. Karagiorgis decided to hold Karditsa for another twenty-four hours, but communications proved a problem and he lost control of the situation. The DAG brigade in the northern part of the town got the order too late and withdrew in the early morning of 13 December and was followed later in the day by another brigade after a skirmish in the town. By this time the beleaguered garrison was beginning to receive reinforcements from other parts of Thessaly, including armored units from Larisa.[4]

Karagiorgis' force was now vulnerable. Burdened with looted supplies and forced recruits, it had become a slow-moving target, and with clear skies was exposed to air attack. Despite these liabilities, Karagiorgis managed to escape with a large part of his force, losing about 600 men and women, by reaching the hills of Agrapha. As had been the case through the civil war thus far, the GNA senior leadership's lethargic response to a communist incursion enabled the DAG to get away. The garrison suffered 200 killed, wounded, and missing. The civilian population, however, paid a steeper price in casualties, with 150 dead and wounded and over 1,000 men and women taken by the DAG.[5]

Woodhouse describes the attack on Karditsa as a combination of Zachariadis' order of battle and the tactics of Vaphiadis—guerrilla warfare applied to a conventional military operation.[6] It was a guerrilla action because the attack was hit-and-run despite the intent to capture and hold a town, and conventional because the DAG units were organized and deployed in regular military formations. Except for the human and material loot, the success at Karditsa achieved little strategic advantage for the communists.

By the end of the year both sides resembled two punch-drunk boxers—one heavy and slow moving and the other leaner and faster, and neither one with the power to deliver a knockout blow. The communist strategy remained the same—to capture an isolated town in order to claim Greek territory and a place for a KKE provisional government and in the interim continue to wage a campaign of skirmishes and raids. The DAG hit-and-run successes, however, were not a demonstrable yardstick of victory. Zachariadis had decided to transform the DAG into a conventional force and abandon guerrilla tactics to fight a positional battle. Furthermore, time was running out for the insurgents. Although the DAG was still resilient and mobile, at a tactical level much of its achievement relied on the local overt and covert Aftoamyna support units. Just after the limited success of the insurgents in Karditsa, the communists were soon to face a new GNA that overcame the sclerotic chain of command and fought the DAG units in the field while waging a relentless war against the KKE support infrastructure.

In December 1948 the GNA high command decided to conduct a holding action in the north and concentrate on clearing out the communist forces in the Peloponnese as well as in central Greece. Decisive action was necessary because senior commanders in the GNA feared that without significant victories, the Americans would be less inclined to maintain their massive economic and military support. The first step in winning the confidence of the Americans was the success of Operation Pigeon (December 1948–February 1949). The operation represented a single coordinated effort by GNA forces that resulted in the complete destruction of communist units in a particular engagement and region.

On 23 November 1948, General Thrasyboulos Tsakalotos, First Army Corps commander and one of the more competent field commanders in the GNA, had been ordered by the army general staff to proceed with his corps to the Peloponnese and eliminate the communist bands operating in the peninsula.[7] The Greek general was convinced that to succeed with his mission it was imperative to secure the cooperation of the locals both in the towns and in the villages. He knew, however, that the people of the region would not cooperate with the government authorities until the GNA demonstrated that it could ensure the security of individuals and groups who collaborated with the government forces.[8] General Tsakalotos was fully aware that the DAG and its supporters in the towns and countryside had an extensive network and the ability to intimidate the noncommunist residents of the Peloponnese. Although the First Army Corps included almost 20,000 men confronting DAG units, which totaled no more than 3,500 men and women, the communists enjoyed superiority in intelligence and mobility with the support of the Aftoamyna informants.

Two dramatic kidnappings in the autumn of 1948 underscored the extent of communist control over the region and the helplessness of the government forces to maintain security. In October a BBC correspondent, Kenneth Matthews, was captured in Mycenae, and in November DAG guerrillas in Tripolis took an American civilian engineer, Francis L. McShane. Matthews was kept for one week and McShane for eleven days. Both men were given a tour of "Free Greece," which did little to impress either one of the communist claims of total victory. The kidnappings, on the other hand, demonstrated to the victims the sway of the insurgents in the Peloponnese.[9] The abductions were evidence that the DAG units could easily move about the peninsula with impunity.

An extensive web of communist networks provided the DAG with recruits, supplies, money, and intelligence on the movements of the GNA. Remarkably, according to Tsakalotos, the Peloponnese KKE was able to intimidate the local police forces and army units by threats as well as pressure from influential individuals within the political establishment in Athens. The Greek general does not say who these influential people in the capital were, only that they were well placed. The KKE networks, according to Tsakalotos, extended to Athens and Piraeus and the communists had access to supporters in key government positions. He claims, as a result, that the military, civil, and police authorities were afraid to mount any significant operations against the DAG or the KKE support organizations.[10] The peninsula, on the other hand, offered an ideal battleground for the GNA. It is connected to the mainland by a narrow bridge, which gave the advantage to a superior force if it could isolate the region from the mainland Greece.

Consequently, Tsakalotos, on his own initiative, decided that in order to destroy the DAG units he had to isolate the Peloponnese and eliminate the regional KKE networks. He implemented a series of security measures designed to sever the Peloponnese and its population from the mainland. Individuals coming to and from the region had to present special passes issued by the police authorities. All ports, shipping vessels, and cargo were placed under close scrutiny, and passengers as well as their luggage closely inspected. To ensure complete surprise, Tsakalotos ordered the arrest of all suspected communists in the Peloponnese, and on the night of 27–28 December apprehended approximately 4,300–4,500 individuals.[11] To accomplish this operation rapidly and with complete surprise, the general deployed almost all 20,000 men of the First Army Corps.

In another step to guarantee total secrecy and avoid political intervention in his plan, he had ensured that all the telephone lines between the Peloponnese and Athens be cut just before the arrests. He even went so far as to establish a five-hundred-meter cordon sanitaire extending from the door of the corps headquarters, making it impossible for anyone to approach the building before undergoing careful scrutiny by armed guards. Tsakalotos does not offer any explanation of how he knew who was a supporter of the insurgents. One assumption is that the police and gendarmes had lists of possible suspects and under the circumstances suspicion was sufficient grounds for arrest.

The arrests, because of their scale and speed, also included some innocent individuals who were merely sympathetic to the left and not necessarily part of any KKE organizations, in addition to some conservatives who were in the wrong place at the wrong time. Tsakalotos was made aware of this and writes that he understood, yet refused to delay the operation by implementing any screening procedure for fear of tipping off the KKE. Kostantine Rendis, the minister of war and representative for Corinth, in particular, complained bitterly that many of his supporters had been rounded up and sent to the prisons on the islands. Tsakalotos was certain that despite the political fallout, no Greek minister was prepared to take responsibility for the return of the prisoners to the Peloponnese in face of American pressure.[12]

For many of the KKE cadres, the knock on the door came as a complete surprise. Dusk comes early in December, and the arrests, by taking place in the darkness, enhanced the mood of anxiety and fear. Lulled by a sense of false security, the KKE activists and sympathizers expected that the communist network of spies and informants would give them advance warning of any potential threat. At the very least, the unfortunate communists counted on the hope that the reign of fear the DAG had inflicted on the region would have led many locals to warn them of imminent danger. Yet the almost simultaneous arrests made it impossible for the communists to have any advance inkling of the GNA's plans. All with a few exceptions were trapped. By the afternoon of 28 December half of those arrested were transferred to the prison islands of Makronissos and Trikkeri, and the remaining 2,000 confined to detention camps in the Peloponnese.[13]

The arrests gutted the KKE organizations in the Peloponnese, cutting off the DAG forces from supplies, recruits, and information about the movements of the National Army and gendarme units.[14] Tsakalotos launched the operation against the DAG guerrilla groups immediately after destroying the KKE networks, and particularly the Aftoamyna, in two phases. The First Army Corps with 11,000 men confronted about 4,000 DAG fighters organized in bands ranging from 30 to 100 guerrillas. Until December 1948, the strategy of the communists was to attack at a time and place that gave them the best advantage and then withdraw into their mountain hideouts.[15] The Aftoamyna had provided the DAG bands with all manner of supplies and timely intelligence on potential targets and when to fall back in the face of superior government forces. After the mass arrests, the DAG units faced battle without knowing when and where the enemy would strike.

In the first phase of the sweep, the Ninth Division reinforced by the 72nd Brigade advanced against the guerrillas in the north and northwest of the peninsula, with particular concentration along the Gulf of Corinth. Government naval forces secured the northern coast of the Peloponnese, thus preventing both reinforcements and supplies from arriving as well as stopping the communists from escaping across the gulf. Until the GNA and Royal Greek Navy sealed the north coast, the gulf was the primary access route for the DAG guerrillas to their command center in central Greece. Reinforcements and military supplies were ferried to the DAG units in the Peloponnese by small fishing boats. A month prior to Operation Pigeon, for example, the DAG attempted to reinforce the communist bands in the Peloponnese, but in the Gulf of Corinth the Greek navy captured the vessel carrying 1,500 rifles, 100 machine guns, and over 1,000 landmines as well as other explosives.[16]

In the second phase, on 3 January 1949, Tsakalotos' forces advanced along a north-to-south axis, driving the communists away from their strongholds and deployed mountain commando units that ambushed the DAG bands. By the end of February, the GNA had taken most of the insurgents out of action: 679 killed, 1,601 captured, and 628 surrendered.[17] Only a couple of hundred guerrillas escaped temporarily, and within a few months the gendarme and army commando units hunted them down. The significance of the GNA victory in the Peloponnese was underscored by the fact that the DAG leadership ordered the assassination of Tsakalotos, whom they held responsible for the demise of the DAG guerrilla bands in the region.[18]

Operation Pigeon demonstrated that the Greek National Army, when properly led by commanders like Tsakalotos and without interference from the political leadership in Athens, could easily defeat the communist insurgent units in the field. Equally significant, the GNA victory indicated that the insurgents could be readily overcome once they lost the support of the regional communist networks, such as the Aftoamyna. Furthermore, destroying the DAG guerrillas in the Peloponnese secured the southern flank of the GNA, thus enabling the government forces to concentrate on central and northern Greece. The mass arrests of the communists and others demonstrated that the KKE's hold over the countryside and the villagers was in large part based on the ability of the insurgents to coerce the local population through an infrastructure of informants and execution squads.[19] The resort to fear and intimidation by the KKE in 1948 also speaks to loss of popularity and sympathy for the communists.

The GNA, by focusing on the elimination of the communist networks, also sent a strong signal to the residents of the Peloponnese that the government could impose law and order as well as security beyond the large urban centers. To defeat the insurgency throughout Greece, the GNA had to apply the lessons of Operation Pigeon to the rest of the country. A major drawback, however, remained the unwieldy general staff.

The American military advisers constantly faced a situation in which Greek commanders lacked initiative and refused to pursue the enemy. To a great extent, nepotism and political expediency were factors in the appointment of officers even at the battalion level. The chief of the Greek general staff, General Dimitrios Giantzis, was a metaphor of everything wrong with the GNA. He was an elderly officer in poor health and easily dominated by the palace, particularly when King Paul succeeded King George in 1947, and whoever was head of the government in Athens. He was congenial and kowtowed to every demand or suggestion by General James Van Fleet, the head of the American mission to Greece, but lacked the influence and energy to enforce the general's recommendations. Van Fleet, at the instigation of the palace, contrived to secure a dramatic change in the leadership of the military and, in turn, concentrate the direction of the war in the hands of a single commander-in-chief with authority over all the armed forces.[20]

On 21 January 1949, Field Marshal Alexandros Papagos, the hero of the Greek army victories against the Italians, agreed to assume supreme command of the armed forces. Papagos enjoyed the confidence of the military and, as the only field marshal in the Greek army, outranked all the other generals. The field marshal, however, had conditions for accepting the job, which included replacing the large and unwieldy National Defense Council with a smaller organization that would be responsible more for overall military strategy than for day-to-day operations. He demanded complete control over planning, order of battle, the right to make appointments, command of the navy, air force, and gendarmerie in addition to the GNA, the freedom to launch operations, no interference from the allied military missions, strict censorship, and the imposition of martial law throughout the country. King Paul agreed and also gave Papagos considerable authority over economic matters.

Almost immediately after Papagos assumed command he announced that he had no confidence in the government. Papagos' proclamation triggered a political crisis, and Themistokles Sophoulis, the prime minister, immediately resigned. Several attempts by a variety of politicians to form a new coalition government failed. The minuet of government making went into motion as soon as Sophoulis tendered his resignation. Alexander Diomidis, the ex-governor of the Bank of Greece, agreed to head a new coalition with George Papandreou and Sophocles Venizelos. Diomidis, however, could not secure parliamentary support so Sophoulis once again formed an administration with most of the same politicians only with different portfolios.

As had been the case in the 1930s, the army once again intervened in the political arena and set a dangerous precedent for the future. The politicians had made government a game of musical chairs and accomplished little. The notion that the officer corps was the guardian of the state was not a new concept: the Greek army had taken over the country in 1922, 1925, and 1935 under the pretense of exercising the "sacred" right of the military to intervene and preserve national interests. The belief that the military were the custodians of Greece reemerged in the last year of the civil war and quickly became the dogma of the officer corps. An important addition to the raison d'être of the army's conception of stewardship was the imminent threat of Slavic communism. Subsequently, three pillars emerged to form the anticommunist Greek state: the army, the palace, and American intervention, all of which coalesced and underwrote authoritarian regimes until the collapse of the junta in 1974.[21]

In the meantime, Papagos, after assuming command of the army, purged the officer corps of incompetent commanders and with the help of the Americans and the palace neutralized political influence over the military. In time, the reforms improved the morale and discipline of the Greek army. The GNA had the advantage of superior firepower over the DAG, and with energetic and offensive-minded officers it was better prepared to fight the communist forces in 1949. The field marshal was not a gifted strategist nor did he bring any new ideas on how to defeat the insurgents; in fact, neither was necessary. The army needed a steady hand and a shield from political interference in the conduct of the war. Papagos, because of his past victories and his German imprisonment during most of the occupation, had not participated in the resistance and the events immediately after liberation and thus was untainted.

Equally important, Papagos had quickly gained the support of the American advisers in Greece. He had developed a close working relationship with General Van Fleet, which gave the field marshal additional freedom from the country's political leadership. On meeting Papagos for the first time, Van Fleet commented: "I liked the man instantly. Papagos was all soldier, an erect man with striking hazel eyes, a classic Hellenic face, and strong views about how to defeat the Communists—views that coincided with mine."[22] As the American largess in funds and military hardware was keeping the Greek state from economic collapse and the insurgency at bay, the attitude of the American advisers such as Van Fleet was critical. Under these circumstances, U.S. military and diplomatic advisers exercised considerable and increasing influence over the conduct of the war and Greek affairs generally in the decades following the conflict.

Van Fleet proved to be an exceptional commander who used American military aid effectively in reequipping the GNA. He established a series of training centers that prepared Greek officers to lead their troops in battle. Equally significant was his influence on the order of battle, organization, and equipment of the Greek army. Under Van Fleet's direction the Greek army's standard field division was designed for mountain warfare and armed with machine guns, pack artillery and light mortars. Tanks were limited to mopping-up operations, and a small number of motorized vehicles accompanied the GNA divisions; most of the rest were assigned to supply units in the rear areas. Without the impediment of tanks, trucks, and heavy artillery, the GNA divisions were not restricted to roads and could expand their range of operations. Horses and mules carried supplies and ammunition to the fighting forces in the field. Interestingly, Van Fleet opposed the use of air mobile units carried to battle by helicopters, as the United States would use in the Vietnam War.[23] In large measure, the Greek army that took the field in late 1948–1949 was the work of Van Fleet and the other American advisers. Perhaps the best tribute to Van Fleet's contribution to the GNA was the decision by the KKE to order his assassination. In February 1949, the Greek security service arrested twelve DAG guerrillas, who had been part of a group of eighteen sent to Athens to kill the American general.[24]

Until 1949, three problems confronted the Greek government and the American advisers. The first was the low morale plaguing the conscripts of the GNA and lack of aggressive spirit of many of their commanders. The appointment of Papagos and his purges of incompetent and lackluster officers addressed the first. The second problem was the challenge confronting a conventional army fighting guerrillas who could strike and then melt away into the safe havens provided by their Balkan communist allies. Mobility, concentration of force, and firepower as well as battles of encirclement held the prospect of annihilating the DAG. The reorganized and retrained Greek army was in a position to undertake this strategy successfully in 1949, more so than it had been in the previous years of the insurgency. Third was the failure of the Athens regimes to protect the countryside communities from DAG raids.

The Yiafka organization not only acted as the eyes and ears of the KKE and its forces, but also could intimidate the village authorities as well as anyone suspected of assisting the GNA. Initially, the Greek government tried to rely on an alphabet soup of acronyms representing various right-wing groups that had sprung to life after the December Uprising in 1944. Almost all of these organizations were primary interested in seeking revenge and meting out retribution against communists and those who had sided with the left during and after the occupation. Except for terrorizing their neighbors, these right-wing extremists were of little use in defending the villagers.[25] In the fall of 1947, the Greek government established the National Defense Corps (NDC) to address the vulnerability of the countryside. The NDC was organized into regionally based battalions composed of ex-servicemen and older classes' reservists yet led by regular army officers. The American advisers agreed but despite promises to deploy the NDC as a local guard and defend the villages, the GNA committed these units in mobile operations for which they were unsuited.[26]

In 1948, after American pressure, the NDC was redeployed as a static defense force. Concurrently, the Greek government organized a new militia, the Home Guard, to replace the paramilitaries. The Americans supplied 50,000 small arms and the new units, trained in counterinsurgency and exclusively under the control of the GNA, assumed responsibility for defending the villages dotting the countryside and the Greek mountain ranges. Thus in 1949, for the first time since the beginning of the civil war, the inhabitants of the countryside would trust the government for their safety while becoming disenchanted with their treatment by the DAG. The communist failures in 1947 and 1948 to secure a large town as well as the military reverses in the Peloponnese made the DAG less tolerant, and its needs increased particularly as larger formations required more food rations. The constant requisitions of supplies and the forced recruitment of young men and women as well as the brutal treatment of villagers lost the KKE the moral high ground it had enjoyed in the early days of the conflict. To some degree, even in regions where the local population was sympathetic to the communists and the insurgency, the Greek government had emerged in 1949 as the lesser of two evils.

During this period, however, Zachariadis was less interested in winning the hearts and minds of the Greek people than in achieving a conclusive military victory. Toward this aim, the KKE leader was completing a political and military reorganization. By the summer of 1948, Zachariadis had assumed absolute control over the party and the direction of the war. Vaphiadis, Zachariadis' military rival and former head of the DAG, had been removed officially on 4 February 1949. To maintain morale and avoid dissention in the ranks, the communist leadership announced that Vaphiadis was relieved for reasons of health. The same fate befell Andreas Tzimas, a pro-Tito senior member of the KKE leadership, and eventually Karagiorgis, the successful DAG commander, was dismissed and soon condemned as a traitor for supporting Vaphiadis. At the beginning of the year Zachariadis was master of the KKE's policy and military strategy. The communist leader, in the meantime, had become hostage to the Macedonian National Liberation Front (NOF), which was quickly emerging as the representative of Bulgarian interests.[27] In effect, this association further tainted the KKE as a vehicle of Slavic communist machinations in the Balkans.

By the end of 1948 the civil war had reached the second of three stages in the conflict. From 1946 to 1947, the communists waged an effective guerrilla war in the Greek countryside against small and medium-sized urban centers. In late 1947, the insurgents began the actual transition of the guerrilla bands into the Democratic Army of Greece in order to wage a conventional war. A year later, the transition was still in progress and the DAG operated at times as a conventional army, while still using guerrilla tactics. Between the summer of 1948 and early 1949, the DAG had completed its transformation into a traditional military organization, but still faced serious challenges in securing manpower and supplies. In the winter of 1949 the problem of reserves was acute. The DAG was losing 4,000 men per month and only finding 1,000 replacements, of which only a small percentage were actual volunteers.[28]

The DAG had suffered its first serious losses during the first round of the major battles of Grammos and Vitsi mountains in 1948, yet succeeded in repelling attacks by the substantially larger GNA forces. In April 1948, the GNA had begun an offensive in south-central Greece and then wheeled northward to advance against the communist positions in the Grammos mountains. During the course of the fighting the Greek air force pounded the DAG defenses and on 20 June used napalm for the first time in the civil war. Despite severe losses, the DAG units managed a skillful retreat from the Grammos into the safety of Albania. In August the communist forces once again advanced into Greek territory and reestablished a network of strong defenses in the Vitsi mountains. The GNA, under strong pressure from the Americans, attacked the DAG fortifications repeatedly from 22 August to 14 September and, notwithstanding its advantage in numbers and firepower, failed to defeat the communists. In early October with the onset of winter snow and cold in the Greek mountains, the GNA terminated its offensive.[29]

In late 1948 and early 1949 the communists were still able to bring the war to remote and isolated towns. The DAG leadership continued to conduct raids and avoid major skirmishes. During the winter of 1949, guerrilla warfare was the way to secure a constant flow of supplies and recruits, and there was always the possibility of capturing and holding a small remote town in the mountains. Zachariadis used this period to finalize the transition of all the DAG units into conventional military forces, and until the process was complete, the many DAG formations were deployed much the same as they had been at the battle for Karditsa—a combination of conventional order of battle and guerrilla tactics.

Toward this end Zachariadis had ordered Karagiorgis' forces to advance through the Pindus mountains in order to capture Karpanisi, a strategic town located on the road between Larisa and Agrinion. Karpanisi is the highest rural town in Greece and one of the most isolated. Located in the heart of the southern Pindus range, it is encircled by mountains, including the formidable Velouchi. Communication between Karpanisi and Lamia, the nearest large town, was by a single motor road—easily vulnerable to ambush. The geography of Karpanisi made it very difficult to defend or relieve, as had been the case at Karditsa. It was impossible to hold all the heights surrounding the town without a large garrison; the GNA troops were barely able to defend Karpanisi itself. This was an ideal place for the communists to capture and establish their government within Greece.

On 5 January 1949 Karagiorgis' forces reached the area of Karpanisi. On the evening of 19-20 January the DAG force of 3,000–6,000 (more likely closer to the lower figure) quickly overwhelmed the garrison of 1,400 government soldiers. Karagiorgis employed the same tactics he had used at Karditsa, but casualties had reduced his units and the forced recruits had only two weeks' training.[30] Despite these drawbacks the insurgents held the town for eighteen days.[31] This was the longest period the communists held an urban center during the entire civil war. The DAG forces spent that time pillaging, executing government authorities, and eventually burning part of the town. On 29 January 1949, the First Army Corps, led by General Tsakalotos, launched a counterattack from two directions. Part of the corps advanced northeast from Agrinion and the other moved west toward Karpanisi. The attempt failed, and it was the first time in the war that the insurgents held a town successfully against the GNA. It was not until 9 February that Tsakalotos' First

Army Corps finally forced the DAG to abandon the town. A convenient snowstorm enabled the DAG to pull out of Karpanisi quickly and intact.

Karagiorgis nevertheless conducted a fighting retreat over the course of a month dividing his forces into three columns—one heading north toward the Agrapha mountains and the other two moving west separately until all three columns reunited and advanced to the mountains of Vardoussia. The communists took 500 hostages and forced 1,500 others to join the DAG. On this occasion, the government forces arrived too late to save the victims of the DAG, plagued as usual by poor intelligence and planning that gave the advantage to Karagiorgis' forces.[32] Despite Karagiorgis' achievement, this was the last major DAG initiative in central Greece.

Although a tactical success, the attack on Karpanisi was not decisive and beyond the looting and abductions it only demonstrated that the DAG forces were little more than guerrilla units preying on remote communities. It gave considerable fuel to the government propaganda that the insurgents were not an army or a political entity at all, but merely bandits carrying on a tradition of hostage taking, abductions, and extortion that reached back to previous centuries. The other narrative emanating from Athens was that the KKE and DAG were Moscow's creatures pursuing the goals of the "Slavo-Macedonians" and the Bulgarians—Greece's historic Balkan rivals. Significantly, as the DAG pulled back from southern Greece, it had to rely more on Slavophone Macedonian forced recruits as well as volunteers to fill the shrinking ranks of the DAG units. By 1949, Slavophone Macedonians represented almost half of the DAG, which gave the government propaganda more than a ring of truth.

In the winter and early spring, however, the DAG was still a potent force and continued its sporadic raids in northern Greece. On the night of 11–12 January DAG units attacked and captured Naousa and held it for five days. A few days later, on 15 January, the insurgents advanced on Florina.[33] The operation was the brainchild of Zachariadis, with the ultimate aim of eventually taking Thessaloniki and with it northern Greece. This was the first occasion that Zachariadis had direct command of the DAG and it was an opportunity to demonstrate his military ability. The consensus among historians of the Greek civil war is that Zachariadis was an incompetent military leader who was prepared to seize the first opportunity to achieve martial glory. Although Zachariadis had assumed the overall direction of the war, he left tactical control of the DAG to seasoned commanders such as Georgios Gousias, who had replaced Vaphiadis as commander-in-chief of the DAG. Gousias had commanded large ELAS units during the occupation and had taken part in the insurgency from late 1945.[34]

Georgios Gousias had tactical control of the attack against Florina and led the 10th and 11th DAG divisions, totaling 4,000 men, as they advanced on the town in the early hours of 12 February 1949. Preceding the attack, an artillery barrage of almost 1,500 shells dropped on the defenders. The leading brigade of the 11th Division penetrated the southern approaches to the town, while another brigade seized the nearby hills and blocked the access routes. That was the extent of the DAG advance. Although the winter snow slowed the government relief forces, the GNA division was well equipped and well trained. More important, it had access to air support. The Royal Greek Air Force struck the DAG units with rockets, bombs, and napalm. The effect was devastating. The communist advance stopped and the insurgents fell back with heavy casualties. A few days later, GNA reinforcements arrived and drove the DAG units from Florina and out of the surrounding mountains.

On 15 February the DAG units began to fall apart, and shortly afterward the rout turned into panic as the insurgents fell back and scurried up the Pisoderi Gorge. The battle for Florina was an expensive defeat. The DAG losses included 799 killed, 1,500 wounded, and 350 captured or surrendered. In one brigade, 400 men suffered frostbite and their commander was killed. The 425th Battalion (18th Brigade, 11th Division) lost 25 percent of its strength in the first three hours of the battle. The GNA, for its part, suffered significantly lower casualties: 44 dead, 220 wounded, and 35 missing in action.[35] In his post mortem of the battle Zachariadis concluded: "We lost the Battle of Florina on account of inadequacy in war technique and lack of leadership all along the line."[36]

On this occasion, the GNA had advance warning and easily managed to beat back the DAG. At the end of February, a small band managed to gain a temporary foothold in Larisa and a day later was forced to retreat. In March, communist units attempted to attack Arta, and during April they launched several abortive raids in central Macedonia and the Khalkidiki Peninsula. By the end of the month, however, the communists terminated their activities in this part of Greece and concentrated their forces in their stronghold in the northwest along the Albanian frontier. Van Fleet summarized the GNA victory: "The defeat of the guerrilla forces at Florina was the first successful operation against bandit attacks on large villages. . . . I consider the operation very successful, first, because plans had been drawn for the defense of Florina, second orders were issued and obeyed, third, the training paid off, fourth, morale of the GNA and Greek civilians was improved."[37] Two critical ingredients for the GNA victory were access to good intelligence and air power.[38] The attack against Florina was the last assault on a large defended town by the

DAG and the final offensive outside the communist stronghold in Grammos-Vitsi. The advantage now passed to the Greek National Army, which held the initiative until the end of the civil war. By June the GNA had cleared central Greece of DAG bands, and the survivors were no longer active guerrillas but fugitives.[39]

After three years of war, the KKE was politically divided, it had failed to establish a foothold in Greece, and as a result of keeping faith with Stalin it had severed relations with Yugoslavia, a critical ally and an important source of supplies as well as a base of operations adjacent to Greek Macedonia. The losses of the Peloponnese and central Greece forced the insurgents to concentrate in the northwest. The DAG still had the option of crossing the border and regrouping in Albania, but that would have meant resuming a guerrilla war. Zachariadis, however, had decided otherwise and prepared for a decisive engagement that he could win with strong fortifications. Besides, falling back on Albania was not an appealing alternative. Despite communist solidarity, the Albanians lacked the resources of the Yugoslavs and the DAG would have had to rely upon the Soviet Union through its clients in the eastern bloc for supplies. As long as Stalin refused to identify publicly with the cause of the Greek communists, the DAG's logistics were hostage to a long and complex supply system subject to the whims of the Soviet Union's satellites.

By the summer of 1949, Zachariadis had more or less completed the transition of the DAG into a conventional force, while conducting some limited hit-and-run operations. The KKE leader had ordered a series of minor actions in Greek (eastern) Macedonia and Thrace. On 5 May two DAG brigades, about 1,000 men and women, captured the village of Neon Petritsi and held it for twenty-four hours. Ten days later on 15 May another brigade numbering approximately 700 seized the village of Metaxades and this time was able to hold it for three days until GNA forces drove the DAG out. On 20 June a DAG unit captured a Greek army frontier post in the Beles mountains and once again the GNA forced the communists to withdraw.

Despite the KKE siding with Stalin, the Yugoslavs had permitted the Greek communists limited access across their border and had continued to supply the DAG with food and ammunition as well as use of camps and hospitals. Perhaps, as Edgar O'Balance suggests, "Tito thought that this magnanimous attitude might win the KKE over to his side, and it can only be wondered why he was so patient for so long and did not clamp down on Greek insurgent activities sooner."[40] When the KKE leadership, however, announced openly that they supported Stalin and that the Greek communists agreed to accept a

Bulgarian controlled Slavo-Macedonian state that would include the Greek province of Macedonia, it was the last straw. On 10 July Tito officially closed the Yugoslav-Greek border. This was a major setback; in addition to the loss of supplies and bases, at least 4,000 DAG fighters were interned by the Yugoslavs.[41] Stalin consequently ordered Bulgaria and Rumania to increase supplies and provide the DAG with bases and hospital facilities.

The KKE suffered a further setback in early July when the GNA advanced against the DAG brigade defending the Kaimakchalan mountains that extended eastward from the Monastir Gap to the Yugoslav border. In seven days the GNA drove the communists from their defenses inflicting over 400 deaths, while the survivors escaped across the border to Yugoslavia. The GNA victory drove a wedge into the DAG, separating the main army that operated in the northwest frontier along the Greek-Albanian border from the communist forces in the Beles mountains in the northeast that protected access to Bulgaria. In effect, the DAG was now forced to wage battle from two widely separated bases, which meant a duplication of supplies and communications.[42]

Over June and July, the DAG constructed strong defenses in the northwest frontier around the Vitsi massif that could also serve as a jumping-off point for offensive operations into Greece. The area encompassed approximately 250 square miles, with Albania in the west and Yugoslavia in the north. Steep mountains strewn with rocks and cut by valleys with thick forests marked the region, which proved to be a natural defensive terrain. The communists built concrete emplacements for their artillery, which they covered with barbed wire and reinforced with machine guns. Now, for the first time in the war, the Greek army confronted static communist forces along a broad front of approximately forty miles.[43] The Greek army and security services carried out extensive sweeping operations, arresting thousands of communist sympathizers and suspected informers throughout the countryside, severing the DAG from sources of intelligence and local support.[44]

The DAG had about 7,000 troops concentrated in the Vitsi bastion and another 5,000 in the south positioned along the Grammos mountain range. An additional 3,000 reinforcements were located in close proximity to the main force—a total of 15,000 men and women. The Greek army, thanks to massive American aid, was able to field over 160,000 troops in eight divisions and two independent brigades. The First Corps with three divisions was assigned the task of clearing the Vitsi mountain range, the Second Corps (also consisting of three divisions) was to capture the Grammos mountain range, and the Third Corps, which included two divisions and two

independent brigades, was assigned the task of eliminating the Beles mountains pocket.

The GNA managed to advance quickly and attack before Zachariadis
could deploy all his forces. On 5 August 1949, the three divisions of the Second Corps attempted a diversionary attack against the communist defenses in
the Grammos in order to mask the primary offensive aimed at Vitsi, but after
one week of fighting they made little progress.[45] Thick woods, in particular,
made it difficult for the GNA units to move forward quickly and provided
the insurgents with natural cover.

On 10 August, the main offensive of the GNA spearheaded by the
First Corps struck the communist forces in Vitsi in a three-pronged attack.
The fighting was bitter and the communists clung grimly to their positions
along the mountainsides and in the valleys, but the superior firepower of the
Greek Army eventually dislodged and finally overwhelmed the insurgents.
Although the GNA killed and captured over 2,000 rebels, their victory was
not complete because a large number escaped to Albania and Bulgaria. A few
managed to cross into Yugoslavia even after Tito had closed the border
and only because local Yugoslav officials had some empathy for their former
communist allies.[46] However, the Yugoslav authorities interned the DAG
refugees.

On 19 August the Third Corps, supported by substantial air power,
advanced against the DAG brigade in the Beles mountains and in three days
captured the communist stronghold. Only sixty-five DAG soldiers were
killed, with an equal number of wounded and prisoners. The rest, about 1,000
insurgents, slipped across the frontier into Bulgaria. The survivors succeeded
in escaping because Bulgarian troops provided cover, and even during the
fighting Bulgarian artillery had supported the DAG unit.[47]

The Grammos stronghold, however, continued to stand, and on
25 August the Second Corps of the Greek army launched a fresh offensive,
this time supported by fifty-one Curtiss Helldivers armed with cannons,
machine guns, and rockets and able to drop napalm bombs on the DAG
positions. The insurgents fought stubbornly and, using the advantage of the
terrain and camouflage, at first repulsed the Greek government forces. The
rugged Grammos mountaintops provided excellent cover for the defenders
and almost insurmountable obstacles for the attackers. Greek soldiers, on
both sides, hunted each other on the barren hillsides and in the thick woods
almost to a stalemate, but eventually the firepower of the Greek army, and
their sheer numbers, prevailed.

Greek National Army artillery pounded the communist positions, and the Helldivers machine-gunned the defenders. Where bullets and soldiers could not reach, napalm incinerated any lingering opposition. After only one day, the insurgents began to give way, and the government forces captured several of the heights. On 27 August, Mount Grammos fell to the GNA; the rebel forces began to disintegrate, and soon about 8,000 insurgents were fleeing across the border into Albania. The Yugoslavs had already closed the border to the Greek communists, and the Albanians now began to restrict their movements as well—only the Bulgarians were prepared to continue to support the insurgents.

Despite the defeats at Grammos and Vitsi, Zachariadis was prepared to resume the struggle in the form of a long guerrilla war, but Stalin intervened and ordered the Greek communists to declare a cease-fire. The Greek civil war had by the early fall of 1949 become a dangerous luxury for the Soviets in their overall policy toward the West. In early October a flotilla of small boats (chartered by the British Secret Service), carrying twenty-six Albanian freedom fighters, landed on the coast of Albania with the aim of overthrowing the country's communist regime. Little came of it; upon reaching the shoreline they were ambushed and most were killed.[48]

Similar attempts by parachute drops had also failed, and years later Kim Philby, the notorious communist mole in Britain's intelligence service, hinted that he had betrayed the operations to his Soviet masters. There is little doubt, however, that Stalin was unsettled by the Anglo-American efforts to undermine the Albanian regime and assumed that was in response to Albania's support of the Greek insurgents. The Tito-Stalin split also left Albania, the sole Soviet ally with access to the Mediterranean, isolated. Furthermore, the Soviet dictator was becoming increasingly apprehensive over American maneuvers to encourage a Greek-Yugoslav-Turkish anti-Soviet Balkan pact.[49]

On 16 October 1949, the insurgents' radio station announced a temporary halt to the fighting in order to prevent the destruction of Greece. The voice of the KKE then proclaimed that the Democratic Army of Greece had not given up, as it was forced to back down only temporarily due to the material advantage of the Athens government and Tito's treachery. A few isolated pockets of resistance continued throughout the fall and the Greek civil war sputtered to an end. A little later, Soviet ships steamed into the harbors of Albania and collected the remnants of the Democratic Army; among them was Kostas Katsuris, who would remain in exile for almost twenty years. He was one of the lucky ones; many others spent the rest of their lives in the remote parts of the USSR and were returned to Greece only after the first Socialist Greek government (PASOK) declared a general amnesty in 1982.[50]

It is estimated that as many as 158,000 people lost their lives as a direct result of the civil war. Losses in the Greek armed services and the Democratic Army of Greece were 11,000 and 38,000 killed, respectively. Soldiers and guerrillas were not the only casualties—or even the majority. Some 700,000 people, approximately 10 percent of Greece's population, either fled from their homes or were forcibly relocated by the Greek authorities in order to deny the communists both recruits and supplies from the mountain villages.[51] Most did not return to their small communities and remained in Athens, creating a permanent shift in Greece's urban-rural population distribution. As a result of this relocation, Athens has become a sprawling metropolis that comprises almost 50 percent of the population of Greece. Close to 50,000 Greeks were condemned to exile, and almost 28,000 children were abducted or forced to flee Greece with the communist forces to Balkan and Eastern European communist states. Eventually, only 10,344 were repatriated after the war.[52] The rest faced a dreary life in the orphanages of Eastern Bloc countries. Victims of the conflict nursed their enmity against their opponents for years afterward.

Did the KKE have any chance of victory? David Galula, a French military officer who influenced the development, theory, and practice of counterinsurgency warfare, provides the best analysis. In 1948 Galula was a member of the United Nations Special Committee on the Balkans (UNSCOB) and had the opportunity to observe the Greek civil war. Later he studied the war in Indochina and took part in the French campaign in Algeria, during which he was able to apply successfully his theories of counterinsurgency warfare.[53] As a theorist, observer, and practitioner, Galula concludes:

> The 1945–50 Communist insurgency in Greece, a textbook case of everything that can go wrong in an insurgency, is an example of failure due, among other less essential reasons, to the lack of a cause. The Communist Party, the EAM and its army ELAS, grew during World War II, when the entire population was resisting the Germans. Once the country was liberated, the EAM could find no valid cause. Greece had little industry and consequently no proletariat except the dockers [sic] of Piraeus and tobacco-factory workers; the merchant sailors, whose jobs kept them moving about, could provide no constant support. There was no appalling agrarian problem to exploit. The wealthy Greek capitalists, whose fortunes had usually been made abroad, were

an object of admiration rather than hostility in a trade-minded nation. No sharply fixed classes existed; the minister of the navy might well be the cousin of a café waiter. To make matters worse, the Greek Communists were perforce allied to Bulgaria, Greece's traditional enemy; to Yugoslavia, which claims a part of Macedonia; to Albania from which Greece claims part of Epirus. With national feelings running as high as they do in the Balkans, these associations did not increase the popularity of the Greek Communists.[54]

Galula adds, with respect to the tactics of the Greek communists:

Using what forces they had at the end of the war, taking advantage of the difficult terrain, withdrawing into the safe asylum across the satellites' borders when necessary, the communist insurgents were able to wage commando-type operations but not true guerrilla warfare; in fact, their infiltrating units had to hide from the population when they could not cow it, and their operations lasted generally as long as the supplies they carried with them. The ELAS [sic] was obliged to enlist partisans by force. Whenever the unwilling recruits found the political commissar behind their back less dangerous than the nationalist forces in front, they deserted.[55]

The forced recruitment of young men and women in particular cost the KKE the support of most of the villages within the DAG's areas of operations. The policy of press-ganging exposed the underlying weakness of the communists' insurgency. The dilemma of the KKE leadership was that without press-ganging recruits it would not have been possible to transform the guerrilla bands into a conventional army. The commander of the DAG concluded by the middle of 1947 that willing volunteers represented only 10 percent of the Democratic Army.[56]

The continuing manpower shortage also forced the insurgents to rely more and more on female recruits, which by 1949 made up 20–25 percent of the DAG forces and as much as 90 percent of the personnel in the administrative and logistics units.[57] Without forced recruitment, the DAG would have lacked the manpower to take the field as a conventional army. One important consideration is that insurgents failed to attract large numbers of volunteers from the cities. The KKE supporters in Athens and in the other cities and towns could not be convinced to join their comrades in the mountains and take part in the fighting, perhaps because they did not believe there was a chance of victory.[58]

The manpower shortage effectively reflected the lack of confidence for the KKE to assume control of the Greek state. The unpopularity of the communists intensified further when in 1949 the KKE proclaimed the self-determination of the Slavophone Macedonians.

The postmortem of the DAG must include Zachariadis, the man who directed the political and military fortunes of the KKE during the course of the Greek civil war. Zachariadis, remarkably for the impact he had on the country, did not know Greece very well. He lived in Athens for only short periods, and for part of that time he was confined to the claustrophobic world of Greek communists languishing in prison. When not incarcerated, the KKE leader lived in the narrow working-class districts of Athens and Piraeus. These areas represented only a small part of Greek society and gave him a distorted impression of the Greek people and their interests. Greece was a society of small entrepreneurs, shopkeepers, small farmers, fishermen, and a limited number of professionals, mostly teachers, civil servants, engineers, architects, military officers, and lawyers with a handful of university professors. Low-paid teachers and academics lured by Marxist ideology gravitated to the KKE and gave the party a handful of educated cadres who tried, but failed, to incorporate into the party's platform the justification for waging war and killing fellow Greeks.

Until the very end of his life Zachariadis essentially remained an outsider from the mainstream of Greek society thus hindering his understanding of Greek social and political dynamics, which threw off his timing. He miscalculated in 1940, by underestimating the pride of the Greek people in defeating the Italian army. He published a letter supporting the war and then a second letter, under pressure from the Comintern, condemning it as a fascist conflict. Although he lacked formal military training and experience in guerrilla warfare during the occupation, Zachariadis had understood the strategic conundrum confronting the KKE and the DAG. A protracted guerrilla war had little appeal unless it led to a political settlement on the KKE's terms leading to a socialist state. The alternative was a long, drawn-out insurgency confined to the Greek mountains with little chance of military victory. The Vaphiadis notion of an indefinite guerrilla war, consequently, made little sense, especially in the aftermath of the Truman Doctrine. U.S. support, on the scale that the Americans poured money, arms, and advisers into Greece, meant it would only have been a matter of time before the reinforced and retrained GNA would have eventually destroyed the communist forces, especially when the GNA transformed into battalion- and division-sized formations.[59]

Perhaps as significant as the problems of logistics and firepower, Zacharia-dis misunderstood his idol. Stalin had agreed to sign Greece over to the Brit-ish in October 1944 and ultimately stood by that agreement in December 1944. When the United States replaced Great Britain in Greece, the geopo-litical dynamic of the region did not change and Stalin faced the same strate-gic and tactical dilemmas. Perhaps the Balkans was not the place where Stalin wanted to confront the United States. In the words of the historian Simon Montefiore, "Stalin was determined to test American resolve in Berlin, not in some obscure Balkan village."[60]

The Soviet dictator was certainly opportunistic, and if the Greek com-munists had achieved complete victory he may have afforded them diplo-matic recognition. The Truman Doctrine, in contrast, raised the stakes for Stalin. Greece was no longer the concern of Britain's declining empire, as it had come under the protection of the most powerful state to emerge out of World War II: the United States. Stalin was not prepared to challenge Amer-ica in Greece, particularly without significant naval forces in the Mediterra-nean. Without Soviet intervention, or massive infusion of war material from the eastern bloc countries, the Greek communist insurgency was doomed.

Zachariadis' misfortune was that Greece's location in the Balkans and eastern Mediterranean was vital to the Anglo-Americans and not vital to the Soviets, at least for the foreseeable future. At the same time, broad-based sup-port for the KKE was a short-term by-product of discontent and disappoint-ment over the failure of the immediate postwar governments to address the economic crisis and the backlash from the suppression of the broad-based EAM resistance movement followers. Hundreds of thousands of EAM sup-porters had felt cheated by the return of the inept prewar political establish-ment after liberation.

Disappointment turned to anger when the ranks of the Greek resistance watched the spectacle of collaborators picking up their lives with only the minor inconvenience of waiting to resume their vocations between the Ger-man withdrawal and the conservative regimes following on the heels of the British Army. Anger turned to hatred in response to the White Terror—such intensity of feelings subsided during the course of the civil war leaving only the memory of past wrongs for future generations. The KKE's call for civil war did not inspire the large number of EAM followers to fight and die in the Greek mountains for the communists. This, ultimately, was the greatest mis-judgment of Zachariadis and the KKE leadership.

Epilogue

A war of extermination on the part of the poor against the deadly poor.
—Joyce N. Loch

A fundamental question that has to be addressed in a history of the Greek civil war is whether the fratricide was inevitable. There are essentially two narratives of the Greek civil war, and both are filtered through an ideological lens. There is the narrative that the left-wing resistance was betrayed and persecuted by the reinstalled politicians of prewar Greece and the British, leaving the followers of EAM-ELAS little choice but to fight. Then there is the story of the right, which claims that the communists who dominated the leadership of the left-wing resistance had planned all along to seize power after liberation. Part of the left-wing narrative also alludes to class differences and a clash between the collaborators, who were welcomed back into the state system by the Papandreou government of national unity, and those who had fought the Axis powers.

The left-wing narrative underscores the point that almost all who collaborated were individuals from the prewar establishment and the members of Greece's middle-class professionals who had staffed the civil service during the occupation. In fairness, many had kept their jobs in order to survive and operate the essential functions of the state machinery. The most conspicuous, for example, were policemen, who continued to provide a modicum of law and order, albeit under the jurisdiction of the occupation authorities. Some chose to assist the Italians and Germans and hunt down resistance fighters, while many more covertly facilitated the work of opposition groups in the

291

cities and towns. Yet they hardly constituted a majority of the middle class. Hundreds of professionals also joined the ranks of the left- and right-wing resistance, which did not label any particular organization according to class.

To understand the social dynamics, one must realize that in the twentieth century Greece lacked (and continues to lack) the distinct class divisions prevalent in other European countries. At one end of the social spectrum are wealthy groups that make up a plutocracy rather than an aristocracy, and at the other end are a highly unionized working class and small-scale land farmers. The groups that were least organized and most susceptible to economic downturns or cataclysmic events were the small entrepreneurs and professionals. During the course of the Axis occupation these groups faced repression and quickly tumbled into the chasm of insolvency and instant poverty. An untold number from this part of society died of starvation or as the fodder of reprisals; some survivors joined the left, and others, because of fear or greed, worked for the occupation authorities. In effect, they gravitated to the polar extremes that had come to divide Greece in the 1940s.

In 1944, and during the course of the occupation, Winston Churchill was determined to bring back the Greek king to his throne because he believed that a monarchy could restore legitimacy to the war-torn Greek state. After 1947, the Americans reached the same conclusion, only in their case they assumed that a monarchy was the best guarantee of preventing the communists from taking control of Greece. The Greek left and many from the center-left, however, rejected the monarchy because they believed that the crown and the prewar political establishment were devoid of any legitimate authority to govern Greece. King George II had been reinstated on the throne in 1935 after a rigged referendum and a year later sanctioned the equally illegitimate regime of Ioannis Metaxas. Although carelessly described as a dictator, Metaxas relied on neither a mass-based party nor the power of the military, but was a Greek strongman leading the government at the sufferance of the king.

In December 1944, the communists tried to exploit the antimonarchist and anti-Metaxas sentiments of the Greek people as well as their hatred of collaborators in order to force the British-backed government of George Papandreou to concede a greater role in the government for the left. The attempt failed, but it did facilitate the return of the prewar political leadership as well as enable a number of collaborators to reassert their control of the state. During and in the aftermath of the 1944 December Uprising, when Greek government forces fired on unarmed leftist demonstrators, both sides engaged in terrorist activities, cementing the political schism and adding an element of blood feud that practically guaranteed another round of fighting.

Although the road to perdition had started with the emergence of a fragmented and politically charged resistance, civil war was not the inevitable outcome of liberation. Most of the European resistance movements had been plagued by ideological rifts and lacked a clear consensus on the future direction of their respective countries, but their differences did not lead them to armed conflict. The French resistance, for example, had to contend with not only the occupation but also the Vichy regime—a puppet of the Nazis and, for most of the war, the legitimate government of France.

General Charles de Gaulle, however, the leader of the Free French, managed to avoid postwar political confrontation because he had forced the Allies to accept him as the representative of France and, eventually, the leader of the legitimate government. Indeed, de Gaulle's aloofness and arrogance, though they infuriated the Allies, set him apart from the other leaders of governments-in-exile. After the liberation of Paris, de Gaulle faced a divided French people and a powerful communist movement. The Communist Party of France, as was the case with the KKE, had orders from Moscow not to make a grab for power. This was hardly known to all the Allies, let alone to the post-liberation governments. Certainly, there was the unknown factor that the rank and file of the communist resistance fighters was not a disciplined army and led by their regional leaders might easily have taken matters into their own hands.

De Gaulle had to convince thousands of armed men and women to stand down and turn over the administration of France to his appointed representatives. Instead of alienating those who had had a hand in liberating France, the general invited them to join the French army and channel their energies toward the fight against the Germans.[1] De Gaulle offered the resistance fighters recognition and the opportunity to continue the war or resume civilian life—in effect, marginalization from the main French armed forces with honor.[2] In so doing he avoided the showdown that confronted the Greek government of national unity in December 1944. De Gaulle, as was the case with Greek and other European governments-in-exile, feared that insurrection against the Germans would lead to chaos. The liberation of Paris in August 1944 by its citizens was exemplary, but to de Gaulle it set a terrible precedent that could inspire other resistance groups to seize French cities and towns. His stature as the leader of the Free French and his charisma enabled the general to assume power, but it was precarious until he could reestablish the institutions of prewar France—the army and the civil service. In both cases de Gaulle had to address the failure of many French officers to join the resistance and the fact that thousands of civilians had collaborated with the Nazis and Vichy. He dealt with the problem of the collaborators and saved the dignity of France by proclaiming "only a handful behaved badly under the German occupation: the rest could look each other confidently in the eyes as patriots."[3] In actual practice de Gaulle moved swiftly to punish collaborators, and over 160,000 men and women were accused of collaborating with the Nazis. Of these almost 120,000 were tried, and 94,000 were found guilty and either imprisoned (24,000) or deprived of their rights (50,000). Approximately 1,600 were executed, but Marshal Pétain, the head of the Vichy regime, although condemned to death, served a life sentence.[4]

Unlike de Gaulle, Prime Minister George Papandreou lacked international and national political stature and was completely beholden to the British as well as to King George II for his authority. Furthermore, he had to contend with Greek royalist officers who envisioned a new Greek army purged of republicans and leftists. The officers who had followed the king into exile and enlisted in the Greek forces in the Middle East had little respect or sympathy for the Greek resistance. Those who disagreed with the monarchy were weeded out from the armed forces of the Greek government-in-exile over the course of the war so that by liberation the military was small in number but cohesive ideologically and loyal to the monarchy.

Almost immediately after the liberation of Greece, those appointed to organize the army by the government of national unity decided to exclude any officers who had taken part in the left's resistance or who had a history of republican sympathies. This discrimination deprived these men of their dignity and also of their livelihood. In so doing the government lost control over a body of well-trained and well-armed men vulnerable for recruitment by the communists. At the same time, the Papandreou government failed to arrest the collaborators and bring them to justice, giving the communist-led EAM a powerful political issue with which to undermine the legitimacy of the government. The communists, for their part, and although they had their instructions from Moscow to support the government of national unity, instead chose violence and attempted to seize control of Athens in December 1944. They failed and set the stage for a final and much more destructive confrontation that lasted from 1946 to 1949.

In the weeks and months following the end of the occupation there had been a brief moment of celebration. Sadly, neither side could understand or forgive the other. Instead, Greek society plunged once again into the historic conflict over the constitutional problem of how to or who should govern the Greek state. Unlike previous struggles for control of the state, this outcome had dire consequences for the losers. In effect, political divisions overshadowed the social and economic challenges of a country with limited resources and a dependence on external partners for its security. The center-left and right looked to the West for patrons to safeguard Greek territory, while the communists preferred to bring Greece within the Soviet sphere.

The demonization of the left, which continued after the end of the civil war and was intensified by the onset of the Cold War and its anticommunist paranoia in the United States under McCarthyism, directly affected U.S. allies such as Greece, which had been one of the main inspirations for the Truman Doctrine. In addressing the U.S. Congress in 1947, President Harry S. Truman had promised substantial help to countries struggling to remain free of communist influence. Like their American patrons, the successive Greek governments gave no one on the left the benefit of the doubt, nor did they treat avowed communists leniently. To some extent the communists played into the hands of the right. As John Karpozilos observes, when the Radio Free Greece KKE broadcast from Bucharest announced the end of hostilities on 15 October 1949, less than two weeks later on 28 October the DAG's leadership proclaimed that the Democratic Army did not surrender and "[we] have our guns at the ready."[5] The "guns at the ready" phrase, notes Karpozilos, was to haunt the Greek left for decades, inspiring the suppression of left-wing dissidents on the grounds of a potential communist insurrection from the north.

The American legacy in the Greek civil war was the conviction that the success of the anticommunist struggle in Greece could be replicated in other troubled regions. The United States emerged from the Greek civil war victorious in its first indirect showdown with the Soviet Union. The confrontation, however, was a matter of perception. Stalin had little interest in Greece and even less inclination to challenge the United States in the Balkans, but American policy makers were convinced that they had stayed the fall of the first domino to Soviet communism and aggression. Further opportunities to halt Soviet intervention and expansion presented themselves in the Middle East and in Asia. Howard Jones writes, "America's experience in Greece provided a glimmer of a policy that would later become known in the 1950s as nation building."[6] After North Korea attacked South Korea in 1950, Truman declared, "Korea is the Greece of the Far East. If we are tough enough now, if we stand up to them like we did in Greece three years ago, they won't take over the whole Far East."[7]

The stalemate in Korea further reinforced the notion of a worldwide communist conspiracy, with countries such as Greece serving as frontline states in a new global conflict. In 1952, Greece and Turkey were admitted to NATO, and in the fall of that year the Americans established military bases in both countries. The formation of the Greek anticommunist state was complete and another legacy of the civil war. The U.S. bases became a symbol of America's commitment to fighting communism not only on the battlefield, but also within the social and political fabric of individual states.

Accordingly, the Greek example served as a model for America's intervention in Central and South America, in the Middle East, and, perhaps most dramatically, in Vietnam and later in Iraq and Afghanistan.[8] In 1950, Douglas Dillon, the U.S. chargé d'affaires in Saigon, wrote in a report criticizing the French failure to contain the Vietminh that, for the United States, it "may eventually become necessary to assume some responsibilities in Indochina as in [the] case of Greece, the threat of spreading Communist political contagion East and West . . . should influence our action." He went on to recommend the "limited use of U.S. force" and "our going as far as we did in Greece and farther than was ever announced we could go."[9] In the same year Secretary of State John Foster Dulles, even before the Korean War, connected the situation in Asia, and particularly Southeast Asia, with that in the Middle East and Greece. He concluded that the fall of Greece to the communist rebels would have resulted in the encirclement of Turkey and ultimately the Soviet domination of the eastern Mediterranean and the Middle East.[10]

In 1957, President Dwight D. Eisenhower, claiming that he understood the lesson learned from the Greek civil war, agreed to expand the U.S. role in Vietnam. Henry Cabot Lodge Jr., the American ambassador to the United Nations, also proclaimed, "We of the free world won in Greece . . . and we can win in Vietnam."[11] The Greek-Vietnam nexus, however, was not confined to the Republicans. According to John F. Kennedy's speechwriter Theodore Sorensen, President Kennedy "at times compared the Vietnam War to the long struggles against Communist guerrillas in Greece and Asia."[12] Likewise, in his memoirs President Lyndon B. Johnson considered the Truman Doctrine in Greece part of America's international inheritance and his justification for committing additional U.S. forces in Vietnam, stating, "In 1947 the British were able to pass on to us their responsibilities in Greece and Turkey. In 1954 the French knew they could transfer the problem of Southeast Asia's security to our shoulders."[13] For American cold warriors, the U.S. experience in Greece—a successfully fought proxy war against communist guerrillas—became, to a degree, a model for involvement in Vietnam.

The failure of the United States in Vietnam is complex and beyond the scope of this study. Two decades of war in Vietnam caused 58,178 U.S. deaths and, in the process, triggered social and political upheavals whose aftershocks continue to reverberate to this day. The American presence in Greece and in Southeast Asia, however, are differentiated by the willingness of most Greeks (despite later anti-Americanism) to welcome U.S. intervention in their civil war. Critical to the American experience in Greece was the absence of active U.S. combat troops. As a result, any anti-Americanism that remains in Greece is superficial because there is no memory of direct killing of Greeks by Americans. The sentiment is based more on the perception that the United States was responsible for the colonels' junta (1967–74) as well as the Turkish invasion of Cyprus in 1974.

There is little doubt that the Truman Doctrine saved Greece from slipping into the Soviet sphere, and Greece thus escaped decades of economic and cultural stagnation. Yet America's grand strategy of Soviet containment in the Balkans held back and distorted the political evolution of the Greek state. Indeed, after Greece became a member of NATO in 1952, the role of the armed forces was to act as a trip wire to alert the alliance of a sudden Soviet attack against southeastern Europe. Beyond that, the Greek army was to guard against an internal communist threat, which gave the military a political role in the management of the country. The Cold War threat also conveniently dovetailed with the memory of the 1946–1949 communist insurrection and was exploited by the conservative regimes in Athens to suppress legitimate dissent in the name of Western security.

In the years after 1949, the KKE remained an outlaw organization, and ultra-right-wing gangs tormented anyone suspected of leftist activity. Greek schools and universities excluded from their curriculum any course on the resistance or the civil war—Greek history came to an abrupt halt with the glorious victories of the Greek army in Albania in 1940–41. References to the 1946–49 period described the conflict as the "bandit war" and as part of Bulgarian, Yugoslav and Albanian plots inspired by the Soviets to destroy Greece.

The execution of Nikos Beloyannis, a key figure in the KKE, on charges of espionage in 1952 brought into focus the fear of another attack by the DAG and the determination of the victorious right to exact revenge on the communists for the civil war.[14] Beloyannis captured the sympathy of many Greeks and even the international community by becoming the face of thousands of communists and leftists who were either marching to the firing squad or languishing in prison. Pleas for clemency from a range of disparate individuals, including Jean-Paul Sartre, Charles de Gaulle, Charlie Chaplin, Pablo Picasso, 159 members of Britain's Parliament, and thousands of ordinary people, fell on deaf ears.[15] Ironically, the only member of the military court who voted to commute the death sentence was George Papadopoulos, later one of the more prominent colonels in the junta.

The trial of Beloyannis attracted international sympathy for an individual communist, while also exposing the fissures within the Greek Communist Party and its leadership. Just before the execution, Nikos Ploumpidis, the leader of the KKE's underground organization, wrote a letter to the authorities offering to turn himself over to them if they would commute Beloyannis' sentence to life imprisonment. The party's leadership in exile denounced the letter as a forgery on their clandestine radio broadcast and thus consigned Beloyannis to his fate.[16] In recent years, sources suggest that the execution of Beloyannis may have served a useful purpose for the KKE secretary general, Nikos Zachariadis. According to Elli Pappas, Beloyannis' wife, Zachariadis's condemnation of Ploumpidis was politically responsible for the death of Beloyannis (the sacrificial lamb). She further claimed that the "man with the red carnation" (as Beloyannis was known) was more popular than the KKE leader, and that Zachariadis may have felt threatened by individuals who had the stature and popularity within the party to displace him. Furthermore this course of events was convenient for Zachariadis, for Beloyannis' plight drew attention away from his own mistakes, particularly his decision to have the KKE stay out of the 1946 elections.[17] To what extent her charges are true is buried in the former Soviet archives in which the Zachariadis' KGB file remains classified.

It took several decades after the war's end, but changes became perceptible in the political landscape. The Greek electorate in the 1960s supported moderate politicians and began to edge toward electing center-left coalitions. These tendencies alarmed the monarchy and the army, both of which maintained independent relations with the United States, and plans were set in motion to preempt the election of a government that appeared too far from the right. Ironically, the man who elicited such fears was centrist politician George Papandreou, the man who defeated EAM-ELAS and the KKE in the December Uprising. In April 1967, the army seized control of the state and imposed a military dictatorship. For seven years, the military junta applied all the instruments of fear and repression against the left and the moderate right. The prison islands were once again filled to capacity, the torture chambers were reactivated, and a web of informants spied on Greeks at home and abroad.

For most Greeks the cruel legacy of the civil war began to dissipate slowly after the collapse of the junta in 1974, accelerated by the election in October 1981 of PASOK, the first socialist party to rule Greece, and by the recognition of the resistance a year later. During the 1990s the schism between the left and the right blurred: In 1989, an ecumenical government that also included the conservative and communist parties breached, albeit temporarily, the barriers of mistrust, fear, and hatred that had polarized Greek society since the occupation. The shadow of the civil war, however, continued to linger, and occasionally emotions flared up in response to events in the Balkans.

The breakup of the Yugoslav Federation in 1991 and the establishment of a so-called Macedonian republic (across the border from the Greek province of Macedonia) caused waves of hysteria in Greece and throughout the Greek diaspora. The overreaction to the breakup of Yugoslavia and the exaggerated fears of a Balkan conflagration spilling into Greece were, to a great extent, a reflex reaction rooted in Slavophone Macedonian participation in the civil war.

The scars of the civil war overlay a series of fault lines and other divisions that occasionally inflamed political passions, whether as reactions to authoritarian rule or to economic hardship. Two recent examples from contemporary Greece, which is currently in the throes of a severe economic crisis, illustrate that the divisions that have plagued Greek society may at times be papered over but are never dormant.

The KKE continued to adhere to a rigid Stalinist line long after the ideology was abandoned by other European communist parties, but is now trying to reinvent itself and take advantage of the current economic problems. The KKE has provided its own dogmatic interpretation of the reasons for the collapse of socialism, the road to the global economic collapse in the early part of the twenty-first century, and the crisis of capitalism, the latter two providing new opportunities for putting out its ideological message. Remarkably, in March 2011, its leadership proceeded to rehabilitate its main civil war icons: Zachariadis (both politically and in terms of party-line doctrine) and Veloukhiotis (politically only).[18] Thus, from messiah turned to outcast, the memory of the controversial leader of the left during the civil war was conjured up and posthumously reinstated on the pedestal of failed tragic hero.

These same turbulent socioeconomic and political crises also helped give rise to the extreme right-wing party Chrysi Avgi (Golden Dawn) and the electoral obliteration of PASOK in favor of the more radical left Syriza. It is in this new polarized political environment that the ghosts of the civil war again resurface as part of the country's political discourse. During a verbal altercation in the Parliament in 2013, a Golden Dawn member shouted the slogan "Sto Vitsi kai sto Grammo sas hosame stin ammo" (In Vitsi and Grammos [civil war battles] we shoved you in the ground). At the same time, during left-wing public protests, the chanting of "EAM-ELAS-Meligalas" (referring to a place in the Peloponnese where Security Battalion troops were ambushed and massacred by ELAS fighters) has also been heard.[19] Indeed, extreme ideologies, a bloated and unresponsive civil service, and chronic political corruption are testaments to a broken civil society—another legacy of civil strife and war.

Notes

PREFACE AND ACKNOWLEDGMENTS

1. Alan Bullock, *Ernest Bevin: Foreign Secretary, 1945–1957* (London: Heinemann, 1983), 160.
2. Ritchie Ovendale, *Britain, the United States and the Transfer of Power in the Middle East, 1945–1962* (London: Leicester University Press, 1996), 4.
3. Nikos Marantzidis, *Demokratikos Stratos Elladas (DSE), 1936–1949* (Athens: Ekdoseis Alexandria, 2010); Charles R. Shraeder, *The Withered Vine: Logistics and the Communist Insurgency in Greece, 1945–1949* (Westport, CT: Praeger, 1999).
4. Giorgos Margaritis, *Istoria tou Ellinikou Emphiliou Polemou 1946–1949*, 2 vols. (Athens: Bibliorama, 2000).
5. Edgar O'Balance, *The Greek Civil War, 1944–1949* (New York: Frederick A. Praeger, 1966); C. M. Woodhouse, *The Struggle for Greece, 1941–1949* (London: Hurst, 2002).
6. Stanley G. Payne, *Civil War in Europe, 1905–1949* (New York: Cambridge University Press, 2011); Philip B. Minehan, *Civil War in World War in Europe: Spain, Yugoslavia, and Greece, 1936–1949* (New York: Palgrave, 2006).
7. Loring M. Danforth and Riki Van Boeschoten, *Children of the Greek Civil War: Refugees and the Politics of Memory* (Chicago: University of Chicago Press, 2011); John Sakkas, *Britain and the Greek Civil War, 1944–1949: British Imperialism, Public Opinion and the Coming of the Cold War* (Mainz: Franz Philipp Rutzen, 2013).

PROLOGUE

1. For a detailed and compelling account in Greek of the trial and execution, see Stelios Protaios, *E Diki ton Exi* (Athens: Chrisima Vivlia, n.d.). Protaios includes, along with

his own account, the minutes of the extraordinary court-martial. Michael Llewellyn Smith, in his study of the Greek expedition in Turkey, includes some discussion in English on the trial and execution of The Six: Michael Llewellyn Smith, *Ionian Vision: Greece in Asia Minor, 1919–1922* (Ann Arbor: University of Michigan Press, 1973).

2. On 28 September 1922, part of the main army (12,000 men) marched into the capital: see Smith, *Ionian Vision,* 314.

3. The leaders of the coup ordered the arrest of Gounaris, Theotokis, Protopapadakis, Stratos, and Goudas, whom they planned to execute immediately and then declare a general amnesty. They also arrested Prince Andrew, one of Constantine's younger sons. After protests from the British and French ambassadors, they decided to delay the executions. Subsequently, they arrested Baltazzis, Hatzianetis, and Stratigos. The court-martial began deliberations in the Greek Parliament on 13 September 1922 and concluded with guilty verdicts on the 28th. The military court consisted of ten officers and was headed by General Othonaios.

4. Smith, *Ionian Vision,* 323; David Lloyd George, *The Truth about the Peace Treaties* (London: Gollancz, 1938), 2:1348.

5. According to Smith, it was Colonel Neokosmos Grigoriadis, the officer in charge of the execution, who read the judgment to the accused: Smith, *Ionian Vision,* 327.

6. This version of Andrew's escape has been supplanted by a more fanciful and dramatic report in which Talbot persuaded one of the leaders of the government, Colonel Nikolaos Plastiras, to have another person, General Theodore Pangalos, personally escort Andrew to the British warship. Pangalos was considered a hard-liner and an implacable foe of the monarchy and its supporters; thus his presence guaranteed Andrew's safety.

7. According to Markezinis, Talbot had served as a naval attaché at the British Embassy in Athens during World War I but was working for Britain's Secret Service. In this capacity, Talbot managed to get close to Venizelos as well as to other prominent members of the Greek Liberal Party, and, claimed Markezinis, was present at all significant international meetings that concerned Greek affairs. A few years later, Talbot used his contacts in Greece on behalf of Whitehall Securities to secure a profitable agreement with the short-lived dictatorship of Theodoros Pangalos. Spiros Markezinis, *Politiki Istoria tis Ellados, Seira B: Sygchronos Elinismos* (Athens: Papyros, 1973), 2:121. Prince Andrew had links to the British royal family through his mother, a granddaughter of Queen Victoria. If Andrew had been executed it would have had a serious impact on the British royal family. His mother was a granddaughter of Queen Victoria, and Andrew was the father of Philip, Duke of Edinburgh and Queen Elizabeth's consort. Prince Philip was a year old in 1922.

8. There is some confusion about whether Hatzianestis was degraded before the execution. Protaios (*E Diki ton Exi,* 819) states that according to some accounts, Hatzianestis removed his own epaulets; others claim he was degraded in prison. Smith relies on A. F. Frangoulis, who was not present but was closely associated with the condemned men. According to this version, the degrading was to take place just before the execution, but as the officers approached the general to remove his military insignia, he

ripped off his epaulets and decorations. Protaios writes that most of the eyewitnesses of the execution did not comment on this. Hatzianestis was wearing a civilian trench coat, which casts some doubt on the theory that the general suffered this vital humiliation before the firing squad ended his life. See Smith, *Ionian Vision*, 428; A. F. Frangoulis, *La Grèce, son statut international, son histoire diplomatique*, 2nd ed., 2 vols. (Paris: Académie diplomatique internationale, 1927).

CHAPTER 1. ORIGINS

Epigraph: George Orwell, *Nineteen Eighty-Four* (New York: Harcourt, Brace, 1949), 35.

1. This was particularly the case with Smyrna (modern-day Izmir), Resat Kasaba, "Economic Foundations of a Civil Society: Greeks in in the Trade of Western Anatolia, 1840–1876" in *Ottoman Greeks in the Age of Nationalism in the Nineteenth Century*, ed. Dimitri Gondicas and Charles Issawi (Princeton, NJ: Darwin Press, 1999), 46–77.

2. The name means lighthouse. The lighthouse district in Constantinople was the center of the Orthodox Church and the residence of the wealthy Greeks.

3. Christine M. Phillipou, *Biography of an Empire: Governing Ottomans in an Age of Revolution* (Berkeley: University of California Press, 2011), 6.

4. L. S. Stavrianos, *The Balkans since 1453* (New York: New York University Press, 1958), 111.

5. On this point see Bernard Lewis, *What Went Wrong? Western Impact and Middle Eastern Response* (Oxford: Oxford University Press, 2002).

6. Most of the diaspora communities in Europe were small in number and eventually assimilated or returned to Greece. The communities that remained in the Ottoman Empire were considerably larger than even the population of Greece in 1830. Those in Russia were also significant in number, at least until 1917.

7. J. A. Petropoulos, *Politics and Statecraft in the Kingdom of Greece, 1833–1843* (Princeton: Princeton University Press, 1968), 28–30.

8. Ibid., 29.

9. Petropoulos' *Politics and Statecraft in the Kingdom of Greece* provides an erudite and exhaustive study of the factions and their role in the period of 1833–1843.

10. The town of Surgut in Siberia was founded in 1594. It is located in a remote area with distinctive physical beauty. During Zachariadis' stay, his son suggests that the local population was approximately two thousand people, mostly fishermen. Daily life was filled with hardships, particularly in the winter, when the temperature could drop to -52 C: Sifis Zachariadis, interview with the author, Piraeus, 16 July 2013.

11. This is mentioned in the publications of Alexis Parnis, *Geia Chara Nikos: I Allilographia mou me to Niko Zachariadi* (Athens: Ekdoseis Kastaniotis, 2011), 29. The poet Alexis Parnis was a comrade and trusted friend of Zachariadis. For the report indicating the cause of death and letter of his first wife to his family in Greece, see Petros Anataios, *Nikos. Zachariadis: Thytis kai Thyma* (Athens: Fytrakis, 1991).

12. He had tried three times to escape. The first, with the help of a neighbor, a Siberian named Vilikseniev, who lived two houses away. Using the latter's truck they drove for

one kilometer. While searching for Zachariadis, local officers interrogated Vilikseniev's wife on her husband's whereabouts and then located both of them. On the second occasion, Zachariadis flew to another city in Siberia, but the person who sold him the ticket also informed the authorities. Finally, Zachariadis managed to board a ship. It appeared that one of the two officers stationed in front of his house must have alerted the authorities. Zachariadis made it to Omsk but was soon apprehended. According to Sifis Zachariadis, the "KGB worked well. All was reported." Zachariadis' attempts are indicative of his growing desperation and exasperation with his prolonged exile. It was perhaps inevitable that he would one day turn to more extreme measures: Sifis Zachariadis, interview with the author, Piraeus, 16 July 2013.

13. According to statements made by his second wife, Roula Koukoulou, Charilaos Florakis attempted to discuss the case of Zachariadis in one of his meetings with members of CPSU but was not successful: Frenty Germanos, *To Antikeimeno (Nikos Zachariadis)* (Athens: Ekdoseis Kastaniotis, 2000), 204. The title of the book translates as "The Object" and was how Soviet authorities referred to Zachariadis in their reports.

14. Sifis Zachariadis, interview with the author, Piraeus, 16 July 2013.

15. For details, see Lampros Stauropoulos, "Poios 'Autoktonise' ton Zachariadi," *To Vima*, 27 July 2003.

16. Lampros Stauropoulos, "O 'Megalos Archigos' Dialekse tin Kremala," *To Vima*, July 28, 2013; Sifis Zachariadis, interview with the author, Piraeus, 16 July 2013.

17. Ibid.

18. Agis Stinas, *Anamniseis; Ebdominta Chronia Kato Ap'ti Simaia tis Sosialistikis Epanastasis* (Athens: Ypsilon Vivlia, 1985), 173–175.

19. Leuteris Apostolou, *Nikos Zachariadis: I Poreia Enos Igeti, 1923–1949* (Athens: Philistor Press, 2000), 44–45.

20. Yiotopoulos became an influential member of the Trotsky organization in Paris and Trotsky's second in command (Stinas, *Anamniseis,* 173–175).

21. Ibid., 170–171. The Archive Marxists, between 1929 and 1930, created committees in Athens and Thessaloniki and gained considerable support, but also clashed violently with the authorities. Violence appeared to be an integral part of Archive Marxism even when it came to internal opposition. See also Antoni Flountzi, *1937–1943: Akronafplia kai Akronafpliotes* (Athens: Themelio, 1979), 216–224.

22. Biographical information provided in an interview with historian and journalist Giorgos Petropoulos, interview with the author, Athens, 15 September 2013.

23. Dominique Eudes, *The Kapetanios; Partisans and Civil War in Greece, 1943–1949* (New York: Monthly Review Press, 1972), 246–248.

24. Nikos Zachariadis, *Theseis gia tin Istoria tou KKE* (Athens: Ekdoseis tis Kentrikis Epitropis tou KKE, 1945), 7.

25. The letters are part of Zachariadis' legacy that the KKE is still trying to fathom. For example, see KKE's official newspaper, *Rizospastis,* 30 October 2011.

26. "To the People of Greece: Open Letter," written on 30 October 1940 (two days after the declaration of war by Italy), and published on 2 November 1940 in the Greek press: Nikos Zachariadis, *Istorika Dilimmata, Istorikes Apantiseis: Apanta ta Dimosievmena, 1940–1945,* ed. Giorgos Petropoulos (Athens: Kastaniotis, 2011), 31.

27. In Dachau he associated with veteran German communists also held there and assumed the unofficial leadership of the prisoners. See Vangelis Papanikos, *O Nikos Zachariadis sto Dachau: Martyria mias Epohis* (Athens: Philistor Press, 1999), 32–34.

28. Yiannis Stefanidis, "Greece in the Second World War (1940–1944)," in *Elliniki Istoria,* vol. 7 (Athens: Ekdotiki Athinon, 2007), 75.

29. Ibid., 67–68.

30. Zachariadis' survival and relative good physical condition after his liberation from Dachau triggered accusations that he had collaborated with the enemy in exchange for better treatment.

31. He maintained the necessity of signing the Varkiza Accord even in 1946: Nikos Zachariadis, *I Simerini Economiki kai Politiki Katastasi stin Ellada kai ta Provlimata tou Dimokratikou Kinimatos kai Agona,* 12 February 1946, ASKI 1; Apostolou, *Nikos Zachariadis Igeti,* 97–98. Other historians claim that Zachariadis was convinced from the beginning of the need for an armed revolutionary struggle in typical Leninist-Stalinist fashion and that he simply masked his true intentions to confuse his enemies: Solon N. Grigoriadis, *Istoria tis Synchronis Elladas, 1941–1974: Nikos Zahariadis: O Moiraios Igetis,* vol. 4 (Athens: Kapopoulos, 1974), 62–63.

32. In early June 1945, shocked readers of KKE's official newspaper, *Rizospastis,* read the following bulletin: "The KKE's leader, the co-fighter Nikos Zachariadis, announced that the Central Committee of KKE decided to denounce publicly as suspect and opportunist the activities of Aris Velouhiotis." The fate of the once popular ELAS commander was sealed. Cut off from EAM and the KKE and pursued by government troops, he was eventually trapped, some suggest betrayed. A few days after the denouncement by Zachariadis, he allegedly committed suicide: Grigoriadis, *Istoria tis Synchronis Elladas,* 67.

33. Zachariadis had a deep antipathy for Velouhiotis before the occupation, which may explain his condemnation of the guerrilla leader. One of his inmates in Dachau recalls: "Upon arriving at Dachau, I told Zachariadis what I knew, that there were two organizations: Zerva's (EDES) under the English and the King, and ours, of EAM-ELAS with Aris Velouhiotis as the leader. Upon hearing Aris' name, he jumped up as if bitten by a snake and said: 'Ari, the traitor, the miserable, the opportunist, [is that] the commander they found to put as leader? Shame for our movement." Papanikos, *O Nikos Zachariadis sto Dachau,* 77.

34. This was evident in his positions both during KKE's 12th plenum and its 7th Congress, in the fall of 1945. During the course of the 7th Congress, Zachariadis disapproved of "the tendencies of some comrades to present the issue [in a] one-sided [manner] when they talk about a peaceful transition [to Socialism]. It has to be immediately stressed that there is a possibility for a peaceful transition, but not a certainty . . . one possibility that is becoming more distant more and more every day that passes." Grigoriadis, *Istoria tis Synchronis Elladas,* 73.

35. Ibid., 132.

36. In January 1946, a delegation of EAM representatives led by M. Partsalidis visited the USSR. Partsalidis had discussed with members of the Soviet leadership the issue of participating in the elections, and the Soviets suggested that the KKE not abstain:

Giorgos Petropoulos, interview by the author, Athens, 15 September 2013. Zachariadis' official position was that the elections would not be conducted properly. Several senior KKE leaders disagreed, but Zachariadis imposed his view. Vasou Georgiou, *I Zoi Mou* (Athens, 1992), 480–481.The latter suggests that a myth was created regarding the plenum; namely, that it was decided at that time to have an armed struggle. Interestingly, in the first volume of the concise history of the KKE covering 1918–1949, it is stated that it was in fact during that specific plenum that a decision was reached about the gradual commencement of the armed struggle, while criticizing the lack of planning with regards to the armed struggle, thus losing valuable time and momentum. It also clearly stated that under the circumstances it was a serious mistake to abstain from the elections: Ekdosi tis Kentrikis Epitropis tou KKE, *Syndomi Istoria tou KKE; Schedio, Meros A, 1918–1949* (Athens: Ekdoseis Synchroni Epochi), 245–246.

37. According to sources cited by Grigoriadis (*Istoria tis Synchronis Elladas,* 143), the decision was finalized during the second plenum of KKE's central committee, but the critical paragraph was omitted from the minutes released to the press. In it, the central committee declared that, having evaluated domestic and international, as well as Balkan factors, it decided to organize a new armed people's struggle against the monarchist-fascist delirium. Vasou Gerogiou states that during that same plenum, in February 1946, a smaller meeting took place with selected members of the party and Zachariadis; the latter asked them whether there was a possibility to commence a general uprising in Athens, Piraeus, Thessaloniki, and other major cities. The answer was negative: Georgiou, *I Zoi Mou,* 481–483.

38. The sixteenth plenum of the KKE central committee in 1956 accused Zachariadis of "the erroneous decision of abstaining from the 1946 elections," in addition, for mischaracterizing "the democratic, national liberating, anti-imperialist struggle [the civil war] as a Socialist Revolution, assuming that DAG is fighting to bring about the dictatorship of the Proletariat"; for his "too leftist line of thought and its sectarian-producing tendencies"; for "cultivating an intense cult of personality"; and, finally, for his "dictatorial way of imposing his 'infallible' opinion, and for persecuting anyone opposing him." Kentriki Epitropi tou KKE, *I Ekti Platia Olomelia tis KE tou KKE: 11–12 Marti 1956,* 22–26.

39. Parnis himself had been accused as an accessory, as reported in a three-page letter on his indictment: Parnis, *Geia Chara Nikos,* 267, 272.

CHAPTER 2. AUTHORITARIANISM, WAR, AND OCCUPATION

1. Cyprus, the Italian-occupied Dodecanese, and northern Epirus (southern Albania), remained as the three outstanding issues of Greek foreign policy until the end of World War II. In the postwar settlement of the Treaty of Paris in 1947, Greece took possession of the Dodecanese Islands, but failed to secure Cyprus and northern Epirus.

2. The republic was proclaimed on 25 March 1924, the anniversary of the outbreak of the Greek War of Independence.

3. In 1909 the army demanded that the king and government accept a series of military and economic reforms. At this critical juncture, the military stopped short of establishing a dictatorship and turned to Venizelos to implement their demands.

4. Thanos Veremis, *Oi Epemvaseis tou Stratou stin Elliniki Politiki* (Athens, 1983), 75–92. Veremis also makes the point that during the crises in the early part of the twentieth century, the majority of the officers did not necessarily support the monarchy or a particular politician, but remained on the sidelines and followed the faction that won control of the army (ibid., 83).

5. The division originated in 1915 with the resignation of Venizelos over the king's refusal to permit the Greek army to participate in the Anglo-French attack on the Dardanelles. In the June 1915 elections Venizelos won an impressive majority (184 out of 310 seats) with a pro-Entente campaign platform. In October, however, Venizelos once again resigned, bringing about a constitutional crisis. This time, Venizelos stepped down because the king refused to honor the Greek-Serbian treaty of 1913 invoked by the Bulgarian attack against Serbia. Venizelos' second resignation was followed by another election, but his party (the Liberals) abstained.

6. According to Veremis (*Oi Epemvaseis tou Stratou stin Elliniki Politiki*, 59), the officer corps in 1916 was made up of two categories of officers: the first included graduates of the military academy and those who had attained permanent status in the army. This group, having achieved its position in the army, was generally loyal to the king. The second category was mostly nonprofessional, lower-ranked officers and had achieved permanent status as a result of the Balkan wars, but their position would be less secure if there was ever a general demobilization. The latter group became staunch supporters of Venizelos and eventually proved to be the most fanatical republicans.

7. The purge of royalist officers in 1922 was followed by the dismissal of 1,800 republican officers because of the unsuccessful coups of 1933 and 1935. See André Gerolymatos, "The Role of the Greek Officer Corps in the Resistance," *Journal of the Hellenic Diaspora* 11, no. 3 (1984), 71, n. 7.

8. George Dafnis, *I Ellas Metaxi Dio Polemon 1923–1940,* vol. 2 (Athens, 1955; Athens: Ikaros, 1974), 369. Dafnis attributes the populist victory to the strong backing of the middle class. He points out, however, that this support did not translate into an endorsement of the monarchy but rather the rejection of the Liberal party.

9. A critical factor in the victory of the populists was the boycott of the elections by the Venizelists.

10. According to the American ambassador—Lincoln MacVeagh, *Ambassador MacVeagh Reports: Greece, 1933–1947,* ed. J. O. Iatrides (Princeton: Princeton University Press 1980), 60—the number given for the monarchist vote was 400,000 votes higher than the total vote cast by all parties in any previous election. According to Hagen Fleischer, the Danish ambassador in Athens commented that the entire process was a farce and "the greatest comedy performed on the European scene for a long time." Hagen Fleischer, *Stemma kai Swastika* (Athens: Papazisis, 1988), 54.

11. J. S. Koliopoulos, *Greece and the British Connection, 1935–1941* (Oxford: Oxford University Press, 1977), 6.

12. The breakdown of seats in the new parliament of 1936 was: 143 Populists, 141 Liberals (Venizelists), and fifteen Communists. Dafnis, *I Ellas Metaxi Dio Polemon*, 2:402.

13. Koliopoulos, *Greece and the British Connection*, 40.

14. Dafnis, *I Ellas Metaxi Dio Polemon*, 2:423 ff.

15. Metaxas confided to his diary that the country was on the eve of a communist revolution. Communist propaganda, he wrote, had already infiltrated the civil service and threatened to paralyze the state, and it had started eroding the discipline of the armed forces. Ioannis Metaxas, *To Prosopiko tou Imerologio*, ed. P. Vranas (Athens: Ekdoseis Gkobosti, 1960), 4:222–223.

16. Metaxas considered this the successor to the classical and Byzantine civilizations. There are several works published in Greek that are sources on the Metaxas dictatorship, but as Koliopoulos points out in *Greece and the British Connection*, 51, they are either polemics against Metaxas or apologias for his regime. These include D. Kallonas, *Ioannis Metaxas: Mathitis-Stratiotis-Politikos-Agonistis Kyvernitis* (Athens, 1938); B. P. Papadakis, *I Chethesini kai i Avriani Ellas* (Athens, 1946); T. Nikouloudis, *Ioannis Metaxas* (Athens, 1941), and *I Elliniki Krisis* (Cairo, 1945); A. P. Tabakopoulos, *O Mythos tis Dictatorias* (Athens, 1945); M. Malainos, *I 4i Avgoustou, pos kai Giati Epivlithi I Dictatoria tou I. Metaxa* (Athens, 1947); I. G. Koronakis, *I Politeia tis 4is Avgoustou, Fos eis Mian Plastographimenin Periodon tis Istorias mas* (Athens, 1950); S. Linardatos, *Pos Eftasame stin 4i Avgoustou* (Athens, 1965), *I 4i Avgoustou* (Athens, 1966), and *I Esoteriki Politiki tis 4is Avgoustou* (Athens, 1975); N. Psiroukis, *O Fassismos kai i 4i Avgoustou* (Athens, 1974); G. Chiotakis, *Politikes Thyelles: 2. I Dictatoria 4is Avgoustou, oi Protagonistes tis, o Polemos 1940–1941* (Athens, 1983); and in English, Jon V. Kofas, *Authoritarianism in Greece: The Metaxas Regime* (New York: Columbia University Press, 1983). A reliable addition to the bibliography of the period is Hagen Fleisher and Nikolaos Svoronos, eds., *Praktika tou Diethnous Istorokou Synedriou, I Ellada 1936–44: Diktatoria, Katochi, Andistasi* (Athens: Morphotiko Institouto, 1989), and the biography of Metaxas by P. J. Vatikiotis, *Popular Autocracy in Greece 1936–41: A Political Biography of General Ioannis Metaxas* (London: Frank Cass, 1998).

17. On this point and the debate over the nature of the Metaxas regime see Vatikiotis, *Popular Autocracy in Greece*.

18. Metaxas, *To Prosopiko tou Imerologio*, vol. 4, 553; also in Vatikiotis, *Popular Autocracy in Greece*, 156.

19. Kofas, however, argues that the Metaxas regime evolved from a conservative dictatorship to an authoritarian quasi-fascist state. By 1938, Kofas writes, Metaxas had purged most of the royalists from his government and replaced them with his own followers, thus gradually becoming independent of the king (Kofas, *Authoritarianism in Greece*, 53–54). Regardless, the army was loyal only to the king and could easily remove Metaxas and his followers at the king's discretion.

20. Koliopoulos attributes the passivity of the politicians to several factors: the weakness of the parties and their inability to galvanize popular opposition to the dictatorship. Some in the Liberal party even entertained the hope that Metaxas would reinstate the cashiered Venizelist officers. Another consideration was the fear that the reaction of Metaxas to vociferous opposition would be to create his own party. John S.

Koliopoulos, "Esoterikes Exelixeis apo tin Protin Martiou os tin 28 Octovriou 1940," in *Istoria tou Ellinikou Ethnous: Neoteros Ellinismos apo 1913 os 1941* (Athens: Ekdotiki Athenon, 1978), 393.

21. Gerolymatos, "The Role of the Greek Officer Corps in the Resistance," 71.

22. Anticommunist policy was nothing new in Greek politics. Previous administrations had been as fervent in combating communism. Between 1929 and 1932, the Venizelos government made 11,000 arrests resulting in 2,130 convictions. A. Elefandis, *I Epangelia tis Adinatis Epanastasis: KKE kai Astismos ston Mesopolemon* (Athens: Themelio, 1976), 56.

23. John Loulis, *The Greek Communist Party, 1940–1944* (London: Croom Helm, 1982), 4–5.

24. Fleischer, *Stemma kai Swastika*, 128. One historian, D. G. Kousoulas, contends that there were over 45,000 such declarations during the period of the dictatorship. D. G. Kousoulas, *Revolution and Defeat: The Story of the Greek Communist Party* (London: Oxford University Press, 1965), 130.

25. Loulis, *The Greek Communist Party*, xiv, Table I.

26. According to the official history of the KKE, the process of decapitating the leadership of the party was completed in November 1939 with the arrest of Siantos and George Skafida. Approximately 2,000 communists were imprisoned throughout the dictatorship. *Syndomi Istoria tou KKE, Meros A 1918–1949*, 142; Elefandis, *Epangelia tis Adinatis Epanastasis*, 257.

27. According to D. H. Close, "The Police in the Fourth of August Regime," *Journal of the Hellenic Diaspora* 13, nos. 1–2 (Spring–Summer 1986), 93, two departments of the gendarmerie, the Eidiki Asfalia (Special Security) and the Yeniki Asfalia (General Security), formed the political or secret police responsible for counterespionage and anticommunism.

28. Loulis, *The Greek Communist Party*, 4; D. G. Kousoulas, *KKE: Ta Prota Chronia, 1918–1949* (Athens: Elliniki Euroekdotiki, 1987), 158.

29. On the underground activities of one prominent member of the KKE during this period, see Vasilis Bartziotas, *Exinda Chronia Kommounistis* (Athens: Sygchroni Epochi, 1986), 151–153. Some of these cells established contact with noncommunist underground organizations, including that of a group of serving officers who had socialist sympathies. Elefandis, *Epangelia tis Adinatis Epanastasis*, 257.

30. Bartziotas, *Exinda Chronia Kommounistis*, 159–168; A. Phlountzes, *Akrovafplia kai Akronafpliotes* (Athens: Themelio, 1979), 213–216; Linardatos, *I 4i Augoustou*, 415–417; A. Stinas, *Anamniseis*, 235–238; Markos Vafeiadis, *Apomnimonevmata*, vol. 1 (Athens: Diphros, 1948), 308–311.

31. Elefandis, *Epangelia tis Adinatis Epanastasis*, 258, remarks that the collective imprisonment of the communists enabled many of them to form lasting personal relationships, thus solidifying their unity and their affiliation with the KKE.

32. *Documents on British Foreign Policy 1919–1939, Series I*, vol. 18 (London: Foreign Office, 1972), 984–989.

33. R. Vansittart, *The Mist Procession* (London: Hutchinson, 1958), 289.

34. C. M. Woodhouse, *Modern Greece: A Short History* (London: Praeger, 1968), 210.

35. In 1929, a delegation of Cypriots in London petitioned the British government for the unification of Cyprus with Greece, but the request was rejected. In 1931 the combined votes of the Turkish minority representatives and British officials defeated a vote on the budget by the Cypriot Legislative Council. In response, Greek Cypriots declared a boycott of British goods and refused to pay their taxes. On 21 October a demonstration in Nicosia, the capital of Cyprus, grew violent, resulting in the burning of Government House. This led to numerous uprisings throughout the island requiring the use of British troops to restore order. Despite the strong sympathy that the people of Greece had for Cyprus, the Venizelos government refused to make any kind of protest against the British. Dafnis, *I Ellas Metaxi Dio Polemon*, 2:74–82.

36. Royal Institute of International Affairs, *The Balkan States: A Review of the Economic and Financial Development of Albania, Bulgaria, Greece, Romania and Yugoslavia since 1919* (London: Oxford University Press, 1936), 139–140; Alexander Cadogan, *The Diaries of Sir Alexander Cadogan 1938–1945*, ed. David Dilks (London: Putnam, 1971), 117–118.

37. Mogens Pelt, "Greece and Germany's Policy towards South-Eastern Europe 1932–1940," *Epsilon* 2, no. 2 (1988), 56.

38. According to Pelt, in order to guarantee supplies of chrome, cotton, olives, and bauxite, the Germans had to secure Greece as a source of these products. Using the clearing accounts, however, ran counter to Greece's economic interests since the goods saved currency or were traded for foreign currency, and therefore the Greeks were reluctant to sell them to Germany. The trade agreement of 1937 was one means by which the Germans were able to force the Greeks to sell them a higher percentage of these products. Pelt, "Greece and Germany's Policy towards South-Eastern Europe," 67.

39. Koliopoulos, *Greece and the British Connection*, 23.

40. Foreign Office Telegram, 15 October 1935, FO 371/19508.

41. Fleischer, *Stemma kai Swastika*, 187; S. Markezinis, *Politiki Istoria tis Neoteros Ellados: I Syngchronos Ellas 1932–1936* (Athens: Payros, 1978), 4:64.

42. Vansittart, *Popular Autocracy in Greece*, 537. According to the American ambassador in Athens, MacVeagh, the British Ambassador in Athens, Sir Sydney Waterlow, confided to him that the return of King George II would be a "calamity." Once, however, Waterlow was informed that the restoration of the monarchy would take place, he immediately told the Greek Minister for Foreign Affairs that the king "would have the full support of the British Legation and of himself personally." Waterlow later confessed to MacVeagh that he had not changed his views on the return of the king, but since the Greeks were going to restore the monarchy it seemed best to try and help them make it a success. MacVeagh, *Ambassador MacVeagh's Reports*, 56–58.

43. Memorandum by the Foreign Secretary 16 October 1935, FO 371/19508; Koliopoulos, *Greece and the British Connection*, 24.

44. Viscount Templewood, *Nine Troubled Years* (London: Collins, 1954), 160–161.

45. The Earl of Avon, *Facing the Dictators: The Memoirs of Anthony Eden, Earl of Avon* (Boston: Cassell, 1962), 386. On 1 July, Eden made a similar declaration at Geneva.

46. Larry Pratt, *East of Malta, West of Suez: Britain's Mediterranean Crisis, 1936–1939* (Cambridge: Cambridge University Press, 1975), 38; COS Memorandum, 29 July 1936, in FO 371/20383.

47. Koliopoulos, *Greece and the British Connection*, 33.

48. Joint Planning Sub-Committee Report, 21 July 1936, FO 371/20383.

49. Koliopoulos, *Greece and the British Connection*, 35.

50. Athens Dispatch No. 281, FO 371/20390.

51. Koliopoulos, *Greece and the British Connection*, 60.

52. *DGFP*, Series D, vol. V, pp.316–318.

53. Metaxas, *Imerologio*, vol. 7, 359.

54. Waterlow also began to include in his reports descriptions of the repressive measures taken by the Metaxas regime, especially the compulsory enrollment of young people in the dictatorship's youth movement, EON. See: Athens Dispatch No. 485, 19 December 1938, FO 371/22371; Letter from Waterlow to Alexander Cadogan, 17 October 1938, FO 371/22363.

55. Athens Telegram No. 185, 6 October 1938, FO 371/22362.

56. Metaxas, *Imerologio*, vol. 7, 311.

57. *Documents on British Foreign Policy, 1919–1939*, Third Series, Vol. 5, Nos. 95, 101, 109–110 (Crolla/Halifax); 97, 111–112, 117 (Greek fears); 118 (Italian assurance to Greece); N. H. Gibbs, *Grand Strategy*, vol. 1, *Rearmament Policy: History of the Second World War* (London: Public Stationery Office, 1976), 709.

58. Koliopoulos, *Greece and the British Connection*, 111. The guarantees offered by the British government to Greece, adds Pratt, *East of Malta, West of Suez*, 160, indicated a partial shift in British diplomacy from appeasement to containment, but it did not lead to Anglo-Greek alliance. According to N. H. Gibbs (*Grand Strategy*, vol. 1, *Rearmament Policy*, 713): "It is important to emphasize that these new guarantees were almost entirely political in scope and immediate in purpose. There was no detailed analysis of their military implications during preliminary discussions, and no follow up staff talks once the guarantees had been given."

59. Cadogan, *The Diaries of Sir Alexander Cadogan*, 170–175.

60. War Cabinet: Chiefs of Staff Committee, "Greek Cooperation Report," 22 September 1939, FO 371/23782 R7921.

61. Metaxas, *Imerologio*, 4: 406. In December, Metaxas confided again in his diary that he was pleased with the state of affairs in Greece considering what was going on in the rest of the world: Ibid., 41.

62. FO 371/24910.

63. W. J. M. Mackenzie, *The Secret History of SOE: The Special Operations Executive, 1940–1945* (London: St. Ermin's Press, 2000), 138. Mackenzie's work was in effect an internal history of the SOE completed in 1948. The last head of the SOE, Sir Colin Gubbins, commissioned the work intended for future directors of any successor organization and thus it was kept secret until fifty-two years later.

64. FO 371/24982.

65. Ibid.

66. *DGFP*, Series D, Vol. XI, No. 323, "Directive 18," p. 530.

67. *DGFP*, Series D, Vol. XI, No. 511, "Directive 20: Operation Marita."

68. Part of the inducement for the Greeks to accept the presence of British intelligence representatives was their role in organizing secret meetings between British and Greek

military authorities. Bickham Sweet-Escott, *Baker Street Irregular* (London: Methuen, 1962), 61–62.

69. Ibid., 60–62; N. Hammond, *Venture into Greece: With the Guerrillas, 1943–1944* (London: William Kimbers, 1983), 13; Col. Julian Dolbey, *Report on SOE Activities in Greece and the Islands of the Aegean Sea* (1947); Richard Clogg, "The Special Operations Executive in Greece," in *Greece in the 1940s: A Nation in Crisis,* ed. John O. Iatrides (Hanover, NH: University Press of New England, 1981), 110–111.

70. These activities were concealed from the Greek General Staff partly because of security and partly because postoccupation planning might have undermined the will of the Greek military by implying that the defeat of Greece was inevitable (Clogg, "The Special Operations Executive in Greece," 111). All the preparations made by MIR and the Greek General Staff amounted to very little, Dolbey, *Report on SOE Activities in Greece and the Islands of the Aegean Sea.* MIR also attempted to establish links with groups hostile to the Metaxas regime. In the summer of 1940, a MIR agent went to Crete to make plans with General Emmanouil Mandakas, a leading opponent of Metaxas, in order to prepare for a possible rebellion in Crete in the event that the Greek government gave in to Axis pressure. Unfortunately the agent was caught, causing some embarrassment for the British diplomats in Athens (Clogg, "The Special Operations Executive in Greece," 110).

71. Keith Jeffery, *The Secret History of MI6, 1909–1949* (New York: Penguin Press, 2010), 415–416.

72. C. M. Woodhouse, *Apple of Discord* (London: Hutchinson, 1948), 37. In another text, however, Woodhouse emphasizes that the SOE gave priority to recruiting cashiered republican officers since "such officers were readily available . . . and were perhaps thought not to be so dangerous politically as the Communists." Woodhouse, *Struggle for Greece,* 29.

73. Hammond, *Venture into Greece,* 13–14.

74. R. Clogg, "The Special Operations Executive in Greece," 111.

75. His actual name was Count Dobrski.

76. Dolbey, *Report on SOE Activities in Greece and the Islands of the Aegean Sea,* 21. Part of his report and other classified memos as well as segments of one lengthy account on the history of British intelligence operations Greece in the later 1930s and early 1940s by Ian Pirie were included in Mackenzie's *Secret History of SOE.* Although extremely useful, it is not a comprehensive history of the SOE and only offers an overview, albeit with some intriguing occasional details, on operations in Greece. Dolbey, *Report on SOE Activities in Greece and the Islands of the Aegean Sea,* along with Ian Pirie's *Greek History* (HS 7/268 89846: also declassified) and C. M. Woodhouse, *History of the Allied Military Mission in Greece, Sep 1942-Dec 1944,* provide considerable details on British espionage, sabotage, and relations with the Greek resistance, both left and right.

77. Dolbey, *Report on SOE Activities in Greece and the Islands of the Aegean Sea,* Appendix II, "Directives," 5.

78. Colin Gubbins, who became the executive director of the SOE in 1943, had also supported the concept. The Poles and the Czechs who had organized secret armies particularly had impressed Gubbins, and he believed that these could serve as a model

for other countries in occupied Europe (Sweet-Escott, *Baker Street Irregular,* 47–48). The difficulty, however, was that Britain lacked the industrial capacity to manufacture millions of weapons that would have been required to arm the mass armies.

79. Dolbey, *Report on SOE Activities in Greece and the Islands of the Aegean Sea,* Appendix I, "Origin and Constitution of SOE," 2; Woodhouse, *Apple of Discord,* 92.

80. Michael Ward, correspondence with the author, 15 November 2004.

81. Phoivos N. Grigoriadis, *Germanoi Katoxi Andistasis,* vol. 5 (Athens: Neokosmos, 1973), 217. The publication of the SOE's internal history, Mackenzie, *The Secret History of SOE,* has added considerable information on the organization.

82. Mackenzie, *Secret History of SOE,* 140.

83. After the German attack, SOE's activities were limited to a number of demolitions by a group sent from Egypt, led by Peter Fleming, and the destruction of several bridges near Thebes by another SOE officer, David Pawson. As the front was collapsing, SOE representatives in Greece were desperately attempting to equip their embryonic cells with radios and explosives but were only able to organize a few small groups. The speed of the German advance permitted only the most rudimentary plans for the organization of clandestine networks. According to Sweet-Escott, the SOE managed to "bully" seven wireless transmitters from SIS, but of these only one, left by Pawson to Bakirdzis, ever made contact with the SOE in Cairo. With the exception of Prometheus, the code name used by Bakirdzis, all other information concerning Greece came from escaped British soldiers and Greeks who managed to leave the country. Bickham Sweet-Escott, "SOE in the Balkans," in *British Policy towards Wartime Resistance in Yugoslavia and Greece,* ed. Phyllis Auty and Richard Clogg (London: Macmillan, 1975), 7.

84. Koliopoulos, *Greece and the British Connection,* 214; FO 371/29862.

85. "Greek Military Situation," FO 371/24884 R74320.

86. *DGFP,* Series D, XII, No. 195, "Directives of the High Command of the Wehrmacht," 338ff; F. H. Hinsley and Edward Thomas, eds., *British Intelligence in the Second World War: Its Influence on Strategy and Operations* (London: HMSO, 1979), 347–348.

87. John Keegan, *The Second World War* (Toronto: Penguin, 1989), 152.

88. M. van Creveld, *Hitler's Strategy 1940–1941: The Balkan Clue* (Cambridge: Cambridge University Press, 1973), 158.

89. Great Britain Cabinet Office, *Principal War Telegrams and Memoranda 1940–1943,* vol. 1, *Middle East, From the Occupation of Cyrenaica to the Fall of Keren and Harar,* Cabinet History Series (Nendeln: KTO Press, 1976), nos. 39, 40, 69, 73.

90. Hinsley and Thomas, *British Intelligence in the Second World War,* 1:361.

91. Martin Gilbert, *Finest Hour: Winston Churchill, 1939–1941* (London: Heinemann, 1983), 1014. In a minute to General Wavell, Churchill emphasized the point that the American newspapers were full of reports of the British sending forces to Greece (Winston S. Churchill to Wavell, 4 April 1941 in Martin Gilbert, *The Churchill Papers: The Ever Widening War* [New York: W.W. Norton, 2000], 3:448).

92. *Great Britain Cabinet Office,* vol. 1, nos. 36, 39; Sir Llewellyn Woodward, *British Foreign Policy in the Second World War* (London: HMSO, 1970), 1:511.

93. Woodward, *British Foreign Policy in the Second World War,* 1:526.

94. Evacuation of the BEF began on the night of 24–25 April and continued for the next five nights. See S. W. Roskill, *The War at Sea 1939–1945* (London: HMSO, 1954), 436.

95. Tsolakoglou initiated unauthorized discussions with Sepp Dietrich, the commander of the Adolf Hitler Division, and surrendered his forces on 20 April 1941.

96. The British Mediterranean Fleet provided a force of six cruisers, twenty destroyers, and thrity other ships to facilitate the evacuation. Slightly over 50,000 men were rescued by the Royal Navy at a cost of two destroyers and four transports.

97. Papagos requested that he should be relieved of his command and put on the retired list. According to Koliopoulos the reason given for Papagos' resignation was that no one should be left in a high position who could make terms with the Germans. The Foreign Office, however, interpreted the resignation of Papagos and the dismissal of the Greek General Headquarters as an indication of the Greek government's lack of trust in the General. Koliopoulos, *Greece and the British Connection,* 292; FO 371/29820 R4615.

98. The surviving Greek fleet included one old cruiser, nine destroyers, one torpedo boat, five submarines, and one depot and repair ship. In addition to the fleet, some land forces were evacuated or made their way to Egypt along with 900 air force personnel, of whom 200 were pilots. FO 371/29816 R74220.

99. Emmanouil Tsouderos, *Logoi* (Athens: Aetos, 1946), 73; FO 371/33167 R 1362; Fleischer, *Stemma kai Swastika,* 179.

100. P. Papastratis, "Diplomatika Paraskinia tis Ipografis tis Stratiotikis Symfonias Vretanias—Elladas stis 9 Martiou 1941," *Mnimon* 7 (1979), 174–182.

101. The constitution of 1911 was a variation of that of 1864, when Prince George of Denmark became King George I of Greece. In 1927, after the abolition of the monarchy, the constitution was again revised, but in 1935, with the restoration of George II, the constitution of 1911 was reinstated. In 1936, Metaxas, with the support of the king, suspended eight articles of the constitution and established the dictatorship.

102. FO 371/33160, p. 59ff.; GAK E 13.

103. Emmanouil Tsouderos, *Ellinikes Anomalies stin Mesi Anatoli* (Athens, 1945), 47–48; Fleischer, *Stemma kai Swastika,* 159–160.

104. Thanasis Hadzis, *E Nikifora Epanastasi pou Chathike: Ethnikoapeleftherotikos Agonas 1941–45,* (Athens: Dorikos, 1982), A:107–108; Alexandros Zaousis, *Oi Dio Ochthes 1939: Mia Prospathia gia Ethniki Symfiosi* (Athens: Papzisis, 1987), part B, 34.

105. Fleischer, *Stemma kai Swastika,* 157–159; J. Petropoulos, "The Traditional Political Parties of Greece During the Axis Occupation," in *Greece in the 1940s: A Nation in Crisis,* ed. J. O. Iatrides (Princeton: Princeton University Press, 1981), 27–28.

106. The famine took a greater toll of life than the war of 1940–41, all the bombings, the casualties from resistance activity, and the victims of reprisals exacted by the Axis forces combined. Fleischer, *Stemma kai Swastika,* 194. In a recent study, Violetta Hionidou argues that the famine was not confined to 1941–1942 but continued until 1944. Violetta Hionidou, *Famine and Death in Occupied Greece, 1941–1944* (Cambridge: Cambridge University Press, 2006).

107. Emmanouil Tsouderos, *O Episitismos 1941–1944: Mesi Anatoli* (Athens: Papazisis, 1948), 3. On the reaction to the famine by the Greek government-in-exile, see GAK A6-A17; B1-B4; E1-E3.

108. As early as June 1941 Tsouderos began to argue that a blockade would have serious implications for Greece. He accepted the policy of denying the enemy any supplies of food, but he pointed out that the situation in Greece would become desperate and that a way around the problem was to supply Greece through the International Red Cross or even simply by sending food secretly and unofficially. Fleischer suggests that Tsouderos has received a great deal of criticism for his role in the crisis, but that for the most part he has been blamed for the delays of food shipments from Turkey caused by R. Raphael, the Greek ambassador in Istanbul. Tsouderos, *Logoi*, 17–18 and passim; Fleischer, *Stemma kai Swastika,* 206, n. 58.

109. Another possible source of supply acceptable to the British was Russia, but the German invasion in 1941 eliminated that option: P. Papastratis, *British Policy towards Greece during the Second World War* (Cambridge: Cambridge University Press, 1984), 115–116.

110. Why, and if, the British ambassador made such a promise, knowing full well the blockade policy, is not known, but the matter of 30,000 tons of grain per month is mentioned by Ilias Venezis and supported by Fleischer: Ilias Venezis, *Archiepiskopos Damaskinos* (Athens: Estias, 1981), 110; Fleischer, *Stemma kai Swastika,* 204. Before the war, Greece annually imported 400,000–500,000 tons of grain, but the problem was compounded by a poor harvest in 1941 and the additional burden of feeding the BEF. Just before the collapse of Greece, the Greek government had purchased over 350,000 tons of grain from abroad, but most of these supplies had been consumed: Fleischer, *Stemma kai Swastika,* 204. According to Peter Hoffmann, a shipment of 47,000 tons of grain from Australia, which was to have replaced what the British forces had confiscated and consumed in Greece, was prevented from reaching Greece: Peter Hoffmann, "Roncalli in the Second World War: Peace Initiatives, the Greek Famine and the Persecution of the Jews," *Journal of Ecclesiastical History* 40, no. 1 (1989), 78.

111. FO 371/29817 R 8810. From his first meetings with Churchill and Eden, Tsouderos had brought up the subject of Greek territorial claims, but both avoided giving the Greek prime minister any commitments and sidestepped the proposal of an Anglo-Greek alliance (Papastratis, *British Policy towards Greece,* 16).

112. FO 371/29817 R8810; Papastratis, "Diplomatika Paraskinia," 176, n. 5, and *British Policy towards Greece,* 16–17. Papastratis comments that the objections of the Foreign Office were a reaction to Tsouderos' requests for Greek territorial claims and border adjustments in northern Greece. On the Greek claims see E. Tsouderos, *Diplomatika Paraskinia* (Athens: Aetos, 1950), 116; *The Greek White Book: Diplomatic Documents Relating to Italy's Aggression Against Greece* (London: Greek Foreign Ministry, 1942), introduction. For the basis of the Greek claims to northern Epiros, see B. P. Papadakis, *Diplomatiki Istoria tou Ellinikou Polemou* (Athens, 1956), 221–222.

113. Papastratis, "Diplomatika Paraskinia," 177, n. 7; Tsouderos, *Diplomatika Paraskinia,* 188.

114. The main articles called for the Greek armed forces to come under the command of the Britain's Middle East Theater of Operations, which also became responsible for their organization and direction. On the other articles see Tsouderos, *Diplomatika Paraskinia,* 164–167; and Papastratis, "Diplomatika Paraskinia," 178–179.

115. Papastratis, *British Policy towards Greece,* 11.

116. Ibid.

117. Woodward, *British Foreign Policy in the Second World War,* 3: 383.

118. Ibid.

119. Woodhouse, *Apple of Discord,* 49.

120. Ibid., 50.

121. Winston S. Churchill, *The Second World War, Closing the Ring* (London: Houghton Mifflin, 1951), 5: 458 and 465.

122. Ibid. 466.

123. Henri Michel, *The Shadow War: Resistance in Europe 1939–1945,* trans. Richard Barry (London: Andre Deutsch, 1972) 53–54; D. Stafford, *Britain and European Resistance 1940–1945: A Survey of the Special Operations Executive, with Documents* (London: Macmillan, 1980), 33–34.

124. Lord Hubert Miles Gladwyn Jebb, *The Memoirs of Lord Gladwyn* (London: Weidenfeld and Nicolson, 1972), 103 and 105–106.

125. *DGFP,* Series D, 12: no. 463, p. 722.

126. *DGFP,* Series D, 12: no. 463, p. 722.

127. Fleischer, *Stemma kai Swastika,* 117–118.

128. Christos Zalokostas, *To Chroniko tis Sklavias* (Athens: Estia, 1949), 14; Fleischer, *Stemma kai Swastika,* 118.

129. Fleischer, *Stemma kai Swastika,* 118.

130. In a report to King George II, Prince Peter stated that the Germans, unlike the Italians, initially were not hated. On the contrary, a large part of the population, especially the upper class, sympathized with and even admired Germany (FO 371/37216 R 3924). Fleischer (*Stemma kai Swastika,* 118, n. 7) also points out that half the faculty of the University of Athens and four-fifths of the faculty of the Polytechnic School had studied in Germany.

131. Ch. Christidis, *Chronia Katochis: Martyries Imerologion, 1941–1944* (Athens, 1971), 5.

132. Ibid., 10; Fleischer, *Stemma kai Swastika,* 121.

133. Athenians were not permitted outdoors after 10:00 P.M. Dionysios Benetatos, *To Chroniko tis Sklavias, 1941–1944* (Athens, 1963), 28; Christidis, *Chronia Katochis,* 5–6; Fleischer, *Stemma kai Swastika,* 121.

134. Raphael Lemkin, *Axis Rule in Occupied Greece: Laws of Occupation, Analysis of Government Proposals for Redress* (New York: H. Fertig, 1973), 190.

135. Benetatos, *To Chroniko tis Sklavias,* 27.

136. Particularly irritating for the Germans was that the allied radio networks hailed the taking down of the German flag as a major act of resistance for all of occupied Europe: Fleischer, *Stemma kai Swastika,* 119–120. The individuals who took down the German flag were two students, Manolis Glezos and Apostolos Santas. Dimitris Gatopoulos, *Istoria tis Katochis* (Athens: Melissa, 1949), A:131.

137. Venezis, *Archiepiskopos Damaskinos,* 195–197.

138. Damaskinos had been elected archbishop under Metaxas but the election was technically invalidated, and Chrysanthos replaced him. Ironically, the Germans replaced Chrysanthos with Damaskinos.

139. FO 371/29909 R8414; FO 371/29842 R10894.

140. K. Pyromaglou, *O Georgios Kartalis kai i Epochi tou, 1934–1944* (Athens, 1965), A: 140. Archbishop Damaskinos concluded that the government-in-exile's neglect of its supporters allowed the communists to seize the initiative; by the time the government reacted to the problem, it was too late. FO 371/37206 R10450.

141. J. L. Hondros, *Occupation and Resistance: The Greek Agony, 1941–1944* (New York: Pella, 1983), 101.

142. Edmund Myers, *Greek Entanglement* (Gloucester: Sutton, 1985), 103.

143. Fleischer (*Stemma kai Swatsika,* 179–181) suggests that the means of accomplishing this was the return of the king after the war and that the Tsouderos government from the very beginning attempted to exclude from the government all those who opposed the monarchy. Hondros (*Occupation and Resistance,* 101) states that the aim of the government-in-exile was to use the officer corps in order to support the monarchy in the postwar period. K. Pyromaglou (*O Georgios Kartalis kai i Epochi tou,* 140–141) also maintains that the government-in-exile had the express goal of reimposing the prewar political system and finds little difference between the puppet governments and that of Tsouderos and the king. On 6 November 1941, Alexander Sakellariou, the vice premier and commander-in-chief of the Greek fleet, warned Tsouderos that the Greek nation considered the government-in-exile nothing more than the continuation of the 4 August regime: Alexander Sakellariou, *Enas Navarchos Thimatai* (Athens: Dimokratos, 1971), 392.

144. Georgios Tsolakoglou, *Apomnemonevmata* (Athens, 1959); K. Logothetopoulos, *Idou i Alitheia* (Athens, 1948); Ioannis Rallis, *O Ioannis Rallis Omilei ek tou Tafou* (Athens, 1947); N. Louvaris, "Golgothas enos Ethnous," *Ethnikos Keryx,* 2 April–11 June 1950; Woodhouse, *Apple of Discord,* 27.

145. In April 1940 the number of permanent officers reached 4,980. Later, because of the war, 300 senior cadets from the military academy were prematurely graduated, and 50 warrant officers were advanced to the rank of second lieutenant, which increased the number of officers to 5,180. The Greek armed forces also included 10,000 reserve officers and 1,150 ipoaxiomatikoi (subofficers), Alexandros Papagos, *O Ellinikos Stratos kai i pros Paraskevi tou* (Athens: Ekdosis Deifthynseos Istorias Stratou, 1969), 412 and passim.

146. By the beginning of the war, 4,500 professional officers had been purged from the armed forces. During the war 3,000 of these were recalled to active service, but approximately 1,500, most of whom were of higher rank, were excluded from serving (Gerolymatos, "The Role of the Greek Officer Corps in the Resistance," 71 and nn. 7 and 8).

147. As a body, the professional active officers suffered a much higher casualty rate than the ordinary soldiers or the reserve officers. According to established figures, casualties amongst professional officers reached 6.9 percent dead and 9 percent wounded.

In contrast, the rate for the reserve officers was 1.7 percent dead (figures not available for wounded), while for the permanent reserve officers (those who had been forced to retire) recalled to active duty, the rate was 1.1 percent dead and 1.8 percent wounded. The lower casualty rate among this group was due to the reluctance of the Metaxas regime to place them in command of combat units (Gerolymatos, "The Role of the Greek Officer Corps in the Resistance," 70–71).

148. K. Pyromaglou, "Ta Tagmata Asphalias," *Istoriki Epitheoresis* 6 (October–December 1964), 539. See also Konstantinos Th. Bakopoulos, *I Omeria ton Pende Andistratigon: I Zoe ton—Stratopeda Sygendroseos* (Athens, 1948), 26–27.

149. See Tsouderos, *Ellinikes Anomalies stin Mesi Anatoli*; Hagen Fleischer, "The Anomalies in the Greek Middle East Forces, 1941–1944," *Journal of the Hellenic Diaspora* 5, no. 3 (1978), 5–36.

CHAPTER 3. THE POLITICS OF VIOLENCE

Epigraph: C. P. Cavafy, "Waiting for the Barbarians," *Collected Poems,* trans. Daniel Mendelsohn (New York: Alfred A. Knopf, 2010), 193.

1. W. K. Klingaman, *1941: Our Lives in A World on the Edge* (New York: Harper and Row, 1966), 210. There is no other evidence for this event, it may be urban legend or even wishful thinking on the part of Klingaman. However, considering the heroism of the Greek army, it may also have taken place.

2. This was particularly irritating for the Germans, since it was hailed by the British BBC radio as a major act of resistance for all of occupied Europe: Fleischer, *Stemma kai Swastika,* 119–120. The individuals who took down the German flag were two students, Manolis Glezos and Apostolos Santas. Gatopoulos, *Istoria tis Katochis,* vol. A, 131.

3. The thousands of young women who joined the left-wing ELAS, on the other hand, eschewed identification with tradition and preferred military attire and when not possible just ordinary trousers.

4. The SOE had secretly trained about 350 saboteurs in northern Greece and hid three and a half tons of explosives. In the Athens area, seven groups were established and supplied with one and a half tons of explosives. According to a secret SOE report all the groups had accepted money but only one agreed to maintain a radio set: HS 7/268 89846, *Major Pirie's Report: A History of SOE Activities in Greece May 1940–November 1942,* 443.

5. Ibid., 444.

6. Alexatos, although a key figure in the development of espionage, sabotage, and guerrilla activity organizations in Greece, remains a mystery. It is not clear when he was recruited by the SOE, but it was before the occupation (Richard Clogg, "The Special Operations Executive in Greece," in *Greece in the 1940s: A Nation in Crisis,* ed. John O. Iatrides (Hanover, NH: University Press of New England, 1981), 113). According to Fleischer, Alexatos was a smuggler with considerable experience in getting in and out of Greece as well as other countries in the Middle East. Between 1941–1942 he brought funds into Greece and instructions for several groups working for different

British intelligence services: Fleischer, *Stemma kai Swastika*, 240–241. It is evident from one source that Alexatos was sympathetic to the Left and of considerable assistance to both EAM and the KKE: A. Levidis, "Yia Hare tis Alithias: Intelligence kai Andistasi" (unpublished manuscript: Athens, 1975), 29. In August 1943, Tsimas travelled to Cairo as part of a guerrilla delegation and used the opportunity to look for Alexatos, but to no avail. He concluded that Alexatos was terminated: Fleischer, *Stemma kai Swastika*, 241, n. 75. Odysseus, however, survived; the reason for his disappearance was that he had resumed his earlier career in smuggling, which he continued after the war: Michael Ward, *Greek Assignments: 1943 SOE–1948 UNSCOB* (Athens: Lycabettus Press, 1990), 132–133.

7. HS7/268 89846, *Major Pirie's Report: A History of SOE Activities in Greece May 1940–Nov. 1942*, 445.
8. Ward, *Greek Assignments*, 254–255.
9. FO 74038 HS 5/524.
10. Michael Ward, correspondence with the author, 15 November 2004.
11. HS 7/151 89846.
12. G. H. N. Seton Watson, "Afterword," in *British Policy towards Wartime Resistance in Yugoslavia and Greece*, ed. Phyllis Auty and Richard Clogg (London: Macmillan, 1975), 289.
13. According to M. R. D. Foot and J. M. Langley, Atkinson's first name was not John, but they only provide the initials of G. D. See: M. R. D. Foot and J. M. Langley, *MI9: Escape and Evasion, 1939–1945* (London: Bodley Head, 1979), 92. The secondary Greek sources covering this particular episode all use the name of "John." See Zaousis, *Oi Dio Ochthes: 1939–1945*, 73; Gatopoulos, *Istoria tis Katochis*, 207–216; and G. V. Ioannidis, *Ellines kai Xenoi Kataskopoi stin Ellada* (Athens: Ekdosis A. Mavridis, 1952), 22–40. The sources dealing with Atkinson and his activities at Antiparos are not in agreement concerning his role in Greece or even the period of time he spent there. According to the accounts listed above, Atkinson arrived in Greece in October 1941 and was captured by the Italians in January 1942. The British sources refer to Atkinson's presence in Greece and his capture but do not provide any details. Foot and Langley state that his mission was to assist British soldiers to escape from Greece and that almost all the members of the team were captured in January 1942: Foot and Langley, *MI9*, 92. In addition, the submarine *Triumph* sent to facilitate the rescue was lost at Antiparos. According to S. W. Roskill, the *Triumph* was sunk by a mine on 14 January 1942 in the Gulf of Athens (presumably the Saronic Gulf): Roskill, *The War at Sea, 1939–1945*, 443. On the other hand, *Janes Fighting Ships* lists the submarine as lost on 16 January 1942 in the Aegean: *Janes Fighting Ships of World War II*, ed. Anthony Preston (New York: Military Press, 1989). Sweet-Escott, on the other hand, suggests that this event took place in the spring of 1942 and that its purpose was to make contact with Greeks willing to work for the British. He also adds that the group was brought to Antiparos by submarine, but he does not indicate that it was lost: Sweet-Escott, *Baker Street Irregular*, 119. In a later account, Sweet-Escott mentions the capture of a single British officer at Antiparos in February 1942. Woodhouse writes about the arrest of a British officer at Antiparos but adds no further information:

Woodhouse, *Apple of Discord,* 8. The Greek sources cited base their facts from the account of Alexander Zannas, although they include some aspects not covered by Zannas: Alexander Zannas, *I Katochi: Anamniseis-Epistoles* (Athens: Estias, 1964), 74ff; Admiral Panagiotis E. Konstas, *I Ellas tis Dekaetias 1940–1950* (Athens, 1955), 244–246. The head of the Greek secret service in Cairo, Konstas bases his account not only on his own recollections, but also on the transcripts of the postwar trial of the collaborators. Another reliable source, although it only provides a brief reference to the Atkinson affair, is *IAEA* (Athens, n.d.), 2:2:38–39.

14. FO 74038 HS5/524.

15. Zannas, *I Katochi,* 73.

16. FO 74038 HS5/524.

17. According to Zannas, Atkinson arrived by submarine at Euboia and made his way on foot to Athens. He was able to reach Zannas through a mutual friend, Panagiotis Sifnaios. Zannas and Atkinson met at the home of Sifnaios, where Atkinson was staying and where he had found refuge in the course of his escape in April. Zannas, *I Katochi,* 74.

18. In the summer of 1941, Zannas purchased four bombs from a communist organization (for 280,000 drachmas), which he turned over to Nikos Nikolaidis and Stavros Margaritis. Both of these men had found employment at the Elefsina airport, which was used by the German air force, and wished to try their hand at sabotage. They planted the first two bombs in German aircraft bound for Crete or North Africa and set them to explode one hour after the planes were in the air. The third bomb, however, exploded on the ground next to a loaded bomber, which caused the destruction of several aircraft: ibid., 76–77.

19. Zannas' role in the underground movement was the link between several groups involved with espionage and sabotage. As the head of the Greek Red Cross, he was under constant surveillance and could only be involved indirectly. He had direct access to Evert, the commander of the Athenian police, and to the archbishop of Athens, both of whom aided many of the different clandestine groups set up in Athens. Zannas' brother, Sotiris, had been an agent of Section D in 1940–41 but was forced to leave Greece because of his involvement with the Maleas organization, another group that hid British soldiers and assisted them to escape to the Middle East; see below. Levidis, "Yia Hare tis Alithias," 20.

20. Zannas, *I Katochi,* 77.

21. Ibid., 78–79.

22. At Antiparos, Atkinson was able to operate from the summer home of a Greek lawyer, Spyros Tzavellas (Ioannidis, *Ellines kai Xenoi Kataskopoi stin Ellada,* 23).

23. Ibid., 24; Zaousis, *Oi Dio Ochthes,* 73–74.

24. Zaousis, *Oi Dio Ochthes,* 73.

25. According to Spyro Kotsis, the explosives were timed to go off at 9:00 a.m.: Spyro Kotsis, *Midas 614* (Athens, 1976), 127. At that time, ships were usually 500 meters from the harbor, and according to Atkinson's calculation they would sink in deeper water. Fortunately for the population of Milos, the German and Italian authorities

assumed the attack against the ships was the work of British commandos and did not exact retribution against the inhabitants of the island: Ioannidis, *Ellines kai Xenoi Kataskopoi stin Ellada,* 127.

26. In Zannas' account Atkinson had left Antiparos and returned from Egypt by submarine in mid-December 1941 in order to organize the escape of another group of twenty British and four Greeks: Zannas, *I Katochi,* 78–80. The group in Athens had already transported the twenty-four escapees to Anavysos and later to Antiparos, but they too were captured by the Italians. Shortly thereafter, the British submarine was also sunk. Ward, who was responsible for sending off agents to Greece, relates in his memoirs that Atkinson left Alexandria for Antiparos in October 1941: Ward, *Greek Assignments,* 180.

27. According to G. B. Ioannidis, Atkinson and his associates were betrayed because someone affiliated with the group had a failed affair with a woman who informed the Italians as an act of revenge: Ioannidis, *Ellines kai Xenoi Kataskopoi stin Ellada,* 26. Kotsis, on the other hand, suggests that the activities of the group had attracted the attention of the Italian garrison: Kotsis, *Midas 614,* 127. This version is corroborated by Konstas, who states that according to the evidence produced in the postwar trial of the collaborators, the presence of the group at Antiparos became known to the Italians through "an unfortunate incident" and by the incredible carelessness of Atkinson, who at one point was fishing by dropping hand grenades in the sea: Konstas, *I Ellas tis Dekaetias,* 246.

28. Konstas, *I Ellas tis Dekaetias,* 246; Zannas, *I Katochi,* 80; Kotsis, *Midas 614,* 128; Zaousis, *Oi Dio Ochthes,* 74; Sweet-Escott, *Baker Street Irregular,* 119.

29. Konstas, *I Ellas tis Dekaetias,* 246–247; Zannas, *I Katochi,* 81; Kotsis, *Midas 614,* 128; Zaousis, *Oi Dio Ochthes,* 74.

30. According to John Patelis, whose father and brother were also part of the Atkinson group on Antiparos, after he was arrested, the Italians paraded him in front of the British prisoners and one of them, named Alec, pointed him out. In an interview Patelis expressed his bitterness toward the British captives whose cowardliness cost the life of his father and brother: "The Betrayal," *Monthly Illustrated Atlantis,* June 1963. I am grateful to Hellen Marinatos for providing me with the *Monthly Illustrated Atlantis* article and for a Greek commemorative publication that adds considerable background to Atkinson's time on Antiparos.

31. Many received long prison sentences; Atkinson and his immediate associates were condemned to death and executed some months later.

32. These others included Captain Theodoros Koundouriotis, the son of one of Greece's most famous admirals and one of those who had helped set up the Bakirdzis cell; Leon Polymenakos, a distinguished physician and Kanellopoulos' doctor; Panagiotis Klapeas, a well-known lawyer; and two senior officers, Aristidis Pallis and Vasilis Angelopoulos: Kotsis, *Midas 614,* 128–129. In addition to Kanellopoulos, Bakirdzis was mentioned in Atkinson's papers; he too had to leave Greece and was succeeded by Koutsogiannopoulos, a naval officer with the code name of Prometheus II: Zaousis, *Oi Dio Ochthes,* 75.

33. Konstas, *I Ellas tis Dekaetias,* 247.

34. Ch. Christidis, *Chronia Katochis,* 27 April 1942, p. 258, Atkinson and those implicated with him were tried in February 1943 (the trial lasted from 9 to 17 February). Atkinson, along with Diamandis Arvanitopoulos, Tzavellas, and two others closely affiliated with the group, was executed on 24 February 1943: Konstas, *I Ellas tis Dekaetias,* 247.

35. According to Alexandros Zaousis, Kanellopoulos had excellent contacts with the officer corps and was in a good position to get Greek officers to participate in a resistance organization: Zaousis, *Oi Dio Ochthes,* 85. Fleischer writes that Kanellopoulos had established links with Greek republican officers such as Bakirdzis, Sarafis, and Psaros as well as with monarchists in order to organize a resistance movement: Fleischer, *Stemma kai Swastika,* 161. At the same time Kanellopoulos refused to cooperate with EAM since he opposed the creation of large organizations and preferred the establishment of a number of small, well-organized groups.

36. For an analysis of the attitudes of the Greek political leaders, see Fleischer, *Stemma kai Swastika,* 155–161; K. Pyromaglou, *I Ethniki Andistasis: EAM-ELAS-EDES-EKKA* (Athens: Dodoni, 1975), 215–221.

37. The committee included Thrasyvoulos Tsakalotos, Spiliotopoulos, Eust. Liosis, St. Kitrilakis, K. Dovas, and Filippidis: Th. Tsakalotos, *40 Chronia Stratiotis tis Ellados* (Athens: Acropolis Edition, 1960), A:369.

38. Ibid., 371.

39. P. Kanellopoulos, *Imerologio: 31 March 1942–4 January 1945* (Athens: Kedros, 1977), 8 May 1943.

40. FO 371/37201 R74220; Kanellopoulos, *Imerologio,* 8 May 1943.

41. Kanellopoulos, *Imerologio,* 5 August 1943.

42. Kanellopoulos also adds that information from the intelligence groups in Greece, although transmitted by Greek agents, was received and interpreted by SOE personnel in Cairo, an arrangement that he wished to change in the near future: ibid., 9 May 1943.

43. Ibid., 8 May 1943.

44. GAK, "Apostoli Gama," No. 4; Kotsis, *Midas 614,* 28–30.

45. GAK, "Apostoli Gama," No. 4; Kotsis, *Midas 614,* 28.

46. Kotsis, *Midas 614,* 32–37.

47. Ibid., 56–57.

48. The death of Tsigantes, killed by the Italians in a gun battle on 15 January 1943, also meant that the first attempt to block the Corinth Canal, code named Thurgoland, did not materialize. A second SOE team, commanded by Lt. Cdr. Cumberledge and codenamed Locksmith, managed to penetrate the canal and succeeded in laying some mines, which had been especially designed for this operation; however, they failed to explode. Unfortunately, Cumberledge and three members of his team were arrested upon their return to the island of Paros. The four were then brought to Athens and later sent to Germany, where they were shot in May 1945.

49. The difficulties of the Greek communists were further compounded by the Italian invasion of Greece. The general secretary of the KKE, Zachariadis, who was in prison at the time, published a letter on 1 October in the government-controlled communist

newspaper, *Rizospastis,* stating that the Communist Party was prepared to accept the direction of the Metaxas regime in the war. On 31 October, he issued a second letter, supporting the government unconditionally in the war against Italy: *Akropolis,* November 2, 1940; *Rizospastis,* September 25, 1943; *Saranda Chronia tou KKE 1918–1958* (Athens: Sygchroni Epochi, 1958), 744; Fleischer, *Stemma kai Swastika,* 130–131. In this, Zachariadis, despite the German-Soviet Pact (on the directives of the Comintern to the KKE, see Fleischer, *Stemma kai Swastika,* 132–133), was supported by the majority of the imprisoned communists and members of the central committee held at Akronafplia. In fact, just prior to Zachariadis' letter, the communist inmates of Akronafplia appealed to Metaxas for their release so that they could fight on the Albanian front: *Rizospastis,* 28 October 1945; N. I. Mertzos, *KKE Episima Keimena, 1940–1945* (Athens: Ekdosis tou KKE Esoterikou, 1979), 4:14–15. The remnants of the central committee still at large, however, declared Zachariadis' letter false and contrary to communist ideology. The Italian-Greek conflict, they claimed, had nothing to do with the protection of Greece but only served the interests of the British: Mertzos, *KKE Episima Keimena,* 4:24–36. However, the policy of the KKE became confused when a month later, Zachariadis published a third letter. This time, he stated that the KKE's support was based on the understanding that the war was antifascist, and after the Greek army crossed the Albanian frontier it became fascist in nature and served British imperialist interests: ibid., 4:22–23. After 1949, the central committee of the KKE concluded that Zachariadis' decision to support the government in 1940 had exceeded the policy guidelines of the Comintern: Fleischer, *Stemma kai Swastika,* 133.

50. Only 1,350 communists were kept in the following prisons and islands: Akronafplia (600), Agio Stratis (230), Anaphi (220), Aigina (170), Pholegandros (130); and another 500 were in various prisons in the Peleponnese and in Kimolo (36), Gavdos (30), Asvestochori (17), Kerkyra (10); and 30 more in Ios, Siphnos, Pylos, and Amorgos: Zaousis, *Oi Dio Ochthes,* 23; G. Ioannidis, *Anamniseis: Provlimata tis Politikis tou KKE stin Ethniki Andistasi, 1940–1945* (Athens: Themelio, 1979), 505.

51. In this case, Kaiti Zevgos, who spoke a little French and German, while hiding the fact that they were communists, convinced the German authorities on the island that they were exiled because they had opposed the Metaxas regime. The Greek commandant of the island also helped by not referring to his inmates as communists. Accordingly, the Germans permitted the exiles to make use of small boats and leave: Kaiti Zevgos, *Me ton Yianni Zevgo sto Epanastatiko* (Athens: Ekdosis Okeanida, 1980), 197–199.

52. According to Vasilis Bartziotas, during the same period seventeen others escaped from other islands; two would play key roles in the resistance: Markos Vafeiadis and Metsos Vladas. In the next two years, adds Bartziotas, four hundred more managed to escape and reestablish contact with the KKE: Vasilis Bartziotas, *Ethniki Andistasi kai Dekemvris 1944* (Athens: Sychroni Epochi, 1979), 74.

53. Another four hundred escaped during the course of the occupation: Zaousis, *Oi Dio Ochthes,* 23.

54. Twenty-seven inmates of Akronafplia prison, called the Marxist University by the communists, found their freedom through the intervention of the German security

services acting on behalf of the Bulgarian embassy. They identified themselves as Bulgarian and were released. Many of these were instrumental in the creation of EAM-ELAS and played a key role in the resistance: Fleischer, *Stemma kai Swastika,* 142; Bartziotas, *Ethniki Andistasi kai Dekemvris 1944,* 74. Some agreed to work for the Bulgarian security services, which acted as a front for the Gestapo, or some, such as Tsipas, may have been Bulgarian agents all along (see below, Chapter 5).

55. Fleischer, *Stemma kai Swastika,* 142–143; Ioannidis, *Anamniseis,* 506.

56. Hadzis, *E Nikiphora Epanastasi pou Chathike,* A:121–122 and n. 5. The organizational difficulties were resolved with the sixth and seventh plena of the central committee and the KKE called upon the Greek nation to form a national liberation front to fight the Axis. According to Hadzis, those present represented the reorganized central committee of the KKE: ibid., A:118–119. The old central committee dissolved itself: Mertzos, *KKE Episema Keimena 1940–1945,* 5: 58–59.

57. Hadzis, *E Nikiphora Epanastasi pou Chathike,* A:150.

58. In early September, Hadzis and Kostas Vidalis met with General Stylianos Gonatas, one of the leading republican officers, and brought up the subject of resistance. The latter not only opposed the idea but threatened the representatives of the KKE personally and stated that he would violently oppose them: Hadzis, *E Nikiphora Epanastasi pou Chathike,* A:152–153.

59. SKE (Socialist Party of Greece); ELD (Union of Popular Democracy); AKE (Agrarian Party of Greece).

60. The first step toward forming a common front was taken by the Greek labor unions which, with the support of the communists, established the National Workers' Liberation Front (EEAM) on 16 July 1941. In addition to its role of looking after the needs of labor during the occupation, EEAM proposed the creation of a common front to instigate resistance: *Avgi,* 13 July 1960; Mertzos, *KKE Episima Keimena,* 5: 66–67; Fleischer, *Stemma kai Swastika,* 146. On the organization of the EEAM, see also Angelos Avgoustidis, "EEAM: The Workers' Resistance," *Journal of the Hellenic Diaspora* 11, no. 3 (1984), 55–67; Benetatos, *To Chroniko tis Sklavias 1941–1944,* 51–52. For the entire constitution of EAM see G. Augeropoilos et al., eds., *St' Armata St' Armata! Chroniko tis Ethnikis Andistasis 1940–1945* (Athens: Geranikos, 1964), 104–105; Mertzos, *KKE Episima Keimena 1940–1945,* 5: 83–85.

61. Fleischer, *Stemma kai Swastika,* 147.

62. According to Hadzis, who became the political officer of the central committee of ELAS, the KKE proceeded with the creation of armed bands after exhausting every effort to enlist the cooperation of senior Greek officers: Hadzis, *E Nikiphora Epanastasi,* 272–273. On 2 February 1942, EAM decided that it would initiate the armed struggle against the occupation forces by organizing its own units in the mountains. It was agreed by those present—I. Polydoros, Tsimas, and Hadzis—and afterward approved by Siantos, to name these forces the National Popular Liberation Army and that the new organization would come under EAM; the central committee of ELAS would receive its direction from the central committee of EAM.

63. Veloukhiotis was the nom de guerre adopted by Athanasios Klaras, who had been arrested by the Metaxas security service before the occupation. According to his

brother, B. Klaras, he signed the infamous declaration of repentance on instructions from Zachariadis. A. Klaras was not able to substantiate this and during the occupation no one came forward to back his claim; Zachariadis himself was shipped off to Dachau and after the war denounced Klaras. As a result, Klaras was always suspected by the KKE central committee: B. Klaras, *O Adelphos mou o Aris* (Athens: Dorikos, 1985), 112–113. According to Benetatos, the central committee of EAM had not yet made up its mind whether to initiate guerrilla warfare when Klaras on his own initiative formed his band, which was recognized after the fact: Benatatos, *To Chroniko tis Sklavias 1941–1944*, 83–84.

64. In Greek "democratic" also means "republican." Another translation of EDES would therefore be "National Republican Greek League."

65. Pyromaglou, *I Ethniki Andistasis*, 314–315.

66. Pyromaglou, *I Ethniki Andistasis*, 305–306, 315.

67. Fleischer, *Stemma kai Swastika*, 152. In his account of the Greek resistance and his role in EDES, Pyromaglou writes that on 9 September 1941 Plastiras asked him to return to Greece and work with the latter's followers toward establishing a democratic and socialist organization. Upon his arrival in Athens (23 September 1941), Pyromaglou, through the intervention of Gonatas and Ilias Stamatopoulos, met with Zervas and shortly thereafter agreed to become the General Secretary of a five-man governing committee created in October to direct EDES.

68. Pyromaglou, *I Ethniki Andistasis*, 314–315; Benetatos, *To Chroniko tis Sklavias*, 53–54.

69. *IAEA*, 4:46.

70. He was the cousin of the poet Seferis: C. M. Woodhouse, *Something Ventured* (London: Granada, 1982), 29; Levidis, "Yia Hare tis Alithias," 26; Hadzis, *E Nikiphora Epanastasi pou Chathike*, A: 373.

71. The implication in the Greek sources is that contact with Cairo meant contact with the SOE.

72. Levidis, "Yia Hare tis Alithias," 23ff.

73. Leonidas Spais, *Peninda Chronia Stratiotis* (Athens: Melissa, 1970), 225; *IAEA*, 4:35; K. Pyromaglou, *O Georgios Kartalis kai I Epochi tou 1934–1944*, A:150; Fleischer, *Stemma kai Swastika*, 241.

74. Levidis, "Yia Hare tis Alithias," 27; Fleischer, who interviewed Levidis, suggests that the British were not prepared to sever contact with EAM and that is why they decided to support only EDES and EAM and exclude those who refused to cooperate with the left: Fleischer *Stemma kai Swastika*, 241, n. 74.

75. Levidis, "Yia Hare tis Alithias," 30.

76. Fleischer, *Stemma kai Swastika*, 241.

77. Alexatos not only brought 7,100 gold sovereigns to the KKE but also turned over to them at least one wireless set and helped them repair a second: Ioannidis, *Anamniseis*, 124–125; 513, n. 40.

78. Fleischer, *Stemma kai Swastika*, 242, nn. 76, 77, and 78. This account is based on a series of articles published in the newspaper *Akropolis* by both Zervas and Koutsogiannopoulos; see also: Dolbey, *Report on SOE Activities in Greece and the Islands of the Aegean Sea*, Cairo 27 June 1945, 53.

79. Woodhouse, *Something Ventured*, 21.

80. Ibid., 40–41.

81. Ibid., 43. This statement is disputed by Hadzis, who claims that the central commit-tees of the KKE, EAM, and ELAS were more than willing to cooperate with the British: Hadzis, *E Nikiphora Epanastasi*, A:377.

82. *OKW Diaries (Kriegstagebuch des Oberkommando des Wehrmacht, 1940–1945)*, ed. Geführt von Greiner and Percy E. Schramm, vol. 2, 1940 (Frankfurt am Main: Bernard & Graefe Verlag für Wehrwesen, 1961–1966), 141.

83. Over the next two years the SOE established eighty missions in Greece, which em-ployed 611 officers and other ranks. During the same period, the SOE's intelligence activity was carried out by 600 British and 3,000 Greek agents. Dolbey, *Report on SOE Activities in Greece and the Islands of the Aegean Sea*, 7, 17.

84. Woodhouse, *Something Ventured*, 54.

85. FO 371/37201 74220 R 2050, "Political Aspects of the Greek Resistance Movement," 123.

86. Ibid.

87. Ibid.

88. Ibid., 116–117.

89. FO 371/37201 74220 R 2050, "Resistance Groups in Greece," Minute by Dixon, 7 March 1943. Dixon went so far as to recommend that all SOE activity be suspended in Greece.

90. FO 371/37201 74220 R 2332.

91. Woodhouse had prompted Zervas to send a friendly message to the king of Greece on the occasion of Greek National Day, 25 March. To Woodhouse's surprise Zervas went even further and in the telegram assured George II that if the British so desired he would accept the return of the monarch with or without a plebiscite: Woodhouse, *Something Ventured*, 64. Initially this was kept secret, and according to Pyromaglou, had the news become known it would have led to the break-up of EDES: Pyromaglou, *O Georgios Kartalis*, A:544.

92. R. Clogg, "Pearls from Swine," in *British Policy towards Wartime Resistance in Yugoslavia and Greece*, ed. P. Auty and R. Clogg (London: Macmillan, 1975), 175. The SOE used this message from Zervas to prove to the Foreign Office that it was not supporting only antimonarchist resistance organizations: FO 371/3717194 R 2266.

93. FO 371/37201 74220, R 2322.

94. FO 371/37201 74220, R 2050, "Political Aspects of the Greek Resistance Movement."

95. On the strength of these forces see Hondros, *Occupation and Resistance*, 117–118; 144–145.

96. The report was written in June 1943 by J. M. Stevens, who had returned to Cairo from a fact-finding mission in the Greek mountains where he tried to assess the mer-its of ELAS and EDES. Stevens concluded in his report that ELAS was poorly led, since it had mounted a campaign against regular Greek officers, but by the summer of 1943, was attempting to attract such men into its ranks: J. M. Stevens et al., eds., *British Reports on Greece 1943–44* (Copenhagen: Museum Tusculanum Press, 1982), 16, 24.

97. In each village, EAM had set up four organizations: the local EAM central committee, which supervised all political and resistance activity; a group responsible for relief; another responsible for youth; and a division that looked after logistical support for ELAS. The entire EAM apparatus was under the control of the secretary of the central committee, who was usually a member of the KKE. The village secretaries elected a district EAM, which in turn elected regional committees of EAM. Each of the regions then had one representative on the twenty-five-member national central committee of EAM in Athens. Cities, such as Athens and Thessaloniki, had independent representation, and the EAM organizations were based on neighborhood units: Hondros, *Occupation and Resistance,* 118.

98. Sarafis, a well-respected republican officer, had initially taken the field with a new band, but it was soon dispersed and he was captured by ELAS. After some hesitation Sarafis agreed to join ELAS and serve as its military commander.

99. By the summer of 1943, ELAS included 600 professional officers, 1,250 republican officers, and 2,000 lower-ranking reserve officers: Gerolymatos, "The Role of the Greek Officer Corps in the Resistance," 75.

100. Although Zervas' message to King George was kept secret, it was leaked to the Antifascist Military Organization (ASO), based in the Middle East, which passed it on to Athens where it was published in the communist newspapers: Fleischer, *Stemma kai Swastia,* 393; *Kommounistiki Epitheoresi,* February 1944, 15; *Rizospastis,* 15 November 1944.

101. When ELAS captured Sarafis on 7 March 1943, Zervas requested permission from the BMM to effect a rescue, but Myers feared it would lead to war between ELAS and EDES. He was convinced, however, that Zervas' forces would prove superior and advised the SOE that the destruction of ELAS would have little impact upon the guerrilla war. He also added that this was the last opportunity to check the growing power of ELAS and recommended all-out support for EDES: Fleischer, *Stemma kai Swastika,* 391; FO 371/37202 R 4209.

102. Stevens, *British Reports on Greece 1943–44,* 120.

103. On the text of the agreement, see Woodhouse, *Apple of Discord,* Appendix C, 299–300.

104. FO 371/37203 R 5573.

105. According to Hadzis, another reason the British were forced to recognize ELAS as an Allied force was that they were afraid of complications in the Balkans, because ELAS was coming into contact with Albanian and Yugoslavian partisans and might form a military and perhaps even a political alliance. Hadzis adds that the British recognition of ELAS was considered a significant political victory. Hadzis, *E Nikiphora Epanastasi,* B:139.

106. Myers, *Greek Entanglement,* 228.

107. Operation Animals was one element of a much greater effort, Operation Minced Meat, implemented to persuade the Germans that the Allies had targeted Greece for their offensive in the Mediterranean. See Charles Cruickshank, *Deception in World War II* (Oxford: Oxford University Press, 1979), chapter 4; Hinsley and Thomas, eds., *British Intelligence in the Second World War: Its Influence in Strategy and Operations,* 3:120.

108. Between March and the time of the Allied landings in Sicily, the total number of German divisions in the Balkans rose from eight to eighteen and those in Greece from one to eight: Hinsley and Thomas, eds., *British Intelligence in the Second World War: Its Influence in Strategy and Operations,* 3:11, 80, and 144–145; According to Dolbey there were six German and twelve Italian divisions contained in Greece during this period: Dolbey, *Report on SOE Activities in Greece and the Islands of the Aegean Sea.*

109. Myers had planned to visit Cairo on his own to report to Moyne and discuss the problems of the guerrilla bands, but after he informed Tsimas and Pyromaglou of his trip, both asked whether they could go along. To satisfy EKKA, Myers also had to agree to take George Kartalis. Before Myers could complete the travel arrangements, Siantos, the acting secretary of the KKE, insisted that three other EAM representatives join the group. Although Myers had asked and received permission from Cairo to take Tsimas, Pyromaglou, and Kartalis, when he signaled the SOE about the additional EAM representatives there was not enough time to await a reply: E. Myers, "The Andarte Delegation to Cairo: August 1943," in *British Policy towards Wartime Resistance in Yugoslavia and Greece,* ed. Phyllis Auty and Richard Clogg (London: Macmillan, 1975), 148–149.

110. Myers proposed that the guerrilla bands be recognized as part of the Greek armed forces and recommended that andarte liaison officers be attached to the Greek general staff. He also believed that political matters concerning the resistance organizations should be handled by civilian authorities and hoped that the joint headquarters could be divided into two separate departments, with civil liaison officials attached to the Greek government-in-exile. Myers feared that after the intensive guerrilla activity that preceded the Allied landings in Sicily, the andarte bands would grow restless and begin to attack each other. Therefore, he planned to limit the size of the bands, but provide them with light artillery and other supporting arms, in order to raise both the status and the quality of the guerrillas and focus their attention on training, thus avoiding a civil war in the mountains. Before departing from Greece, Myers held several meetings with the delegation that was to travel to Cairo, and all agreed to accept and collectively support Myers' recommendations: Myers, *Greek Entanglement,* 236–243.

111. Myers, "The Andarte Delegation to Cairo: August 1943," 151.

112. Ibid., 151–152.

113. Dolbey, *Report on SOE Activities in Greece and the Islands of the Aegean,* Appendix III, p. 10.

114. André Gerolymatos, "American Foreign Policy towards Greece and the Problem of Intelligence, 1945–1947," *Journal of Modern Hellenism* 7 (1990), 157–162.

115. Hondros, *Occupation and Resistance,* 175–183. In his account of the Greek resistance, Hondros includes a detailed study of Zervas' contact with the Germans. On links between the Greek guerrilla bands and the Germans in general, see also Hagen Fleischer, "Contracts between German Occupation Authorities and the Major Greek Resistance Organizations: Sound Tactics or Collaboration," in *Greece in the 1940s: A Nation in Crisis,* ed. John O. Iatrides (Hanover, NH: University Press of New England, 1981), 48–60.

116. Hondros, *Occupation and Resistance,* 183.

117. By August 1944, according to General Hubert Lanz, EDES had received consider-able material support from the allies and, under strong pressure from the AMM, attempted to destroy German units in the region of Epiros. As a result, Zervas' forces suffered considerable losses so that by the time of the German withdrawal in October, EDES was down to 8,000 men: General Hubert Lanz, "Partisan Warfare in the Balkans," in Historical Division European Command: Foreign Military Studies Branch, MS No. P-995a, Koenigstein/TS, September 15, 1950).

118. In a memorandum to the Foreign Office on 14 October 1943, it was argued that the British had to work with EAM-ELAS since this was the most effective resistance in Greece. The author of the memorandum also stressed that left-wing groups produce much better results: FO 371/37206 R 10177.

119. FO 371/37208 R 1221; FO 371/37206 74337.

120. FO 371/37206 R 10295; FO 371/37208 R 11753, R 11908.

121. CAB 65/40, W. M. (43), Minutes, 22 November 1943.

122. Anthony Eden, *The Reckoning: The Memoirs of Anthony Eden, Earl of Avon* (Boston: Cassel, 1965), 498–499; FRUS 1943, 4:157–158; MacVeagh, *Ambassador MacVeagh Reports,* 395. For a comprehensive study of American policy toward Greece from 1943, see: Lawrence S. Wittner, *American Intervention in Greece, 1943–1949* (New York: Columbia University Press, 1982). Another useful guide to American-British relations over Greece is Warren F. Kimball, ed., *Churchill and Roosevelt: The Complete Correspondence,* 3 vols. (Princeton: Princeton University Press, 1984).

123. Mary Henderson, *Xenia: A Memoir, Greece 1919–1949* (London: Weidenfeld and Nicolson, 1988), 61.

124. Hondros, *Occupation and Resistance,* 204.

125. Ibid.

126. FO 371/37210 R 13883.

127. Hondros, *Occupation and Resistance,* 206–207.

128. Other stipulations included the resumption of supplies to all the guerrilla forces and the release of prisoners. For the complete articles of the agreement see Woodhouse, *Apple of Discord,* Appendix F, "The Plaka Armistice," 303–304.

129. The other members of PEEA included several academics and Social Democrats, with Siantos serving as the only representative of the KKE. On the history and or-ganization of PEEA, see Basilis Bouras, *I Politiki Epitropi Ethnikis Apeleftherosis PEEA: Eleftheri Ellada 1944* (Athens: Diogenis, 1983), 90. Bouras argues that the participation of some of Greece's most notable academics indicated that the intel-lectuals had become supporters of EAM.

130. Hondros, *Occupation and Resistance,* 211–212.

131. L. S. Stavrianos, "Mutiny of the Greek Armed Forces, April 1944," *American Slavic and East European Review* 9 (December 1950), 307; Harold Macmillan, *The Blast of War, 1939–1945* (London: Macmillan, 1967), 571; Fleischer, "The Anomalies in the Greek Middle East Forces, 1941–1944," 26–27.

132. According to Fleischer, Venizelos had contacts with the mutineers, and he and the other republican politicians were attempting to use the crisis to topple Tsouderos.

By this time, however, both the king and the Foreign Office had become convinced that keeping Tsouderos would aggravate the crisis and found Venizelos the only acceptable alternative: Fleischer, "The Anomalies in the Greek Middle East Forces, 1941–1944," 28–29.

133. Eighteen of the rebels were condemned to death, but their sentences were commuted to life imprisonment by the Greek government in October 1944. The British imprisoned 6,397 Greek seamen and soldiers in camps in Eritrea and in other detention centers in the Middle East. A total of 2,060 were eventually reinstated in the armed forces but confined to garrison duties, while another 1,450, who were offered amnesty, refused it, and were imprisoned for the duration of the war: FO 371/43714 R 7081; Hondros, *Occupation and Resistance*, 214.

134. Hondros, *Occupation and Resistance*, 216.

135. The conference had been arranged by Tsouderos before the arrival of Papandreou.

136. R. Leeper, *When Greek Meets Greek* (London: Chatto and Windus, 1950), 51.

137. According to Leeper, Papandreou simply managed to postpone the question of the monarchy: ibid., 54.

138. A summary of these points is found in Woodhouse, *Apple of Discord*, 305–306; Leeper, *When Greek Meets Greek*, 53–54.

139. Leeper, *When Greek Meets Greek*, 56.

140. Hondros, *Occupation and Resistance*, 224–226.

141. On 12 June, according to Leeper, Papandreou convinced his cabinet to state publicly that it was the view of the national government that the king would return to Greece only after a plebiscite and that the king had agreed to this in advance, both by his letter to Tsouderos on 8 November 1943 and by approving the Lebanon Charter, in which this policy was implicit. George II had little choice but to accept or face the resignation of the government: Leeper, *When Greek Meets Greek*, 57–58.

142. For a detailed analysis of the tactics of the German military operations, see Hondros, *Occupation and Resistance*, 153–159.

143. Ibid., 153.

144. André Gerolymatos, "The Security Battalions and the Civil War," *Journal of the Hellenic Diaspora* 12, no. 1 (Spring 1985), 17.

145. NARA RG 226:83476; E. Wiskemann, *The Rome Berlin Axis: A History of the Relations between Hitler and Mussolini* (London: Oxford University Press, 1949), 278; F. W. Deakin, *The Brutal Friendship* (London: Weidenfeld and Nicolson, 1962), 253.

146. Gerolymatos, "The Security Battalions and the Civil War," 18.

147. NARA RG 226:83476. Professional considerations were certainly a motive, since the mutinies among the Greek armed forces in the Middle East had caused the removal of many republican officers. A postwar Greek army, it was assumed, would also have to accommodate officers who had fought in North Africa and those who had participated in the resistance, at least with right-wing groups. This would leave little room for officers who had remained outside these forces: A. Stavrou, *Allied Politics and Military Interventions: The Political Role of the Greek Army* (Athens: Papazisis, 1970), 24.

148. According to Pyromaglou, although the Security Battalions were envisioned as a means of controlling the immediate postwar period in Greece, they were not intended to be used as an anticommunist force. Pyromaglou adds that their deployment against EAM-ELAS not only betrayed the republican leaders who had supported the organization of these units but served to divide the republican movement in a manner that was irreconcilable: Pyromaglou, "Ta Tagmata Asfalias," 543.

149. Gerolymatos, "The Role of the Greek Officer Corps," 76.

150. Bakopoulos, *I Omeria ton Pende Andistratigon*, 34–38.

151. Hondros, *Occupation and Resistance,* 172–173.

152. Ibid., 173.

153. Hondros adds that although EAM-ELAS did not publicly denounce British contacts with the Rallis government, shortly after the outbreak of the civil war they made strong protests to Cairo that British officers were working with collaborators: ibid., 173–174.

154. John L. Hondros, "Too Weighty a Weapon: Britain and the Greek Security Battalions, 1943–1944," *Journal of the Hellenic Diaspora* 15, nos. 1–2 (1988), 36–37.

155. FO 371/43706.

156. Gerolymatos, "The Security Battalions and the Civil War," 21.

157. General Infante, the commander of the Pinerolo Division, immediately changed sides after the Italian surrender and signed an agreement with ELAS recognizing his unit as an allied force. The Pinerolo Division had a complement of 12,000 well-equipped men. Within one month, ELAS divided the Italian division into small units that were subsequently disarmed: Woodhouse, *Apple of Discord,* 101.

158. Papastratis, *British Policy towards Greece during the Second World War,* 210.

159. Gerolymatos, "The Security Battalions and the Civil War," 21, n. 23.

160. The EAM ministers were sworn in on 3 September 1944 and received the following portfolios: Svolos was made minister of finance; Nikos Askoutsis received communications; Ilias Tsirimokos, Militiadis Porphyrogenis, and Zevgos were made ministers of economy, labor, and agriculture, respectively; while Angelos Angelopoulos became undersecretary for finance.

161. Hondros, *Occupation and Resistance,* 230; Woodhouse, *Apple of Discord,* 86. For a detailed study of the Soviet Mission in Greece and its possible role in the decision of EAM-ELAS to join the Greek government, see Lars Baerentzen, "The Arrival of the Soviet Military Mission in July 1944 and KKE Policy: A Study of Chronology," *Journal of the Hellenic Diaspora* 13, nos. 3–4 (Fall–Winter 1986), 77–111.

162. FO 371/43715 R 12457; Force 133 MEF Reports, GSOE/94506.

163. Harold Macmillan, *War Diaries: Politics and War in the Mediterranean, January 1943–May 1945* (New York: St. Martin's Press 1984), 524–525.

164. The Greek government was to arrive in Athens on 17 October 1944, but when it was realized that the 17th fell on a Tuesday, the day that Constantinople fell to the Ottomans and thus was considered unlucky, the trip was postponed to the 18th. The Greek government was transported by a Canadian ship from Taranto to the island of Poros, where, for the sake of propriety, the passengers were transferred to the Greek cruiser *Averoff.* Although a very old ship only able to make ten knots, the

Averoff was the pride of the Greek navy in the Balkan wars and thus had the honor of bringing the Greek government to Athens: Leeper, *When Greek Meets Greek*, 73–74.

165. Force 133 MEF Reports, Ref GSOE/94/505, "Maintenance of Law and Order in Greece."

166. NARA RG 226: L49838; L49839; XL 2683.

167. Gerolymatos, "The Security Battalions and the Civil War," 23.

168. According to Hondros, the decisions made at Tehran by Roosevelt, Churchill, and Stalin regarding war crimes worked to the advantage of those who served in the Security Battalions: Hondros, "Too Weighty a Weapon," 35. The criteria for charging war criminals instituted by the United Nations commission set up by the allies omitted atrocities conducted by traitors or Quislings of allied nations against their own country. The allies eventually agreed to three categories of collaborators: allied nationals in German uniform, allied nationals in military or paramilitary Quisling formations, and allied nationals who actively collaborated but did not take up arms against the allies. The United States, writes Hondros, wanted to treat members of the first two categories as prisoners of war who would be screened for war crimes and turned over to their national governments for trial. The British chiefs of staff agreed but requested that "after thorough investigation, those found suitable" for incorporation into their national forces or formation into labor units be transferred to their own governments. In 1945 the Greek courts trying collaborators ruled that the formation of the Security Battalions did not fall under the category of collaboration since their function had been to maintain law and order and to act against criminal elements: Gerolymatos, "The Security Battalions and the Civil War," 25.

169. On this issue, see Papastratis, *British Policy towards Greece*, 213–216.

170. M. Gilbert, *The Road to Victory: Winston Churchill, 1939–1941* (Toronto: Stoddard, 1986), 7:882.

CHAPTER 4. BLOODY DECEMBER

Epigraph: Churchill's retort to a Labour member of Parliament with respect to the British intervention during the December Uprising, UK Parliamentary Debates, Commons, 5th series (1909–80), 8 December 1944, columns 934–47.

1. W. H. McNeill, *The Greek Dilemma: War and Aftermath* (New York: Lippincott, 1947), 163.

2. The disproportionate number of young women participating in the demonstrations as well as their extreme behavior is a phenomenon mentioned by several Greek and non-Greek witnesses. See: Henderson, *Xenia: A Memoir, Greece 1919–1949*, 122; W. Byford-Jones, *Greek Trilogy: Resistance, Liberation, Revolution* (London: Hutchinson, 1945), 138.

3. Henderson, *Xenia*, 123.

4. There are several accounts of the demonstration at Papandreou's residence; most of them, however, were either recorded after the event or heard about it almost immediately afterward. It is also indicative of the confusion and mythology of the December

Uprising that the explosion caused by the hand grenades was used as evidence by opponents of EAM that some of the demonstrators at Constitution Square were armed:
Henry Maule, *Scobie: Hero of Greece, The British Campaign 1944–45* (London: Arthur
Barker, 1975).

5. Kanellopoulos, *Imerologio: 31 March 1942–4 January 1945,* 703.

6. Byford-Jones, *Greek Trilogy,* 138.

7. Ibid.

8. Some accounts say that he used an automatic weapon. If that were the case, however,
the number of dead would have been much higher.

9. Byford-Jones, who generally is even-handed about the crisis, accounts for the twelve
killed. The EAM, ELAS, and KKE sources are not in agreement over the precise number of dead and wounded, but they range from 16 to 54 killed and up to 140 wounded:
Byford-Jones, *Greek Trilogy,* 139. On the various sources discussing the December casualties, see Spyros G. Gasparinatos, *Apeleutherosi, Dekemvriana, Varkiza,* 2 vols.
(Athens: I. Sideris, 1998), 1: 261, n. 16. Kanellopoulos, a moderate member of the
right, claims in his diary that only 11 were killed that Sunday: Kanellopoulos,
Imerologio, 701–703.

10. Byford-Jones, *Greek Trilogy,* 139–140.

11. Precise numbers are difficult to verify. McNeill suggests that about 60,000 filled
Constitution Square: McNeill, *Greek Dilemma,* 170. Left-wing accounts claim that
the total number of demonstrators ranged from 500,000 to 600,000: Gasparinatos,
Apeleutherosi, Dekemvriana, Varkiza, 1: 257, n. 7.

12. McNeill, *Greek Dilemma,* 170.

13. Ibid.

14. The principal sources in English for the events of 3 December 1944 are based in part
on McNeill, *Greek Dilemma,* 165–171; and John O. Iatrides, *Revolt in Athens: The
Greek Communist "Second Round," 1944–1945* (Princeton: Princeton University Press,
1972), 187–194. A personal interpretation of the December uprising is found in Nigel
Clive, *A Greek Experience 1943–1948* (Salisbury, Wilts.: Russell, 1985), 152–153, and a
subsequent analysis is provided by Lars Baerentzen, "The Demonstration in Syntagma
Square on Sunday the 3rd of December, 1944," *Scandinavian Studies in Modern Greek*
2 (1978), 3–52; Byford-Jones, *The Greek Trilogy.*

15. The leading editorial in *Rizospastis* on 5 December 1944 underlined that the hundreds
of thousands of demonstrators denounced Papandreou as a murderer and claimed
that the funeral of Sunday's victims also represented the political and national funeral
of the "pathetic" premier.

16. Zaousis, *Oi Dio Ochthes,* 2: 692.

17. Hadzis states that the ELAS men were instructed to use their weapons only in self-
defense: Hadzis, *E Nikiphora Epanastasi pou Chathike,* A:215.

18. Zaousis, *Oi Dio Ochthes,* 2:693.

19. Maule, *Scobie,* 11–12.

20. Ibid. 126.

21. Rigas Rigopoulos, interview with the author, Athens, 27 May 2002.

22. Ibid.

23. Ibid. Also see his account of his wartime experiences in Rigas Rigopoulos, *The Secret War: Greece—Middle East, 1940–1945, The Events Surrounding the Story of Service 5-16-5* (Paducah, KY: Turner, 2003).

24. Gilbert, *The Road to Victory*, 1100.

25. Clive's comments regarding Papandreou were related to the author during a delightful lunch in Athens a few years before Clive passed away.

26. Bartziotas, *Exinda Chronia Kommounistis*, 340–341.

27. Hadzis, *E Nikiphora Epanastasi pou Chathike*, 211.

28. Ibid., 211–212.

29. Richard O'Brien, "Recollections" (unpublished manuscript, London, n.d.), 2.

30. Gilbert, *Road to Victory*, 1086.

31. On this point see Woodhouse, *The Struggle for Greece*, 119.

32. McNeill suggests that the right wing's opposition to disbanding the Third Brigade was strongly backed by Leeper, the British ambassador, and General Scobie: McNeill, *Greek Dilemma*, 158.

33. Ibid.

34. The *EAM White Book* claims that Papandreou stated that "until our regular army is organized, and in order to continue the participation of Greece in the common allied struggle, besides the Mountain (Third) Brigade and the Sacred Squadron there will also be organized from the forces of our national resistance a brigade of ELAS and a proportion unit of EDES." However, there is no reference as to where or under what circumstances Papandreou made these comments: *EAM White Book, May 1944– March 1945* (New York: Greek American Council, 1945), 24.

35. Woodhouse, *Something Ventured*, 80.

36. Baerentzen, "The Arrival of the Soviet Military Mission in July 1944 and KKE Policy," 79.

37. Peter Stavrakis, *Moscow and the Greek Communism, 1944–1949* (Ithaca: Cornell University Press, 1989), 38.

38. Hammond, *Venture into Greece*, 162–163.

39. Woodhouse, *The Apple of Discord*, 198.

40. Ioannidis, *Anamniseis*.

41. Petros Rousos, *I Megali Pendaetia 1940–1945: I Ethniki Andistasi kai O Rolos tou KKE*, 2 vols. (Athens: Ekdoseis: Synchroni Epochi 1978), 203.

42. Georgiou, *I Zoi Mou*, 414–416.

43. Iatrides, *Revolt in Athens*.

44. Record of Meetings at the Kremlin, Moscow, October 9th, at 10 p.m.: FO 800/303, folios 227–35, quoted in Martin Gilbert, *Road to Victory*, 991.

45. Ibid.

46. Winston S. Churchill, *The Second World War: Triumph and Tragedy* (London: Houghton Mifflin, 1953), 6:196–197.

47. Record of Meetings at the Kremlin, Moscow, October 9th, at 10 p.m.: FO 800/303, folios 227–35 quoted in Gilbert, *Road to Victory*, 991.

48. Churchill, *The Second World War*, 6:197.

49. Giorgis Vontitsos-Gousias, *Oi Aities Gia tis Ittes ti Diaspasi tou KKE kai tis Ellinikis Aristeras* (Athens: Na Ypiretisoume to Lao, n.d.), 12.

50. Record of Meetings at the Kremlin, Moscow, October 9, at 10 P.M.: FO 800/303, folios 227–35, quoted in Gilbert, *Road to Victory,* 992.

51. Georgiou, *I Zoi Mou,* 408.

52. Woodhouse, *Struggle for Greece,* 14.

53. Ioannidis, *Anamniseis,* 267.

54. Ole Smith, "History Made to Fit All Occasions: The KKE View of the December Crisis," *Journal of the Hellenic Diaspora* 22, no. 2 (1996), 67.

55. Nikos Zachariadis, *Provlimata Kathodigisis* (Athens: Exodos, 1978), 80.

56. Vasilis Bartziotas, "I Politiki Stelekhon tou KKE sta Teleutea," in *Deka Chronia,* ed. Nikos Zachariadis (Athens: Poria, 1978), 13–14.

57. Woodhouse, *Struggle for Greece,* 20.

58. Ole Smith, one of the most knowledgeable scholars of the KKE, and one who had access to KKE archives, commented: "There is more to this issue than merely the question of Siantos' role." Smith was convinced that "either the KKE knows the motives behind Siantos' strange behaviour during the December events or at least some individuals in the party leadership suspect there were reasons for that behaviour which would not be wise to reveal." Whatever these reasons, Smith concludes that the KKE strategy in December 1944 was to avoid a fight with the British and confine the battle against the Papandreou government. Smith, "History Made to Fit All Occasions," 67.

59. Kenneth Matthews, *Memories of a Mountain War: Greece 1944–1949* (London: Longman, 1972), 79; Svetozar Vukmanović-Tempo, *How and Why the People's Liberation Struggle of Greece Met with Defeat* (London: Merlin Press, 1950), 14–16.

60. Loulis, *The Greek Communist Party, 1940–1944,* 161.

61. Ibid.

62. Woodhouse, *Struggle for Greece,* 115.

63. Ioannidis, *Anamniseis,* 339.

64. "Crowd Fired on in Athens," *The Times* (London), 4 December 1944.

65. "A Tragedy of Errors," *The Times* (London), 7 December 1944.

66. Drew Pearson, "Daily Washington Merry-Go-Round," *Washington Post,* 11 December 1944.

67. Woodhouse, *Something Ventured,* 93.

68. Ibid., 95.

69. McNeill, *Greek Dilemma,* 178.

70. Gilbert, *Road to Victory,* 1056.

71. J. Ehrman, *Grand Strategy* (London: HMSO, 1956), 61.

72. Ibid.

73. On the ELAS order of battle see the "Secret Report" of Makridis in Gregory Pharakos, *Mystiki Ekthesi [1946] kai Ala Dokoumenta* (Athens: Ellinika Grammata, 2000), 2:115.

74. Ioannidis, *Anamniseis,* 339.

75. Ehrman, *Grand Strategy,* 62.

76. On this point see Smith, "History Made to Fit All Occasions," 67.

77. McNeill, *Greek Dilemma,* 175.

78. According to McNeill, as late as 12 or 13 December EAM leaders still hoped for a diplomatic settlement: McNeill, *The Greek Dilemma*, 179.

79. Ibid., 179–180.

CHAPTER 5. THE POGROM OF THE LEFT

Epigraph: Theophilos Frangopoulos, *The Silent Border* (Athens: Ekdositon Philon, 1995).

1. At the time of the interview (West Vancouver, January 17, 2004), Ron McAdam was a retired physician living in West Vancouver, but in 1944 he was a second lieutenant with the 11th Battalion of the prestigious King's Royal Rifle Corps. He passed away on February 20, 2010.

2. Ron McAdam, interview by the author, West Vancouver, January 17, 2004.

3. Ibid.

4. Ibid.

5. Major J. C. H. Beswick, "Eleventh Battalion, 'Liberation of Greece and Civil War,' King's Royal Rifle Corps," in *Swift and Bold: The Story of the King's Royal Rifle Corps in the Second World War, 1939–1945*, ed. H. Wake and W. F. Deeds (Aldershot: Gale and Polden, 1949), 87.

6. Ibid.

7. Operation Mincemeat, the deception operation implemented in the early summer of 1943 to fool the Germans into believing that the Allies were planning an invasion of Greece instead of Italy, included the use of a corpse with fake documents washed ashore in neutral Spain. In addition, the SOE employed women operatives who, out of uniform, did not hesitate to kill the enemy. British commandos, during hit-and-run tactics, rarely took prisoners. For more information see Denis Smyth, *Deathly Deception: The Real Story of Operation Mincemeat* (Oxford: Oxford University Press, 2010).

8. Beswick, "Eleventh Battalion," 87.

9. McAdam, interview by the author, West Vancouver, 17 January 2004.

10. Byford-Jones, *Greek Trilogy*, 198–199.

11. Beswick, "Eleventh Battalion," 87.

12. McAdam, interview by the author, West Vancouver, 17 January 2004.

13. Byford-Jones, *Greek Trilogy*, 169.

14. Ibid., 170.

15. Maule, *Scobie*, 122.

16. Byford-Jones, *Greek Trilogy*, 170.

17. Petros Makris-Staikos, *Kitsos Maltezos, O Agapimenos ton Theon* (Athens: Okeanida 2000), 133–134.

18. Ibid., 201–202 and n. 465.

19. Ibid. 209. This incident is taken from Zalokostas, *To Chroniko tis Sklavias*.

20. Makris-Staikos, *Kitsos Maltezos*, 245–246.

21. Gasparinatos, *Apeleutherosi, Dekemvriana, Varkiza*, 1:271.

22. Dione Dodis, interview by the author, Vancouver, 25 October 2003.

23. Dione Dodis, correspondence with the author, 10 November 2003.

24. Ward, *Greek Assignments*, 215; Dione Dodis, correspondence with the author, October 2003.

25. Ward, *Greek Assignments*, 217.

26. Ibid.

27. Iakovos Chrondymadis, *E Mavri Skia stin Ellada: Ethnikososialistikes kai Fasistikes Organosis stin Ellada tou Mesopolemou kai tis Germanikis Katochis, 1941–1942* (Athens: Monographia tis Stratiotikis Istorias, 2001), 70.

28. An example is Coco Chanel, who became an agent of Walter Schellenberg, the deputy director of the SD, the security service of the SS. After the liberation of France, she escaped punishment because at the time, there was no documentary evidence proving her collaboration with the Germans. Schellenberg was tried by the Nuremberg Military Tribunal and sentenced to six years' imprisonment for war crimes. He was released in 1951 because of incurable liver disease and moved to Italy. Remarkably, Chanel paid for Schellenberg's medical care and living expenses, financially supported his wife and family, and covered the cost of Schellenberg's medical expenses in 1952. We do not know whether she did it out of friendship or fear that if she did not help Schellenberg, he would have exposed their wartime relationship. During the German occupation of Paris she was also the lover of Baron Hans Gunther von Dincklage, an Abwehr agent. On Chanel's collaboration and links to the Nazis, see Hal Vaughan, *Sleeping with the Enemy: Coco Chanel's Secret War* (New York: Knopf, 2011).

29. The process of expelling her had begun on 24 October at a smaller meeting of the Actors Guild. Interview with Manos Eleutheriou, YouTube video, 52:01, posted by varipeponi, 20 March 2014, https://www.youtube.com/watch?v=_d596EQDCkE.

30. Matthews, *Memories of a Mountain War*, 98.

31. George Rallis stated to the author that his father was urged by other politicians to work with the Axis in order to counterbalance the growing influence and power of EAM and the KKE: George Rallis, interview by the author, Athens, 20 June 1990. George, however, could not abide by his father's decision to collaborate and he left home, only to return after the liberation to support his father, who faced charges of treason.

32. Polybias Marsan, *Eleni Papadaki: Mia Photerini Theatriki Porea me Aprosdokito Telos* (Athens: Kastianiotis, 2001), 286–289.

33. *Ellinikon Ema*, 15 October 1943.

34. *Ellinikon Ema*, 6 December 1943.

35. Interview with Manos Eleutheriou.

36. Marsan, *Eleni Papadaki*, 345; interview with Manos Eleutheriou.

37. Interview with Manos Eleutheriou.

38. N. Athanas, a distant relative of Orestes, as a young man during the December Uprising remembers seeing Kaliopi, Orestes' wife, wearing a fur coat. Athanas also recalls that Orestes was always well dressed and did not appear deranged or come across as a fanatic: N. Athanas, interview by the author, 22 August 2014.

39. Interview with Manos Eleutheriou.

40. Marsan, *Eleni Papadaki*, 351.

41. Ibid., 352.

42. Ibid., 360.

43. Ibid., 360.

44. Maule, *Scobie,* 254.

45. On the controversy over the Peristeri mass grave site, see also Zaousis, *Oi Dio Ochtes,* 776.

46. Matthews, *Memories of a Mountain War,* 94.

47. "Ta Eglimata ton Eamokommouniston," *E Ellas* 2 January 1945; Dimitris Garouphalias, *Keimena kai Anamnisis apo ton Tragiko Dekemvrio 1944* (Athens, 1981), 322–324. On the use of wells as makeshift gravesites for those executed by ELAS see Byford-Jones, *Greek Trilogy,* 248.

48. N. Athanas is almost certain that Orestes was not executed: N. Athanas, interview with the author, 23 August 2014.

49. Vasilis Bartziotas, *Ethniki Adistasi kai Dekemvris* (Athens: Sygchroni Epochi, 1979), 403; Spyros A. Kotsakis, *Dekemvris tou 1944 stin Athena* (Athens, 1986), 211–212.

50. I am grateful to Mr. Athanas for sharing with me a copy of Orestes' letter he wrote from prison. N. Athanas, correspondence with the author, 25 August 2006.

51. Phoivos Grigoriadis, *Emphylios Polemos 1944–1949, Dekemvris, Chitokratia* (Athens: Neokosmos, 1975), 9:194.

52. On the persecution and execution of Greek members of the Trotsky organization as well as communists who did not agree with the KKE, see Agis Stinas, *EAM-ELAS-OPLA* (Athens: Dithnis Bibliothiki, 1984).

53. Roy Jenkins, *Churchill* (New York: Farrar, Straus and Giroux, 2001), 771.

54. Churchill, *Triumph and Tragedy,* 276.

55. Zevgos, *Me ton Yianni Zevgo sto Epanastatiko Kinima,* 332.

56. Despina Makka-Photiadis, "Reminiscences from December 1944," unpublished manuscript, Athens, 1990.

57. Ibid.

58. Ibid.

59. Ibid.

60. Maule, *Scobie,* 244.

61. Makka-Photiadis, "Reminiscences."

62. Ward, *Greek Assignments,* 225–226.

63. Dione Dodis, correspondence with the author, 13 November 2004.

64. Ward, *Greek Assignments,* 229.

CHAPTER 6. BALKAN MACHINATIONS

Epigraph: Joseph Stalin, 10 January 1945, quoted in Georgi Dimitrov, *The Diary of Georgi Dimitrov,* ed. Ivo Banac, trans. Jane Hedges (German), Timothy D. Sergay (Russian), and Irina Faion (Bulgarian) (New Haven: Yale University Press, 2003), 352.

1. Prior to the great fire that swept through this part of Thessaloniki it was the location of the city's courts. After the 1917 fire the area was cleared and housed the main bus terminal until 1962. The city government had plans to rebuild the courts, but the

discovery of archaeological remains of the ancient imperial Roman forum delayed construction. Eventually the site became the expansive Thessaloniki Square.

2. Fears of Balkan volatility brought about one of the quickest and most successful peacekeeping operations in the history of the UN. In 1997, Albania, after the ravages of economic collapse brought about by a pyramid scheme and political disintegration, descended into chaos. The army melted away and people looted the armories and caused riots and criminal gangs roamed the country. Thousands of refugees flooded Italy and Greece. Albania was poised to become a failed state, possibly triggering a race by outsiders for parts of its territory. Any grab for Albania's regions was certain to force a confrontation by the country's neighbors leading to a Balkan war. Italy and Greece appealed to the United States and the European Union, and finally the UN Security Council sanctioned a "coalition of the willing." Operation ALBA, led by Italy, included Greece, Turkey, Romania, and Austria—states with a direct interest in maintaining Balkan stability—as well as France, Spain, Denmark, and Spain. The peacekeepers arrived on 15–16 April 1997 and departed four months later on 12 August, after restoring law and order. Greece and Turkey, normally antagonists in the Balkans and the Aegean, cooperated gladly and swiftly because both countries feared another Balkan war. The author was in Albania in 1997 and witnessed firsthand Greek-Turkish military cooperation, which would have seemed impossible a few years earlier.

3. Ipek Yosmaoglu, *Blood Ties: Religion, Violence, and the Politics of Nationhood in Ottoman Macedonia, 1878–1908* (Ithaca, NY: Cornell University Press, 2014), 19–47.

4. On the origins of the Macedonian struggle see Stavrianos, *The Balkans since 1453,* 513–517; Nadine Lange-Akhund, *The Macedonian Question, 1893–1908* (New York: Columbia University Press, 1998), 19–25; Douglas Dakin, *The Greek Struggle in Macedonia, 1897–1913* (Thessaloniki: Institute for Balkan Studies, 1993), 26–34; and Duncan M. Perry, *The Politics of Terror: The Macedonian Liberation Movements, 1893–1903* (Durham: Duke University Press, 1988), 2–8.

5. The Council of the Ecumenical Patriarchate declared the Exarchate as schismatic in September 1872.

6. Stavrianos, *The Balkans,* 518–521; Lange-Akhund, *The Macedonian Question,* 26–33; Dakin, *The Greek Struggle in Macedonia,* 16–23; Perry, *The Politics of Terror,* 27–30; and Dimitrije Djordjevic and Stephen Fischer-Galati, *The Balkan Revolutionary Tradition* (New York: Columbia University Press, 1981), 177.

7. Djordjevic and Fischer-Galati, *The Balkan Revolutionary Tradition,* 177–178.

8. Perry, *The Politics of Terror,* 38; Stavrianos, *The Balkans,* 519–520; Dakin, *The Greek Struggle in Macedonia,* 46–48; and Lange-Akhund, *The Macedonian Question,* 36–37.

9. The Ottoman government is often referred as the "Sublime Porte," technically a metonym for the gate to the buildings of the central Ottoman government.

10. For examinations of the IMRO's ideology, see Perry, *The Politics of Terror;* and Lange-Akhund, *The Macedonian Question,* 93–94.

11. Djordjevic and Fischer-Galati, *The Balkan Revolutionary Tradition,* 190.

12. Lange-Akhund, *The Macedonian Question,* 124.

13. For the Illinden uprising, see Perry, *The Politics of Terror*, 133–140; Lange-Akhund, *The Macedonian Question*, 118–130; and Dakin, *The Greek Struggle in Macedonia*, 92–106.

14. The effects of the Illinden uprising on the IMRO are examined in Perry, *The Politics of Terror*, 141–142; and Lange-Akhund, *The Macedonian Question*, 201–207.

15. For the Muerzsteg Agreement and the subsequent reforms see Lange-Akhund, *The Macedonian Question*, 141–200; and Dakin, *The Greek Struggle in Macedonia*, 112–116. For a more recent and comprehensive study on the Muerzsteg Agreement see Julian Allan Brooks, "Managing Macedonia: British Statecraft, Intervention, and 'Proto-Peacekeeping' in Ottoman Macedonia, 1902–1905" (PhD thesis, Simon Fraser University, 2014).

16. Djordjevic and Fischer-Galati, *The Balkan Revolutionary Tradition*, 194.

17. For a few years, the 1908 Young Turk Revolution inspired hope that Christians in Ottoman Macedonia could achieve local autonomy and better rights. This undercut the propaganda of the various nationalist groups and armed bands, forcing them to contain their activities until the Balkan Wars in 1912–1913.

18. Unfortunate civilians trapped on the wrong side of the battles faced a litany of horrors: at the very least expulsion from their homes, but more likely mass killings, rape, and torture. The *Report of the International Commission to Inquire into the Causes and Conduct of the Balkan Wars* (Washington, DC: Carnegie Endowment for International Peace, Division of Intercourse and Education, Publication No. 4, 1914) offers graphic details on the atrocities.

19. Stevan K. Pavlowitch, *A History of the Balkans, 1804–1945* (London: Longman, 1999), 313.

20. For an example of how the Comintern was supposed to be an agency for promoting international socialism, rather than the CPSU's interests, see "Invitation to the First Congress of the Communist International, 24 January 1919," in *The Communist International, 1919–1943 Documents*, ed. Jane Degras, vol. 1 (London: Frank Cass, 1971), 1–2.

21. For an explanation see Andrew L. Zapantis, *Greek-Soviet Relations, 1917–1941* (New York: Columbia University Press, 1982), 26–32. The decision was taken at the Third Extraordinary Congress of the KKE, organized with representatives of the Comintern, convened in Athens 26 November–3 December 1924: Kousoulas, *Revolution and Defeat*, 14–17.

22. Loulis, *The Greek Communist Party*, 1.

23. Zapantis, *Greek-Soviet Relations*, 168–169.

24. Vladimir Dedijer, *Tito Speaks: His Self-Portrait and Struggle with Stalin* (London: Readers Union, 1954), 110.

25. The Great Purges, one of the defining events for communists in the 1930s, began on 1 December 1934 with the assassination of Sergei Kirov, the head of the Leningrad branch of the Communist Party of the Soviet Union and one of the party's most popular leaders. Although never conclusively proven, most historians now agree that Kirov was assassinated on Stalin's orders. Whether Stalin was responsible for Kirov's death or not, he exploited the killing of Kirov to initiate the Great Purges and eliminate potential rivals by having them accused of terrorism, sabotage, treason, and

espionage against the Soviet Union. The purges were not limited to Stalin's political opponents, however; they included all the communist parties loyal to the USSR. Milan Gorkic, the secretary general of the Communist Party of Yugoslavia, was one of thousands of foreign nationals executed by the NKVD. By the time the purges unofficially concluded in 1938, approximately 1.5 million individuals had been killed, including many of the Bolshevik old guard, thus giving Stalin absolute control of both the party and the state. For the most influential works in the English language on the subject see Robert Conquest, *Stalin and the Kirov Murder* (New York: Oxford University Press, 1987), 10; Zora Steiner, *The Triumph of the Dark: European International History, 1933–1939* (Oxford: Oxford University Press, 2011), 460.

26. Prior to contact with the KKE, the CPY-led Nationalist Liberation Army (NLA) had survived four major offensives by the Germans aimed at eliminating partisan activity in occupied Yugoslavia and engaged in an ongoing civil war with the Mihailović's Chetniks. See Stevan K. Pavlowitch, *Hitler's New Disorder: The Second World War in Yugoslavia* (New York: Columbia University Press, 2008), 21–72 and Christophe Chiclet, *Les Communistes Grecs dans la Guerre: Histoire du Parti Communiste de Grèce de 1941 à 1949* (Paris: Editions L'Harmattan, 1987), 25–50.

27. See Swain, "Tito and the Twilight of the Comintern," 213.

28. This is according to Artiem Ulunian, "The Communist Party of Greece and the Comintern: Evaluations, Instructions and Subordination," in *International Communism and the Communist International, 1919–43*, ed. Tim Rees and Andrew Thorpe (Manchester: Manchester University Press, 1998), 201.

29. Lazar Koliševski, *Political Report to the First Congress of the Communist Party of Macedonia. I Kongres na KPM* (Zagreb: Kultura, 1950), 57–58.

30. "Tito complains to Moscow about the attitude of the Macedonian and Bulgarian communists and requests for clarification of Comintern policy, 4 September 1941," in Stephen Clissold, ed., *Yugoslavia and the Soviet Union, 1939–1973: A Documentary Survey* (London: Oxford University Press, 1975), 153.

31. *Yugoslavia and the Soviet Union, 1939–1973*, 153.

32. Josip Broz Tito, *V Kongress, Kommuntićke Partije Jugoslavije: Izveštije i Referati* (Belgrade: Kultura, 1948) 14.

33. Report cited in Stephen E. Palmer, Jr., and Robert R. King, *Yugoslav Communism and the Macedonian Question* (Hamden, CT: Archon Books, 1971), 69.

34. Ibid.

35. Ibid.

36. Ibid., 75.

37. Report cited in ibid., 75–76.

38. Svetozar Vukmanović-Tempo, *Struggle for the Balkans* (London: Merlin Press, 1990), 188.

39. Ibid.

40. Ibid.

41. James Horncastle, "The Dekemvriana and the Slavo-Macedonian Question," paper presented at *December to Varkiza: Memory, Political Discourse, and the Greek Civil War*, in Burnaby, Canada, 20 February 2015.

42. Giannis Zevgos, "The National Minorities and National Demagogy," *Kommounistiki Epitheoresi*, July 1944, 632.

43. Vukmanović-Tempo, *Struggle for the Balkans*, 71–72.

44. Ibid., 71.

45. No complete extant minutes of the meeting have survived although some sections are reproduced in Vukmanović's writings (ibid., 69–70).

46. Ibid., 69–79.

47. Ibid., 76.

48. Ibid., 77.

49. Stefanos Sarafis, *ELAS: Greek Resistance Army* (London: Merlin, 1980), 151.

50. Also in attendance was Brigadier Edmund Myers, who congratulated ELAS on their role in sabotaging "rail, road, and telephone lines" . . . and declared "HQ Middle East [was] entirely satisfied" with their work. Sarafis, *Greek Resistance Army*, 150–151.

51. Sarafis, *Greek Resistance Army*, 150–151.

52. Woodhouse, *The Struggle for Greece*, 49.

53. Vukmanović-Tempo, *Struggle for the Balkans*, 124.

54. Ibid., 125.

55. Milovan Djilas, *Wartime* (New York: Harcourt Brace Jovanovich, 1977), 122.

56. Hugh Seton-Watson and Elizabeth Barker, *Britain and Relations between Balkan Resistance Movements*, cited in Vukmanović-Tempo, *Struggle for the Balkans*, 220–221.

57. Palmer and King, *Yugoslav Communism*, 98.

58. Sarafis, *Greek Resistance Army*, 410.

59. D. Zapheiropoulos, *O Antisymmoriakos 'Agon* (Athens, 1956), 118.

60. In 1944 the KKE ordered the disbandment of the SNOF. After the failure of the December Uprising and the subsequent White Terror, persecuted Slavophones escaped to the mountains and formed the National Liberation Front (NOF) on 23 April 1945. Some KKE in northern Greece also sought refuge and joined the NOF bands. In October 1946 NOF merged with the DAG.

61. Koliopoulous, *Plundered Loyalties*, 130.

62. OSS XL817, 24 June 1944, cited in Stavrakis, *Moscow and Greek Communism*, 130. Ulunian, "The Communist Party of Greece and the Comintern," 22. Until the Popov mission arrived in Greece on 28 July 1944, the CPY continued to be the only way the KKE could contact Moscow—an issue of utmost importance for the KKE, as had been demonstrated by their repeated failed efforts. In desperation the KKE even tried, with the assistance of communist sympathizers, to use the Greek army radio in Cairo, but all to no avail.

63. "Makedonija u Narodnooslobodilačkom Ratu i Narodnoj Revoluciji 1941–1944," in *Istorijski Arhiv Komunističke Partije Jugoslavije*, 7:330–331.

64. "Zapisnik sa Sednice Politbiroa CKKPJ," in *Dokumenti Centralnih Organa KPJ NOR i Revolucija (1941–1945): Knjiga 21*, ed. Milovan Dželebdžić (Belgrade: Izdavački Centar Komunist, 1987), 125–126.

65. In 1963 it became the Socialist Republic of Macedonia.

66. Cited in Evangelos Kofos, *Nationalism and Communism in Macedonia: Civil Conflict, Politics of Mutation, National Identity* (New Rochelle, NY: Aristide D. Caratzas, 1993), 137.

67. Dimitar Vlahov, *Iz Istorije Makedonskog Naroda* (Belgrade: Prosveta, 1950), IX.

68. I have made several efforts to track down which KKE member would have taken part in this meeting. Based on current evidence from the memoirs of KKE leaders it is most probable that it was Stergios Anastasiadis, Andreas Tzimas, or Bartziotas. See Bartziotas' and Tzimas' memoirs for more information.

69. Tito 636 KMJ I-2–9/39.

70. Tito 636 KMJ I-2–9/39.

71. Christina J. M. Goulter, "The Greek Civil War: A National Army's Counter-Insurgency Triumph," *Journal of Military History* 78 (July 2014): 1025.

72. Stavrakis, *Moscow and Greek Communism,* 49.

73. Springe communicated Zachariadis' declaration to Theodoridis in confidence, until its publication in the *Manchester Guardian,* but the latter could not resist and published it in the Thessaloniki paper *Nea Alithia,* FO 371/ 48419, "Zachariadis: Interview with Mrs. Springe," British Consulate-General Salonica to the Chancery, British Embassy in Athens, 30 August 1945.

74. Grigoriadis, *Emphylios Polemos, 1944–1949,* 10:76–77.

75. The oath stated: "I, the child of the People of Greece and fighter of DSE, swear to fight with a weapon in hand, to spill my blood and to give my own life so as to rid from the soil of my Fatherland the very last foreign occupier. To eradicate each sign of fascism. To secure and to defend the national independence and the territorial integrity of my Fatherland. So as to secure and defend Democracy, the honor, the labor, the property/fortune and progress of my People. I swear/pledge to be good, brave and a disciplined soldier, to obey all the orders of my superiors, to adhere to all the ordinances of the rule and to keep the secrets of DSE. I swear/pledge to be an example of good behavior to the People, a carrier and encourager to the Unity of the People and reconciliation and to avoid each action that will compromise me and will dishonor me as an individual and as a fighter. I have as my ideal the free and strong democratic Greece and the progress of the People. And in the service of my ideal I place my weapon and my life. If I ever appear disloyal and from bad intention violate my pledge let the avenging hand of my Fatherland and the hatred and the scorn fall upon me relentlessly" (*Rizospatis,* 28 October 2001).

76. In May 1945, writes Kousoulas, Zachariadis stated that there would be a "people's democracy" in Greece, but only through the ballot. This was certainly in line with Stalin's wishes with respect to the policy of the KKE and adhered to the Soviet leader's policy of gradualism. A war against the British would not contradict Stalin's advocacy of gradual assumption of power because the battle would not be against the Greek government but directed at a foreign power (Kousoulas, *Revolution and Defeat,* 227).

77. Mitsos Partsialidis, *Dipli Apokatastasi tis Ethnikis Andistasis* (Athens: Themelio, 1978), 195 and 199.

78. Vladislav Zubik and Constantine Pleshakov, *Inside the Kremlin's War: From Stalin to Khrushchev* (Cambridge, MA: Harvard University Press, 1996), 126.

79. "E Defteri Olomeleia tis Kendrikis Epitropis tou KKE," Saranda Chronia tou KKE (The Second Plenary of the Central Committee of the KKE, Forty Years of the KKE, 1918-1958), Epilogi Dokoumenton, 554–551. Vasilis Bartziotas, *O Agonas tou Dimokratikou Stratou Elldas* (Athens: Sychroni Epochi, 1982), 28.

80. Ole Smith, "The Greek Communist Party, 1945–1949," in *The Greek Civil War, 1945–1950: Studies in Polarization*, ed. D. H. Close (London: Routledge, 1993), 137.

81. Nikos Zachariadis, *Kainourgia Katastasi, Kainourgia Kathikonda* (Nicosia, 1950), 38.

82. Artiem Ulunian, "The Soviet Union and the Greek Question," in *The Soviet Union and Europe in the Cold War, 1943–1953*, ed. F. Gori and S. Pons (New York: St. Martin's Press, 1996), 150.

83. Tito and the Yugoslav Communist Party had been the favorites in Moscow, a position of *primus inter pares* among communist parties, which had been held first by the German Communist Party in the 1920s and then by the French in the 1930s. This afforded the CPY, in effect Tito, predominance in the affairs of the Comintern until Stalin dismantled it in 1943. The Yugoslav leader came to prominence in the first year of the Soviet-German war (1941), the darkest period in Soviet history; see Geoffrey Swain, "Tito and the Twilight of the Comintern," in *International Communism and the Communist International 1919–1943*, ed. Tim Rees and Andrew Thorpe (Manchester: Manchester University Press, 1998), 205, 215.

84. John Koliopoulos argues that "these were not the actions of persecuted and desperate men: they were part of a drive to force the authorities to their knees by destroying the productive capacity of the region and drive all who could bear arms into the mountains." John S. Koliopoulos, *Plundered Loyalties: World War II and Civil War in Macedonia* (London: Hurst, 1999), 254.

85. The source that is generally taken as authoritative on this subject is C. M. Woodhouse's *The Struggle for Greece*, 262. Woodhouse estimated that the Slavophone Macedonians rose to "11,000 out of a total 25,000 of all ranks in the DAG in 1948, but their proportion increased to 14,000 out of less than 20,000 by 1949." Woodhouse's numbers are given credence by an internal Yugoslav memo, dated to 28 July 1948, which calculated that the number of Slavophone Macedonians in the Democratic Army of Greece as approximately one-half. While not mirroring Woodhouse, the number is close enough that it lends additional credence to Woodhouse's estimate. Although there is considerable evidence to support Woodhouse's assessment of the number of Slavophone Macedonians, Risto Kirjazovski, using documents from the Macedonian Archives, argues that near the end of the Greek civil war the Macedonian Slavophones numbered 14,000. He claims that these were part of a DAG force of 35,000. This number would indicate a much larger DAG and is significantly higher than Woodhouse's estimate during the same period. While the overall number of Slavophone Macedonians in the DAG does not change between the two accounts, their proportion is reduced from 70 percent to 40 percent. Certainly, Woodhouse was not in Greece during the conflict and could have miscalculated the Slavophone Macedonian numbers, but he had access to reliable sources. Kirjazovski, in contrast, greatly inflates the DAG, whose size was considerably less than 35,000 by the end of the war. Significantly, both agree that the number of Slavophone Macedonians in the DAG reached 14,000 men and women. Risto Kirjazovski, *Narodnoosloboditelniot Front i Drugite Organizacii na Makedoncite od Egejska Makedonija, 1945–1949* (Skopje: Kultura, 1985), 176.

86. Samuel B. Griffith, "Strategy, Tactics, and Logistics in Revolutionary Warfare," in Mao Tse-tung, *On Guerrilla Warfare* (Mineola, NY: Dover, 1937 [2005]), 20–26.

87. Svetozar Vukmanović-Tempo, *Bulletin* (Skopje), 10 August 1945.

88. Josip Broz Tito, AYE A/24581/G2–1945.

89. The CPY took control of Yugoslavia after the signing of the Tito-Subasic Agreement, also known as the Vis Agreement, on 17 June 1944.

90. Zapheiropoulos, *O Antisvmmoriakos 'Agon,* 321–322.

91. Charles R. Shrader, *Withered Vine: Logistics and the Communist Insurgency in Greece, 1945–1949* (Westport, CT: Greenwood Press, 1999), 173.

92. Woodhouse, *Struggle for Greece,* 155.

93. Shrader, *The Withered Vine,* 173.

94. Report on Yugoslav press articles, 2 February 1945 AYE A/1869/Mac/1945, cited in Kofos, *Nationalism and Communism,* 159.

95. Reported by Mr. Houstoun-Baswell in his telegram No. 3 Saving of the 4th February. Mr. Clutton to Mr. Bevin, R 8973/298/67.

96. The average income in Macedonia in 1947 was 62 percent of the Yugoslav average. The only region whose per-capita income was lower was Kosovo. See Fred Singleton and Bernard Carter, *The Economy of Yugoslavia* (New York: St. Martin's Press, 1982), 221.

97. Mr. Peake to Mr. Bevin R 13507/298/67.

98. The British, who were not sympathetic to the idea of Yugoslavia annexing Greek Macedonia, noted that Vlahov's "best points (with respect to Macedonian irredentist claims) [were] scored when he turns to economic history and the disastrous consequences in that respect of the partition of Macedonia and the establishment of the present Greek frontier." Belgrade Chancery to Southern Department, "Macedonian Problem," R 8828/407/92.

99. "E Defteri Olomeleia tis Kendrikis Epitropis tou KKE," 529–541.

100. Nikos Zachariadis, *Apofasi tou Politkou Grafeiou tis K.E tou KKE* (Athens: Kentrikis Epitropis tou KKE, 1945), 48.

101. "Zachariadis' Introductory Speech before the Seventh Party Congress," in *To 7º Synedrio,* Issue C (Athens: Kentrikis Epitropis tou KKE, 1945), 30.

102. "Macedonian Problem," R 8828/407/92.

103. Georgi Dimitrov, *Political Report Delivered [sic] to the V Congress of the Bulgarian Communist Party* (Sofia: Ministry of Foreign Affairs, 1949), 67.

104. Sir G. Peake, "Yugoslav-Bulgarian Dispute over Macedonia," R 10222/4155/67.

105. Palmer and King, *Yugoslav Communism and the Macedonian Question,* 137.

106. AYE A/59224.Bb1 1948, dated November 3, 1948.

107. Bitolan, 836 KMJ I-3–6/659.

108. Kofos, *Nationalism and Communism,* 176.

109. Phoivos Grigoriadis, *Istoria tou Emphyliou Polemou, 1945–49—To Dephtero Andartiko,* vol. 4 (Athens: Neokosmos, 1975), 1211.

110. Woodhouse, *Struggle for Greece,* 255.

111. This effectively removed Vaphiadis from power. Although Vaphiadis possessed little influence from this point on, Zachariadis only succeeded in securing his removal on 8 February 1949, ostensibly for the health reasons previously cited, according to the KKE press: Zachariadis cited in Eudes, *The Kapetanios,* 338, 342.

112.   Evangelos Averoff-Tossizza, *By Fire and Axe: The Communist Party and the Civil War in Greece, 1944–49* (New Rochelle, NY: Caratzas Brothers, 1978), 319.

113.   For an excellent example of how these arguments are typically presented see Vladimir Dedijer, *The Battle Stalin Lost: Memoirs of Yugoslavia, 1948–1953* (New York: Viking Press, 1971).

114.   Ivo Banac, *With Stalin against Tito: Cominformist Splits in Yugoslav Communists* (Ithaca, NY: Cornell University Press, 1988), 255.

115.   *Sixteenth Plenum of the BCP CC*, 12 July 1948. Cited in Palmer and King, *Yugoslav Communism and the Macedonian Question*, 126.

116.   Dimitrov, *The Diary of Georgi Dimitrov*, 70.

117.   Rankovic, cited in C. Peake, "Future of Macedonia," R 6531/1081/67.

118.   For a breakdown of expulsions, see Paul S. Shoup, *Communism and the Yugoslav National Question* (New York: Columbia University Press, 1968), 101–144, 173.

119.   C. Peake, *Future of Macedonia*, R 6531/1081/67.

120.   507 IX CKSKJ 33/I-48.

121.   Matthews, *Memories of a Mountain War*, 231.

122.   507 IX CKSKJ 33/I-62.

123.   Central Committee of the KKE, 507 IX CKSKJ 33/I-63.

124.   Text in AYE A/G5/Bb1/1949.

125.   Text repeated in C. Peake, "Future of Yugoslavia," R 6531/1081/67.

126.   "Tito's Greek Move Laid to Cominform," *New York Times*, 24 July 1949, 23.

127.   Ibid.

128.   Djilas, *Conversations with Stalin*, 141.

129.   Ibid., 140–141.

CHAPTER 7. THE POLITICS OF HATE AND RETRIBUTION

Epigraph: Shakespeare, *Julius Caesar*, 3.1.273.

1.   Grigoris Staktopoulos, *Ypothesi Polk: E Prosopiki mou Martiria* (Athens: Ekdosis Gnosi 1984), 25. Panayiotis Kanellopoulos, the veteran and well-respected politician, wrote the prologue to Staktopoulos' war memoirs. On Mouskoundis' personality, see also Edmund Keeley, *The Salonika Bay Murder: Cold War Politics and the Polk Affair* (Princeton: Princeton University Press, 1989), 14. For the less reliable and gossipy account of Kati Marton, *The Polk Conspiracy: Murder and Cover-Up in the Case of CBS News Correspondent George Polk* (New York: Random House, 1990), 166–167. For a recent examination of the Polk murder and of Staktopoulos see John O. Iatrides, "The Polk/Staktopoulos Case Six Decades Later," in Edmund Keeley, *Fonos ston Thermaiko: Ypothesi Polk* (Athens: Ellinika Grammata, 2010). Like Keeley's account, Iatrides provides a somber and balanced analysis of the Polk murder as well as bringing some new material to light, in addition to a survey of the books on the murder. However, the mystery remains.

2.   Keeley, *The Salonika Bay Murder*, 131: Keeley quotes another source who described Staktopoulos as "a softy, afraid of his own shadow."

3. Ibid.

4. Ibid.

5. Ibid., 132.

6. Ibid., 18–19.

7. Ibid., 19.

8. Elias Vladas and Zak Mettger, *Who Killed George Polk? The Press Cover Up, A Death in the Family* (Philadelphia: Temple University Press, 1996), 177 ff. Although a plausible theory, it would have been unlikely for so many individuals to be involved, witness the murder, or have taken part and kept it secret for so many decades.

9. Keeley, *The Salonika Bay Murder,* 22.

10. Howard Jones, *"A New Kind of War": America's Global Strategy and the Truman Doctrine in Greece* (Oxford: Oxford University Press, 1989), 163–164.

11. Ibid., 164.

12. Staktopoulos, *Ypothesi Polk,* 20.

13. Ibid., 86–87.

14. Ibid., 81–90: Staktopoulos describes in detail the various types of torture he suffered.

15. Ibid., 79.

16. Ibid., 88–89.

17. The authorities also imprisoned Staktopoulos' mother and sisters and threatened to link them to the murder as part of the pressure to force the unfortunate man to give a false confession.

18. The PASOK government of Andreas Papandreou recognized the resistance in 1982.

19. *British Documents on Foreign Affairs: Reports and papers from the Foreign Office confidential print. Part III, From 1940 through 1945. Series F, Europe,* ed. Paul Preston and Michael Partridge (Bethesda, MD: University Publications of America, 1997–1998), 26:69.

20. Ibid., 26:80.

21. David Close, "The Reconstruction of a Right-Wing State," in *The Greek Civil War, 1943–1950: Studies in Polarization,* ed. David Close (London: Routledge, 1993), 156–165; Mark Mazower, "The Cold War and the Appropriation of Memory: Greece after Liberation," in *The Politics of Retribution in Europe: War and Its Aftermath,* ed. Istavan Deak et al. (Princeton: Princeton University Press, 2000), 214.

22. NARA, RG 226, Entry 172, Box 4, Folder 227, 4 December 1944.

23. British Embassy Estimates, 14 November 1949, FO 371/78373 R 11085.

24. British Embassy, Athens, to Foreign Office, "Monthly Intelligence Review, Greece," 15 May 1948, PRO FO 371/ 72212 R6706.

25. FO 371/ 72213 R7618, Monthly Intelligence Review, 15 June 1948; Bickham Sweet-Escott, *Greece: A Political and Economic History* (London: Royal Institute of International Affairs, 1954), 91.

26. Central Intelligence Agency, "Greece," March 1948, Truman Library, President's Secretary File, Box 259.

27. British Embassy, Athens, to Foreign Office, 14 November 1949, PRO FO 371/783373/ R11085.

28. For a detailed analysis of the impact of the occupation, see Amikam Nachmani, *International Intervention in the Greek Civil War: The United Nations Special Committee on the Balkans, 1947–1952* (New York: Praeger, 1990).

29. Patrikios' niece and the daughter of his third sister, Katina: Efthimia Phannou, interview by the author, Athens, 15 January 2004.

30. Ibid.

31. Ibid.

32. Stylianos Perrakis undertook a systematic investigation in order to determine why a communist death squad executed his maternal uncle. In the process he uncovered a history of murder, atrocities, torture, and revenge in the region of Argoida: Stylianos Perrakis, *The Ghosts of Plaka Beach: A True Story of Murder and Retribution in Wartime Greece* (Madison, NJ: Fairleigh Dickinson University Press, 2006), 152–154.

33. Matthews, *Memories of a Guerrilla War*, 187.

34. Henderson, *Xenia*, 128.

35. Ibid., 127–128.

36. Leeper, *When Greek Meets Greek*, 112.

37. Sarafis, *Greek Resistance Army*, 161–162.

38. Gerolymatos, "The Security Battalions and the Civil War," 17–28.

39. For a recent study of Makronisos, see Stavros Alvanos, *To Phenomeno Makronisos: Ena Protogono Egklematiko Peirema* (Athens: Ellinka Grammata, 1998).

40. Artemis Leontis, *Topographies of Hellenism: Mapping the Homeland* (Ithaca, NY: Cornell University Press, 1995), 231.

41. As part of the surrender, ELAS handed over 100 artillery pieces, over 200 mortars, 419 heavy machine guns, 1,412 light machine guns, 713 automatic weapons, 48,973 rifles and pistols, and various other types of weapons, radio transmitters, small boats, and thousands of hand grenades. An assortment of as many as 40,000 weapons was hidden in the mountains. T. Gerozisis, *To Soma ton Axiomatikon kai E Thesi tou stin Sygchroni Elliniki Koinonia, 1821–1975* (Athens: Dodoni, 1996), 794.

42. Smith, "The Greek Communist Party, 1945–1949," 135.

43. Ibid.

44. Ibid., 136.

45. H. Montgomery Hyde, *Stalin, The History of a Dictator* (New York: Farrar, Straus and Giroux, 1971), 549.

46. David Close, *Greece since 1945: Civil War and Reconstruction, 1945–1950* (London: Longman, 2002), 27.

47. Plymeris Voglis, "Between Negation and Self-Negation: Political Prisoners in Greece," in *After the War Was Over: Reconstructing the Family, Nation, and State in Greece*, ed. Mark Mazower (Princeton: Princeton University Press, 2000), 81. Voglis also cites British sources indicating that 3,003 individuals were sentenced to death by the extraordinary military tribunals and later executed, in addition to another 378 by civil courts.

48. Ibid., 81–82.

49. Ibid., 82.

50. The second law was in response to the formation of a provisional government by the insurgents in December. Ibid., 81–82.

51. Interview with Leo Katsuris, Vancouver, 8 March 2004.

52. In the absence of polling, one possible indication of the political sympathies of the Greek people was the 1 September 1946 referendum on the monarchy. Although King George II and the monarchy were not popular, 68.4 percent voted in favor and 31.6 percent opposed. The plebiscite was monitored by foreign observers and 86.6 percent of registered voters turned out to cast a ballot. Dieter Nohlen and Philip Stover, *Elections in Europe: A Data Handbook* (Baden-Baden: Nomos Verlagsgesellschaft, 2010), 830. The period of uncertainty after liberation and the fear of civil war were contributing factors that encouraged the majority of Greeks to vote for the return of the monarchy.

CHAPTER 8. FROM INSURGENCY TO CIVIL WAR

Epigraph: Croesus to Cyrus the Great, Herodotus, 1.87.4.

1. According to the official history of the KKE, the raid was published by the DAG newspaper, *Exormisi,* on 28 October 1947: "the first spoils of the armed attack of the people." See Giorgi Katsouli, *History of the Greek Communist Party of Greece,* vol. 6, 1946–1949 (Athens: Ekdoseis Nea Synora, n.d.), 94. Historians are not certain if the KKE officially initiated the civil war on that date or it was chosen in hindsight for propaganda effect and for the sake of posterity. Woodhouse elaborates on whether Zachariadis chose the attack on Litochoro to launch the conflict. That it was hindsight on the part of *Exormisi* is underscored by the date of the published account of the raid. 28 October is the date that Fascist Italy invaded Greece and the Greek army not only defended the country but launched a successful counterattack. See Woodhouse, *The Struggle for Greece,* 170.

2. Zachariadis confided to Markos Vaphiadis, the subsequent commander of the DAG: Woodhouse, *The Struggle for Greece,* 170.

3. The lore of the Greek Klephts (bandits) includes the heroic deeds after the transition of the bandits to foot soldiers in the Greek War of Independence, but also their alternate incarnations as Armatoli, who were former outlaws. In effect Ottoman militia paid to protect caravans and travelers from Klephts, whom the Ottomans had given amnesty and employed to suppress banditry. On the history and analysis of the Klephts and Armatoli, see John S. Koliopoulos, *Brigands with a Cause: Brigandage and Irredentism in Modern Greece, 1821–1912* (Oxford: Oxford University Press, 1987).

4. Vaphiadis was instructed, writes Kousoulas, "at the insistence of Zachariadis, to leave for the mountains to coordinate the activities of the bands." Kousoulas, *Revolution and Defeat,* 240.

5. Another possible choice would have been General Stephanos Saraphis, a professional Greek officer before the occupation. He had organized and directed ELAS during the occupation, but he was not a member of the KKE and it is doubtful that the KKE and especially Zachariadis would have trusted him.

6. Supplies in general remained a problem for the DAG throughout the civil war and Vaphiadis had to make the rounds in the Balkan communist countries to plead for material aid. See O'Balance, *The Greek Civil War,* 131.

7. Perhaps Zachariadis was also trying to remain loyal to Stalin's policy of gradualism.

8. Yiafka or Yiafkes, effectively meaning a place of conspiratorial meeting. Its origin is Russian. Also it meant clandestine meeting place, safe house, or refuge. The names of the DAG logistical and intelligence organizations are often confusing. The general term for the organization responsible for logistical support to the DAG was the Aftoamyna (self-defense), in addition the Aftoamyna also included the Popular Civil Guard that was a static unit, which facilitated material support for the DAG in the field and was based in the villages under KKE control. The Aftoamyna looked after the sick and wounded, providing guides and couriers, and carried ammunition, among other tasks. In the cities and large towns the Yiafka acted as the liaison between secret Aftoamyna volunteers, who collected essential supplies (medicines, money, and gold). The Yiafka cells could also use members of the Aftoamyna as couriers to communicate intelligence gathered in the urban centers. See Shrader, *The Withered Vine*, 118–119.

9. The KKE in the cities and large towns, for security, maintained three-men cells originally devised by Zachariadis in the 1930s. The Yiafka reported to the security service (YSA), which in turn was under the control of the personnel (security) directorate of the DAG. See ibid., 118–119.

10. Ibid., 119.

11. Ibid., 119, contends, basing this on the U.S. military attaché reports, that combatants represented 40 percent of the DAG. According to this, at the peak of the communist army the number of Aftoamyna would have been 50,000.

12. Edward Wainhouse, "Guerrilla Warfare in Greece, 1946–49," *Military Review* 36 (June 1957), 22, states that the Yiafka was supported by 750,000 Communist sympathizers, while Shrader, *The Withered Vine*, 118–119, gives a number of 250,000.

13. After the war, most of those who did not leave Greece with the remnants of the Democratic Army found themselves incarcerated in island concentration camps or in prisons on the mainland. Some were executed, particularly members of OPLA. Others managed to keep their KKE activities secret and reintegrated into Greek society. Many of their grandchildren, as well as some of the great-grandchildren of the insurgents, are the backbone of the contemporary radical left Syriza political party that is governing Greece in 2015. Remarkably, they are also joined by a small number of the grandchildren of the veterans of the Greek National Army, including Euclid Tsakalotos, the grand-nephew of General Tsakalotos, commander of the First Greek Army Corps that destroyed the communist forces in the Peloponnese and later the DAG at Grammos and Vitsi.

14. Goulter provides a comprehensive insight into the DAG's intelligence capabilities. See Goulter, "The Greek Civil War."

15. O'Balance, *The Greek Civil War*, 126.

16. Ibid.

17. Marantzidis, *Demokratikos Stratos Elladas*, 105–106.

18. Ibid.

19. Shrader, *The Withered Vine*, 265.

20. Ibid., 122–124.

21. Angeliki E. Laiou, "Population Movements in the Greek Countryside during the Civil War," in *Studies in the History of the Greek Civil War, 1945–1949*, ed. Lars Baerentzen, John O. Iatrides, and Ole Smith (Copenhagen: Museum Tusculanum Press, 1987), 64–75.

22. Dimitrios Vladas, "Triamisi Chronia Palis," in *Pros tin III Syndiaskepsi tou KKE*, (Central Committee of the Communist Party of Greece, 1951), 109.

23. Philipos Iliou, *Emphylios Polemos: E Embloki tou KKE* (Athens: Themelio, 2005), 83, writes that there were negotiations in Athens at a political settlement between February and August 1947, but these were unsuccessful.

24. Margaritis, *Istoria tou Ellinikou Emphiliou Polemou 1946–1949*, 1: 334–335.

25. Iliou, *Emphylios Polemos*, 183–184. At the meeting only six members of the central committee were present: Nikos Zachariadis, Markos Vapheiadis, Leonidas Stringos, Ioannis Ioannidis, Petros Rousos, and Georgis Eryphriadis. Shortly after, the rest of the central committee hiding out in the mountains and those not under arrest in Athens approved the decisions taken in Yugoslavia.

26. Mertzos, *KKE Episema Keimena*, 5, 245–247. According to Iliou, *Emphylios Polemos*, 81–86, the Third Plenum of September 1947 was one of the most significant meetings of the KKE and one that legitimized the actions of the Communist Party undertaken from August 1946 to September 1947.

27. Iliou, *Emphylios Polemos*, 181–203.

28. John O. Iatrides, "Revolution or Self-Defense? Communist Goals, Strategy, and Tactics in the Greek Civil War," *Journal of Cold War Studies*, 7, no. 3 (Summer 2005), 27, also adds that the success of Limnes would have enabled the Soviet Union to recognize the KKE government.

29. Iatrides also cites Ioannis Ioannidis in which the senior communist instructed Vaphiadis on 14 April 1947 to transform the guerrilla bands into a conventional army and seize Thessaloniki, resulting in a decisive shift in the military and political situation. See Iatrides, "Revolution or Self-Defense?" 23 n.70.

30. Ulunian, "The Soviet Union and the Greek Question," 150, attests to the meeting and claims that Stalin decided to support the KKE in its conflict because he believed that the Greek civil war would tie down the Anglo-Americans in Europe and prevent them from actively intervening in the ongoing conflict in China. Iliou refers to the meeting between Stalin and Zachariadis but writes that there is no surviving documentation that offers any details on what exactly the two communists discussed. He quotes a telegram from Ioannidis in which the prominent KKE leader informed Stergios Anastasiadis, "In the last couple of weeks, Koukos (Zachariadis) met with the Old Man (Stalin) during which they discussed definitively our requests. As a result of these discussions, we will be completely satisfied." See Iliou, *Emphylios Polemos*, 88.

31. Although Yugoslavia was a major supplier to the DAG, Bulgaria provided substantial aid, training, food, paper, and 15 trucks: Elizabeth Barker, "The Yugoslavs and the Greek Civil War of 1946–1949," in *Studies in the History of the Greek Civil War, 1945–1949*, ed. Lars Baerentzen et al. (Copenhagen: Museum Tusculum Press, 1987), 263–295. For a detailed analysis of aid to the KKE during the civil war from the Communist bloc, see Marantzidis, *Demokratikos Stratos Elladas*, chap. 2.

32. O'Balance, *The Greek Civil War,* 130 n. 1.

33. Bulkes is a village in Serbia's Vojvodina province, now known as Maglic. Before World War II it had a German population dating back to when that region of Serbia was part of the Austro-Hungarian Empire. After the liberation of Yugoslavia, the Germans were expelled and the village remained abandoned until it was turned over to the KKE. Almost immediately in the post–Varkiza Agreement period, the Yugoslavs had used it to house several thousand Greek communists (some with their families) who had fled Greece. Factionalism plagued the inhabitants and they had their own civil war; a bloody three-day battle that forced the Yugoslav authorities to intervene. More than likely Tito's break with Stalin was the main cause, as the community was divided between supporters of Tito and Stalin: Alexander Bilinis, "Bulkes: The Greek Republic in Yugoslavia," *Neokosmos,* 15 March 2013, http://neoskosmos.com/news/en/bulkes-the-greek-republic-in-yugoslavia.

34. The transportation and accommodation of the Greek refugees was conducted by the State Security Service, which by early 1945 brought 2,702 men, women, and children to the refugee center. At its peak Bulkes housed 4,500 people. The Greek communist authorities at Bulkes maintained their own governing bodies as well as a security service. The autonomy of Bulkes is underscored by references to the community as the seventh republic of Yugoslavia. The Tito-Stalin split and the decision of the KKE to stay loyal to Stalin ended the Greek communist community in Bulkes. At the end of August 1949 the first group of inhabitants (1,200) left Yugoslavia for Hungary. During the first half of September the remaining Greek residents were transferred to Czechoslovakia through Hungary.

35. Milan Ristovic, "The Bulkes Experiment: A 'Greek Republic' in Yugoslavia 1945–1949," *Journal of Balkan Studies* 46 (2012), 126–143, offers a detailed although not a complete account of the Bulkes story.

36. There were 2,800 KKE members in Bulkes between 1947–1948. See Ristovoc, "The Bulkes Experiment," 132.

37. Matthews accompanied the United Nations Inquiry Commission to Bulkes, but he and the commission representatives only had limited access to the inhabitants. The KKE and the Yugoslav authorities, however, choreographed all of the meetings. See Matthews, *Memories of a Mountain War,* 138–142.

38. Matthews comments: "The ineradicable zest of the Greek for free enterprise, private profit and the accumulation of capital had proved stronger than all the fire generated by Communist ideals and the comradeship of revolution." See ibid., 143.

39. Ristovic, "The Bulkes Experiment," 143. As a publication in a communist country, *Borba* was more likely to keep up with the Yugoslav Communist Party line, but some of its assertions concerning the KKE in Bulkes are substantiated by Matthews, *Memories of a Mountain War,* 159.

40. Matthews, *Memories of a Mountain War,* 159.

41. O'Balance, *The Greek Civil War,* 133.

42. Between 21 and 22 September 1944 ELAS extrajudicial courts tried and executed dozens of Security Battalion personnel in the Peloponnese, and in some cases as many as 800 collaborationist forces were lynched by crowds or shot by ELAS fighters. See

Dimitris Kousouris, *Dikes ton Dosilogon, 1944–1949: Dikeosini, Synehia tou Kratous kai Ethniki Mnimi* (Athens: Polis, 2014), 111.

43. Ibid.

44. Shrader, *The Withered Vine*, 119.

45. Larry E. Cable, *Conflict of Myths: The Development of Counter-Insurgency Doctrine and the Vietnam War* (New York: New York University Press, 1986), 13. According to Goulter, during 1946 the GNA launched large-scale operations in northern Greece operating in brigade strength, according to British army doctrine. Although some of the GNA's operations took place with brigade-sized units, the training was deficient and there was almost no coordination. See Goulter, "The Greek Civil War," 1017–1055.

46. Alexandros Papagos, "Guerrilla Warfare," in *Modern Guerrilla War*, ed. Mark Osana (New York: Free Press, 1962), 237.

47. O'Balance, *The Greek Civil War*, 129.

48. Cited in Nachmani, *International Intervention*, 15.

49. Ibid.

50. Major General Rawlings, "Review of the Anti-Bandit Campaign, NA FO 371/72244/ R14153/G, pp. 2–3.

51. American Embassy, Athens, to the Secretary of State, 8 June 1948, NA 868.00/6-848.

52. Kousoulas, *Revolution and Defeat*, 242.

53. There were three senior British advisers on the Greek Supreme Council of National Defense. The three were nonvoting members, but since the Greek governments from 1944 to 1947 were entirely dependent on Britain for military and economic assistance, the advisers had considerable influence over the training and deployment of the GNA. Major William D. Harris, Jr., *Arts of War Papers: Instilling Aggressiveness: U.S. Advisors and Greek Combat Leadership in the Greek Civil War, 1947–1949* (Fort Leavenworth: Combat Studies Institute Press, 2013), 23.

54. O'Balance, *The Greek Civil War*, 129.

55. Woodhouse, *Something Ventured*, 93.

56. The Rimi Brigade and what was originally the Sacred Company, named after an elite unit in the ancient Theban army in the fourth century BC.

57. In 1946, sixty officers and other ranks were arrested and court-martialed because of ties to the KKE: Cable, *Conflict of Myths*, 11.

58. Harris, *Art of War Papers*, 43.

59. Loose minute, British Air Ministry, 21 June 1947, THA, AIR 46/30 in Nachmani, *International Intervention*, 16.

60. Goulter, "The Greek Civil War," 1027–1028.

61. The accords were the result of a conference in Geneva which included the United States, the USSR, France, Great Britain, and China and was initially organized to settle outstanding issues dealing with the Korean Peninsula. At the end of the meeting, although no new resolutions or declarations were made regarding the Korean issue, the participants agreed on ending the conflict between the French and the Vietminh.

62. The regime of Ngo Dinh Diem by 1956 had destroyed most of the former Vietminh (the name of the Vietnamese forces fighting the French after World War II) networks

in the Mekong Delta. Those that survived withdrew into the jungles and swamps. Yet Diem's indiscriminate campaign against the Vietminh drove many underground and into the arms of the communists who would have otherwise become peaceful citizens. On this analysis see Stanley Karnow, *Vietnam: A History* (New York: Penguin Books, 1991), 243; Mark Moyar, *Triumph Forsaken: The Vietnam War, 1954–1956* (Cambridge: Cambridge University Press, 2006), 83; Fredrick Logevall, *Embers of War: The Fall of an Empire and the Making of America's Vietnam* (New York: Random House, 2012), 679.

63. The North Vietnamese made the decision to begin hostilities against South Vietnam at the Fiftieth Plenum of the Communist Party Central Committee. Ho Chi Minh, the leader of North Vietnam, advocated a strategy of political organization in the villages of the South and small guerrilla raids. Ho Chi Minh, like Zachariadis, had a difficult time securing support from the Soviets and the Chinese. Moscow opposed an uprising and Beijing, although favorable, cautioned that the time was not right for offensive military operations. See Moyar, *Triumph Forsaken* 60–61, 83.

64. The official British notification came in two notes on 21 February 1947 from the British embassy to the American Secretary of State informing the U.S. government that aid from Britain to Greece was to end. For a recent study of the Truman Doctrine see Judith S. Jeffery, *Ambiguous Commitments and Uncertain Policies: The Truman Doctrine in Greece, 1947–1952* (New York: Lexington Books, 2000).

65. All quotes in the preceding paragraph cited from NARA, Entry 421, Folder 400, 336 (20 March 1947), Sec 1-A, pp. 4 and 7. "Memorandum by the State-War-Navy Coordination Committee to the Joint Chiefs of Staff on Policies for Execution of Assistance Program to Greece," 18 August 1947.

66. Jones, *"A New Kind of War,"* 1.

67. David McCullough, *Truman* (New York: Simon and Schuster, 1992), 545.

68. F. C. Pogue, *George C. Marshall, Statesman* (New York: Viking, 1987), 4:162; Marshall's Speech File, ML. Appendix 525–528.

69. Pogue, *George C. Marshall,* 165–167; Wittner, *American Intervention in Greece,* 78–79; McCullough, *Truman,* 546–547.

70. Wittner, *American Intervention in Greece,* 71; Dean Acheson, *Present at the Creation: My Years in the State Department* (New York: Norton, 1969), 219.

71. McCullough, *Truman,* 542.

72. Wittner, *American Intervention in Greece,* 73.

73. Ibid., 78–79.

74. The initial draft of this speech was thought by Clark Clifford, Truman's special counsel, to be too weak, while Marshall (who was in Paris, en route to Moscow) found the final draft too aggressive. Truman wanted to avoid sounding as if he was reading an "investment prospectus"; Marshall was known for shying away from bad rhetoric. Various changes were made over the multiple drafts, and some direct references to the Soviets were made obscure, but overall, Marshall was told that the communist threat had to remain tangible in the wording. Pogue, *George C. Marshall,* 4:165–167; McCullough, *Truman,* 545–546.

75. Jones, *"A New Kind of War,"* 1.

76. Wittner, *American Intervention in Greece,* 80–81.

77. Pogue, *George C. Marshall,* 164; *Foreign Relations of the United States, 1947, The Near East and Africa* (Washington, DC: Government Printing Office, 1971), 5:60–62.

78. Wittner, *American Intervention in Greece,* 178–18.

79. Jones, *"A New Kind of War,"* 94.

80. Ibid., 127–128.

81. Ibid., 127–129.

82. United Press story in "Note for Record," 11 February 1948, in P & O 000.7 (TS), sect. I, case I, Army Staff Records, NA, cited in Jones, *"A New Kind of War,"* 128–129.

83. Constantine Poulos, "The Lesson of Greece," *Nation,* 27 March 1948, 343–345, cited in Jones, *"A New Kind of War,"* 129.

84. Ibid., 131.

85. Cable, *Conflict of Myths,* 19.

86. By this time, the Greek special forces expanded to 2,000 men in four groups that also included an air-mobile unit. Cable, *Conflict of Myths,* 18–19.

87. Letter, COMJUSMAPG to JCS, 31 March 1948, CCS 02, BP 2, cited in Cable, *Conflict of Myths,* 19, n. 37.

88. Cable, *Conflict of Myths,* 19.

89. Ibid., 141.

90. Although predominantly Greek, the Dodecanese remained under Ottoman control after the establishment of the Greek state. The Italians occupied the islands when Italy defeated the Ottoman Empire in 1911 and held them until the Germans took them over in the fall of 1943. The British, with Italian cooperation in many cases, easily occupied Kastelorizo, Kos, Leros, Samos, Kalymnos, Syri, and Astypalaia, but failed to defend the islands against the German counterattacks. For a detailed discussion of the battle for Leros and the Eastern Aegean, see Anthony Rogers, *Churchill's Folly: Leros and the Aegean, the Last Great Defeat of World War Two* (London: Cassell, 2003).

91. Operation Shingle, the code name for the allied landings on Anzio on 22 January 1944, was intended to outflank the German winter line and facilitate an advance on Rome. The allied landings could not break out and during the course of the battle the Ranger battalions suffered heavy losses. In the Battle of Cisterna on 29 January, the First and Second Ranger Battalions lost 761 men killed or captured.

92. Shrader suggests four phases, which overlap those of Kousoulas, but with some variation of dates. In effect, Shrader includes the period of winter 1945 to summer 1946, during which uncoordinated leftist bands were operating in the Greek mountains and slowly were coming under the control of the KKE by August 1946. See Shrader, *The Withered Vine,* 77–86.

93. The brigades were armed with 963 rifles, 393 submachine guns, 81 light machine guns, 6 heavy machine guns, 27 light mortars, and 6 medium mortars: Kousoulas, *Revolution and Defeat,* 240, n. 6; Cable, *Conflict of Myths,* 17.

94. Woodhouse represents the view that Markos favored a guerrilla war of attrition or even a pause, while Zachariadis was determined to force the issue by switching to conventional warfare. See Woodhouse, *The Greek Civil War,* 230.

95. O'Balance argues that the combination of the change of tactics by the DAG, Tito's closing of the Yugoslav border with Greece, and the transition to conventional warfare by the DAG led to the defeat of the Greek communists. See O'Balance, *The Greek Civil War*, 179. Woodhouse also concluded that the combination of these factors contributed to the defeat of the DAG. He claims, however, that a strategy of guerrilla warfare cannot by itself bring victory unless it can be augmented by external support or the guerrilla forces transition into a conventional army. See Woodhouse, *The Struggle for Greece*, 276. This was the dilemma that confronted Zachariadis, who had little choice but to risk everything in a conventional battle against a far superior force.

96. Ole Smith, "A Turning Point in the Greek Civil War, 1945–1949: The Meeting between Zachariadis and Markos," *Scandinavian Studies in Modern Greek* 3 (1976), 44.

97. Ibid., 42.

98. Zapheiropoulos, *O Andisymmoriakos Agon*, 62–63; Woodhouse, *The Struggle for Greece*, 254.

CHAPTER 9. THE CAULDRON OF BATTLE

1. Shrader, *The Withered Vine*, 230.

2. Initially, Edmund Myers, the head of the SOE Mission in Greece, had organized the construction of the landing strip in 1943 to facilitate the transport of representatives of the resistance organization to Cairo. (ELAS had constructed a landing field that serviced planes that supplied arms, food, and ammunition as well as transported ELAS and SOE agents in and out of the country.) See Woodhouse, *The Struggle for Greece*, 53, 256.

3. Woodhouse, *Struggle for Greece*, 256.

4. Zapheiropoulos, *O Andisymoriakos Agon*, 544–545.

5. Zapheiropoulos, *O Andisymoriakos Agon*, 547.

6. Woodhouse, *Struggle for Greece*, 257.

7. Tsakalotos was further instructed that after completing this operation, the First Corps was to "cleanse" the regions of Roumelis, Thessaly, and Epiros. Thrasyvoulos Tsakalotos, *40 Chronia Stratiotis tis Ellados: Istorikes Anamniseis, Pos Ekerdisame tous Agonas, 1940–1949* (Athens: Acropolis Edition, 1960), 2:198.

8. Ibid., 200. Prior to 1946, Tsakalotos commanded the Third Mountain Brigade (the Rimi Brigade), which was formed in the Middle East after the mutiny of the Greek armed forces.

9. Both were released on the orders of Karagiorgis, a senior commander in the DAG. See Matthews, *Memories of a Mountain War*, 217–258, and Shrader, *The Withered Vine*, 124. Woodhouse points out that the exercise backfired since both men reported on the impossibility of the KKE victory. See Woodhouse, *Struggle for Greece*, 235.

10. Tsakalotos, *40 Chronia*, A:201. Paul F. Braim, *The Will to Win: The Life of General A. Van Fleet* (Annapolis, MD: Naval Institute Press, 2001), 167, supports Tsakalotos' claims that well-placed communist sympathizers provided information to the insurgents and adds that they were joined by some in government and in the civil service who opposed the monarchy.

11. To ensure complete secrecy, Tsakalotos only issued the order a few days before the arrests. He only informed the general staff of his intentions a day after (28 December) the arrests had taken place, fearing that if it had become known to the political establishment in Athens, the order would have been cancelled. He admits that among the 4,500 there were innocent people. See Tsakalotos, *40 Chronia*, 207.

12. Ibid., 204–205.

13. Any doubts that Tsakalotos had about incarcerating the communists were eliminated when a communist group tried to sabotage the radio transmission center of the Army Corps headquarters on the evening of 25 December. See Tsakalotos, *40 Chronia*, 202.

14. Margaritis, *Istoria tou Ellinikou Emphiliou Polemou*, 303–304, claims that almost all of those arrested were either innocent or simply sympathetic to the left. He adds that it would have been a major asset if the DAG had so many supporters. The intention of Tsakalotos was, according to Margaritis, to terrorize the population and conduct total war in the Peloponnese. Part of the general's scheme was also to bring to the government side many of the prominent families, and that is why he had many of the heads of these families arrested. Remarkably, Margaritis, although he goes into considerable details of the fate of each DAG band, does not explain the complete victory of the First Army Corps. Certainly, during the period that the DGA enjoyed predominance in the region, many noncommunists assisted the insurgents out of fear.

15. Frank J. Abbot, *The Greek Civil War, 1947-1949: Lessons for the Operational Artist in Foreign Internal Defense*, School for Advanced Military Studies thesis (Fort Leavenworth, Kansas: School of Advanced Military Studies, U.S. Army Command and General Staff College, May 1994), 30.

16. Kousoulas, *Revolution and Defeat*, 261.

17. Woodhouse, *The Struggle for Greece*, 261.

18. The new commander-in-chief, at least in name, of the DAG, Georgios Vrondisios (Goussias), ordered the assassination of Tsakalotos. Coincidently, Tsakalotos and Vrondisios both came from a village near Ioannina. See Tsakalotos, *40 Chronia*, 212.

19. Zaphiropoulos, *O Antisymmoriakos Agon*, 511 as well as Tsakalotos, *40 Chronia*, 212.

20. Braim, *The Will to Win*, 189.

21. The junta, or the colonels' junta, was established in 1967 and imposed military rule for seven years.

22. Braim, *The Will to Win*, 188.

23. Andrew J. Birtle, *U.S. Army Counterinsurgency Operations, 1942–1976* (Washington, DC: Center of Military History United Sates Army) Kindle Book, 2006.

24. The leader of the team was Captain Barbas (nom de guerre) already under suspended sentence of death. As head executioner of the KKE prisoner camp in Piraeus he was responsible for the murder of 600 Greek civilians during the December Uprising in 1944. This was the second attempt; shortly after his arrival KKE assassins had placed explosives on the railway tracks to detonate when the train he was on passed over. See Braim, *The Will to Win*, 185–186.

25. By 1948 the right-wing paramilitaries numbered 48,000 (Wittner, *American Intervention*, 245).

26. Birtle, *U.S. Army Counterinsurgency Operations*.

27. Woodhouse, *The Struggle for Greece*, 262.

28. Ibid., 263.

29. In terms of numbers, the GNA had 147,000 troops while the communist forces only 23,000. The GNA enjoyed air supremacy and an abundance of artillery and mortars and constant resupply of ammunition and rations (Wittner, *American Intervention*, 243). Another important advantage was that the GNA soldiers had medical support units as well as medical supplies. The DAG had serious deficiencies in both medical supplies and support.

30. Zaphiropoulos, *O Antisymmoriakos Agon*, 551–552, assessed the communist forces at approximately 2,900, while Tsakalotos, *40 Chronia*, 223, estimated 6,000.

31. On 23 January an American plane conducting reconnaissance was shot down near Karpanisi. Later the mutilated body of the pilot was found. The unfortunate man was the first American casualty killed by communist forces. According to Woodhouse, *Struggle for Greece*, 260–261, the KKE interpreted this incident as proof of American participation in the fighting.

32. Papagos blamed General Ketseas, one of Tsakalotos' divisional commanders, for the setback. Ketseas was relieved of his command and court-martialed.

33. On 27 January the mouthpiece of the KKE, Radio Free Greece, located outside of the country, announced an offer of peace. The conditions included the removal of all foreign military missions, a general amnesty, the guarantee of political freedom, free trade unions, and negotiations on the establishment of a new government acceptable to both sides. The government rejected these terms.

34. Woodhouse, *The Struggle for Greece*, 262, and Shrader, *The Withered Vine*, 232, who repeats Woodhouse, in particular emphasize Zachariadis' limitations and ambition to secure a reputation as a military commander.

35. In addition to the dead, wounded, and surrendered, the DAG lost a significant number of weapons, including large mortars, mines, heavy and light machine guns, as well as hundreds of thousands of rounds of ammunition. Shrader, *The Withered Vine*, 262, offers a comprehensive list of sources on the battle for Florina.

36. Shrader, *The Withered Vine*, 235.

37. Ibid., 234, n. 87.

38. Woodhouse, *The Struggle for Greece*, 262.

39. O'Balance, *The Greek Civil War*, 194.

40. Ibid., 195.

41. Wittner, *American Intervention*, 252.

42. Ibid., 196.

43. O'Balance, *The Greek Civil War*, 196.

44. Wittner, *American Intervention*, 250–251.

45. Leo Katsuris, who took part in the diversionary attack against the Grammos defenses, remembered that his division struck deep behind the flanks of the rebels and some units had crossed the border into Albania. "The moment we crossed," he recalls, "the Albanians attacked us and as our unit fell back towards the Greek frontier we stumbled on a minefield. We lost four hundred men that day." Leo Katsuris, interview by the author, Vancouver, 8 March 2004.

46. O'Balance, *The Greek Civil War*, 196–197. The Yugoslavs interned most of the Greek communists and sent them to other eastern bloc countries, particularly to Czechoslovakia. See Ristovic, "*The Bulkes Experiment*," 142–143.
47. Ibid., 198.
48. Richard J. Aldrich, *The Hidden Hand: Britain, America, and Cold War Secret Intelligence* (New York: Overlook Press, 2002), 163.
49. Ulunian, "The Soviet Union and the Greek Question," 154. In 1952, Greece and Turkey joined NATO, and between 1953 and 1954 Greece, Yugoslavia, and Turkey concluded a series of treaties laying the foundation for a Balkan pact.
50. Kosta Katsuris emigrated to Canada from the Soviet Union in 1967.
51. U.S. advisers had inspired the strategy of shifting populations and relocating entire communities; later this was applied with much less success in Vietnam.
52. Woodhouse, *Struggle for Greece*, 209.
53. In 1958, Galula was transferred to the Headquarters of National Defense in Paris. Galula resigned his commission in 1962 to study in the United States and became a research associate at the Center for International Affairs at Harvard University. He died in 1967 of lung cancer.
54. David Galula, *Counterinsurgency Warfare: Theory and Practice* (Westport, CT: Praeger Security International, 1964), 12.
55. Galula, *Counterinsurgency Warfare*, 12.
56. "E Oportounistiki Platforma tou Markou Vaphiadi," 15 November 1948, *Neos Kosmos* 8 (1950), 476–480 in Marantzidis, *Democratikos Stratos*, 137.
57. During the battle of Grammos and Vitsi, the percentage of female combatants in some units reached as high as 50 percent. See Shrader, *The Withered Vine*, 110.
58. Marantzidis, *Democratikos Statos*, 138–139, comments that those in the DAG units were bitter over the fact that their fellow communists refused to volunteer and remained in the safety of the cities and towns. In an act of desperation the KKE demanded that Greek communist refugees in France present themselves for military service in the DAG; otherwise, they would be disbarred from the Greek Communist Party. The threat, according to Marantzidis, was symbolic since a few dozen or hundreds of KKE refugees would not have made any difference to the outcome of the civil war.
59. The United States supplied the South Vietnamese government with significant military aid and American troops, planes, and naval forces and still failed to defeat the communists. Unlike the Vietcong, the DAG did not have a constant flow of recruits and regular units coming to its aid.
60. Simon Sebag Montefiore, *Stalin: The Court of the Red Tsar* (London: Weidenfeld and Nicolson, 2003), 511.

EPILOGUE

1. Robert Gildea, *Fighters in the Shadows: A New Version of the French Resistance* (London: Faber and Faber, 2015), 409.
2. Initially, de Gaulle ordered the dissolution of the armed resistance units, but after strong objections from the Comité d'Action Militaire he agreed that they could be

incorporated in the Free French Army. Over 200,000 resistance fighters joined or fought in their own units with the Free French Army to the end of World War II (Matthew Cobb, *The Resistance: The French Fight Against the Nazis* [New York: Simon and Schuster, 2009], 276).

3. Gildea, *Fighters in the Shadows,* 409.

4. Cobb, *The Resistance,* 276.

5. Kostis Karpozilos, "The Defeated of the Greek Civil War: From Fighters to Political Refugees in the Cold War," *Journal of Cold War Studies,* 16, no. 3 (2014), 65.

6. Jones, *"A New Kind of War,"* 234.

7. Margaret Truman, *Harry S. Truman* (New York: William Morrow, 1973), 461.

8. In 1961, the Special Operations Research Office of the American University was contracted by the Department of the Army to prepare a study of guerrilla warfare in Greece. Significantly, the study focused on the Greek resistance bands fighting the Axis during the occupation and not on the Greek civil war. D. M. Condit, *Case Study in Guerrilla War: Greece during World War II* (Washington, DC: Special Operations Research Office, 1981).

9. Douglas Dillon, "Chargé at Saigon to the Secretary of State," *Foreign Relations of the United States, 1950, East Asia and the Pacific,* vol. 6 (Washington, DC: Government Printing Office, 1976), 705, 710, 778, 803–4.

10. John Foster Dulles, *War and Peace* (New York: Macmillan, 1950), 44, 231.

11. William J. Miller, *Henry Cabot Lodge: A Biography* (New York: Heinemann, 1967), 373.

12. Theodore Sorensen, *Kennedy* (New York: Harper and Row, 1965), 745.

13. Lyndon Baines Johnson, *The Vantage Point: Perspectives of the Presidency, 1963–1969* (New York: Holt, 1971), 422–423.

14. A notable exception to this policy of retribution was on 15 December 1962 when King Paul pardoned Manolis Glezos, a well-known communist who took down the swastika from the Acropolis in 1941 and became a hero because of it.

15. Pablo Picasso, for example, created the drawing *L'Homme à l'oeillet* (Man with Carnation, 1952) in protest. He was "fascinated by the bravura of Beloyannis, who had appeared before the tribunal with a flower in his hand. This is what he captured in his drawing, which he . . . donated to the amnesty committee in order to raise money to save Beloyannis." Gertje Utley, *Pablo Picasso: The Communist Years* (New Haven: Yale University Press, 2000), 179. Spyridon, archbishop of Athens and all Greece, was quoted as saying that the self-sacrifice of Beloyannis was superior even to the martyrdoms of the first Christians (Foteini Tomai, "Oi Antidraseis gia ti Diki Beloyanni," *To Vima,* 12 February 2006). The immortalization of Beloyannis, for example, in the poems, art, music, films, and writings of Yiannis Ritsos, Alexis Parnis, Kostas Varnalis, Nâzim Hikmet, Picasso, Peter de Francia, Míkis Theodorakis, Dido Sotiriou, and Nikos Tzimas, contributed to the glorification of Beloyannis as an individual and a communist. To a degree, this was similar to the way the death of the young worker Tassos Toussis in 1936 served as an inspiration for Ritsos to create his poem "Epitaphios." For many on the left, faith in communist ideology replaced faith in God and religion; in this respect, Beloyannis became an emblem of the cultural reverence of the heroic, messianic communist.

16. Zachariadis and the KKE also rushed to expel Ploumpidis from the party and publicly denounced him as an "agent of the [domestic] Security Service, and a traitor" (L. Stavropoulos, "To KKE Apokathista Zachariadi-Stalin," *To Vima,* 6 March 2011).

17. Nikos Kiaos, "The Lamb Beloyiannis, the Scapegoat Ploumpidis," *Eleutherotypia,* 13 September 2010. Elli Pappas claims that Zachariadis was envious of and feared Beloyannis. She deposited the material for her book at the Historical Archives of the Benaki Museum, asking that it be published only after her death. This stipulation has led to some skepticism about its accuracy, which reflects the uneasiness that arises when Greek communists write about the KKE and its members. In 1950, Zachariadis had to issue a formal apology to the KKE for keeping the party out of the 1946 election and effectively handing the country over to a series of right-wing regimes. According to Pappas, Beloyannis was sacrificed to atone for Zachariadis' "mistake." See Elli Pappas, *Martyries mias Diadromis* (Athens: Benaki Museum, 2010), 40, 166, 240, 307. Zachariadis may have learned his tactics from his political role model, Joseph Stalin.

18. In contrast, KKE's central committee had rehabilitated both Ploumpides and Siantos in 1958.

19. Kalyvas and Marantzidis, Op-ed, *Kathimerini,* July 2013.

Bibliography

ARCHIVES

Archeia Synchronis Koinonikis Istorias (ASKI)

Zachariadis, Nikos. Eigisi tou N. Zachariadi sti Dodekati Olomelia tis Kentrikis
Epitropis tou KKE. June 1945.
——. I Simerini Economiki kai Politiki Katastasi stin Ellada kai ta Provlimata tou
Dimokratikou Kinimatos kai Agona. 12 February 1946.

Arhiv Jugoslavije (AJ)

507 IX CKSKJ 33/I-48
507 IX CKSKJ 33/I-59
507 IX CKSKJ 33/I-61
507 IX CKSKJ 33/I-62
507 IX CKSKJ 33/I-63
507 IX CKSKJ 33/I-64
507 IX CKSKJ 33/I-66
836 KMJ I-2–9/39
836 KMJ I-3–6/235
836 KMJ I-3–6/241
836 KMJ I-3–6/659

Genika archia tou kratous (GAK)

GAK Files A6-A17; B1-B4; E1-E3; E-13
GAK, "Apostoli Gama." No. 4

Istoriko Archio tou Yrourgio Exoterikon (AYE)

A/24581/G2/1945
A/30946/G5–1947
A/59224.Bb1 1948
A/G5/Bb1/1949

National Archives of the United Kingdom

CAB 65/25 WM (42) 5
CAB 65/40, WM (43), Minutes, 22 November 1943
HS 7/151 89486
HS 7/268 89846. "Major Pirie's Report: A History of SOE Activities in Greece, May
    1940–November 1942"
FO 371/19508
FO 371/20383
FO 371/20390, Athens Dispatch No. 28
FO 371/22362
FO 371/22363
FO 371/22371
FO 371/23782 R 7921, Chiefs of Staff Committee.
FO 371/24884 R 74320 "Greek Military Situation"
FO 371/24910
FO 371/24982
FO 371/29816 R 74220
FO 371/29817 R 8810
FO 371/29820 R 4615
FO 371/29842 R 10894
FO 371/29862
FO 371/29909 R 8414
FO 371/33160
FO 371/33167 R 1362
FO 371/3717194 R 2266
FO 371/37201 74220 R 2050, "Resistance Groups in Greece." Minute by Dixon,
    7 March 1943
FO 371/37201 74220 R 2050, "Political Aspects of the Greek Resistance Movement"
FO 371/37201 74220 R 2322

FO 371/37201 R 74220
FO 371/37203 R 5573
FO 371/37206 R 74337
FO 371/37206 R 10177
FO 371/37206 R 10295
FO 371/37206 R 10450
FO 371/37208 R 11753, R 11908
FO 371/37208 R 1221
FO 371/37210 R 13883
FO 371/37216 R 3924
FO 371/43706
FO 371/43715 R 12457
FO 371/72213 R 7618, Monthly Intelligence Review, 15 June 1948
FO 371/72244/R14153/G
FO 371/78373 R 11085, British Embassy estimates, 14 November 1949
FO 71/37202 R 4209
FO 74038 HS 5/524
FO 800/303, folios 227–235
FO 898/97 R 754320, "Joint SOE/PWE Survey of Resistance in Occupied Europe"
R 6531/1081/67
R 8828/407/92
R 8973/298/67
R 10222/4155/67
R 13507/298/67

National Archives and Records Administration

NARA Entry 16, Folder 110605–110619, 5 January 1945
NARA Entry 421, Folder 400, 336 (20 March 1947) Sec. 1-A ("Memorandum
    by the State-War-Navy Coordination Committee to the Joint Chiefs of
    Staff on Policies for Execution of Assistance Program to Greece." 18 August
    1947).
NARA Entry 421, Folder ABC 400, 336 Greece (20 March 1947) Sec. 1-A,
    Appendix F
NARA RG 226: Entry 172, Box 4, Folder 227, 4 December 1944
NARA RG 226: L49839
NARA RG 226: 83476
NARA RG 226: L49838
NARA RG 226: Xl 2683
NARA Entry 16, Folder 110924–110936, 8 January 1945
NARA Entry 210, Folder I, 31 January 1945

Harry S. Truman Library

Central Intelligence Agency. "Greece." March 1948. Truman Library, President's Secretary File, Box 259, December 1944–January 1945.

OTHER PRIMARY SOURCES

Acheson, Dean. *Present at the Creation: My Years in the State Department.* New York: Norton, 1969.

Bakopoulos, Konstantinos Th. *I Omeria ton Pende Andistratigon: I Zoe ton— Stratopeda Sygendroseos.* Athens: n.p., 1948.

Beswick, Major. C. H., "Eleventh Battalion, 'Liberation of Greece and Civil War,' King's Royal Rifle Corps." In *Swift and Bold: The Story of the King's Royal Rifle Corps." In the Second World War, 1939–1945,* edited by H. Wake and W. F. Deeds. Aldershot: Gale and Polden, 1949.

British Documents on Foreign Affairs: Reports and Papers from the Foreign Office Confidential Print. Gen. ed. Paul Preston and Michael Partridge, *Part III, From 1940 through 1945. Series F, Europe.* Bethesda, MD: University Publications of America, 1997–1998.

British Documents on Foreign Affairs: Reports and Papers from the Foreign Office Confidential Print. Gen. ed. Paul Preston and Michael Partridge, *Part IV from 1946 through 1950, Series F, Europe,* Vol. 5, 1946. Ed. Denis Smyth and André Gerolymatos. University Publications of America, 2000.

British Documents on Foreign Affairs: Reports and Papers from the Foreign Office Confidential Print: South-Eastern Europe, January 1946–June 1946. Gen ed. Paul Preston and Michael Partridge. Ed. Denis Smyth. University Publications of America, 2000.

British Documents on Foreign Affairs: Reports and Papers from the Foreign Office Confidential Print: South-Eastern Europe, July 1946–December 1946. Gen Ed. Paul Preston and Michael Partridge. Ed. Denis Smyth. University Publications of America, 2000.

British Documents on Foreign Affairs: Reports and Papers from the Foreign Office Confidential Print: Italy, The Vatican, Yugoslavia and Albania, South-Eastern Europe (Gen) 1947. Gen ed. Paul Preston and Michael Partridge. Ed. Denis Smith and André Gerolymatos. University Publications of America, 2001.

British Documents on Foreign Affairs: Reports and Papers from the Foreign Office Confidential Print: Bulgaria, Greece, Rumania, Yugoslavia and Albania, 1948. Gen. ed. Paul Preston and Michael Partridge. Ed. Denis Smyth. University Publications of America, 2002.

Byford-Jones, W. *Greek Trilogy: Resistance, Liberation, Revolution.* London: Hutchinson, 1945.

Cabinet Office (Great Britain), *Cabinet History Series: Principal War Telegrams and Memoranda 1940–1943*, Vol. I, "Middle East, From the Occupation of Cyrenaica to the Fall of Keren and Harar." Now. 39, 40, 69, 73.

Cadogan, Alexander. *The Diaries of Sir Alexander Cadogan, 1938–1945.* Edited by David Dilks. London: Putnam, 1971.

Carnegie Endowment for International Peace. *Report of the International Commission to Inquire into the Causes and Conduct of the Balkan Wars.* Washington, DC: Carnegie Endowment for International Peace, Division of Intercourse and Education, Publication No. 4, 1914.

Christidis, Ch. *Chronia Katochis: Martyries Imerologion, 1941–1944.* Athens: n. p., 1971.

Churchill, W. S. *Closing the Ring, The Second World War*, vol. 5. London: Houghton Mifflin, 1951.

———. *Triumph and Tragedy, The Second World War*, vol. 6. London: Houghton Mifflin, 1953.

Clive, Nigel. *A Greek Experience 1943–1948.* Salisbury, Wiltshire: Russell, 1985.

The Communist International, 1919–1943 Documents. Ed. Jane Degras, Vol. 1. London: Frank Cass, 1971.

de Gaulle, Charles. *The Complete War Memoirs of Charles de Gaulle, 1940–1946.* Trans. Jonathan Griffin. New York: Da Capo, 1967.

Dimitrov, Georgi. *The Diary of Georgi Dimitrov, 1933–1949.* Edited by Ivo Banac. Trans. Jane Hedges (German), Timothy D. Sergay (Russian), and Irina Faion (Bulgarian). New Haven: Yale University Press, 2003.

———. *Political Report delivered [sic] to the V Congress of the Bulgarian Communist Party.* Sofia: Ministry of Foreign Affairs, 1949.

Djilas, Milovan. *Conversations with Stalin.* London: Penguin, 1962.

———. *Wartime.* Translated by Michael Petrovich. New York: Harcourt Brace Jovanovich, 1977.

Documents on Foreign German Policy, Series D, Vol. 2, No. 323, "Directive 18."

Documents on Foreign German Policy, Series D, Vol. 2, No. 511, "Directive 20: Operation Marita."

Documents on Foreign German Policy, Series D, Vol. 12, No. 463.

Dokumenti Centralnih Organa KPJ NOR i Revolucija (1941–1945): Knjiga 21. Ed. Milovan Dželebdžić. Belgrade: Izdavački Centar Komunist, 1987.

EAM White Book. May 1944–March 1945. New York, 1944–1945.

Eden, Anthony. *Facing the Dictators: The Memoirs of Anthony Eden, Earl of Avon.* London: Cassell, 1962.

———. *The Reckoning: The Memoirs of Anthony Eden, Earl of Avon.* Boston: Cassel, 1965.

Force 133, MEF Reports, Ref GSOE/94/505, "Maintenance of Law and Order in Greece."

Force 133, MEF Reports, Ref GSOE/94/506.

Foreign Relations of the United States, 1947, The Near East and Africa. Vol. 5. Washington, DC: Government Printing Office, 1971.

Georgiou, Vasos. *I Zoi Mou.* Athens, 1992.

Hammond, N. *Venture into Greece: With the Guerrillas, 1943–1944.* London: William Kimbers, 1983.

Henderson, Mary. *Xenia—A Memoir, Greece 1919–1949.* London: Weidenfeld and Nicolson, 1988.

Istorijski Arhiv Kommunističke Partije Jugoslavije. Vols. 7–8. Belgrade: Kultura, 1951.

Jebb, Lord Hubert Miles Gladwyn. *The Memoirs of Lord Gladwyn.* London: Weidenfeld and Nicolson, 1972.

Johnson, Lyndon Baines. *The Vantage Point: Perspectives of the Presidency, 1963-1969.* New York: Holt, 1971.

Kanellopoulos, P. *Imerologio: 31 March 1942–4 January 1945.* Athens: Kedros, 1977.

Kardelj, Edvard. *Reminiscences: The Struggle for Recognition and Independence: The New Yugoslavia, 1944–1957.* London: Blond & Briggs, 1982.

Katsouli, Giorgi. *History of the Greek Communist Party of Greece,* vol. 6, 1946–1949. Athens: Ekdoseis Nea Synora, n.d.

Kimball, W. F. *Churchill and Roosevelt: The Complete Correspondence,* 3 vols. Princeton: Princeton University Press, 1984.

Klaras, B. *O Adelphos mou o Aris.* Athens: Dorikos, 1985.

Klingaman, W. K. *1941: Our Lives in a World on the Edge.* New York: Harper and Row, 1966.

Kotsakis, Spyros A. *Dekemvris tou 1944 stin Athena.* Athens: Stin Athena, 1986.

Lanz, General Hubert. "Partisan Warfare in the Balkans." In *Historical Division European Command: Foreign Military Studies Branch,* MS No. P-995a, Koenigstein/Ts 15 September 1950.

Leeper, R. *When Greek Meets Greek.* London: Chatto and Windus, 1950.

Lloyd George, David. *The Truth about the Peace Treaties.* London: Victor Gollancz, 1938.

Loch, Joyce N. *A Fringe of Blue: An Autobiography.* London: John Murray, 1968.

Macmillan, Harold. *The Blast of War, 1939–1945.* London: Macmillan, 1967.

———. *War Diaries, The Mediterranean 1943–1945.* London: Macmillan, 1984.

MacVeagh, Lincoln. *Ambassador MacVeagh Reports: Greece, 1933–1947.* Ed. J. O. Iatrides. Princeton: Princeton University Press, 1980.

Makka-Photiadis, Despina. *Reminiscences from December 1944.* Unpublished manuscript, Athens, 1990.

Matthews, Kenneth. *Memories of a Mountain War: Greece 1944–1949.* London: Longman, 1972.

McNeill, W. H. *The Greek Dilemma: War and Aftermath.* New York: Lippincott, 1947.

Metaxas, Ioannis. *To Prosopiko tou Imerologio.* Edited by C. Christidis (Vols. 1–2, 1896 1920), by P. M. Siphnaios (Vol. 3, 1921–1932), by P. Vranas (Vol. 4, 1933–1941). Athens: Ekdoseis Gkobosti, 1951–1964.

Nohlen, Dieter and Philip Stover. *Elections in Europe: A Data Handbook.* Baden-Baden: Nomos Verlagsgesellschaft, 2010.

O'Brien, Richard. "Recollections." Undated unpublished manuscript. London.

OKW Diaries, Band II (Kriegstagebuch des Oberkommando des Wehrmacht, 1940–1945, 4 vols. ed. H. Greiner and Percy E. Schramm. Frankfurt am Main, 1961–1966.

Parliament of the United Kingdom, *Hansard,* December, 8, 1944.

Partsialidis, Mitsos. *Dipli Apokatastasi tis Ethnikis Andistasis.* Athens: Themelio, 1978.

Protaios, Stelios. *E Diki ton Ex.* Athens: Chrisima Vivlia, n.d.

Rallis, Ioannis. *O Ioannis Rallis Omilei ek tou Tafou.* Athens, 1947.

Report on SOE Activities in Greece and the Islands of the Aegean Sea, Appendix I, "Origin and Constitution of SOE."

Roskill, S. W. *The War at Sea 1939–1945.* London: HMSO, 1954.

Rousos, Petros. *I Megali Pendaetia 1940–1945: I Ethniki Andistasi kai O Rolos tou KKE.* 2 vols. Athens: Ekdoseis: Synchroni Epochi, 1978.

Sarafis, Stafanos. *ELAS, Greek Resistance Army.* London: Merlin Press, 1980.

Stevens, J. M. "Report of Lt.-Col. J. M. Stevens on Present Conditions in Central Greece." In *British Reports on Greece 1943–44,* edited by Lars Baerentzen. Copenhagen: Museum Tusculanum Press, 1982.

Stinas, A. *Anamniseis: Ebdomitda Chronia Kato apo ti Semaia tis Sosialistikis Epanastasis.* Athens: Dithnis Bibliothiki, 1985.

——. *EAM-ELAS-OPLA.* Athens: Dithnis Bibliothiki, 1984.

Templewood, Viscount. *Nine Troubled Years.* London: Collins, 1954.

Tito, Josip Broz. *V Kongress, Kommuntičke Partije Jugoslavije: Izveštije i Referati.* Belgrade: Kultura, 1948.

Tsakalotos, Thrasyvoulos. *40 Chronia Stratiotis tis Ellados: Istorikes Anamniseis, Pos Ekerdisame tous Agonas, 1940–1949.* 2 vols. Athens: Acropolis Edition, 1960.

Tsolakoglou, Georgios. *Apomnemonevmata.* Athens, 1959.

Tsouderos, Emmanouil, *Diplomatika Paraskinia.* Athens: Aetos, 1950.

——. *Ellinikes Anomalies stin Mesi Anatoli.* Athens, 1945.

——. *Logoi.* Athens: Aetos, 1946.

——. *O Episitismos 1941–1994: Mesi Anatoli.* Athens: Papazisis, 1948.

UK Parliamentary Debates, Commons, 5th Series (1909–80), December 8, 1944, Columns 934–47.

United Nations. General Assembly. "Report of the United Nations Special Committee on the Balkans." Official Records: Third Session, Supplement No. 8 (A/574). Lake Success, NY: United Nations General Assembly, 1948.

United States Army Command and General Staff College. *Internal Defense Operations: A Case History, Greece 1946–49.* Fort Leavenworth, KS: United States Army and General Staff College, 1967.

Vafeiadis, M. *Apomnimonevmata.* Vol. 1. Athens: Diphros, 1948.

Ward, M. *Greek Assignments: 1943 SOE–1948 UNSCOB.* Athens: Lycabettus Press, 1990.

Woodhouse, C. M. *Something Ventured.* London: Granada, 1982.

Zachariadis, Nikos. *"Apofasi tou Politkou Grafeiou tis K.E tou KKE."* Athens: Kentrikis Epitropis tou KKE, 1945.

——. "Zachariadis' Introductory Speech before the Seventh Party Congress." *To 7º Sunedrio,* Issue C. Athens: Kentrikis Epitropis tou KKE, 1945.

——. *Istorika Dilimmata, Istorikes Apantiseis: Apanta ta Dimosievmena, 1940–1945.* Edited by Giorgos Petropoulos. Athens: Kastaniotis, 2011.

——. *Kainourgia Katastasi, Kainouryia Kathikonda.* Nicosia, 1950.

——. *Problimata Kathodigisis.* Athens: Exodos, 1978.

——. *Thesis gia tin Istoria tou KKE.* Athens: Ekdoseis tis Kentrikis Epitropis tou KKE, 1945.

Zalokostas, Christos. *To Chroniko tis Sklavias.* Athens: Estia, 1949.

SECONDARY SOURCES

Abbot, Frank J. *The Greek Civil War, 1947–1949: Lessons for the Operational Artist in Foreign Internal Defense,* School for Advanced Military Studies thesis. Fort Leavenworth, Kansas: School of Advanced Military Studies, U.S. Army Command and General Staff College, May 1994.

Aldrich, Richard J. *The Hidden Hand: Britain, America and Cold War Secret Intelligence.* New York: Overlook Press, 2002.

Alvanos, Stavros. *To Phenomeno Makronisos: Ena Protognoro Egklematiko Peirema.* Athens: Ellinka Grammata, 1998.

Anataios, Petros. *N. Zachariadis: Thytis kai Thyma.* Athens: Fytrakis, 1991.

Apostolous, Leuteris. *Nikos Zachariadis: I Poreia Enos Igeti, 1923–1949.* Athens: Philistor Press, 2000.

Augeropoilos, G., et al., eds. *St'Armata St'Armata! Chroniko tis Ethnikis Andistasis 1940–1945.* Athens: Geranikos, 1964.

Averoff-Tossizza, Evangelos. *By Fire and Axe: The Communist Party and the Civil War in Greece, 1944–49.* New Rochelle, NY: Caratzas Brothers, 1978.

——. *Fotia kai Tsekouri.* Athens: Estia, 2010.

Avgoustidis, Angelos. "EEAM: The Worker's Resistance." *Journal of the Hellenic Diaspora* 11, no. 3 (1984): 55–67.

Baerentzen, Lars. "The Arrival of the Soviet Military Mission in July 1944 and KKE Policy: A Study of Chronology." *Journal of the Hellenic Diaspora* 13, nos. 3–4 (1986): 77–112.

——. "The Demonstration in Syntagma Square on Sunday the 3rd of December, 1944." *Scandinavian Studies in Modern Greek* 2 (1978): 3–52.

Banac, Ivo. "The Impact of the Macedonian Question on Civil Conflict in Greece, 1943–1949." In *Greece at the Crossroads: The Civil War and its Legacy.* University Park: Pennsylvania State University Press, 1995.

——. *With Stalin against Tito: Cominformist Splits in Yugoslav Communists.* Ithaca, NY: Cornell University Press, 1988.

Barker, Elizabeth. "The Yugoslavs and the Greek Civil War of 1946–1949." In *Studies in the History of the Greek Civil War, 1945–1949.* Ed. Lars Baerentzen et al. Copenhagen: Museum Tusculum Press, 1987. 263–295.

Bartziotas, V. *O Agonas tou Dimokratikous Stratou Elladas.* Athens: Synchroni Epochi, 1982.

——. *Ethiniki Andistasi kai Dekemvris 1944.* Athens: Synchroni Epochi, 1979.

——. *Exinda Chronia Kommounistis.* Athens: Synchroni Epochi, 1986.

——. "*I Politiki Stelekhon tou KKE sta Teleutea Deka Chronia.*" In *Deka Chronia Palis,* edited by Nikos Zachariadis. Athens: Poria, 1978.

Benetatos, D. *To Chroniko tis Sklavias 1941–1944.* Athens, 1963.

Birtle, Andrew J. U.S. Army Counterinsurgency Operations, 1942–1976 (Washington, DC: Center of Military History United States Army, 2006), Kindle edition.

Bouras, Basilis. *I Politiki Epitropi Ethnikis Apeleftherosis PEEA: Aleftheri Ellada 1944.* Athens: Diogenis, 1983.

Braim, Paul F. *The Will to Win: The Life of General A. Van Fleet.* Annapolis: Naval Institute Press, 2001.

Brooks, Julian Allan. "Managing Macedonia: British Statecraft, Intervention, and 'Proto Peacekeeping' in Ottoman Macedonia, 1902–1905." PhD thesis, Simon Fraser University, 2014.

Bullock, Alan. *Ernest Bevin: Foreign Secretary, 1945–1957.* London: Heinemann, 1983.

Cable, Larry. *Conflict of Myths: The Development of Counter-Insurgency Doctrine and the Vietnam War.* New York: NYU Press, 1988.

Cavafy, C. P. *Collected Poems.* Trans. D. Mendelsohn. New York: Alfred A. Knopf, 2010.

Chiclet, Christophe. *Les Communistes Grecs dans la Guerre: Histoire du Parti Communiste de Grèce de 1941 à 1949.* Paris: Editions L'Harmattan, 1987.

Chiotakis, G. *Politikes Thyelles: 2. I Dictatoria 4is Avgoustou, oi Protagonistes tis, o Polemos 1940–1941.* Athens, 1983.

Chondrymadis, Iakovos. *E Mavri Skia stin Ellada: Ethnikososialistikes kai Fasistikes Organosis stin Ellada tou Mesopolemou kai tis Germanikis Katochis, 1941–1942.* Athens: Monographia tis Stratiotikis Istorias, 2001.

Clissold, Stephen, ed. *Yugoslavia and the Soviet Union, 1939–1973: A Documentary Survey.* London: Oxford University Press, 1975.

Clogg, R., "Pearls from Swine." In *British Policy towards Wartime Resistance in Yugoslavia and Greece,* edited by P. Auty and R. Clogg. London: Macmillan, 1975.

——. "The Special Operations Executive in Greece." In *Greece in the 1940s: A Nation in Crisis.* Edited by John O. Iatrides. Hanover, NH: University Press of New England, 1981.

Close, David. *Greece since 1945: Civil War and Reconstruction, 1945–1950.* London: Longman, 2002.

——. "The Police in the Fourth of August Regime." *Journal of the Hellenic Diaspora* 13, nos. 1–2 (1986): 91–106.

——. "The Reconstruction of a Right-Wing State." In *The Greek Civil War, 1943– 1950: Studies in Polarization,* edited by David Close. London: Routledge, 1993.

Condit, D. M. *Case Study in Guerrilla War: Greece During World War II.* Washington, DC: Special Operations Research Office, 1981.

Conquest, Robert. *Stalin and the Kirov Murder.* New York: Oxford University Press, 1987.

Creveld, M. Van. *Hitler's Strategy 1940–1941: The Balkan Clue.* Cambridge: Cambridge University Press, 1973.

Cruickshank, Charles. *Deception in World War II.* Oxford: Oxford University Press, 1979.

Dafnis, G. *I Ellas Metaxi Dio Polemon 1923–1940.* 2 vols. Athens: Ikaros, 1974.

Dakin, Douglas. *The Greek Struggle in Macedonia, 1897–1913.* Thessaloniki: Institute for Balkan Studies, 1993.

Danforth, Loring M., and Riki Van Boeschoten. *Children of the Greek Civil War: Refugees and the Politics of Memory.* Chicago: University of Chicago Press, 2011.

Deakin, F. W. *The Brutal Friendship.* New York: Harper & Row, 1962.

Dedijer, Vladimir. *The Battle Stalin Lost: Memoirs of Yugoslavia, 1948–1953.* New York: Viking Press, 1971.

——. *Tito Speaks: His Self-Portrait and Struggle with Stalin.* London: Readers Union, 1954.

Djordjevic, Dimitrije, and Fischer-Galati. *The Balkan Revolutionary Tradition.* New York: Columbia University Press, 1981.

Ehrman, J. *Grand Strategy.* London: HMSO, 1956.

Ekdosi tis Kentrikis Epitropis tou KKE. *Syntomi Istoria tou KKE: Schedio, Meros A, 1918–1949.* Athens: Ekdoseis Synchroni Epochi.

Elefandis, A. *I Epangelia tis Adinatis Epanastasis: KKE kai Astismos ston Mesopolemon.* Athens: Themelio, 1976.

Eudes, Dominique. *The Kapetanios: Partisans and Civil War in Greece, 1943–1949.* New York: Monthly Review Press, 1972.

Fleischer, Hagen. "The Anomalies in the Greek Middle East Forces, 1941–1944." *Journal of the Hellenic Diaspora* 5, no. 3 (1978): 5–36.

———. "Contracts between German Occupation Authorities and the Major Greek Resistance Organizations: Sound Tactics or Collaboration." In *Greece in the 1940s: A Nation in Crisis,* edited by John O. Iatrides. Hanover, NH: University Press of New England, 1981.

———. *Stemma kai Swastika.* Athens: Papazisis, 1988.

Fleischer, Hagen and Nikolas Svoronos, eds. *Praktika tou Diethnous Istorokou Synedriou, I Ellada 1936–44: Dikatoria, Katochi, Andistasi.* Athens: Morphotiko Institouto, 1989.

Flountzi, Antoni. *1937–1943: Akronafplia kai Akronafpliotes.* Athens: Themelio, 1979.

Foot, M. R. D. and J. M. Langley. *MI9: Escape and Evasion 1939–1945.* London: Bodley Head, 1979.

Frangopoulos, Theophilos. "Betrayals." In *The Silent Border.* Athens: Ekdosiston Philon, 1995.

Frangoulis, A. F. *La Grèce, son statut international, son histoire diplomatique.* 2nd edition. 2 vols. Paris: Académie diplomatique internationale, 1927.

Galula, David. *Counterinsurgency Warfare: Theory and Practice.* Westport, CT: Praeger, 1964.

Garouphalias, Dimitris. *Keimena kai Anamnisis apo ton Tragiko Dekemvrio 1944.* Athens: Privately published, 1981.

Gasparinatos, Spyros G. *Apeleutherosi, Dekemvriana, Varkiza.* 2 vols. Athens: I. Sideris, 1998.

Gatopoulos, Dimitris. *Istoria tis Katochis.* Vol. A. Athens: Melissa, 1949.

Germanos, Frenty. *To Antikeimeno (Nikos Zachariadis).* Athens: Ekdoseis Kastaniotis, 2000.

Gerolymatos, André. "American Foreign Policy towards Greece and the Problem of Intelligence, 1945–1947." *Journal of Modern Hellenism* 7 (1990): 147–162.

———. *The Balkan Wars: Conquest, Revolution, and Retribution from the Ottoman Empire Era to the Twentieth Century and Beyond.* New York: Basic Books, 2003.

———. "Greek Democracy on Trial: From Insurgency to Civil War." *Review of International Affairs: Center for Eurasian Studies* 2, no. 3 (2003): 119–134.

———. *Red Acropolis, Black Terror: The Greek Civil War and the Origins of Soviet-American Rivalry.* New York: Basic Books, 2004.

———. "The Role of the Greek Officer Corps in the Resistance." *Journal of the Hellenic Diaspora* 11, no. 3 (1984): 69–80.

———. "The Security Battalions and the Civil War." *Journal of the Hellenic Diaspora* 12, no. 1 (1985): 17–28.

Gerozisis, T. *To Soma ton Axiomatikon kai E Thesi tou stin Sygchroni Elliniki Koinonia, 1821 1975.* Athens: Dodoni, 1996.

Gibbs, N. H. *Grand Strategy: History of the Second World War.* Edited by J. R. M. Butler. Vol. 1. London: Public Stationery Office, 1976.

Gilbert, M. *The Road to Victory: Winston Churchill 1939–1941*. Vol. 7. Toronto: Stoddard, 1986.

Goulter, Christina J. M. "The Greek Civil War: A National Army's Counter-insurgency Triumph." *Journal of Military History* 78 (July 2014): 1017–1055.

Grigoriadis, Phoivos. *Emphylios Polemos 1944–1949*. Vols. 9–10. Athens: Neokosmos, 1975.

———. *Germanoi Katoxi Andistasis*, vol. 5. Athens: Neokosmos, 1973.

———. *Istoria tou Emphyliou Polemou, 1945–49—To Dentero Andartiko*. Vol 4. Athens: Neokosmos, 1975.

Grigoriadis, Solon Neok. *Istoria tis Synchronis Elladas, 1941–1974: Nikos Zachariadis: O Moiraios Igetis*. Vol. 4. Athens: Kapopoulos, 1974.

Hadzis, Thanasis. *I Nikiphora Epanastasi pou Chathike: Ethnikoapeleutherotikos Agonas, 1941–1945*. Athens: Dorikos, 1982.

Harris, William D. Jr., Major. *Arts of War Papers: Instilling Aggressiveness: U.S. Advisors and Greek Combat Leadership in the Greek Civil War, 1947–1949*. Fort Leavenworth: Combat Studies Institute Press, 2013.

Herodotus. *The Landmark Herodotus: The Histories*. Ed. Robert B. Strassler. Trans. Andrea L. Purvis. New York: Pantheon Books, 2007.

Hinseley, F. H. et al. *British Intelligence in the Second World War: Its Influence in Strategy and Operations*. 3 vols. London: HMSO, 1984.

Hionidou, Violet. *Famine and Death in Occupied Greece, 1941–1944*. Cambridge: Cambridge University Press, 2006.

History of the Great Patriotic War. Vol. 1. Moscow: Military Publishing House of the Ministry of Defense of the USSR, 1960–1965.

Hoffmann, Peter. "Roncalli in the Second World War: Peace Initiative, the Greek Famine and the Persecution of the Jews." *Journal of Ecclesiastical History* 40, no. 1 (1989): 74–99.

Hondros, J. L. *Occupation and Resistance: The Greek Agony 1941–1944*. New York: Pella, 1983.

———. "Too Weighty a Weapon: Britain and the Greek Security Battalions, 1943–1944." *Journal of the Hellenic Diaspora* 15, nos. 1–2 (1998): 33–48.

Horncastle, James. "The Dekemvriana and the Slavo-Macedonian Question." Paper presented at *December to Varkiza: Memory, Political Discourse, and the Greek Civil War*. Burnaby, Canada, 20 February 2015.

Hyde, H. Montgomery. *Stalin: The History of a Dictator*. New York: Farrar, Straus and Giroux, 1971.

Iatrides, John O. *Revolt in Athens: The Greek Communist "Second Round." 1944–1945*. Princeton: Princeton University Press, 1972.

———. "Revolution or Self-Defense? Communist Goals, Strategy, and Tactics in the Greek Civil War." *Journal of Cold War Studies* 7, no. 3 (Summer 2005): 3–33.

Iliou, Philipos. *Emphylios Polemos: E Embloki tou KKE*. Athens: Themelio, 2005.

Ioannidis, G. *Anamniseis: Provlimata tis Politikis tou KKE stin Ethniki Andistasi, 1940–1945*. Athens: Themelio, 1979.

——. *Ellines kai Xenoi Kataskopoi stin Ellada*. Athens: Ekdosis A. Mavridis, 1952.

Jeffery, Judith S. *Ambiguous Commitments and Uncertain Policies: The Truman Doctrine in Greece, 1947–1952*. New York: Lexington Books, 2000.

Jeffery, Keith. *The Secret History of MI6, 1909–1949*. New York: Penguin Press, 2010.

Jenkins, Roy. *Churchill*. New York: Farrar, Straus and Giroux, 2001.

Jones, Howard. *"A New Kind of War": America's Global Strategy and the Truman Doctrine in Greece*. Oxford: Oxford University Press, 1989.

Kallonas, D. *Ioannis Metaxas: Mathitis-Stratiotis-Politikos-Agonistis* Kyvernitis. Athens, 1938.

Kalyvas, Stathis N. *The Logic of Violence in Civil War*. New York: Cambridge University Press, 2006.

Karis-Staikos, Petros Kitsos Maltezos. *O Agapimenos ton Theon*. Athens: Okeanida, 2000.

Karnow, Stanley. *Vietnam: A History*. New York: Penguin Books, 1991.

Karpozilos, Kostis. "The Defeated of the Greek Civil War: From Fighters to Political Refugees in the Cold War." *Journal of Cold War Studies* 16, no. 3, (2014): 62–87.

Kedros, A. *I Elliniki Andristasi 1940–44*, vol. 1. Athens: Themelio, 1981.

Keegan, John. *The Second World War*. Toronto: Penguin, 1989.

Keeley, Edmund. *Fonos ston Thermaiko*. Ypothesi Polk. Athens: Ellinika Grammata, 2010.

——. *The Salonika Bay Murder: Cold War Politics and the Polk Affair*. Princeton: Princeton University Press, 1989.

Kentriki Epitropi tou KKE. *I Ebdomi Platia Olomeleia tis KE tou KKE: 18–24 Flevari 1957*. Athens: Synchroni Epochi, 2011.

——. *I Ekti Platia Olomelia tis KE tou KKE: 11–12 Marti 1956*. Athens: Synchroni Epochi, 2010.

Kirjazovski, Risto. *Narodnoosloboditelniot front I drugite organizacii na makedoncite od Egejska Makedonija, 1945–1949*. Skopje: Kultura, 1985.

Kofas, Jon V. *Authoritarianism in Greece: The Metaxas Regime*. New York: Columbia University Press, 1983.

Kofos, Evangelos. *The Impact of the Macedonian Question on Civil Conflict in Greece, 1943–1949*. Athens: Hellenic Foundation for Defense and Foreign Policy, 1989.

——. *Nationalism and Communism in Macedonia: Civil Conflict, Politics of Mutation, National Identity*. New Rochelle, NY: Aristide D. Caratzas, 1993.

Koliopoulos, J. S. *Brigands with a Cause: Brigandage and Irredentism in Modern Greece, 1821–1912*. Oxford: Oxford University Press, 1987.

———. "Esoterikes Exelixeis apo tin Protin Martiou os tin 28 Octovriou 1940." In *Istoria tou Ellinikou Ethnous: Neoteros Ellinismos apo 1913 os 1941*. Athens: Ekdotiki Athenon, 1978.

———. *Greece and the British Connection 1935–1941*. Oxford: Oxford University Press, 1977.

———. *Plundered Loyalties: Axis Occupation and Civil Strife in Greek West Macedonia, 1941–1949*. London: Hurst, 1999.

Koliševski, Lazar. *Political Report to the First Congress of the Communist Party of Macedonia*. I Kongres na KPM. Zagreb: Kultura, 1950.

Konstas, Panagiotis E. *I Ellas tis Dekaetias 1940–1950*. Athens, 1955.

Kotsis, Spyro. *Midas 614*. Athens, 1976.

Kousoulas, D. G. *KKE: Ta Prota Chronia, 1918–1949*. Athens: Elliniki Euroekdotiki, 1987.

———. *Revolution and Defeat: The Story of the Greek Communist Party*. London: Oxford University Press, 1965.

Kousouris, Dimitris. *Dikes ton Dosilogon, 1944–1949: Dikeosini, Synehia tou Kratous kai Thniki Mnimi*. Athens: Polis, 2014.

Laiou, Angeliki E. "Population Movements in the Greek Countryside during the Civil War." In *Studies in the History of the Greek Civil War, 1945–1949*, ed. Lars Baerentzen, John O. Iatrides, and Ole Smith. Copenhagen: Museum Tusculanum Press, 1987.

Lange-Akhund, Nadine. *The Macedonian Question, 1893–1908*. New York: Columbia University Press, 1998.

Lazari, Vasili. *I Trixroni Epopoiia tou Dimokratikou Stratou Elladas, 1946–49*, 5th ed. Athens: Rizospastis-Sugxroni Epoxi, 2011.

Lemkin, Raphael. *Axis Rule in Occupied Greece: Laws of Occupation, Analysis of Government Proposals for Redress*. New York: H. Fertig, 1973.

Leontis, Artemis. *Topographies of Hellenism: Mapping the Homeland*. Ithaca, NY: Cornell University Press, 1995.

Levidis, A. "Yia Hare tis Alithias: Intelligence kai Andistasi." Unpublished manuscript, Athens, 1975.

Lewis, Bernard. *What Went Wrong? Western Impact and Middle Eastern Response*. Oxford: Oxford University Press, 2002.

Linardatos, S. *I 4i Augoustou*. Athens: Ekdosi Dialogos, 1975.

———. *I Estoeriki Politiki tis 4is Avgoustou*. Athens, 1975.

———. *Pos Eftasame stin 4i Avgoustou*. Athens, 1965.

Logevall, Fredrick. *Embers of War: The Fall of an Empire and the Making of America's Vietnam*. New York: Random House, 2012.

Logothetopoulos, K. *Idou I Alitheia*. Athens, 1948.

Loulis, J. *The Greek Communist Party, 1940–1944*. London: Croom Helm, 1982.

Lukács, Georg. *The Historical Novel*. London: Penguin, 1962.

Machiavelli, Niccolo. *The Prince*. Trans. William K. Marriott. New York: Everyman's Library, 1992.

Mackenzie, W. J. M. *The Secret History of SOE: The Special Operations Executive, 1940–1945*. London: St. Ermin's Press, 2000.

Makris-Staikos, Petros and Kitsos Maltezos. *O Agapimenos ton Theon*. Athens: Okeanida 2000.

Malianos, M. *I 4i Avgoustou, pos kai Giati Epivlithi I Dictatoria tou I. Metaxas*. Athens, 1947.

Mao-Tse Tung. *On Guerrilla Warfare*. Champaign: University of Illinois Press, 2001.

Marantzidis. *Demokratikos Stratos Elladas (DSE), 1936–1949*. Athens: Ekdoseis Alexandria, 2010.

Margaritis, Giorgos. *Istoria tou Ellinikou Emphuliou Polemou 1946–1949*. Vol. 1. Athens: Bibliorama, 2000.

Markezinis, S. *Politiki Istoria tis Neoteros Ellados: I Synchronos Ellas, 1932–1936*. Vol. 4. Athens: Papyros, 1978.

———. *Politiki Istoria tis Ellados,* Seira B,' Synchronos Elinismos, vol. 2. Athens: Papyros, 1973.

Marsan, Polybias. *Eleni Papadaki: Mia Photerini Theatriki Porea me Aprosdokito Telos*. Athens: Kastiaiotis, 2001.

Marton, Kati. *The Polk Conspiracy: Murder and Cover-Up in the Case of CBS News Correspondent George Polk*. New York: Random House, 1990.

Maule, H. *Scobie: Hero of Greece, the British Campaign 1944–45*. London: Arthur Barker, 1975.

Mazower, Mark. "The Cold War and the Appropriation of Memory: Greece after Liberation." In *The Politics of Retribution in Europe: War and Its Aftermath*, edited by Istvan Deak et al. Princeton: Princeton University Press, 2000.

Mazower, Mark, ed. *After the War Was Over: Reconstructing the Family, Nation, and State in Greece*. Princeton: Princeton University Press, 2000.

McCullough, David. *Truman*. New York: Simon and Schuster, 1992.

Mertzos, N. I. *KKE Episema Keimena 1940–1945*, 5 vols. Athens: Ekdosis tou KKE Esoterikou, 1979.

Michel, Henri. *The Shadow War: Resistance in Europe 1939–1945*. Translated by Richard Barry. London: Andre Deutsch, 1972.

Miller, William J. *Henry Cabot Lodge: A Biography*. New York: Heinemann, 1967.

Minchan, P. *Civil War and World War in Europe: Spain, Yugoslavia, and Greece, 1936–1949*. New York: Palgrave Macmillan, 2006.

Montefiore, Simon Sebag. *Stalin: The Court of the Red Tsar*. London: Weidenfeld and Nicolson, 2003.

Moyar, Mark. *Triumph Forsaken: The Vietnam War, 1954–1956*. Cambridge: Cambridge University Press, 2006.

Myers, E. "The Andarte Delegation to Cairo: August 1943." In *British Policy towards Wartime Resistance in Yugoslavia and Greece*. Edited by Phyllis Auty and Richard Clogg. London: Macmillan, 1975.

———. *Greek Entanglement*. Gloucester: Sutton, 1985.

Nikouloudis, T. *I Elleniki Krisis*. Cairo, 1945.

———. *Ioannis Metaxas*. Athens, 1941.

O'Balance, Edgar. *The Greek Civil War, 1944–1949*. New York: Praeger, 1966.

Orwell, George. *Nineteen Eighty-Four*. Suffolk: Penguin Modern Classics, 1954.

Ovendale, Ritchie. *Britain, the United States and the Transfer of Power in the Middle East, 1945–1962*. London: Leicester University Press, 1996.

Palmer, Jr., Stephen E., and Robert R. King. *Yugoslav Communism and the Macedonian Question*. Hamden, CT: Archon Books, 1971.

Papadakis, B. P. *Diplomatiki Istoria tou Ellinikou Polemou*. Athens, 1956.

———. *I Chethesini kai I Avriania Ellas*. Athens, 1946.

Papagos, Alexander. "Guerrilla Warfare." In *Modern Guerrilla War*, edited by Mark Osana. New York: Free Press, 1962.

———. "I pros Polemous Proparaskevi tou Ellinikou Stratou 1923–1940." In *Archigeion Stratou Diefthnisis Stratou*. Athens: Ekdosis Diefthynseos Istorias Stratou, 1969.

———. *O Ellinikos Stratos kai I pros Paraskevi tou*. Athens, 1945.

Papanikos, Vangelis. *O Nikos Zachariadis sto Dachau: Martyria mias Epohis*. Athens: Philistor Press, 1999.

Papastratis, P. *British Policy towards Greece during the Second World War 1941–1944*. Cambridge: Cambridge University Press, 1984.

———."Diplomatika Paraskinia tis Ipografis tis Stratiotikis Symfonias Vretanias— Elladas stis 9 Martiou 1941." *Mnimon* 7 (1979): 174–182.

Pappas, Elli. *Martyries mias Diadromis*. Athens: Benaki Museum, 2010.

Parnis, Alexis. *Geia Chara Nikos: I Allilographia mou me to Niko Zachariadis*. Athens: Ekdoseis, 2011.

Pavlowitch, Stevan K. *A History of the Balkans, 1804–1945*. London: Longman, 1999.

———. *Hitler's New Disorder: The Second World War in Yugoslavia*. New York: Columbia University Press, 2008.

Payne, Stanley G. *Civil War in Europe, 1905–1949*. Cambridge: Cambridge University Press, 2011.

Pelt, Mogens. "Greece and Germany's Policy towards South-Eastern Europe 1932–1940." *Epsilon* 2, no. 2 (1988): 55–76.

Perrakis, Stylianos. *The Ghosts of Plaka Beach: A True Story of Murder and Retribution in Wartime Greece*. Madison, NJ: Fairleigh Dickinson University Press, 2006.

Perry, Duncan M. *The Politics of Terror: The Macedonian Liberation Movements, 1893–1903*. Durham, NC: Duke University Press, 1988.

Petropoulos, J. A. *Politics and Statecraft in the Kingdom of Greece, 1833–1843.*
    Princeton: Princeton University Press, 1968.
——. "The Traditional Political Parties of Greece During the Axis Occupation." In
    Greece in the 1940s: A Nation in Crisis, edited by J. O. Iatrides. Hanover, NH:
    University Press of New England, 1981.
Petros, Antaios. *N. Zachariadis: Thytis kai Thyma.* Athens: Fytrakis, 1991.
Phlountzes, A. *Akrovafplia kai Akronafpliotes.* Athens: Themelio, 1979.
Pogue, F. C. *George C. Marshall: Statesman.* New York: Viking, 1987.
Pratt, Larry. *East of Malta, West of Suez: Britain's Mediterranean Crisis, 1936–1939.*
    Cambridge: Cambridge University Press, 1975.
Psiroukis, N. *O Fassismos kai I 4i Avgoustou.* Athens, 1974.
Pyromaglou, K. *I Ethniki Andistasis: EAM-ELAS-EDES-EKKA.* Athens: Dodoni,
    1975.
——. *O Georgios Kartalis kai I Epochi tou, 1934–1944.* Vol. A. Athens, 1965.
——. "Ta Tagmata Asphalias." *Istoriki Epitheoresis,* 6 (October–December 1964).
Pyromaglou, K., ed. *Istorikon Archion Ethnikis Andistasis,* Vol. 2. Athens, n.d.
Rees, Tim and Andrew Thorpe, eds. *International Communism and the Communist
    International, 1919–43.* Manchester: Manchester University Press, 1998.
Rigopoulos, Rigas. *The Secret War: Greece–Middle East, 1940–1945, The Events
    Surrounding the Story of Service 5–16–5.* Paducah: Turner, 2003.
Ristovic, Milan. "The Bulkes Experiment: A "Greek Republic in Yugoslavia
    1945–1949." *Journal of Balkan Studies,* 46 (2012) 126–143.
Rogers, Anthony. *Churchill's Folly: Leros and the Aegean, the Last Great Defeat of
    World War Two.* London: Cassell, 2003.
Royal Institute of International Affairs. *The Balkan States: A Review of the Economic
    and Financial Development of Albania, Bulgaria, Greece, Roumania and
    Yugoslavia since 1919.* London: Oxford University Press, 1936.
Sakellariou, Alexander. *Enas Navarchos Thimatai,* 2 vols. Athens: Dimitrakos, 1971.
Sakkas, John. *Britain and the Greek Civil War 1944–1949: British Imperialism, Public
    Opinion and the Coming of the Cold War.* Mainz: Franz Philipp Rutzen, 2013.
Saloutsos, Th. *The Greeks in the United States.* Boston: Cambridge University Press,
    1964.
Saranda Chronia tou KKE 1918–1958. Athens: Synchroni Epochi, 1958.
Seton Watson, G. H. N. "Afterword." In *British Policy towards Wartime Resistance in
    Yugoslavia and Greece.* London: Macmillan, 1975.
Shahgedanova, Maria. *The Physical Geography of Northern Eurasia.* New York:
    Oxford University Press, 2002.
Shoup, Paul S. *Communism and the Yugoslav National Question.* New York:
    Columbia University Press, 1968.
Shrader, Charles R. *The Withered Vine: Logistics and the Communist Insurgency in
    Greece, 1945–1949.* Westport, CT: Praeger, 1999.

Singleton, Fred and Bernard Carter. *The Economy of Yugoslavia.* New York: St. Martin's Press, 1982.

Smith, Michael Llewellyn. *Ionian Vision: Greece in Asia Minor 1919–1922.* Ann Arbor: University of Michigan Press, 1973.

Smith, Ole. "The Greek Communist Party, 1945–1949." In *The Greek Civil War, 1945–1950: Studies in Polarization,* edited by D. H. Close. London: Routledge, 1993.

——. "History Made to Fit All Occasions: The KKE View of the December Crisis." *Journal of the Hellenic Diaspora* 22, no. 2 (1996): 57–68.

——. "A Turning Point in the Greek Civil War, 1945–1949: The Meeting Between Zachariadis and Markos." *Scandinavian Studies in Modern Greek* 3 (1979): 35–46.

Smyth, Denis. *Deathly Deception: The Real Story of Operation Mincemeat.* Oxford: Oxford University Press, 2010.

Sorensen, Theodore. *Kennedy.* New York: Harper and Row, 1965.

Spais, Leonidas. *Peninda Chronia Stratiotis.* Athens: Melissa, 1970.

Stafford, D. *Britain and European Resistance 1940–1945: A Survey of the Special Operations Executive, with Documents.* London: Macmillan, 1980.

Staktopoulos, Grigoris. *Ypothesi Polk: E Prosopiki mou Martiria.* Athens: Ekdosis Gnosi, 1984.

Stavrakis, Peter. *Moscow and Greek Communism, 1944–1949.* Ithaca, NY: Cornell University Press, 1989.

Stavrianos, L. S. *The Balkans since 1453.* New York: New York University Press, 1958.

——. "Mutiny of the Greek Armed Forces, April 1944." *American Slavic and East European Review* 9 (1950): 302–311.

Stavrou, A. *Allied Politics and Military Interventions: The Political Role of the Greek Army.* Athens: Papazisis, 1970.

Stefanidis, Yiannis. "Greece in the Second World War (1940–1944)." In *Elliniki Istoria.* Vol. 7. Athens: Ekdotiki Athinon, 2007.

Steiner, Zora. *The Triumph of the Dark: European International History, 1933–1939.* Oxford: Oxford University Press, 2011.

Stinas, A. *Anamniseis: Ebdominta Chronia Kato Ap'ti Simaia tis Sosialistikis Epanastasis.* Athens: Ypsilon Vivlia, 1985.

Swain, Geoffrey. "Tito and the Twilight of the Comintern." In *International Communism and the Communist International, 1919–43,* edited by Tim Rees and Andrew Thorpe. Manchester: Manchester University Press, 1998.

Sweet-Escott, Bickham. *Baker Street Irregular.* London: Methuen, 1962.

——. *Greece: A Political and Economic History.* London: Royal Institute of International Affairs, 1954.

——. "SOE in the Balkans." In *British Policy towards Wartime Resistance in Yugoslavia and Greece.* London: M University of London Press, 1975.

Syndomi Istoria tou KKE, Meros A 1918–1949. Athens: Ekdosi ticke tou KKE, 1988.

Tabakaopoulos, A. P. *O Mythos tis Dictatorias.* Athens, 1945.

Thucydides, *History of the Peloponnesian War, Books III and IV.* Trans. C. F. Smith. Cambridge: Harvard University Press, 1975.

Truman, Margaret. *Harry S. Truman.* New York: William Morrow, 1973.

Ulunian, A. "The Communist Party of Greece and the Comintern: Evaluations, Instructions and Subordination." In *International Communism and the Communist International, 1919–43.* Edited by Tim Rees and Andrew Thorpe, 187–204. Manchester: Manchester University Press, 1998.

———. "The Soviet Union and the Greek Question." In *The Soviet Union and Europe in the Cold War, 1943–1953.* Edited by F. Gori and S. Pons. New York: St. Martin's Press, 1996.

Utley, Gertje. *Pablo Picasso: The Communist Years.* New Haven, CT: Yale University Press, 2000.

Vansittart, R. *The Mist Procession.* London: Hutchinson, 1958.

Vatikiotis, P. J. *Popular Autocracy in Greece 1936–41: A Political Biography of General Ioannis Metaxas.* London: Frank Cass, 1998.

Vaughan, Hal. *Sleeping with the Enemy: Coco Chanel's Secret War.* New York: Knopf, 2011.

Venezis, Ilias. *Archiepiskopos Damaskinos.* Athens: Estias, 1981.

Veremis, Thanos. *Oi Epemvaseis tou Stratou stin Elliniki Politiki.* Athens: n.p, 1983.

Vladas, Dimitrios. "Triamisi Chronia Palis." In *Pros tin III Syndiaskepsi tou KKE.* Central Committee of the Communist Party of Greece, 1951.

Vladas, Elias and Zak Mettger. *Who Killed George Polk? The Press Cover Up, A Death in the Family.* Philadelphia: Temple University Press, 1996.

Vlahov, Dimitar. *Iz Istorije Makedonskog Naroda.* Belgrade: Prosveta, 1950.

Voglis, Plymeris. "Between Negation and Self-Negation: Political Prisoners in Greece." In *After the War Was Over: Reconstructing the Family, Nation, and State in Greece,* edited by Mark Mazower. Princeton: Princeton University Press, 2000.

Vontitsos-Gousias, Giorgis. *Oi Aities Gia tis Ittes ti Diaspasi tou KKE kai tis Ellinikis Aristeras.* Athens: Na Ypiretisoume to Lao, n.d.

Vukmanović-Tempo, Svetozar. *How and Why the People's Liberation Struggle of Greece Met with Defeat.* London: Merlin Press, 1950.

———. *Struggle for the Balkans.* London: Merlin Press, 1990.

Wainhouse, Edward. "Guerrilla Warfare in Greece 1946–49." *Military Review* 36 (June 1957).

Wake, H. and W. F. Deeds, eds. *Swift and Bold: The Story of the King's Royal Rifle Corps in the Second World War, 1939–1945.* Aldershot: Gale and Polden, 1949.

Wallace, D. J. "Conditions in Zervas-Held Territory." In *British Reports on Greece 1943–1944.* Copenhagen: Museum Tusculanum Press, 1982.

Wiskemann, E. *The Rome-Berlin Axis: A History of the Relations between Hitler and Mussolini*. London: Oxford University Press, 1949.

Wittner, Lawrence S. *American Intervention in Greece, 1943–1949*. New York: Columbia University Press, 1982.

Woodhouse, C. M. *The Apple of Discord*. London: Hutchinson, 1948.

———. *Modern Greece: A Short History*. London: Praeger, 1968.

———. *The Struggle for Greece 1941–1949*. London: Hurst, 2002.

Woodward, Sir L. *British Foreign Policy in the Second World War*. Vol. 1. London: HMSO, 1970.

Yosmaoglu, Ipek. *Blood Ties: Religion, Violence, and the Politics of Nationhood in Ottoman Macedonia, 1878–1908*. Ithaca, NY: Cornell University Press, 2014.

Zannas, Alexander. *I Katochi: Anamniseis-Epistoles*. Athens: Estias, 1964.

Zaousis, A. L. *Oi Dio Ochthes: 1939–1945*. Athens: Papzisis, 1987.

Zapantis, Andrew L. *Greek-Soviet Relations, 1917–1941*. New York: Columbia University Press, 1982.

Zapheiropoulos, D. *O Antisvmmoriakos 'Agon*. Athens, 1956.

Zevgos, Giannis. "The National Minorities and National Demagogy." *Kommounistiki Epitheoresi*, July 1944.

Zevgos, Kaiti. *Me ton Yianni Zevgo sto Epanastatiko Kinima*. Athens: Ekdosis Okeanida, 1980.

Zubik, Vladislav, and Constantine Pleshakov. *Inside the Kremlin's War: From Stalin to Khrushchev*. Cambridge, MA: Harvard University Press, 1996.

NEWSPAPERS AND PERIODICALS

Akropolis

Avgi

Bulletin (Skopje)

E Ellas

Eleutherotypia

Elinikon Ema

Ethnikos Keryx

Exormisi

Kommounistiki Epitheoresi

Nation

Neos Kosmos

Politika

Rizospastis

To Vima

The Times (London)

Washington Post

INTERVIEWS AND PERSONAL CORRESPONDENCE

Athanas. Correspondence with André Gerolymatos, 25 August 2006.

———. Interview with André Gerolymatos, 22 August 2014.

Dodis, Dione. Correspondence with André Gerolymatos. 10 November 2003, 13 November 2002.

———. Interview by André Gerolymatos. Vancouver, 25 October 2003.

Katsuris, Leo. Interview by André Gerolymatos. Vancouver, 8 March 2004.

McAdam, Ron. Interview by André Gerolymatos. West Vancouver, 17 January 2004.

Petropoulos, Giorgos. Interview by André Gerolymatos. Athens, 15 September 2013.

Phannou, Efthimia. Interview by André Gerolymatos. Athens, 15 January 2004.

Rallis, George. Interview by André Gerolymatos. Athens, 5 June 1989.

Rigopoulos, Rigas. Interview by André Gerolymatos. Athens, 27 May 2002.

Zachariadis, Sifis. Interview by André Gerolymatos. Piraeus, 16 July 2013.

Index

Printed and bound by CPI Group (UK) Ltd, Croydon, CR0 4YY

25/03/2025

14647356-0002